Managing Expatriates

Beiträge zur
Bevölkerungswissenschaft
–
Series on Population Studies

Book series published by the
Federal Institute for Population Research, Germany
(Bundesinstitut für Bevölkerungsforschung)

Volume 50

Brenton M. Wiernik
Heiko Rüger
Deniz S. Ones (Eds.)

Managing Expatriates
Success Factors in Private and Public Domains

Barbara Budrich Publishers
Opladen • Berlin • Toronto 2018

A CIP catalogue record for this book is available from
Die Deutsche Bibliothek (The German Library)

© 2018   by Barbara Budrich Publishers, Opladen, Berlin & Toronto
www.barbara-budrich.net

ISBN   **978-3-8474-2031-6 (Hardcover)**
eISBN   978-3-8474-1017-1 (eBook)

Die Deutsche Bibliothek – CIP-Einheitsaufnahme
Ein Titeldatensatz für die Publikation ist bei der Deutschen Bibliothek erhältlich.

Verlag Barbara Budrich Barbara Budrich Publishers
Stauffenbergstr. 7. D-51379 Leverkusen Opladen, Germany

86 Delma Drive. Toronto, ON M8W 4P6 Canada
www.barbara-budrich.net

Picture credits/Titelbildnachweis: Cover image: "Atlas catalan", Abraham Cresques, Bibliothèque Nationale de France [http://gallica.bnf.fr/ark:/12148/btv1b55002481n]
Jacket illustration/Umschlaggestaltung: Bettina Lehfeldt, Kleinmachnow, Germany –
www.lehfeldtgraphic.de and BiB
Editorship/Schriftleitung: Dr. Jasmin Passet-Wittig, BiB
Typesetting/Satz: Sybille Steinmetz, BiB

Series Editors' Preface

In the last decades, the mobility demands placed on the workforce have become greater and more important. This is true in particular for expatriate employees. The high relevance of analyzing international work-related mobility behaviors becomes evident in its interplay with various spheres of life such as family, social mobility, and quality of life. The present peer reviewed volume of the Series of Population Studies edited by Brenton M. Wiernik, Heiko Rüger, and Deniz S. Ones compiles international state-of-the-art research on factors determining the success of international expatriate employment.

At the end of 2011, the Federal Institute for Population Research (BiB), together with the Federal Foreign Office carried out the Mobility Skills in the German Foreign Service (GFS) study, which examines factors that promote success among diplomats in the GFS. On this occasion, the BiB hosted a scientific meeting in January 2012 with the participation of Jürgen Deller, Deniz S. Ones, and Stephan Dilchert, who belong to the team of the International Generalizability of Expatriate Success Factors (iGOES) Project, which examines German-speaking employees of multinational corporations working in 28 countries. At the meeting, it became clear that both studies pursue a common innovative approach by analyzing diverse expatriate outcomes such as job performance, job satisfaction, well-being, personal relationships, and family life, in addition to expatriate adjustment. This gave rise to the idea of a jointly edited volume providing comparative analyses on public and private sector expatriates. We are now pleased to present the results of these considerations.

The seventeen contributions in this book examine expatriate employment from various angles. The compilation is divided into four coherent thematic sections bringing together contributions that study psychological individual differences, age and experience, support and preparation, and gender and family. The findings presented in this book are based on empirical analyses that draw on four large and innovative research projects that assess international employees from a wide range of populations, cultural backgrounds, and host country contexts. Thereby, the volume not only considers the cultural specificity of expatriate experiences but also studies the generalizability of relations across countries.

The publication of such a volume demands a lot from everyone involved. First of all, thanks is owed to the editors of this volume for accepting the at times demanding challenge to compile such a coherent and high quality volume. Without the dedication of the authors and the people involved in collecting the data on which the articles are based, this book wouldn't have been possible. Furthermore, four blind reviewers supported this volume with their expertise which contributed to ensuring high quality of all articles. Typesetting and formatting of this manuscript was carried out professionally by Sybille Steinmetz.

For scientists and students with an interest in international mobility, the current volume offers important insights into the determinants of expatriate success. The book is also relevant for organizations in the public and private sectors that regularly work with expatriates and are concerned with aligning their operations with evidence-based best practices. We wish all readers an informative and stimulating read.

Wiesbaden, Germany, October 2017

Norbert F. Schneider
(Director of the Federal Institute for Population Research)

Jasmin Passet-Wittig
(Managing Editor)

Editors' Preface

Expatriates have played a long and important role in global economics and culture, dating at least as far back as Marco Polo and other traders who travelled the Silk Road between Asia, Europe, and eastern Africa from before the common era until the 15th century (illustrated on the cover of this book). Today, as the world economy continues to globalize, expatriate employees sent on long-term international assignments are becoming an increasingly important part of organizations' global strategies. International assignments present a myriad of unique challenges for employees, including adapting to a new culture, changing job responsibilities, blurring of work–non-work boundaries, and logistical challenges of moving one's life and family to a new location. Over the past 80 years, a voluminous research literature in applied psychology, management, organizational behavior, and allied fields has developed, exploring the processes through which expatriates respond to these challenges and the factors that promote (or hinder) expatriate success. We are proud to present this book of multiple empirical studies employing diverse conceptual models and analytic techniques. In this book, researchers examine the impact of gender, family, age, experience, preparation, support, and psychological individual differences on expatriate adjustment, satisfaction, performance, and well-being. Using large multinational samples, psychometrically rigorous measures, and straightforward analytic approaches, the studies in this volume make important strides toward understanding the expatriate experience with implications for international human resource management and enhancing the well-being of expatriates around the globe.

Wiesbaden, Germany, October 2017
Brenton M. Wiernik, Heiko Rüger, and Deniz S. Ones

Acknowledgements

There are many groups of individuals without whom this book would not have been possible.

First and foremost thanks goes to Norbert Schneider, the director of the Bundesinstitut für Bevölkerungsforschung (BIB; German Federal Institute for Population Research), who hosted an invitational workshop dedicated to expatriate management research. Jürgen Deller was instrumental in shaping the selection of participants and the content of the research presented. The idea of a book centering on the presented research arose from the discussions during that workshop. Dr. Schneider's encouragement and support brought the idea to fruition. Dr. Deller's insights helped us avoid minefields associated with this cross-national undertaking. We are grateful to both.

One of the important features of this book is that it draws on four large multi-study research efforts. Many supportive individuals were involved in each.

The iGOES team's efforts were led by Jürgen Deller, with support for funding student researcher travels provided by Deutscher Akademischer Austauschdienst (DAAD), Haniel-Stiftung, and Universitätsgesellschaft Lüneburg e.V. The equal opportunity office of Leuphana Universität Lüneburg also funded instrumental material for the iGOES research. The iGOES team also wishes to acknowledge the following students who contributed to their data collection: Claudia Bassarak, Gina Becher, Anna Beil, Veronika Bruchner, Miriam Callegari, Svenja Drossert, Elisa Foit, Niklas Frank, Lisa Fromm, Karen Geitner, Clara Hellweg, Karin Hofmann, Sophia Kammer, Stefanie Klauser, Julia Knobloch, Julia Lauenroth, Sylvia Lehmann, Stefanie Maaß, Maren-Katharina Mittrenga, Stefanie Nitsche, Esther Ostmeier, Nina Pache, Ulrike Pastoor, Katrin Petr, Miriam Pourseifi, Arne Prokandt, Martin Puppatz, Dorothee Rauber, Martin Scheunemann, Theresa Schnieders, Lasse Schulze, Katharina Schuster, Anna-Christina Schwenk, Sehri Silav, Martin Stöckl, Elke Strade, Katharina Strüber, Lars Thurow, Milan Uhe, Richard Vahlhaus, Ines Vetter, Carmen Wesch, Sunnhild Wichern, Sabine Winters, Sandra Wittlinger, and Kathrin Wolf.

Heiko Rüger, Stine Waibel, Herbert Fliege, and Maria Bellinger wish to acknowledge Norbert Schneider, Silvia Ruppenthal, Julika Hillmann, Malte Kaukal, Peter Hilker, Katharina Micheel, Thomas Skora, and Moritz Niehaus who significantly contributed to the realization of the Mobility Skills in the German Foreign Service (GFS) study.

Jack Kostal, Brenton Wiernik, and Deniz Ones wish to thank their colleagues at Korn Ferry, especially Joy Hazucha, for making data available for the global comparisons of expatriate and domestic employees described in this volume.

Hannah Foldes, Deniz Ones, Handan Sinangil, and Brenton Wiernik wish to thank the many students without whose efforts during data collection the studies of expatriate success in Turkey described in this volume could not have been possible.

We also note that all the chapters in this volume have undergone external peer review. As customary, the editors of the volumes critically reviewed the chapters they did not co-author. We also relied on contributing authors reviewing chapters they were not involved in. Each chapter was also reviewed by external reviewers. Our heartfelt thanks go to Casey Giordano, Brenda Ellis, Jeff Dahlke, and Oren Shewach for providing additional blind peer reviews of the chapters in this book. Their contributions have greatly enhanced the quality of the final work.

We hope that the productivity, well-being, and indeed lives of expatriates and the millions who depend on or benefit from their work will be enhanced by the research presented in this book.

Table of contents

Advancing Expatriate Research in Public and Private Sectors

Brenton M. Wiernik, Heiko Rüger, and Deniz S. Ones

Abstract

This volume draws on four large and diverse investigations of expatriate employees to rigorously examine factors that contribute to expatriate success across cultural contexts, economic sectors, and expatriate populations. In this introduction, we present the studies contributing to these investigations, describe the research questions addressed in each thematic section of the book, and situate the studies in the broader expatriate research literature. We conclude with a discussion of the implications of rigorous research for global human resource management practice.

1   Introduction

Globalization is a complex and ongoing challenge for contemporary organizations. Foreign markets continually grow in importance as sources of business revenues. Organizations increasingly rely on employees sent on international assignments to forge international connections, set up and manage foreign establishments, fix problems, and otherwise manage their global business operations (BGRS 2016). As companies come to rely on expatriates for running their foreign investments, they are confronted with the unique challenges of managing an international workforce. Companies capable of meeting these challenges have a distinct competitive advantage and outperform those that cannot (Guthridge/Komm 2008). At the same time, global human resource management is also growing increasingly important and challenging in other sectors, including non-profit, governmental, diplomatic, and military organizations (Anderson 2001). Employees sent abroad by these organizations face similar challenges as corporate expatriates, but they also must manage organizational and situational factors that are unique to non-profit and public sector international assignments. Accordingly, this book explores critical factors that contribute to expatriate success and failure across diverse contexts.

The chapters in this volume draw on four rigorous investigations assessing international employees from a wide range of populations, cultural backgrounds, and host country contexts. In this introduction, we first describe the four large data gathering efforts contributing to this book, highlighting their unique strengths that allow them to complement and extend existing knowledge in the expatriate literature. Next, we introduce the thematic sections of the book, summarize each chapter, and connect their findings to previous expatriate meta-analyses and other research. Finally, we consider the broad conclusions we can draw from the studies in this volume and offer key questions for continuing expatriate research and practice.

2 Investigations Contributing to this Book

2.1 *International Generalizability of Expatriate Success Factors (iGOES) Project*

The iGOES project was designed as an in-depth, rigorous cross-cultural examination of the factors that promote and detract from expatriate success. It was initiated to resolve a puzzling discrepancy between expatriate management research and practice. In *practice*, organizations often rotate managers from one remote subsidiary to another, assuming that "the same attributes and behaviors that [make] a manager successful in one country will allow [them] to be effective in another" (House et al. 2001: 490). In contrast, expatriate *research* (and cross-cultural psychology in general) assumes that "cultural paradigms guide construction of meaning across many domains of social life" (Lehman et al. 2004: 695). That is, cultural differences in values, perceptions, and behaviors lead different factors to drive success and failure in each country. Relations between variables are not expected to generalize from one cultural context to the next (cf. Atwater et al. 2009; Torelli/Shavitt 2010). Thus, the iGOES project sought to resolve this research–practice gap by empirically examining whether relations of critical individual and environmental factors to expatriate success outcomes are, in fact, consistent across cultures. To this end, iGOES gathered data using the same measures from expatriates living in 28 countries across the world, covering all of the GLOBE cultural clusters (House et al. 2004). iGOES sampled only German-speaking expatriates (i.e., German, Austrian, and Swiss). This design allowed iGOES to systematically examine the generalizability of predictor-criterion relations while controlling for the confounding influence of expatriates' home cultures (Ones et al. 2012a).[1]

A key strength of the iGOES project is that it examined a wide array of criterion constructs. Most expatriate research focuses exclusively on international adjustment – the degree of comfort and absence of stress expatriates feel in their host countries (Bhaskar-Shrinivas et al. 2005). For decades, researchers have called for a more inclusive consideration of the expatriate criterion space (e.g., Deller 1997; Hippler et al. 2014; Mol et al. 2005b; Ones/Viswesvaran 1997; Thomas/Lazarova 2006). iGOES aimed to address these calls by measuring not only adjustment, but also job performance and job and life satisfaction. Previous research has demonstrated that while adjustment is related to performance and satisfaction, these relations are moderate at most (e.g., correlations corrected for unreliability [ρ] range .11 to .21 for non-self-rated job performance, .22 to .44 for job satisfaction; Bhaskar-Shrinivas et al. 2005; Hechanova et al. 2003). Thus, by examining predictor relations with additional criteria, iGOES provides a clearer picture of the factors promoting the full scope of "expatriate success".

Moreover, iGOES used construct valid and psychometrically rigorous methods to assess each expatriate criterion. iGOES researchers assessed multiple specific dimensions of international adjustment (Black et al. 1991) and job performance (Campbell/Wiernik 2015; Viswesvaran/Ones 2000), and measured performance using ratings from host country nationals, reducing common method bias and incorporating the most culturally-relevant perceptions and evaluations of performance behaviors (Sinangil/Ones 1997; Takeuchi 2010). Finally, whenever possible, iGOES applied cutting-edge meta-analytic methods to analyze predictor–criterion relations and accurately estimate whether observed differences in relations across countries are from statistical artefacts or true cross-cultural variability (Ones et al. 2012a). Altogether, these strengths permit iGOES to draw strong conclusions about the

---

[1] Additional information about the iGOES project research design and procedures are available in Albrecht et al. (2018b, Appendix A, this volume), as well as Ones et al. (2012a) and Albrecht et al. (2014).

contributions of various factors to expatriate success with key implications for organizations seeking to select, train, develop, manage, and support international employees.

2.2   *Mobility Skills in the German Foreign Service (GFS) Study*

Most expatriate research focuses on managerial employees of multinational corporations. This literature has yielded key insights into how employees adapt during international mobility and how sending organizations can best manage employees to maximize success. However, international assignments are not only practiced by profit-oriented enterprises. Non-profit organizations, such as charities and NGOs, and public sector governmental units, such as military, diplomatic service, and foreign development and aid departments, also send employees on international assignments that vary widely in terms of their duration, adaptation challenges, work responsibilities, interaction with local culture, and other characteristics (Brandt/Buck 2005; Chang 2005; Claus et al. 2015; Fisher/Hutchings 2013; Selmer/Fenner 2009a). The frequency and intensity of these non-profit and public sector international rotations are increasing at similar rates as private sector expatriation (Brandt/Buck 2005; Fenner/Selmer 2008; Selmer/Fenner 2009b). Non-profit and public sector international assignments are similar in many ways to private sector secondments, but employees sent on these assignments also have unique challenges not faced by corporate expatriates. Thus, while many findings from private sector expatriates may generalize to the public sector, there is a need also for research specifically on these unique populations of international employees. The aim of this project was thus to study factors that promote success among diplomats in the German Foreign Service (GFS).

Diplomacy has been a central motivation for international travel for thousands of years; indeed, in many ways, diplomats and ambassadors were the first "expatriates" (Albrecht et al. 2018a; Arnold 1998). Employees of the GFS work worldwide in a rotation system. Employees are deployed to a new country every three to five years. Employees cycle between domestic posts in Germany and international posts spanning all degrees of comfort, difficulty, desirability, and safety (Brandt/Buck 2005). Virtually all GFS employees in all roles and hierarchical levels are part of the rotation, and each employee faces the constant challenge of learning and adapting to new contexts and demands. In the GFS, mobility is profoundly institutionalized, professionalized, and accompanied by a "unique transnational vocational culture" (Niedner-Kalthoff 2006).

Using an online confidential survey of 35.5% percent of all GFS employees ($N = 2,598$), this project explored how employees respond to these frequent rotations throughout their careers. The GFS project thus examines a critical, but under-researched population of international employees. Given the intensity of GFS rotations, the investigators were particularly interested in impacts on employees' health, well-being, personal relationships, and family life. Thus, like iGOES, the GFS project also extended the expatriate criterion space to include not only adjustment, but also job satisfaction, stress, mental and physical health, work–life conflict, and other outcomes. The project explored a variety of psychological, social, sociodemographic, environmental, and preparatory factors that may mitigate or exacerbate the adverse consequences of rotations.[2]

---

[2]   For additional details on the GFS project, see Rüger et al. (2018, Appendix B, this volume), Rüger et al. (2013), and Fliege et al. (2016).

2.3   Global Comparisons of Expatriate Strengths Study

International assignments are a unique type of work environment in expatriate employees must manage not only their work responsibilities but also ongoing challenges with adapting their personal and family lives to their new location. Expatriates often find that the line between work and non-work blurs on international assignments (Albrecht et al. 2018a; Lazarova et al. 2010; Takeuchi et al. 2002). The unique challenges and features of international assignments raise the question of whether expatriates are a similarly *unique population* of employees. Do expatriates systematically differ from their domestic counterparts in their home countries? Who are the individuals who apply for and accept international assignments, and which employee characteristics influence organizations' decisions to send specific employees abroad? Similarly, do expatriates differ from host country national (HCNs) employees? Do expatriates bring a unique suite of psychological characteristics and experiences to their host countries? Answering these questions has not only theoretical implications for modeling the expatriation process, but also practical implications for international human resource management research and practice. For example, how do personality differences for employees willing to accept international assignments affect organizational recruitment procedures? Does range restriction among expatriates on personality traits and experience variables change their validity and utility for criterion prediction? What are the implications for multinational organizations choosing to hire expatriates over HCNs? Previous research comparing expatriates to domestic employees has usually focused on sociodemographic characteristics (e.g., gender, age, family structure, education; van der Velde et al. 2005), job characteristics and anticipated benefits (e.g., Konopaske/ Werner 2005; van der Velde et al. 2005), or outcomes (e.g., job satisfaction, mental health; Bonache 2005; Truman et al. 2011), rather than psychological and human capital variables that are likely to be antecedents of expatriate success (Albrecht et al. 2018a).

This study sought to address these questions by systematically comparing expatriates to home and host country domestic employees. The study used archival data from a large multinational HRM consulting firm to examine the characteristics of 1,679 expatriates originating from 86 countries and working in 79 countries. The investigators compared expatriates to nearly 20,000 domestic employees working in their home and host countries. Expatriate and domestic employees in these samples represented a wide range of industries, functional roles, and hierarchical levels. Like the iGOES project, this study used cross-cultural psychometric meta-analysis (Ones et al. 2012a) to examine within-country expatriate–domestic mean and variance differences on various predictors. This approach allowed for accurate estimation of differences unbiased by country-level mean differences or cultural factors. This approach also allowed the degree of variation in expatriate–domestic differences (and thus the space available for possible moderators) to be empirically estimated.

2.4   Studies of Expatriate Success in Turkey

The final studies contributing to this volume examined two samples of professional expatriates employed in Turkey. Turkey is an intriguing context for expatriate research. It has a cultural history that straddles Western and Middle Eastern ideas and practices (House et al. 2004; Müftüler-Bac 1999). At the time that these studies were conducted, it had a rapidly developing economy. Living and working in Turkey can be a challenge for Western expatriates, perhaps even more so than in Eastern and Southern Asia and other contexts that are more common in expatriate research. As a result, Turkey is an ideal context for studying whether conflicting cultural factors change relations between predictor and criterion variables among expatriates. The expatriates in this study were employed in a wide variety of industries and held a range of hierarchical levels. The major aim of this research was to examine the contribution of social and psychological factors to a wider range of criteria than typically considered in expatriate research (e.g., including job satisfaction and job performance). The studies particularly sought to generalize well-established findings from domestic employee research (such as the contribution of personality traits to job performance; Barrick et al. 2001) to the expatriate context using traditional and rigorous validation procedures.

Study/sample 1 examined 220 expatriates working in Turkey and 220 host country national coworkers who reported on expatriates' work behaviors. The study included qualitative investigations of expatriates' and host country nationals' experiences and perspectives on expatriate success (Sinangil/Ones 1997), as well as quantitative estimation of predictor–criterion relations. Expatriates completed measures of their international adjustment, stay intentions, and job satisfaction. Unlike most expatriate job performance research, which uses short (often self-rated) measures of "overall job performance" (Bhaskar-Shrinivas et al. 2005; Mol et al. 2005b), host country nationals rated expatriates' performance on 10 specific performance dimensions. Such multifactor performance measures are more construct-valid (Viswesvaran/Ones 2000), more conducive to feedback, training, and decision-making (Campbell/Wiernik 2015), and permit investigators to examine the divergent nomological networks of different types of effective expatriate performance behaviors (Hough/Dunnette 1992; cf. Hogan/Holland 2003). Study/sample 2 of the study included 311 expatriates and was gathered several years later using the same sampling design and an even more comprehensive performance measure.

3   Sections of this Book

This book is organized around four thematic sections. Each section draws studies and findings from different sets of the investigations described above.

3.1   *Thematic Section A: Psychological Individual Differences*

The first thematic section of this book considers what psychological characteristics lead individuals to become expatriates and how these traits impact expatriate success, satisfaction, and well-being once they arrive. Compared to domestic employee research, very few studies have investigated relations of stable individual differences characteristic with expatriate success (Albrecht et al. 2018a). Basic questions about role of broad traits such as Emotional Stability, Openness, and Extraversion in driving expatriate outcomes remain unanswered. The state of this literature stands in contrast to widespread beliefs among international human resource managers about the importance of personality traits and other psychological characteristic for expatriate adjustment, performance, and persistence (Ones/Viswesvaran 1999). The chapters in this section explore a variety of psychological individual differences, including traits unique to expatriate settings and broader traits that have been studied in many employment contexts (Barrick et al. 2001).

First, Kostal et al. (*Expatriate Personality: Facet-Level Comparisons with Domestic Counterparts*) consider what types of employees seek out, accept, and are chosen for international assignments. They use data from their large consulting database, the iGOES project, and the studies of expatriates in Turkey to compare expatriate and domestic employees on general personality traits used widely in human resource management research and practice, including the Big Five traits and lower-order personality dimensions. Second, Waibel et al. (*Antecedents and Consequences of Mobility Self-Efficacy*) consider the impact of a psychological individual differences construct unique to the expatriate context. They compare the relative validity of international mobility-specific self-efficacy beliefs versus decontextualized, domain-general self-efficacy for understanding expatriate satisfaction and well-being outcomes. Third, Albrecht et al. (*Tolerance of Ambiguity: Relations with Expatriate Adjustment and Job Performance*) examine tolerance of ambiguity, a trait developed in the earliest days of personality research (Frenkel-Brunswik 1949) and widely believed to be critical for expatriate success (Caligiuri 2000); they find no evidence of criterion-related validity for this oft-cited expatriate competency. Fourth, Ones et al. (*Validity of Big Five Personality Traits for Expatriate Success: Results from Turkey*) broaden the scope of psychological individual differences considered in expatriate research by examining Big Five personality trait validities for expatriate adjustment and job performance. Fifth, Fliege and Wiernik (*Core Self-Evaluative Traits: Self-efficacy, Locus of Control, Optimism and Diplomat Success*) consider another set of constructs that have received wide attention across numerous psychological literatures. They examine how core self-evaluative traits (Judge et al. 1997) can serve as an important psychological resource supporting diplomats' adjustment, satisfaction, and well-being. Finally, Sinangil et al. (*Integrity: Generalizing Findings from Domestic to Expatriate Contexts*) examine integrity, a compound personality trait demonstrated to be one of the best predictors of performance among domestic employees (Ones et al. 1993, 2012b; Schmidt et al. 2016), but which heretofore has been unexamined among expatriates. Together, the chapters in this section provide new insights into the validity of psychological characteristics for a variety of expatriate success outcomes and offer guidance for future expatriate research and practice.

3.2   Thematic Section B: Age and Experience

The second thematic section considers the impacts of employee career stage on their experiences during international assignments, as well as how different types of professional experiences can prepare expatriates for success. Employee age and job-relevant experience are highly influential variables in expatriate management practice. Previous international experience is one of the most-often considered factors during expatriate selection (Anderson 2005; Deller 1997; Harris/Brewster 1999), and such experience is widely-assumed to be highly beneficial for future adjustment and performance (Black et al. 1991; Caligiuri et al. 2001). However, employee age is also associated with a myriad of negative stereotypes, including that older expatriates are unwilling and unable to adjust and more prone to ethnocentrism and other close-minded biases (Olsen/Martins 2009; Wu/Bodigerel-Koehler 2013). Existing empirical evidence has questioned these assumptions, however. Meta-analyses have found zero relationship between age and expatriate success and experience–success relations that were at most small (Hechanova et al. 2003; Mol et al. 2005a). However, the total sample sizes for these analyses were small, necessitating additional studies to provide stable and nuanced estimates of the role of age and experience in expatriate success. This section continues these critical examinations of age and experience-related assumptions by examining the impact of these time-related variables on new expatriate criteria, in new expatriate populations, and from new perspectives.

First, Albrecht et al. (*The Impact of Age and Experience on Expatriate Outcomes*) study the impact of age and six forms of job-relevant experience on job satisfaction and multiple dimensions of expatriate adjustment and job performance in the iGOES samples; they observe negligible to small effects for most relations. Second, Waibel et al. (*Impacts of Age, Tenure, and Experiences on Expatriate Adjustment and Job Satisfaction*) examine similar questions among GFS diplomats. They also find mostly negligible impacts of temporal variables on outcomes, but do observe that increasing tenure can lead to dissatisfaction for high-level diplomats if their realized work experiences fail to meet their expectations. Third, Kostal et al. (*Expatriate Leadership Experience: Host Country Burden or Resource?*) consider the host country perspective by examining whether expatriate managers' leadership experience backgrounds are likely to be an opportunity or liability for HCNs. Across specific forms of experience, they find that expatriates have more experience than either HCNs or domestic managers in their home countries. This supports a resource view of expatriate employees.

3.3 Thematic Section C: Support and Preparation

The third thematic section of this book continues along the expatriation journey by exploring how organizations prepare their employees for international assignments and support them after arrival. The methods for and impacts of such expatriate preparation and support practices have been the primary focus of expatriate research (Albrecht et al. 2018a; Bhaskar-Shrinivas et al. 2005; Harrison et al. 2004). Meta-analytic evidence supports the substantial role that organizational and social support play in expatriate adjustment (unreliability-corrected correlations [ρ] range .07–.22 across dimensions of support and adjustment; Bhaskar-Shrinivas et al. 2005). Similarly, multiple meta-analyses have found small to large positive effects of pre-departure training programs on expatriate adjustment and performance (Deshpande et al. 1994; Deshpande/Viswesvaran 1992; Morris/Robie 2001). However, each of these meta-analyses observed substantial variability in training effectiveness across samples and called for more nuanced research into the benefits of specific types of pre-departure training. This section extends these findings by examining the benefits of preparation and support for new criteria and by considering a variety of important moderators of these effects.

First, Albrecht et al. (*Success Among Self-Initiated Versus Assigned Expatriates*) compare expatriates from two populations assumed to differ in their degree of organizational support and investment – self-initiated versus organizationally-assigned expatriates. They find few differences between these groups and call for more nuanced consideration of expatriate subgroups and more construct-valid measures of initiative in future expatriate research. Second, Wiernik et al. (*Lingua Necessaria? Language Proficiency and Expatriate Success*) examine language proficiency, a form of preparation often regarded as a key enabling factor for expatriate success. They find that while language proficiency is beneficial for adjustment, it has a modest effect on other criteria. Third, Kostal et al. (*Expatriate Training: Intercontextual Analyses from the iGOES Project*) explore the relative effectiveness of different types of expatriate training programs and the moderating effects of training design factors on dimensions of adjustment, job performance, and satisfaction. Finally, Bellinger et al. (*Organizational and Social Support Among Foreign Service Diplomats*) consider the impacts of a variety of organizational and social support systems on diplomat adjustment, family, and well-being outcomes. They find that the benefits of support vary for diplomats with different family structures.

3.4   Thematic Section D: Gender and Family

In the final thematic section of this book, authors consider how gender and family status can affect expatriates' experience while abroad. These factors are a common concern for sending organizations. Between 70–80% of expatriates are accompanied by their spouses, partners, children, or other family members (BGRS 2012), but an increasing number of expatriates choose to leave their families in their home countries, either out of concern that an international move will be harmful to families' well-being, safety, or career prospects (BGRS 2016) or out of fear that having their families present will interfere with expatriates' ability to adjust, perform, and complete their international assignments (BGRS 2012; Haslberger/Brewster 2008). Many organizations also fear that female expatriates will be unable to adjust and succeed abroad, particularly in countries perceived as hostile to women (Baruch/Reis 2015; Caligiuri/Cascio 1998; Sinangil/Ones 2003; Vance/McNulty 2014). These preconceptions result in fewer women being chosen for international assignments compared to men (Andresen et al. 2015; BGRS 2016). This discrepancy is particularly concerning given that international experience is increasingly regarded as a critical factor for advancement into higher ranks of organizational leadership (BGRS 2016; Stahl et al. 2002; Vance 2005).

Despite the pervasiveness of organizational practical concerns about female expatriates and expatriate families, previous expatriate research has only rarely examined these factors. For example, Hechanova et al.'s (2003) meta-analysis of expatriate adjustment included only 4–5 studies of gender and 2–4 studies of family variables (cf. Bhaskar-Shrinivas et al. 2005, who meta-analyzed a somewhat larger sample of studies reporting expatriate employee–spouse adjustment relations [individual analyses included between $k = 3$–11 studies each]). Similarly, Mol et al.'s (2005a) meta-analysis of expatriate job performance included only 5 studies of gender and no studies of family variables. Much more academic attention has been given to theoretical and conceptual discussions of gender and family issues than to empirical tests of model predictions (Albrecht et al. 2018a; cf. Lazarova et al. 2010; Takeuchi 2010). Thus, the studies in this section address critical issues about the role of gender and family in supporting and hindering expatriate success, with total sample sizes that are in some cases larger than the entire existing literatures on these questions.

First, Ones et al. (*A Family Affair: Spouse and Children's Role in Expatriate Adjustment and Job Performance*) examine the impacts of family presence, adjustment, and support on expatriate adjustment, performance and stay intentions. They find that being separated from their children has negative consequences for expatriate parents and also observe results consistent with meta-analytic findings on the importance of family adjustment and support during expatriation. Second, Mercado et al. (*Influence of Family Presence on Expatriate Adjustment and Satisfaction*) also consider the impact of family presence and separation on expatriate outcomes. They find that accompanying family members are generally beneficial for expatriates, but can in some contexts interfere with efforts to integrate host country culture. Third, Foldes et al. (*Gender Differences in Job Performance and Adjustment: Do Women Expatriates Measure Up?*) challenge stereotypes about women's inability to succeed in difficult international contexts by showing that male and female expatriates tend to adjust and perform at similar levels. Finally, Waibel and Rüger (*Influence of Gender and Family Status on Expatriate Well-Being*) show that diplomat women and single parents can experience poorer well-being and discuss how organizations can best support expatriates with challenging family demands.

4   Evidence-Based Expatriate Management: Critical Questions for Research and Practice

We believe that this volume makes an important contribution to advancing basic knowledge on factors that promote success across populations of expatriates. The size and complexity of statistical models used in expatriate research continues to grow, but foundational knowledge of relations among many critical variables remains based on only a handful of studies and only a few hundred expatriates (Albrecht et al. 2018a). We hope that the studies in this volume can strengthen the foundation of empirical knowledge in expatriate management and provide direction for future research on international employees. In particular, we hope that the results presented in the current analyses can contribute to future meta-analyses cumulating studies on the impacts of gender, family, age, support, self-efficacy, personality, and other factors on expatriate success.

Furthermore, we also hope that the findings of these studies can inform organizations seeking to apply evidence-based practice in their systems for expatriate selection, development, support, and management. As future expatriate research also seeks to enhance organizational international HRM practices, investigations that provide rigorous estimation and validation of basic variable relationships with multi-source data, psychometrically strong measures, and large diverse samples will be critical. Below, we highlight two additional key challenges for future expatriate research.

4.1   Generalizability Versus Specificity

All expatriate research is unified by the challenges of employees crossing national borders and contending with changing cultural contexts, organizational environments, and work responsibilities. However, a key conceit of much expatriate research is that expatriate success factors are unique and specific to each cultural context (Atwater et al. 2009; Lehman et al. 2004; Takeuchi et al. 2005; Torelli/Shavitt 2010). However, despite the purported emphasis of expatriate research on understanding cultural specificity, studies have neglected to empirically examine whether relations among expatriate-relevant variables are consistent or vary across cultures and geographic regions (Ones et al. 2012a). Culture-specific factors are most often considered only in the introduction and discussion sections of reports and not measured or tested explicitly. Among studies that sample from multiple cultural contexts and make comparisons, nearly all studies are limited to two or three distinct cultures (Franke/ Richey 2010). By systematically comparing relations across cultures, examining multiple populations of expatriates, and comparing expatriate research to domestic employee findings, the studies in this book shed valuable light on the degree to which expatriate success factors vary across contexts and the factors which may (and may not) explain this variation.

The studies in this book found that many relations are highly consistent across cultures (e.g., tolerance of ambiguity, Albrecht et al. 2018d, Chapter 4; language proficiency, Wiernik et al. 2018, Chapter 12). Where studies did find variability (e.g., relations of expatriate age with job performance), the pattern of variation was often unrelated to factors commonly thought to be critical moderators (e.g., age–performance relations were unrelated to cultural attitudes toward the elderly and aging, Albrecht et al. 2018c, Chapter 8). The general findings of consistency in variable relations across cultures supports global HRM practices that emphasize the same factors for expatriates assigned to diverse locations (Brandt/Buck 2005; House et al. 2004). As expatriate research progresses, and as organizations seek data to inform evidence-based expatriate management practice, studies must continue to systematically compare expatriate success-relevant variables across many cultural contexts. Large scale, multinational collaborations, such as iGOES and similar studies (e.g., GLOBE, House et al. 2004; CISMS, Spector et al. 2002) are the ideal research designs for rigorously examining generalizability and specificity across cultures. Critically, comparisons of findings across cultural contexts (whether in intercultural primary studies or as part of literature reviews) must separate true cross-cultural variation from variation due to sampling error, measurement error, range variation, and other statistical artefacts (ideally using psychometric meta-analysis; Ones et al. 2012a).

Studies in this book also reveal that the critical moderators of expatriate success factors may not be culture, but other national, situational, personal, and environmental characteristics. For example, Waibel et al. (2018b, Chapter 3) found that the impacts of mobility self-efficacy on locational adjustment varied across levels of post difficulty – self-efficacy was less effective for promoting adjustment in locations that lacked basic comforts and were dangerous or hostile. Though post difficulty may be related to culture, this effect more likely stems from broader environmental factors, such as harsher stressors. Even more removed from culture, Waibel et al. (2018a, Chapter 9) found that the importance of job design factors varied across diplomat ages and hierarchical levels. Addressing these factors requires not tailoring of expatriate management to a specific culture, but application of HRM and organizational development programs that have been commonplace for domestic establishments for decades. As expatriate research continues, searches for moderators and boundary conditions across contexts should focus not only on cultural factors, but also on specific environmental and situational constraints on behavior, adaptation, and success. Sending organizations must consider not only the culture of host countries, but also whether the organizations' broader human resource management and support systems are conducive to expatriate success.

4.2   Connecting Private Sector and Public Sector Expatriate Research and Practice References

There are some key differences between private sector expatriates and diplomats and other public sector international employees. Whereas corporate expatriates typically complete only one or two international assignments during their careers, diplomats face the prospect of continuous international rotations, requiring them to repeatedly adjust to new cultures and contexts. Public sector expatriates also tend to reflect a more diverse range of occupations, hierarchical levels, and job characteristics than private sector expatriates, and the role of public sector expatriates as part of organizations' overall strategic goals often differs greatly from that of corporate expatriates. However, despite these differences, public and private sector international employees are also similar in many ways and require similar forms of psychological, social, and organizational support resources to be successful. Public and private sector expatriate research and practice can meaningfully inform each other.

The 50-year-old Peace Corps studies notwithstanding (Church 1982; Mischel 1965; Smith 1966; Textor 1966), research on private sector expatriates is more developed than the literature on non-profit and public sector international employees. Many findings on corporate expatriation, such as factors that support adjustment, the predictive validity of socio-demographic and psychological characteristics, and methods for assessing cultural characteristics, individual variables, and success outcomes, can be directly applied to inform HRM practices for diplomats, international aid providers, and other public sector expatriates. Public sector expatriate researchers should also replicate studies on private sector expatriates to examine whether and how relations between various antecedents and expatriate success vary across sectors.

Public sector research and practice can also inform private sector expatriate management practice. There is an emerging population of "rotation" managers in private sector multinational organizations (House et al. 2004). These high-mobility managers face very similar challenges for repeated relocation and adaptation as do foreign service diplomats. The methods that foreign services use to select, train, and support diplomats may be applied in the private sector to help these managers meet the challenges of highly-mobile international careers. For example, the German Foreign Service has implemented a range of support interventions including not only cross-cultural training, but also on-site psychosocial counseling, transition planning, coordinated peer support networks, logistical support, and programs to help diplomat spouses and families adjust and find employment (Bellinger et al. 2018, Chapter 14, this volume). Private sector multinational organizations should consider implementing similar programs into their international HRM practice. However, like many private sector HRM practices, public sector expatriate support programs are rarely subjected to empirical validation of their efficacy (cf. Campbell et al. 2018; Cohen 2007; Mendenhall et al. 2004; Ones et al. 2017; Perez et al. 2017; Rynes et al. 2007). The GFS study reported in this volume is among the first critical evaluations of human resource management practices in a foreign service department. Future expatriate research and practice should draw on the institutional knowledge accumulated in foreign services and other government departments, while using rigorous methods to determine which practices are actually effective and which practices might be fruitfully applied to business expatriates.

More generally, the support practices of foreign services around the world demonstrate strong values for investing in employees and having concern for their satisfaction, well-being, and personal and career development. Though management research often focuses on trends toward weakening psychological contracts between employers and employees (Sullivan/Baruch 2009) and on the increasing responsibility individuals must take for their own career development (Hall 2004; Wiernik/Kostal 2017), talent management, succession planning, and employee career development and management remain critical issues for organizations (cf. Wiernik/Wille 2018). As international assignments become an increasingly important part of organizational leadership development programs (BGRS 2016; Cartus 2016), understanding how these assignments can be made developmental, rather than harmful, is critical. Again, foreign services' and other non-profit and public sector organizations' expertise on investing in international employees can inform private sector organizations seeking to do the same, but the efficacy of such recommendations must be empirically validated.

Finally, knowledge from public sector expatriate research and practice can also inform research and practice on the diverse populations of expatriate employees. Nearly all private sector expatriate research has focused on managerial- or executive-level employees. Studies of the international relocation process for non-managerial (e.g., engineers, researchers, education and health care professionals) and non-professional (e.g., secretarial staff, skilled tradespeople, agricultural workers, unskilled laborers) employees are sorely needed (cf. Goldin/Reinert 2007; OECD 2006, 2008). Diplomatic, governmental, military, and non-profit organizations have grappled with managing mobility among diverse populations for decades; insights from these organizations' experiences should inform expatriate research for these groups.

International mobility continues to grow in its importance and global impact. Strong empirical investigations and communication between researchers and practitioners across sectors will enable multinational organizations of all types to meet these challenges.

References

Albrecht, Anne-Grit et al. (2014): Openness in Cross-Cultural Work Settings: A Multicountry Study of Expatriates. In: *Journal of Personality Assessment*, Special Issue: Openness to Experience 96,1: 64–75. [https://doi.org/10.1080/00223891.2013.821074].

Albrecht, Anne-Grit; Ones, Deniz S.; Sinangil, Handan Kepir (2018a): Expatriate Management. In: Ones, Deniz S. et al. (Eds.): The SAGE Handbook of Industrial, Work and Organizational Psychology. Volume 3: Managerial Psychology and Organizational Approaches. 2nd ed. London, United Kingdom: Sage: 429–468.

Albrecht, Anne-Grit et al. (2018b): Design, Implementation, and Analysis of the iGOES Project. In: Wiernik, Brenton M.; Rüger, Heiko; Ones, Deniz S. (Eds.): Managing Expatriates: Success Factors in Private and Public Domains, Series on Population Studies 50. Opladen, Germany: Barbara Budrich Publishers.

Albrecht, Anne-Grit et al. (2018c): The Impact of Age and Experience on Expatriate Outcomes. In: Wiernik, Brenton M.; Rüger, Heiko; Ones, Deniz S. (Eds.): Managing Expatriates: Success Factors in Private and Public Domains, Series on Population Studies 50. Opladen, Germany: Barbara Budrich Publishers.

Albrecht, Anne-Grit et al. (2018d): Tolerance of Ambiguity: Relations with Expatriate Adjustment and Job Performance. In: Wiernik, Brenton M.; Rüger, Heiko; Ones, Deniz S. (Eds.): Managing Expatriates: Success Factors in Private and Public Domains, Series on Population Studies 50. Opladen, Germany: Barbara Budrich Publishers.

Anderson, Barbara A. (2005): Expatriate Selection: Good Management or Good Luck? In: *International Journal of Human Resource Management* 16,4: 567–583. [https://doi.org/10.1080/09585190500051647].

Anderson, Barbara A. (2001): Expatriate Management: An Australian Tri-Sector Comparative Study. In: *Thunderbird International Business Review* 43,1: 33–52. [https://doi.org/10/d54w7d].

Andresen, Maike; Biemann, Torsten; Pattie, Marshall Wilson (2015): What Makes Them Move Abroad? Reviewing and Exploring Differences between Self-Initiated and Assigned Expatriation. In: *International Journal of Human Resource Management* 26,7: 932–947. [https://doi.org/10.1080/09585192.2012.669780].

Arnold, Hans (1998): Diplomatie. In: Woyke, Wichard (Ed.): Handwörterbuch Internationale Politik. Wiesbaden: VS Verlag für Sozialwissenschaften: 49–54. [https://doi.org/10/b6k8].

Atwater, Leanne et al. (2009): Are Cultural Characteristics Associated with the Relationship between Self and Others' Ratings of Leadership? In: *Journal of Applied Psychology* 94,4: 876–886. [https://doi.org/10.1037/a0014561].

Barrick, Murray R.; Mount, Michael K.; Judge, Timothy A. (2001): Personality and Performance at the Beginning of the New Millennium: What Do We Know and Where Do We Go Next? In: *International Journal of Selection and Assessment* 9,1/2: 9–30. [https://doi.org/10/frqhf2].

Baruch, Yehuda; Reis, Cristina (2015): Global Career Challenges for Women Crossing International Borders. In: Broadbridge, Adelina M.; Fielden, Sandra L. (Eds.): Handbook of Gendered Careers in Management: Getting in, Getting on, Getting Out. Cheltenham, United Kingdom: Elgar: 341–356. [https://doi.org/10.4337/9781782547709].

Bellinger, Maria M.; Wiernik, Brenton M.; Fliege, Herbert (2018): Organizational and Social Support among Foreign Service Diplomats. In: Wiernik, Brenton M.; Rüger, Heiko; Ones, Deniz S. (Eds.): Managing Expatriates: Success Factors in Private and Public Domains, Series on Population Studies 50. Opladen, Germany: Barbara Budrich Publishers.

BGRS (2016): Breakthrough to the Future of Global Talent Mobility: 2016 Global Mobility Trends Survey Report. Woodridge, IL: Brookfield Global Relocation Services. [http://globalmobilitytrends.brookfieldgrs.com].

BGRS (2012): Global Relocation Trends: 2012 Survey Report. Woodridge, IL: Brookfield Global Relocation Services. [http://globalmobilitytrends.brookfieldgrs.com].

Bhaskar-Shrinivas, Purnima et al. (2005): Input-Based and Time-Based Models of International Adjustment: Meta-Analytic Evidence and Theoretical Extensions. In: *Academy of Management Journal* 48,2: 257–281. [https://doi.org/10.5465/AMJ.2005.16928400].

Black, J. Stewart; Mendenhall, Mark E.; Oddou, Gary R. (1991): Toward a Comprehensive Model of International Adjustment: An Integration of Multiple Theoretical Perspectives. In: *Academy of Management Review* 16,2: 291–317. [https://doi.org/10/fn7m8b].

Bonache, Jaime (2005): Job Satisfaction among Expatriates, Repatriates and Domestic Employees: The Perceived Impact of International Assignments on Work-related Variables. In: *Personnel Review* 34,1: 110–124. [https://doi.org/10.1108/00483480510571905].

Brandt, Enrico; Buck, Christian (2005): Auswärtiges Amt: Diplomatie als Beruf. 4th ed. Wiesbaden, Germany: VS Verlag für Sozialwissenschaften. [https://doi.org/10/b6k9].

Caligiuri, Paula M. et al. (2001): The Theory of Met Expectations Applied to Expatriate Adjustment: The Role of Cross-Cultural Training. In: *International Journal of Human Resource Management* 12,3: 357–372. [https://doi.org/10.1080/09585190121711].

Caligiuri, Paula M. (2000): Selecting Expatriates for Personality Characteristics: A Moderating Effect of Personality on the Relationship between Host National Contact and Cross-Cultural Adjustment. In: *MIR: Management International Review* 40,1: 61–80. [https://www.researchgate.net/publication/234021408].

Caligiuri, Paula M.; Cascio, Wayne F. (1998): Can We Send Her There? Maximizing the Success of Western Women on Global Assignments. In: *Journal of World Business* 33,4: 394–416. [https://doi.org/10.1016/S1090-9516(98)90024-4].

Campbell, John P.; Kuncel, Nathan R.; Kostal, Jack W. (2018): Training and Learning in Work Roles. In: Ones, Deniz S. et al. (Eds.): The SAGE Handbook of Industrial, Work and Organizational Psychology. Volume 1: Personnel Psychology and Employee Performance. 2nd ed. London, United Kingdom: Sage: 533–610.

Campbell, John P.; Wiernik, Brenton M. (2015): The Modeling and Assessment of Work Performance. In: *Annual Review of Organizational Psychology and Organizational Behavior* 2: 47–74. [https://doi.org/10/bc4k].

Cartus (2016): Trends in Global Relocation: 2016 Global Mobility Policy & Practices Survey. Danburry, CT: Cartus Corporation. [http://guidance.cartusrelocation.com/global-mobility-policy-and-practices-survey-2016.html].

Chang, Wei-Wen (2005): Expatriate Training in International Nongovernmental Organizations: A Model for Research. In: *Human Resource Development Review* 4,4: 440–461. [https://doi.org/10.1177/1534484305281035].

Church, T.A. (1982): Sojourner Adjustment. In: *Psychological Bulletin* 91,3: 540–572.

Claus, Lisbeth et al. (2015): Social Capital and Cultural Adjustment of International Assignees in NGOs: Do Support Networks Really Matter? In: *International Journal of Human Resource Management* 26,20: 2523–2542. [https://doi.org/10.1080/09585192.2014.1003083].

Cohen, Debra J. (2007): The Very Separate Worlds of Academic and Practitioner Publications in Human Resource Management: Reasons for the Divide and Solutions for Bridging the Gap. In: *Academy of Management Journal* 50,5: 1013–1019. [https://doi.org/10/fh8xg4].

Deller, Jürgen (1997): Expatriate Selection: Possibilities and Limitations of Using Personality Scales. In: Aycan, Zeynep (Ed.): Expatriate Management: Theory and Research, New Approaches to Employee Management 4. Greenwich, CT: JAI Press: 93–116.

Deshpande, Satish P.; Joseph, Jacob; Viswesvaran, Chockalingam (1994): Does Use of Student Samples Affect Results of Studies in Cross-Cultural Training: A Meta-Analysis. In: *Psychological Reports* 74,3: 779–785. [https://doi.org/10.2466/pr0.1994.74.3.779].

Deshpande, Satish P.; Viswesvaran, Chockalingam (1992): Is Cross-Cultural Training of Expatriate Managers Effective: A Meta Analysis. In: *International Journal of Intercultural Relations* 16,3: 295–310. [https://doi.org/10.1016/0147-1767(92)90054-X].

Fenner, Charles R., Jr.; Selmer, Jan (2008): Public Sector Expatriate Managers: Psychological Adjustment, Personal Characteristics and Job Factors. In: *International Journal of Human Resource Management* 19,7: 1237–1252. [https://doi.org/10.1080/09585190802110026].

Fisher, Kelly; Hutchings, Kate (2013): Making Sense of Cultural Distance for Military Expatriates Operating in an Extreme Context. In: *Journal of Organizational Behavior* 34,6: 791–812. [https://doi.org/10.1002/job.1882].

Fliege, Herbert et al. (2016): Diplomats' Quality of Life: The Role of Risk Factors and Coping Resources. In: *International Journal of Intercultural Relations* 51: 14–28. [https://doi.org/10.1016/j.ijintrel.2016.01.001].

Franke, George R.; Richey, R. Glenn (2010): Improving Generalizations from Multi-Country Comparisons in International Business Research. In: *Journal of International Business Studies* 41,8: 1275–1293. [https://doi.org/10.1057/jibs.2010.21].

Frenkel-Brunswik, Else (1949): Intolerance of Ambiguity as an Emotional and Perceptual Personality Variable. In: *Journal of Personality* 18,1: 108–143. [https://doi.org/10.1111/j.1467-6494.1949.tb01236.x].

Goldin, Ian; Reinert, Kenneth (2007): Globalization for Development: Trade, Finance, Aid, Migration and Policy. Revised. Washington, DC: The World Bank. [https://doi.org/10.1596/978-0-8213-6929-6].

Guthridge, Matthew; Komm, Asmus B. (2008): Why Multinationals Struggle to Manage Talent. In: *The McKinsey Quarterly* May,4: 1–5.

Hall, Douglas T. (2004): The Protean Career: A Quarter-Century Journey. In: *Journal of Vocational Behavior* 65,1: 1–13. [https://doi.org/10.1016/j.jvb.2003.10.006].

Harris, Hilary; Brewster, Chris (1999): The Coffee-Machine System: How International Selection Really Works. In: *International Journal of Human Resource Management* 10,3: 488–500. [https://doi.org/10.1080/095851999340440].

Harrison, David A.; Shaffer, Margaret A.; Bhaskar-Shrinivas, Purnima (2004): Going Places: Roads More and Less Traveled in Research on Expatriate Experiences. In: Cable, Daniel M. (Ed.): Research in Personnel and Human Resources Management. Volume 23. Amsterdam: Elsevier: 199–247. [https://doi.org/10/c9ddbd].

Haslberger, Arno; Brewster, Chris (2008): The Expatriate Family: An International Perspective. In: *Journal of Managerial Psychology* 23,3: 324–346. [https://doi.org/10/dwb3vt].

Hechanova, Regina; Beehr, Terry A.; Christiansen, Neil D. (2003): Antecedents and Consequences of Employees' Adjustment to Overseas Assignment: A Meta-Analytic Review. In: *Applied Psychology* 52,2: 213–236. [https://doi.org/10/d4f4xv].

Hippler, Thomas et al. (2014): The Development and Validation of a Theory-Based Expatriate Adjustment Scale. In: *International Journal of Human Resource Management* 25,14: 1938–1959. [https://doi.org/10.1080/09585192.2013.870286].

Hogan, Joyce; Holland, Brent (2003): Using Theory to Evaluate Personality and Job-Performance Relations: A Socioanalytic Perspective. In: *Journal of Applied Psychology* 88,1: 100–112. [https://doi.org/10.1037/0021-9010.88.1.100].

Hough, Leaetta M.; Dunnette, Marvin D. (1992): US Managers Abroad: What It Takes to Succeed. Presented at the Academy of Management Conference. Las Vegas, NV.

House, Robert J. et al. (Eds.) (2004): Culture, Leadership, and Organizations: The GLOBE Study of 62 Societies. Thousand Oaks, CA: Sage.

House, Robert J.; Javidan, Mansour; Dorfman, Peter W. (2001): Project GLOBE: An Introduction. In: *Applied Psychology* 50,4: 489–505. [https://doi.org/10/dkvp6j].

Judge, Timothy A.; Locke, Edwin A.; Durham, Cathy C. (1997): The Dispositional Causes of Job Satisfaction: A Core Evaluations Approach. In: *Research in Organizational Behavior* 19: 151–188.

Konopaske, Robert; Werner, Steve (2005): US Managers' Willingness to Accept a Global Assignment: Do Expatriate Benefits and Assignment Length Make a Difference? In: *International Journal of Human Resource Management* 16,7: 1159–1175. [https://doi.org/ 10.1080/09585190500143998].

Lazarova, Mila B.; Westman, Mina; Shaffer, Margaret A. (2010): Elucidating the Positive Side of the Work-Family Interface on International Assigments: A Model of Expatriate Work and Family Performance. In: *Academy of Management Review* 35,1: 93–117. [https://doi.org/10.1057/9781137006004_14].

Lehman, Darrin R.; Chiu, Chi-yue; Schaller, Mark (2004): Psychology and Culture. In: *Annual Review of Psychology* 55: 689–714. [https://doi.org/10/cfq2fg].

Mendenhall, Mark E. et al. (2004): Evaluation Studies of Cross-Cultural Training Programs: A Review of the Literature from 1988 to 2000. In: Landis, Dan; Bennett, Janet M.; Bennett, Milton J. (Eds.): Handbook of Intercultural Training. Thousand Oaks, CA: Sage: 129–143. [https://doi.org/10/b6mb].

Mischel, Walter (1965): Predicting the Success of Peace Corps Volunteers in Nigeria. In: *Journal of Personality and Social Psychology* 1,5: 510–517. [https://doi.org/10.1037/h0021915].

Mol, Stefan T. et al. (2005a): Predicting Expatriate Job Performance for Selection Purposes: A Quantitative Review. In: *Journal of Cross-Cultural Psychology* 36,5: 590–620. [https://doi.org/10.1177/0022022105278544].

Mol, Stefan T.; Born, Marise Ph.; van der Molen, Henk T. (2005b): Developing Criteria for Expatriate Effectiveness: Time to Jump off the Adjustment Bandwagon. In: *International Journal of Intercultural Relations* 29,3: 339–353. [https://doi.org/10/dk2vzk].

Morris, Mark A.; Robie, Chet (2001): A Meta-Analysis of the Effects of Cross-Cultural Training on Expatriate Performance and Adjustment. In: *International Journal of Training and Development* 5,2: 112–125. [https://doi.org/10.1111/1468-2419.00126].

Müftüler-Bac, Meltem (1999): Turkish Women's Predicament. In: *Women's Studies International Forum* 22,3: 303–315. [https://doi.org/10.1016/S0277-5395(99)00029-1].

Niedner-Kalthoff, Ulrike (2006): Rotation und Objektivität: Diplomaten als transnationale Migranten. In: Kreutzer, Florian; Roth, Silke (Eds.): Transnationale Karrieren: Biografien, Lebensführung und Mobilität. Wiesbaden, Germany: VS Verlag für Sozialwissenschaften: 83–99. [https://doi.org/ 10.1007/978-3-531-90283-8_4].

OECD (2008): The Global Competition for Talent: Mobility of the Highly Skilled. Paris, France: OECD. [https://doi.org/10.1787/9789264047754-en].

OECD (2006): Where Immigrant Students Succeed. Paris, France: OECD. [https://doi.org/10.1787/9789264023611-en].

Olsen, Jesse E.; Martins, Luis L. (2009): The Effects of Expatriate Demographic Characteristics on Adjustment: A Social Identity Approach. In: *Human Resource Management* 48,2: 311–328. [https://doi.org/10.1002/hrm.20281].

Ones, Deniz S. et al. (2017): Has Industrial-Organizational Psychology Lost Its Way? In: *The Industrial-Organizational Psychologist* 54,4: 67–74. [http://www.siop.org/tip/april17/lostio.aspx].

Ones, Deniz S. et al. (2012a): Cross-Cultural Generalization: Using Meta-Analysis to Test Hypotheses about Cultural Variability. In: Ryan, Ann Marie; Leong, Frederick T.L.; Oswald, Frederick L. (Eds.): Conducting Multinational Research Projects in Organizational Psychology: Challenges and Opportunities, APA/MSU Series on Multicultural Psychology 1. Washington, DC: American Psychological Association: 91–122. [https://doi.org/10/5kz].

Ones, Deniz S.; Viswesvaran, Chockalingam (1999): Relative Importance of Personality Dimensions for Expatriate Selection: A Policy Capturing Study. In: *Human Performance* 12,3/4: 275–294. [https://doi.org/10.1080/08959289909539872].

Ones, Deniz S.; Viswesvaran, Chockalingam (1997): Personality Determinants in the Prediction of Aspects of Expatriate Job Success. In: Aycan, Zeynep (Ed.): Expatriate Management: Theory and Research, New Approaches to Employee Management 4. Greenwich, CT: JAI Press: 63–92.

Ones, Deniz S.; Viswesvaran, Chockalingam; Schmidt, Frank L. (2012b): Integrity Tests Predict Counterproductive Work Behaviors and Job Performance Well: Comment on Van Iddekinge, Roth, Raymark, and Odle-Dusseau (2012). In: *Journal of Applied Psychology* 97,3: 537–542. [https://doi.org/10.1037/a0024825].

Ones, Deniz S.; Viswesvaran, Chockalingam; Schmidt, Frank L. (1993): Comprehensive Meta-Analysis of Integrity Test Validities: Findings and Implications for Personnel Selection and Theories of Job Performance. In: *Journal of Applied Psychology* 78,4: 679–703. [https://doi.org/10/c48t8j].

Perez, Alyssa et al. (2017): Closing the Scientist–Practitioner Gap: Studies from 2016 with Significant Practical Utility. In: *The Industrial-Organizational Psychologist* 54,4: 74–82. [http://www.siop.org/ tip/april17/gap.aspx].

Rüger, Heiko et al. (2013): Mobilitätskompetenzen im Auswärtigen Dienst: Risiken und protektive Faktoren bei der Bewältigung der Auslandsrotation. Beiträge zur Bevölkerungswissenschaft 44. Würzburg, Germany: Ergon.

Rüger, Heiko et al. (2018): Sampling and Procedures for the Mobility Skills in the German Foreign Service Study. In: Wiernik, Brenton M.; Rüger, Heiko; Ones, Deniz S. (Eds.): Managing Expatriates: Success Factors in Private and Public Domains, Series on Population Studies 50. Opladen, Germany: Barbara Budrich Publishers.

Rynes, Sara L.; Giluk, Tamara L.; Brown, Kenneth G. (2007): The Very Separate Worlds of Academic and Practitioner Periodicals in Human Resource Management: Implications for Evidence-Based Management. In: *Academy of Management Journal* 50,5: 987–1008. [https://doi.org/10.5465/AMJ.2007.27151939].

Schmidt, Frank L.; Oh, In-Sue; Shaffer, Jonathan Andrew (2016): The Validity and Utility of Selection Methods in Personnel Psychology: Practical and Theoretical Implications of 100 Years of Research Findings. Fox School of Business Research Paper. Philadelphia, PA: Temple University. [https://doi.org/10.13140/RG.2.2.18843.26400].

Selmer, Jan; Fenner, Charles R., Jr. (2009a): Job Factors and Work Outcomes of Public Sector Expatriates. In: *Human Resource Management Journal* 19,1: 75–90. [https://doi.org/10/dkz5ph].

Selmer, Jan; Fenner, Charles R., Jr. (2009b): Spillover Effects between Work and Non-Work Adjustment among Public Sector Expatriates. In: *Personnel Review* 38,4: 366–379. [https://doi.org/10.1108/00483480910956328].

Sinangil, Handan Kepir; Ones, Deniz S. (2003): Gender Differences in Expatriate Job Performance. In: *Applied Psychology* 52,3: 461–475. [https://doi.org/10/c36tw5].

Sinangil, Handan Kepir; Ones, Deniz S. (1997): Empirical Investigations of the Host Country Perspective in Expatriate Management. In: Aycan, Zeynep (Ed.): Expatriate Management: Theory and Research, New Approaches to Employee Management 4. Greenwich, CT: JAI Press: 173–205.

Smith, M. Brewster (1966): Explorations in Competence: A Study of Peace Corps Teachers in Ghana. In: *American Psychologist* 21,6: 555–566. [https://doi.org/10.1037/h0023607].

Spector, Paul E. et al. (2002): Locus of Control and Well-Being at Work: How Generalizable Are Western Findings? In: *Academy of Management Journal* 45,2: 453–466. [https://doi.org/10.2307/3069359].

Stahl, Günter K.; Miller, Edwin L.; Tung, Rosalie L. (2002): Toward the Boundaryless Career: A Closer Look at the Expatriate Career Concept and the Perceived Implications of an International Assignment. In: *Journal of World Business* 37,3: 216–227. [https://doi.org/10/ddttgr].

Sullivan, Sherry E.; Baruch, Yehuda (2009): Advances in Career Theory and Research: A Critical Review and Agenda for Future Exploration. In: *Journal of Management* 35,6: 1542–1571. [https://doi.org/10.1177/0149206309350082].

Takeuchi, Riki (2010): A Critical Review of Expatriate Adjustment Research through a Multiple Stakeholder View: Progress, Emerging Trends, and Prospects. In: *Journal of Management* 36,4: 1040–1064. [https://doi.org/10.1177/0149206309349308].

Takeuchi, Riki et al. (2005): An Integrative View of International Experience. In: *Academy of Management Journal* 48,1: 85–100. [https://doi.org/10.5465/AMJ.2005.15993143].

Takeuchi, Riki; Yun, Seokhwa; Tesluk, Paul E. (2002): An Examination of Crossover and Spillover Effects of Spousal and Expatriate Cross-Cultural Adjustment on Expatriate Outcomes. In: *Journal of Applied Psychology* 87,4: 655–666. [https://doi.org/10/d2ddkj].

Textor, Robert B. (Ed.) (1966): Cultural Frontiers of the Peace Corps. Cambridge, MA: MIT Press.

Thomas, David C.; Lazarova, Mila B. (2006): Expatriate Adjustment and Performance: A Critical Review. In: Stahl, Günter K.; Björkman, Ingmar (Eds.): Handbook of Research in International Human Resource Management. Cheltenham, United Kingdom: Elgar: 247–263. [https://doi.org/10/b6mc].

Torelli, Carlos J.; Shavitt, Sharon (2010): Culture and Concepts of Power. In: *Journal of Personality and Social Psychology* 99,4: 703–723. [https://doi.org/10.1037/a0019973].

Truman, Sean D.; Sharar, David A.; Pompe, John C. (2011): The Mental Health Status of Expatriate versus U.S. Domestic Workers. In: *International Journal of Mental Health* 40,4: 3–18. [https://doi.org/10.2753/IMH0020-7411400401].

van der Velde, Mandy E.G.; Bossink, Carin J.H.; Jansen, Paul G.W. (2005): Gender Differences in the Determinants of the Willingness to Accept an International Assignment. In: *Journal of Vocational Behavior* 66,1: 81–103. [https://doi.org/10.1016/j.jvb.2003.12.002].

Vance, Charles M. (2005): The Personal Quest for Building Global Competence: A Taxonomy of Self-Initiating Career Path Strategies for Gaining Business Experience Abroad. In: *Journal of World Business*, Global Careers 40,4: 374–385. [https://doi.org/10.1016/j.jwb.2005.08.005].

Vance, Charles M.; McNulty, Yvonne (2014): Why and How Women and Men Acquire Global Career Experience: A Study of American Expatriates in Europe. In: *International Studies of Management & Organization* 44,2: 34–54. [https://doi.org/10.2753/IMO0020-8825440202].

Viswesvaran, Chockalingam; Ones, Deniz S. (2000): Perspectives on Models of Job Performance. In: *International Journal of Selection and Assessment* 8,4: 216–226. [https://doi.org/10/ctcc82].

Waibel, Stine et al. (2018a): Impacts of Age, Tenure, and Experience on Expatriate Adjustment and Job Satisfaction. In: Wiernik, Brenton M.; Rüger, Heiko; Ones, Deniz S. (Eds.): Managing Expatriates: Success Factors in Private and Public Domains, Series on Population Studies 50. Opladen, Germany: Barbara Budrich Publishers.

Waibel, Stine; Rüger, Heiko; Wiernik, Brenton M. (2018b): Antecedents and Consequences of Mobility Self-Efficacy. In: Wiernik, Brenton M.; Rüger, Heiko; Ones, Deniz S. (Eds.): Managing Expatriates: Success Factors in Private and Public Domains, Series on Population Studies 50. Opladen, Germany: Barbara Budrich Publishers.

Wiernik, Brenton M. et al. (2018): Lingua Necessaria? Language Proficiency and Expatriate Success. In: Wiernik, Brenton M.; Rüger, Heiko; Ones, Deniz S. (Eds.): Managing Expatriates: Success Factors in Private and Public Domains, Series on Population Studies 50. Opladen, Germany: Barbara Budrich Publishers.

Wiernik, Brenton M.; Kostal, Jack W. (2017): Protean and Boundaryless Career Orientations: A Critical Review and Meta-Analysis. Manuscript Submitted for Publication.

Wiernik, Brenton M.; Wille, Bart (2018): Careers, Career Development, and Career Management. In: Ones, Deniz S. et al. (Eds.): The SAGE Handbook of Industrial, Work and Organizational Psychology. Volume 3: Managerial Psychology and Organizational Approaches. 2nd ed. London, United Kingdom: Sage: 547–585.

Wu, Wann-Yih; Bodigerel-Koehler, Molortuya (2013): The Mediating Effects of Cross-Cultural Dynamic Competencies on the Relationship between Multicultural Personality and Cross-Cultural Adjustment. In: *International Journal of Human Resource Management* 24,21: 4026–4045. [https://doi.org/10.1080/09585192.2013.781518].

Expatriate Personality: Facet-level Comparisons with Domestic Counterparts

Jack W. Kostal, Brenton M. Wiernik, Anne-Grit Albrecht, and Deniz S. Ones

Abstract

We compared personality trait distributions for expatriates to those of domestic managers and general populations using cross-cultural meta-analysis and three personality inventories. We found that expatriate–domestic manager differences are negligible to moderate in magnitude. Differences varied across lower-order facets within the Big Five domains. Results differed somewhat across personality inventories. Results suggest that expatriate are higher on Experiences-related facets of Openness and Compassion-related facets of Agreeableness, but may be lower on Conscientiousness and Emotional Stability. Our findings indicate that there is likely great opportunity for organizations to enhance expatriate success by incorporating personality traits into expatriate selection procedures.

1 Introduction

Managing expatriates is a challenge for both domestic organizations sending employees on international assignments and the host-country organizations receiving them. Domestic organizations face difficulties providing sufficient support and adapting their management practices to meet expatriates' individual needs. Host organizations are often unprepared to interact with expatriates whose individual characteristics and cultural backgrounds differ from their own employees. A key step in addressing both challenges is understanding the unique ways in which expatriates differ from domestic nationals in their home- and host-countries.

Understanding the personal characteristics expatriates tend to possess can aid both home and host organizations in understanding the unique management challenges and opportunities these employees can present. A variety of personality traits have been linked to different components of expatriate success. For example, among the Big Five traits, Openness has been linked with acceptance of international assignments and with cultural adjustment (Albrecht et al. 2018c; Ones/Viswesvaran 1997), Conscientiousness and Emotional Stability have been linked with cultural and work adjustment and avoiding burnout (Deller/ Albrecht 2006a, 2006b; Hechanova et al. 2003), and Extraversion and Agreeableness have been linked with interactional adjustment (Deller/Albrecht 2006a). If expatriates tend to be deficient in any of these trait domains, then the criteria associated with these domains (e.g., work adjustment for Conscientiousness) represent key areas for organizations to focus on to promote expatriate success. Moreover, deficiencies in these trait domains would suggest avenues for improved selection practices to increase the likelihood of successful expatriation.

Relatively little research has examined the characteristic personality differences between expatriates and domestic employees. Albrecht et al. (2008) compared the iGOES samples (a large sample of German expatriates, see below) to the population normative sample for the German version of the NEO PI-R. They found that expatriates were much higher than the general population on average on Emotional Stability ($d = .84$) and moderately higher on Extraversion and Conscientiousness ($d = .50$ and $.52$, respectively). Expatriates did not differ substantially from the general population on Agreeableness or Openness ($d = -.07$ and $.01$, respectively). These results suggest that expatriates in general tend to be well-equipped in terms of personality characteristics to meet the challenges of expatriate assignments.

However, two issues with Albrecht et al.'s (2008) study urge caution. First, expatriates tend to primarily be employed in managerial positions, and managers tend to be higher than the general population on Extraversion, Conscientiousness, and Emotional Stability (Ones/Dilchert 2009). As a result, these authors are not comparing equivalent populations when examining personality differences between expatriates and domestic norms. Comparing expatriate personality with that of *managers* in the home country would enable a more complete understanding of how expatriates compare with other employees at similar levels of the organizational hierarchy.

Second, increasing research attention is being paid to the role of more specific personality traits in determining workplace behavior. Personality aspects and facets (DeYoung et al. 2007) have been shown to differentially and incrementally predict a variety of workplace outcomes, especially work performance dimensions that are narrower than "overall performance" (Judge et al. 2013). It is conceivable that distinct facets of each Big Five domain are differentially related to expatriate success. For example, the contribution of Extraversion to expatriate interactional adjustment may primarily stem from facets related to outgoingness, such as sociability and warmth, rather than assertiveness-related facets, such as dominance and energy level (Hough/Ones 2001). Indeed, dominance may contribute primarily to successful work adjustment to and performance in expatriates' new work roles, which typically involve increases in managerial and leadership responsibility. Sociability may negatively relate to this form of adjustment, as sociability may undermine expatriates' authority and interfere with their ability to effectively manage their subordinates (Kaiser/Hogan 2011). Opposite relations with performance at the facet level could lead to the zero relationship typically observed between overall Extraversion and expatriate work adjustment. This example suggests that a comprehensive understanding of the challenges and opportunities expatriates bring to their assignments via their personality traits requires a nuanced consideration of lower-order personality facets in addition to the broad Big Five domains. In the context of the present study, it is possible that characteristic patterns of personality traits at the facet level differ from those observed for the Big 5 factors.

In this study, we attempt to address both concerns. Although the importance of expatriate assignments to international organizations might suggest that expatriate employees would be chosen at least in part based on expatriate success-relevant personality traits (e.g., selecting managers with the highest levels of Conscientiousness, resulting in expatriates having higher levels of this trait than their domestic counterparts), non-optimal selection procedures such as reliance on informal recommendations and assessments (Deller 1997; Harris/Brewster 1999), lack of knowledge among organizational policymakers regarding personality correlates of expatriate success, and unwillingness of employees to relocate abroad (Mol et al. 2009) may preclude this from occurring. As such, we frame our study in terms of two research questions:

Research Question 1: Do the personality characteristics of expatriates differ from those of managers in their home country, in terms of the Big 5 factors?

Research Question 2: Do patterns of expatriate personality traits at the facet-level differ in meaningful ways from those observed for the Big 5 factors?

2   Methods

We used 3 expatriate datasets reporting results for 3 personality inventories to address our research questions. We describe the samples, instruments, and analytic methods below.

2.1   Dataset 1: Global Personality Inventory

Sample. The first dataset contained results for 1,679 expatriate managers and 19,646 domestic managers, originating from a total of 86 countries, who completed personality scales and other measures as part of selection, promotion, or development procedures conducted by a global executive recruitment and talent management consultancy. We compared expatriates with domestic managers from their home countries for all within-country samples with $n > 9$ for both expatriates and domestic managers. This resulted in expatriate–domestic manager comparisons being conducted with 1,544 expatriates and 18,940 domestic managers from 36 countries.

Included expatriate managers were from the following countries[1]: Argentina (1%), Australia (6%), Austria (1%), Belgium (2%), Brazil (2%), Canada (6%), China (1%), Colombia (1%), Egypt (1%), Finland (1%), France (8%), Germany (7%), Greece (1%), Hong Kong (2%), India (3%), Ireland (2%), Italy (3%), Japan (2%), Kuwait (1%), Malaysia (2%), Mexico (1%), the Netherlands (2%), New Zealand (1%), Norway (1%), Russia (1%), Saudi Arabia (2%), Singapore (1%), South Africa (2%), South Korea (3%), Spain (1%), Sweden (4%), Switzerland (2%), Taiwan (1%), Thailand (1%), United Kingdom (12%), and United States (13%).

Participants included managers at all hierarchical levels, ranging from first-line managers to senior executives. Among expatriates, 11% were first-line managers, 20% were mid-level managers, 54% were business unit managers, and 15% were senior executives. Among domestic managers, 21% were first-line managers, 27% were mid-level managers, 39% were business unit managers, and 14% were senior executives. Across all samples, 12% of expatriates and 22% of domestic managers were female. Expatriates reported a mean age of 41.74 years ($SD = 6.42$) and a mean organizational tenure of 11.27 years ($SD = 6.73$). Domestic managers reported a mean age of 42.70 years ($SD = 7.17$) and a mean organizational tenure of 12.00 years ($SD = 7.65$).

Participants completed a demographic questionnaire as part of an assessment battery. As part of this questionnaire, participants indicated their country of citizenship (origin country), current location (host country), and expatriate status (yes or no). Expatriates were identified as those individuals who responded "yes" to the expatriate status question. Domestic managers were identified as those individuals responding "no" to this question and who were also currently located in their country of citizenship.

Measure. Participants' personality traits were measured using the Global Personality Inventory (GPI; Schmit et al. 2000). The GPI was developed in response to the need for a personality measure that was easily transportable across countries, with items that focused specifically on behaviors relevant to work contexts. Creation of this instrument involved input from a multi-national team of researchers, to ensure that items were not culture-bound. Scales in U.S. English, British English, German, French, Spanish, Dutch, Swedish, Japanese, Chinese, and Korean were simultaneously developed. To ensure fidelity of item content across cultures, all items were reviewed by bilingual psychologists prior to inclusion

---

[1]   Numbers in parentheses indicate the percent of the total expatriate sample from each country.

in non-English scales. Responses to the GPI can be used to obtain scores on the Big 5 personality traits, as well as various narrower personality facets. Table 1 describes the personality facet scales associated with each Big Five domain on the GPI. Note that the GPI Extraversion composite combines both Extraversion facets and facets typically associated with Industriousness (an aspect of Conscientiousness; DeYoung et al. 2007; Stanek/Ones 2018); it is similar to the compound personality trait of ambition/proactive personality (Fuller/Marler 2009). The GPI also reports scores for several maladaptive personality composites (e.g., narcissism, Machiavellianism, self-deception; cf. Dilchert et al. 2014).

Table 1: Personality Facets contained in the Global Personality Inventory

Emotional Stability

Emotional control (7). Tendency to be even-tempered

Negative affectivity (7). Tendency to be generally unsatisfied with many things, including but not limited to work

Optimism (9). Tendency to believe that good things are possible

Self-confidence (7). Tendency to believe in one's own abilities and skills

Stress tolerance (8). Tendency to endure typically stressful situations without undue physical or emotional reaction

Extraversion

Adaptability (8). Tendency to be open to change and considerable variety

Competitiveness (8). Tendency to evaluate one's performance in comparison to others; desire to outperform others

Desire for achievement (8). Tendency to have a strong drive to realize personally meaningful goals.

Desire for advancement (7). Tendency to be ambitious in the advancement of one's career or position in organization

Energy level (9). Tendency to be highly active and energetic

Influence (9). Tendency to get others to view and do things in a certain way; persuasiveness and tact

Initiative (9). Tendency to take action in a proactive, rather than reactive, manner

Risk-taking (9). Tendency to take chances based on limited information; enjoyment of uncertain situations

Sociability (9). Tendency to be highly engaged by any social situation

Taking charge (10). Tendency to take leadership roles; desire for leadership roles

Openness

Independence (8). Tendency to be autonomous (e.g., desire not to be closely supervised)

Innovativeness/creativity (9). Tendency to produce unique and original things; divergent thinking

↓

Table 1: Personality Facets contained in the Global Personality Inventory – continued

Social astuteness (8). Tendency to accurately perceive social cues and use that information to accomplish goals

Thought focus (7). Tendency to understand ambiguous information by analyzing and detecting systematic themes in the data; convergent thinking

Vision (9). Tendency to have foresight in thinking (e.g., by visualizing outcomes)

Agreeableness

Consideration (10). Tendency to express care about others' well-being

Empathy (7). Tendency to understand what others are feeling and convey that understanding to them

Interdependence (8). Tendency to work well with others

Tolerance/Openness (7). Tendency to accept and respect the individual differences of people

Thought agility (9). Tendency to be open both to multiple ideas and to using alternative modes of thinking

Trust (7). Tendency to believe that most people are good and well-intentioned

Conscientiousness

Attention to detail (9). Tendency to be exacting and precise

Dutifulness (8). Tendency to be filled with a sense of moral obligation

Responsibility (7). Tendency to be reliable and dependable

Work focus (9). Tendency to be self-disciplined in one's approach to work

Maladaptive trait composites

Ego-centered (7). Tendency to be self-centered, narcissistic, egotistical, entitled, arrogant, and condescending

Intimidating (7). Tendency to use power in a threatening way, to be cold, aloof, bullying, abrasive, and fear-inducing

Manipulating (10). Tendency to be self-serving, sly, and Machiavellian, to hide one's mistakes, shift blame, and take advantage of others

Micro-managing (7). Tendency to over-manage when in positions of authority, to be overly involved in decisions, fail to delegate, hinder teamwork development

Passive-aggressive (7). Tendency to avoid confrontation by conveying cooperation/acceptance while also behaving in self-serving or undermining ways

Impressing/Impression management (7). Tendency to try to make a good impression on others, to tell others what they want to hear, use flattery, hide one's true motives, and not be frank or forthcoming

Self-awareness/Self-insight (9). Tendency to be aware of one's strengths and weaknesses, to understand one's habits, motives, values, and behaviors, to avoid self-deception

Note: Adapted from Schmit et al. (2000). Number of items on each scale shown in parentheses.

2.2   Dataset 2: NEO PI-R

Sample. The second dataset was the iGOES samples, which include personality scores for the NEO PI-R (Borkenau/Ostendorf 1993; Costa/McCrae 1992) for 2,105 German-speaking expatriate managers. These expatriates were recruited to voluntarily participate in the iGOES research. Expatriates were working abroad in 28 different countries (Argentina, Austria, China, Costa Rica, Czech Republic, Denmark, Egypt, Finland, France, Ghana, India, Ireland, Italy, Malaysia, Mexico, Morocco, Poland, Russia, Singapore, South Korea, Spain, Sweden, Switzerland, Thailand, the Netherlands, Turkey, United Kingdom, and the United States) representing all cultural clusters as defined by Project GLOBE. For additional information on the iGOES sample, see Albrecht et al. (2018a, Appendix A, this volume).

Expatriates' personality scores were compared to a sample of individuals with managerial responsibility drawn from the norm sample of the German translation of the NEO PI-R ($N = 264$; Borkenau/Ostendorf 1993).[2] We additionally report results from Albrecht et al. (2008) comparing expatriates to the full general population norm sample for the German NEO PI-R.

Measure. Participants' personality traits were measured using the German translation of the NEO PI-R (Borkenau/Ostendorf 1993). The NEO PI-R reports six facet scales for each of the Big Five traits (listed in Table 3). We reverse coded Neuroticism and each of its facet scales to reflect Emotional Stability and make results easier to compare to the GPI and HPI.

2.3   Dataset 3: Hogan Personality Inventory

Sample. The third dataset the sample of expatriates in Turkey described by Ones et al. (2018, Chapter 5, this volume). This sample includes 220 expatriate managers from numerous countries who were employed in Turkey. Expatriates' personality scores were compared to the scores for the United States general employee norm sample for the 1992 version of the Hogan Personality Inventory (HPI; Hogan/Hogan 1992).

Measure. Participants' personality traits were measured using the 1992 Hogan Personality Inventory (Hogan/Hogan 1992). The HPI reports seven primary scales that roughly to the Big Five dimensions of personality (listed in Table 4). The scales are Adjustment (Emotional Stability), Ambition (Extraversion), Sociability (Extraversion), Intellectance (Openness), School Success (Openness), Likeability (Agreeableness), and Prudence (Conscientiousness). It is important to note some unique features of the HPI relative to other measures based on the Big Five. The HPI Ambition scale combines elements of assertiveness (Extraversion) and industriousness (Conscientiousness); like the GPI Extraversion scale, it is similar to the compound personality trait proactive personality (Fuller/Marler 2009). The Sociability scale focuses on sociability and positive emotion facets of Extraversion (the Enthusiasm aspect; DeYoung et al. 2007), and the Prudence scale focuses on cautiousness and order facets of Conscientiousness (the Orderliness aspect; DeYoung et al. 2007). The Intellectance scale is more focused on the Intellect aspect of Openness than on the Experiences aspect (which dominates the NEO PI-R Openness scale; Connelly et al. 2014; Wiernik et al. 2016; Woo et al. 2014). The School Success scale consists primarily of self-ratings of cognitive ability. To aid comparability of the HPI results with the other personality measures, we computed overall Extraversion and Openness scores as unit-weighted composites of Ambition/Sociability and Intellectance/School Success, respectively.

---

[2]   We thank Fritz Ostendorf for generously providing the data for this subsample of the German NEO PI-R norms.

2.4   *Analyses*

For the GPI (dataset 1) and NEO PI-R (iGOES, dataset 2) datasets, expatriates and domestic managers are nested within countries. This data structure introduces the potential for mean-level personality differences across countries to confound expatriate–domestic personality comparisons. To control for this confound, all expatriate–domestic comparisons were conducted within-countries and combined using cross-cultural meta-analysis (Ones et al. 2012). We meta-analyzed d values using the methods described by Schmidt and Hunter (2015). We weighted each d value by its inverse sampling error variance, in response to substantial variability in the ratio of expatriate to domestic managers across countries. Sampling error variance was computed accounting for unequal group sizes (Schmidt/Hunter 2015: 293). We meta-analyzed u values using the method by Hedges and Friedman (1993). Meta-analyses were performed using the log-transformed variance ratios (i.e., $ln\ [u^2]$), weighted by their inverse variance. The mean and residual standard deviation of the meta-analytic distribution of u values were estimated using the method of numerical integration described by Steel (2013).

For the HPI dataset (dataset 3), we computed observed standardized mean differences (Cohen's d) and standard deviation ratios (u values) between expatriates and the United States domestic employee norms. We calculated confidence intervals around each value, accounting for unequal group sizes (Hedges/Friedman 1993; Schmidt/Hunter 2015).

3   Results

Meta-analytic comparisons of expatriates to domestic managers for the GPI are shown in Table 2. Meta-analytic comparisons of expatriates to domestic managers for the NEO PI-R are shown in Table 3. Meta-analytic comparisons of expatriates to the general population for the NEO PI-R are shown in Table 4. Comparisons of expatriates to the United States employee general population for the HPI are shown in Table 5.

3.1   *Research Question 1: Expatriate–domestic Personality Differences for the Big 5*

Comparisons of expatriates to domestic managers and general populations for the Big Five are illustrated in Figure 1. For the GPI, expatriate–domestic manager mean differences for the Big Five were uniformly small (*mean* $|\bar{d}|$ = .09, *range* $|\bar{d}|$ = .00 to .20). Expatriates are weakly but consistently higher on Extraversion than their domestic counterparts at home ($\bar{d}$ = .20, 80% credibility interval [CV] = .02, .38) and slightly higher on Openness ($\bar{d}$ = .14, 80% CV = .14, .14). For the other Big Five, expatriates showed no consistent differences from domestic managers in their home countries ($\bar{d}$ = .08, .06, .00 for Emotional Stability, Agreeableness, and Conscientiousness, respectively; lower bounds of CVs ranged from d = -.25 to d = -.04, while upper bounds of CVs ranged from d = .17 to d = .26).

Differences were somewhat larger for the NEO PI-R, with small differences for Emotional Stability ($\bar{d}$ = -.33) and Extraversion ($\bar{d}$ = .27) and moderate-to-large differences for Openness ($\bar{d}$ = .53) and Conscientiousness ($\bar{d}$ = -.47). Credibility intervals for Big Five differences on the NEO PI-R generally spanned ranges of d values that were small to moderate in magnitude.

Table 2: Expatriates compared to domestic managers in their home countries – GPI

Personality trait	$\bar{d}$	SD_d	$SD_{res.d}$	90% CI	80% CV	$\bar{u}$	SD_u	$SD_{res.u}$	90% CI	80% CV
Emotional Stability	**.08**	.22	.14	.02, .13	-.11, .26	**1.00**	.14	.07	.96, 1.03	.91, 1.09
Emotional control	**.04**	.20	.12	-.02, .09	-.11, .19	**1.02**	.11	.00	.99, 1.05	1.02, 1.02
Low Negative affectivity	**.06**	.21	.13	.00, .11	-.10, .22	**1.01**	.14	.07	.97, 1.05	.92, 1.11
Optimism	**.12**	.22	.15	.06, .18	-.07, .31	**1.00**	.18	.13	.95, 1.04	.84, 1.18
Self-confidence	**.06**	.19	.10	.01, .12	-.07, .20	**.98**	.16	.10	.93, 1.02	.85, 1.12
Stress tolerance	**.04**	.20	.12	-.02, .09	-.11, .18	**1.00**	.10	.00	.97, 1.03	1.00, 1.00
Extraversion	**.20**	.22	.14	.14, .26	.02, .38	**.99**	.16	.11	.95, 1.03	.86, 1.13
Adaptability	**.15**	.21	.13	.10, .21	-.01, .32	**1.00**	.16	.10	.95, 1.04	.88, 1.13
Competitiveness	**.12**	.23	.16	.05, .18	-.09, .32	**.95**	.15	.09	.90, .98	.83, 1.07
Desire for achievement	**.20**	.20	.12	.15, .26	.05, .35	**.98**	.16	.11	.93, 1.02	.85, 1.13
Desire for advancement	**.12**	.21	.14	.07, .18	-.05, .30	**.97**	.12	.04	.94, 1.00	.93, 1.02
Energy level	**.18**	.21	.14	.12, .24	.00, .35	**.98**	.15	.10	.93, 1.01	.85, 1.11
Influence	**.11**	.18	.07	.06, .16	.02, .20	**1.02**	.16	.10	.97, 1.05	.89, 1.15
Initiative	**.10**	.22	.15	.04, .16	-.08, .29	**1.02**	.14	.06	.99, 1.06	.95, 1.10
Risk-taking	**.18**	.19	.09	.13, .23	.07, .30	**.99**	.13	.05	.95, 1.02	.93, 1.05
Sociability	**.08**	.22	.15	.02, .14	-.11, .28	**1.00**	.13	.06	.96, 1.03	.93, 1.07
Taking charge	**.14**	.16	.00	.09, .18	.14, .14	**1.01**	.16	.11	.96, 1.05	.88, 1.15
Openness	**.14**	.15	.00	.09, .18	.14, .14	**1.01**	.14	.07	.98, 1.05	.93, 1.10
Independence	**-.01**	.15	.00	-.05, .03	-.01, -.01	**.99**	.15	.10	.95, 1.03	.87, 1.12
Innovation/creativity	**.16**	.19	.10	.11, .22	.04, .29	**1.02**	.14	.06	.98, 1.05	.94, 1.10
Social astuteness	**.06**	.17	.06	.01, .10	-.02, .13	**1.02**	.16	.11	.97, 1.05	.88, 1.15
Thought focus	**.10**	.16	.00	.06, .15	.10, .10	**1.03**	.16	.11	.98, 1.07	.90, 1.17
Vision	**.12**	.17	.02	.07, .17	.09, .15	**.99**	.14	.07	.95, 1.03	.90, 1.09

Table 2: Expatriates compared to domestic managers in their home countries – GPI – continued

Personality trait	$\bar{d}$	SD_d	$SD_{\text{res.}d}$	90% CI	80% CV	$\bar{u}$	SD_u	$SD_{\text{res.}u}$	90% CI	80% CV
Agreeableness	**.06**	*.18*	*.08*	*.01, .11*	*-.04, .17*	**1.04**	*.17*	*.11*	*.99, 1.08*	*.90, 1.19*
Consideration	**-.01**	.23	.16	-.07, .06	-.21, .20	**1.05**	.14	.05	1.02, 1.09	.99, 1.12
Empathy	**.00**	.19	.09	-.05, .05	-.11, .12	**1.02**	.16	.11	.97, 1.06	.88, 1.16
Interdependence	**.10**	.17	.04	.05, .14	.04, .15	**1.00**	.12	.01	.97, 1.04	.99, 1.02
Though agility	**.08**	.16	.00	.03, .12	.08, .08	**1.05**	.19	.14	.99, 1.09	.88, 1.23
Tolerance/Openness	**.09**	.19	.10	.03, .14	-.04, .21	**1.00**	.16	.10	.95, 1.04	.87, 1.13
Trust	**.01**	.18	.08	-.04, .06	-.09, .11	**1.04**	.15	.09	.99, 1.08	.92, 1.15
Conscientiousness	**.00**	*.26*	*.20*	*-.07, .07*	*-.25, .25*	**1.06**	*.14*	*.06*	*1.02, 1.09*	*.98, 1.13*
Attention to detail	**-.06**	.25	.19	-.13, .01	-.30, .18	**1.04**	.16	.10	.99, 1.08	.92, 1.17
Dutifulness	**.02**	.23	.16	-.04, .08	-.18, .22	**1.03**	.11	.00	1.00, 1.06	1.03, 1.03
Responsibility	**.02**	.26	.20	-.05, .09	-.23, .27	**1.04**	.16	.10	.99, 1.08	.91, 1.17
Work focus	**.02**	.22	.15	-.04, .08	-.17, .22	**1.03**	.13	.06	.99, 1.07	.96, 1.10
Maladaptive trait composites										
Ego-centered	**.02**	.24	.18	-.05, .09	-.21, .25	**1.04**	.16	.09	.99, 1.08	.92, 1.16
Intimidating	**.08**	.21	.13	.02, .14	-.09, .25	**1.02**	.13	.03	.99, 1.06	.98, 1.06
Manipulating	**.01**	.23	.16	-.05, .07	-.19, .21	**1.03**	.11	.00	1.00, 1.06	1.03, 1.03
Micro-managing	**-.09**	.21	.13	-.15, -.03	-.26, .08	**1.03**	.12	.00	.99, 1.06	1.03, 1.03
Passive-aggressive	**-.10**	.24	.17	-.17, -.03	-.32, .12	**1.04**	.14	.06	1.00, 1.07	.96, 1.11
Impressing	**-.04**	.20	.11	-.09, .02	-.18, .10	**1.03**	.14	.06	.99, 1.07	.95, 1.11
Low Self-awareness	**-.07**	.19	.09	-.12, -.02	-.19, .05	**1.03**	.17	.11	.98, 1.07	.89, 1.17

Note: $k = 36$, $N_{\text{Expatriates}} = 1{,}544$, $N_{\text{Domestic Managers}} = 18{,}940$, observed d values and u ratios, positive d values indicate that expatriates score higher, u values greater than 1.0 indicate that expatriates are more variable.

Table 3: Expatriates compared to domestic managers in their home country – NEO PI-R

Personality trait	$\bar{d}$	SD_d	$SD_{res.d}$	90% CI	80% CV	$\bar{u}$	SD_u	$SD_{res.u}$	90% CI	80% CV
Emotional Stability	**-.33**	.21	.17	-.40, -.26	-.54, -.12	**1.02**	.09	.00	.99, 1.05	1.02, 1.02
Low Anxiety	**-.14**	.20	.15	-.20, -.07	-.33, .05	**.97**	.10	.04	.93, 1.00	.91, 1.02
Low Angry Hostility	**-.09**	.13	.00	-.13, -.05	-.09, -.09	**1.01**	.09	.00	.98, 1.03	1.01, 1.01
Low Depression	**-.35**	.20	.15	-.41, -.28	-.54, -.15	**1.09**	.11	.04	1.06, 1.12	1.03, 1.15
Low Self-Consciousness	**-.18**	.17	.11	-.24, -.12	-.32, -.04	**.98**	.09	.00	.95, 1.00	.98, .98
Low Impulsiveness	**-.44**	.17	.11	-.50, -.39	-.58, -.30	**1.06**	.09	.00	1.04, 1.09	1.06, 1.06
Low Vulnerability	**-.35**	.23	.18	-.43, -.28	-.59, -.12	**1.10**	.12	.05	1.06, 1.13	1.03, 1.16
Extraversion	**.27**	.20	.14	.20, .33	.09, .45	**1.07**	.12	.07	1.03, 1.11	.98, 1.16
Warmth	**.37**	.15	.06	.32, .42	.29, .45	**1.13**	.12	.05	1.09, 1.16	1.07, 1.19
Gregariousness	**.24**	.16	.08	.19, .29	.14, .34	**1.05**	.10	.00	1.02, 1.08	1.05, 1.05
Assertiveness	**-.42**	.25	.21	-.50, -.34	-.69, -.15	**1.11**	.11	.03	1.08, 1.14	1.08, 1.15
Activity	**-.04**	.16	.09	-.09, .02	-.15, .08	**1.03**	.10	.04	1.00, 1.06	.99, 1.08
Excitement Seeking	**.31**	.25	.21	.23, .39	.05, .58	**1.03**	.14	.09	.99, 1.07	.92, 1.16
Positive Emotions	**.42**	.17	.11	.36, .47	.27, .56	**1.06**	.21	.18	.98, 1.11	.84, 1.29
Openness	**.53**	.18	.11	.47, .59	.38, .67	**1.04**	.11	.05	1.00, 1.07	.97, 1.10
Fantasy	**.61**	.22	.17	.54, .69	.39, .84	**1.12**	.09	.00	1.09, 1.14	1.12, 1.12
Aesthetics	**.35**	.17	.10	.30, .41	.22, .48	**1.12**	.13	.07	1.08, 1.16	1.03, 1.22
Feelings	**.29**	.15	.08	.24, .34	.20, .39	**1.12**	.13	.07	1.08, 1.16	1.03, 1.21
Actions	**.52**	.14	.04	.48, .57	.47, .58	**.97**	.12	.08	.93, 1.00	.87, 1.07
Ideas	**.04**	.16	.08	-.01, .09	-.06, .15	**1.11**	.09	.00	1.08, 1.14	1.11, 1.11
Values	**.18**	.19	.13	.12, .24	.01, .35	**.93**	.10	.04	.90, .96	.88, .99

$\rightarrow$

Table 3: Expatriates compared to domestic managers in their home country – NEO PI-R – continued

Personality trait	$\bar{d}$	SD_d	$SD_{\text{res.}d}$	90% CI	80% CV	$\bar{u}$	SD_u	$SD_{\text{res.}u}$	90% CI	80% CV
Agreeableness	**.09**	.16	.09	.04, .14	-.02, .20	**.99**	.10	.04	.95, 1.02	.93, 1.04
Trust	**-.07**	.13	.00	-.11, -.03	-.07, -.07	**1.02**	.11	.05	.99, 1.05	.96, 1.09
Straightforwardness	**.00**	.15	.07	-.05, .05	-.09, .08	**.99**	.09	.01	.96, 1.01	.97, 1.00
Altruism	**.24**	.17	.11	.19, .30	.10, .38	**1.00**	.14	.10	.95, 1.04	.88, 1.12
Compliance	**.09**	.16	.09	.04, .14	-.02, .20	**1.02**	.09	.00	.99, 1.04	1.02, 1.02
Modesty	**.01**	.17	.11	-.05, .07	-.12, .15	**.92**	.10	.05	.88, .95	.85, .98
Tender-Mindedness	**.29**	.18	.12	.23, .35	.14, .44	**1.05**	.14	.09	1.00, 1.09	.93, 1.17
Conscientiousness	**-.47**	.21	.16	-.54, -.40	-.68, -.26	**1.15**	.12	.03	1.12, 1.19	1.11, 1.20
Competence	**-.44**	.19	.14	-.51, -.38	-.62, -.27	**1.07**	.12	.06	1.04, 1.11	1.00, 1.15
Order	**-.31**	.18	.13	-.37, -.25	-.48, -.15	**1.12**	.10	.00	1.09, 1.15	1.12, 1.12
Dutifulness	**-.32**	.16	.10	-.37, -.27	-.44, -.20	**1.08**	.09	.00	1.05, 1.10	1.08, 1.08
Achievement Striving	**-.21**	.21	.16	-.27, -.14	-.41, -.01	**1.05**	.09	.00	1.02, 1.07	1.05, 1.05
Self-Discipline	**-.31**	.20	.15	-.38, -.25	-.50, -.13	**1.18**	.14	.09	1.14, 1.22	1.07, 1.30
Deliberation	**-.40**	.15	.07	-.45, -.35	-.50, -.31	**1.06**	.10	.02	1.03, 1.09	1.03, 1.08

Note: $k = 28$, $N_{\text{Expatriates}} = 2{,}106$, $N_{\text{Domestic Managers}} = 264$, observed d values and u ratios, positive d values indicate that expatriates score higher, u values > 1.0 indicate that expatriates are more variable.

Table 4: Expatriates compared to German general population – NEO PI-R

Personality trait	$\bar{d}$	SD_d	$SD_{\text{res}.d}$	90% CI	80% CV	$\bar{u}$	SD_u	$SD_{\text{res}.u}$	90% CI	80% CV
Emotional Stability	**.83**	.17	.13	.67, 1.00	.78, .89	**.82**	.07	.02	.71, .94	.80 , .84
Low Anxiety	**.80**	.18	.13	.63, .97	.74, .86	**.86**	.09	.05	.73, 1.01	.79, .92
Low Angry Hostility	**.52**	.11	.00	.52, .52	.49, .56	**.91**	.08	.03	.78, 1.05	.87, .95
Low Depression	**.72**	.15	.09	.60, .84	.67, .77	**.77**	.08	.05	.65, .91	.71, .83
Low Self-Consciousness	**.65**	.14	.09	.54, .75	.60, .69	**.82**	.07	.02	.71, .95	.79, .86
Low Impulsiveness	**.23**	.15	.10	.10, .35	.18, .28	**.90**	.07	.00	.79, 1.03	.90, .90
Low Vulnerability	**.80**	.16	.11	.66, .94	.74, .85	**.76**	.08	.05	.64, .89	.70, .82
Extraversion	**.52**	.16	.11	.38, .66	.47, .58	**.87**	.10	.07	.73, 1.04	.79, .96
Warmth	**.20**	.12	.03	.16, .24	.16, .24	**.91**	.09	.05	.77, 1.07	.84, .98
Gregariousness	**.17**	.13	.06	.09, .24	.13, .21	**.86**	.08	.03	.74, 1.00	.82, .90
Assertiveness	**.73**	.19	.15	.53, .92	.67, .79	**.83**	.08	.04	.71, .97	.78, .89
Activity	**.47**	.14	.07	.38, .56	.42, .51	**.88**	.09	.04	.75, 1.03	.82, .94
Excitement Seeking	**.16**	.21	.17	-.06, .39	.09, .23	**.88**	.11	.09	.71, 1.08	.77, .99
Positive Emotions	**.24**	.16	.12	.09, .39	.19, .30	**.91**	.17	.16	.66, 1.22	.72, 1.11
Openness	**.03**	.14	.08	-.07, .14	-.01, .08	**.87**	.09	.06	.73, 1.03	.80, .94
Fantasy	**-.33**	.17	.13	-.49, -.17	-.39, -.27	**.88**	.07	.00	.77, 1.00	.88, .88
Aesthetics	**-.31**	.15	.09	-.42, -.19	-.36, -.26	**1.00**	.12	.08	.83, 1.21	.90, 1.11
Feelings	**-.22**	.12	.04	-.27, -.16	-.26, -.18	**.93**	.10	.07	.77, 1.11	.84, 1.02
Actions	**.54**	.12	.04	.50, .59	.50, .58	**.88**	.11	.08	.72, 1.07	.78, .99
Ideas	**.32**	.12	.04	.28, .37	.28, .36	**.87**	.07	.00	.77, .98	.87, .87
Values	**.15**	.17	.12	.00, .31	.10, .21	**.87**	.09	.05	.73, 1.02	.80, .93

Table 4: Expatriates compared to German general population – NEO PI-R – continued

Personality trait	$\bar{d}$	SD_d	$SD_{res.d}$	90% CI	80% CV	$\bar{u}$	SD_u	$SD_{res.u}$	90% CI	80% CV
Agreeableness	**-.07**	*.14*	*.08*	*-.17, .04*	*-.11, -.02*	**.87**	*.09*	*.05*	*.74, 1.02*	*.81 , .94*
Trust	**.38**	.11	.00	.38, .38	.34, .42	**.87**	.09	.05	.73, 1.03	.80, .93
Straightforwardness	**-.07**	.14	.07	-.16, .03	-.11, -.02	**.92**	.09	.04	.79, 1.08	.87, .98
Altruism	**.08**	.16	.11	-.06, .21	.03, .13	**.89**	.12	.09	.71, 1.11	.78, 1.01
Compliance	**.02**	.13	.06	-.06, .10	-.02, .07	**.84**	.08	.03	.73, .98	.81, .88
Modesty	**-.16**	.16	.11	-.30, -.02	-.21, -.11	**.89**	.09	.06	.75, 1.05	.81, .97
Tender-Mindedness	**-.45**	.16	.11	-.59, -.31	-.50, -.39	**.96**	.13	.10	.77, 1.18	.84, 1.08
Conscientiousness	**.55**	*.16*	*.11*	*.41, .68*	*.49, .60*	**.84**	*.08*	*.05*	*.72, .99*	*.79, .91*
Competence	**.65**	.15	.09	.53, .76	.60, .70	**.80**	.09	.06	.67, .96	.73, .87
Order	**.26**	.15	.10	.13, .38	.21, .31	**.89**	.08	.03	.77, 1.03	.86, .93
Dutifulness	**.34**	.13	.05	.27, .41	.30, .39	**.83**	.07	.00	.73, .94	.83, .83
Achievement Striving	**.50**	.17	.13	.34, .66	.45, .56	**.87**	.07	.02	.76, 1.00	.85, .90
Self-Discipline	**.57**	.14	.08	.47, .68	.53, .62	**.81**	.09	.07	.67, .97	.72, .90
Deliberation	**.11**	.13	.06	.03, .19	.07, .15	**.90**	.09	.04	.77, 1.05	.85, .95

Note: $k = 28$, $N_{\text{Expatriates}} = 2,106$, $N_{\text{General Population}} = 11,724$, observed d values and u ratios, positive d values indicate that expatriates score higher, u values > 1.0 indicate that expatriates are more variable.

Table 5: Expatriates compared to U.S. employee general population – HPI

Personality trait	Expat Mean	Expat SD	d	90% CI		u	90% CI	
Adjustment	23.98	6.37	**-.37**	-.48	-.26	**.90**	.83	.97
Extraversion	16.78	6.60	**-.46**	-.57	-.35	**.83**	.77	.90
Ambition	*9.30*	*2.80*	***-2.96***	-3.07	-2.85	***.56***	.52	.61
Sociability	*24.26*	*5.17*	***2.21***	2.10	2.32	***1.06***	.98	1.15
Openness	16.28	6.06	**1.81**	1.70	1.92	**.91**	.84	.98
Intellectance	*14.40*	*4.22*	***-.06***	-.17	.05	***.86***	.79	.93
School Success	*18.16*	*3.17*	***3.02***	2.91	3.13	***1.01***	.93	1.09
Likeability	17.81	4.56	**-.68**	-.79	-.57	**1.93**	1.78	2.09
Prudence	15.60	4.80	**-1.01**	-1.12	-.90	**1.04**	.96	1.13

Note: $N_{\text{Expatriates}} = 220$, $N_{\text{Domestic General Employees}} = 21{,}613$, observed d values and u ratios, positive d values indicate that expatriates score higher, u values > 1.0 indicate that expatriates are more variable.

Comparisons of expatriates to general population norms revealed very different results from comparisons to domestic managers, with expatriates showing elevated Extraversion, Conscientiousness, and Emotional Stability. These divergent findings highlight the importance of not confounding expatriate status with other variables (e.g., occupation, hierarchical level) when investigating factors that distinguish individuals who choose or are selected to work abroad. Expatriate–general population differences were also in some cases much larger than expatriate–domestic manager differences, particularly for the HPI. These differences were far outside the credibility intervals for the GPI and NEO PI-R. Several factors might explain these results. First, as the HPI results are from a single sample, rather than meta-analytic estimates, discrepancies may simply reflect sampling error. Second, whereas each sample for the other analyses was homogeneous on origin country, expatriates in the Turkey study came from many countries and were compared to the United States norms. Discrepancies could thus reflect choice of reference group (e.g., the United States tends to score higher on Extraversion and Conscientiousness than other countries, which may account for the large negative d observed for HPI Ambition; Kostal et al. 2014). Finally, these differences may reflect features of Turkey as a particularly challenging environment for Western expatriates (Sinangil/Ones 2003).

3.2 Research Question 2: Facet-level Personality Comparisons

Facet-level analyses revealed nuance in expatriate–domestic manager personality differences (shown in Tables 2 and 3 and in Figures 2 and 3). For the GPI, the magnitude of expatriate–domestic differences varied across facets. For example, expatriates showed larger differences on Desire for Achievement, Energy Level, and Risk-Taking compared to other Extraversion facets. Similarly, expatriates scored higher on Innovation/Creativity, but differences for other Openness facets were smaller. Facet differences were even more divergent for the NEO PI-R, likely because this inventory covers a wider range of traits than the GPI. Expatriates scored much higher on warmth, positive emotions, excitement-seeking, and other facets associated with the Enthusiasm Extraversion aspect, but lower on Assertiveness facets (DeYoung et al. 2007). Similarly, expatriates scored much higher on Experiences Openness facets, such as fantasy, aesthetics, and actions, but lower on the ideas facet (a marker of the Intellect aspect; DeYoung et al. 2007). Expatriates also scored higher on Compassion Agreeableness facets (tender-mindedness, altruism; DeYoung et al. 2007), but negligibly different on other facets.

Figure 1: Expat–domestic personality differences (Cohen's *d*)

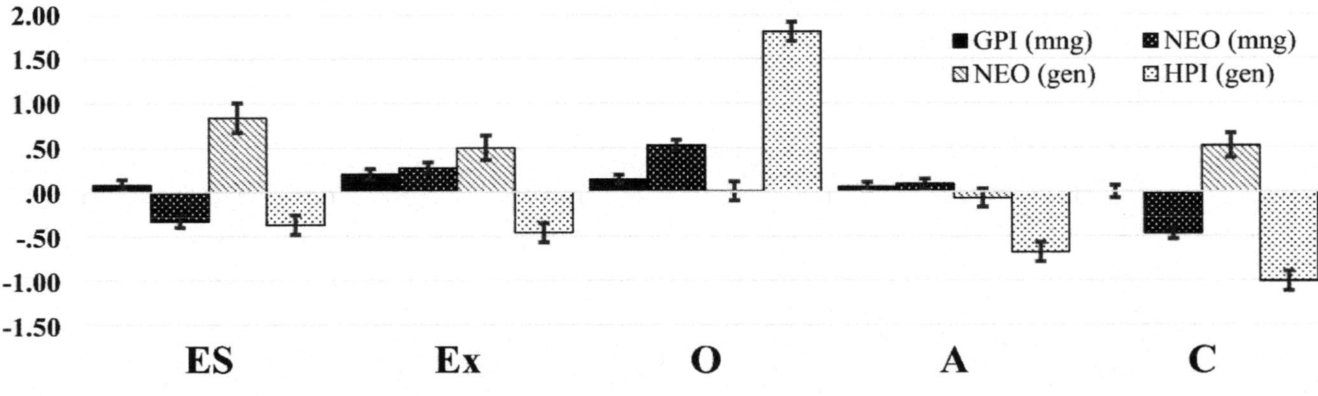

Note: Dark bars (mng) compare expatriates and domestic managers. Light bars (gen) compare expatriates and the general population. Error bars are 90% confidence intervals.

Figure 2: Facet-level expat–domestic manager differences (Cohen's *d*) for GPI

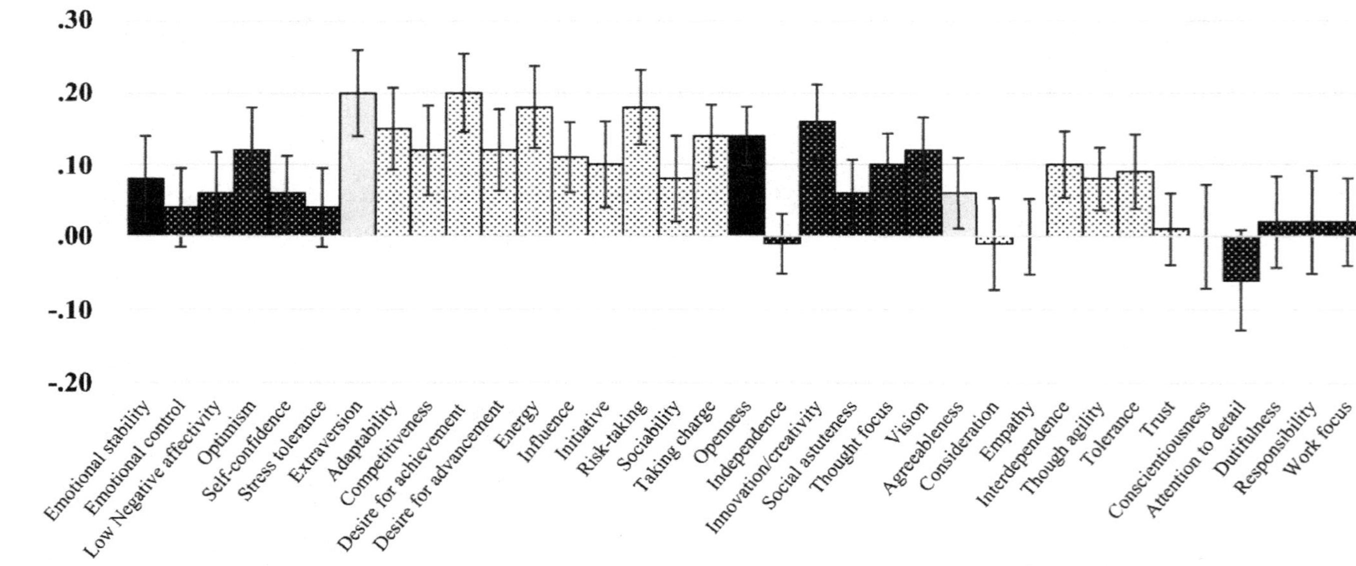

Note: Error bars are 90% confidence intervals.

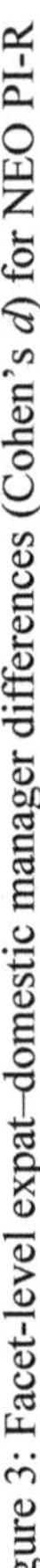

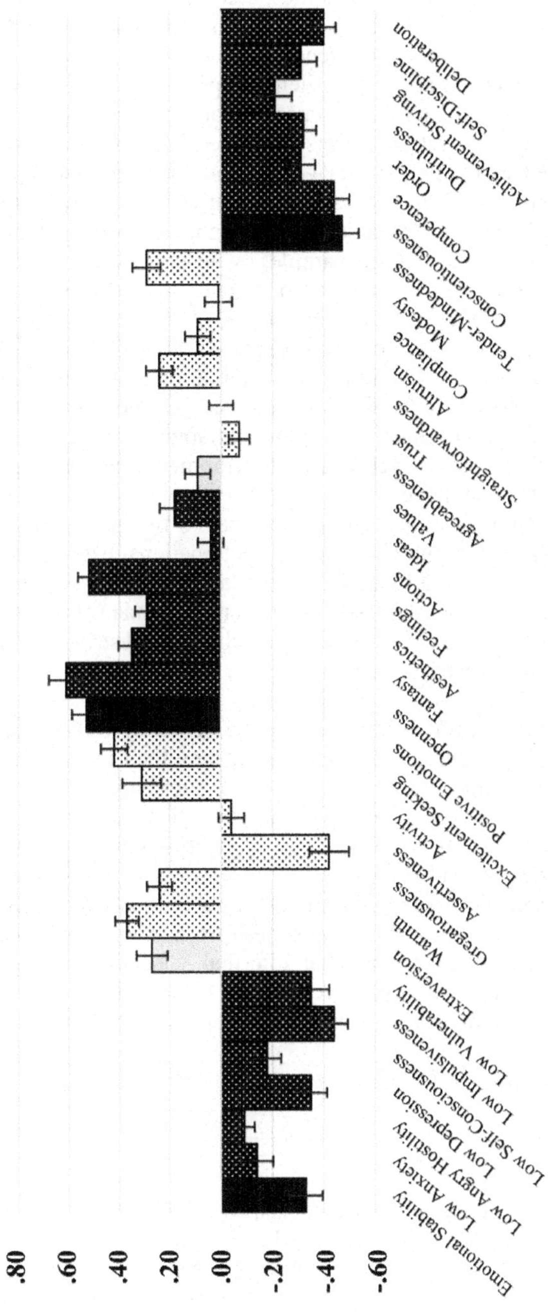

Figure 3: Facet-level expat–domestic manager differences (Cohen's *d*) for NEO PI-R

Note: Error bars are 90% confidence intervals.

4   Discussion

In general, expatriates appear to be quite like their domestic counterparts in their personality characteristics. Expatriates tended to be slightly higher on Openness, especially facets related to creativity, imagination, values, and new experiences, facets which may be especially important for expatriates sent overseas to address challenging problems requiring innovative solutions. Expatriates are also slightly higher than domestic managers on enthusiasm-related facets of Extraversion and compassion-related facets of Agreeableness, traits that can be valuable as expatriates work to interact with and manage international subordinates and peers.

Results for some personality facets differed across the inventories we analyzed. For example, expatriates in our GPI sample scored somewhat higher on achievement-striving and assertiveness, but expatriates in the iGOES samples, who completed the NEO PI-R, scored substantially lower on these traits, as well as on most Emotional Stability facets. Given the importance of Emotional Stability and Conscientiousness for expatriate success (see Ones et al. 2018, Chapter 5, this volume; Ones/Viswesvaran 1997), deficiencies on these traits would represent important liabilities on international assignments. These differences may stem from varying conceptualizations and measurement properties across inventories. Future research should continue to explore personality trait levels among expatriates and identify methods, such as selection and development, that can capitalize on personality strengths and mitigate weaknesses.

It is possible that patterns of personality differences may differ across subgroups of expatriates. For example, expatriates who initiate their own international experiences may be higher on traits related to proactivity, ambition, Openness, and Extraversion compared to organizationally-assigned expatriates or domestic managers (Biemann/Andresen 2010; Doherty et al. 2011). Future research should explore personality trait distributions and their contributions to success across expatriate subpopulations (cf. Albrecht et al. 2018b, Chapter 11, this volume).

Overall, our results suggest that while expatriates may be generally well-suited in some respects for their challenging international assignments (e.g., they tend to be more open to new experiences and sensitive to others' needs and concerns), substantial mean differences between expatriates and domestic managers on some critical traits indicates there is potential for organizations to improve expatriate success outcomes by incorporating personality scores into expatriate selection. Specifically, trait domains that are important to expatriate success but which show negative expatriate–domestic differences (Emotional Stability and Conscientiousness) represent key areas where organizations can benefit from using selection to choose expatriates, rather than relying on volunteers or other informal selection procedures. Even negligible differences on these traits (as were observed for the GPI) indicate that expatriates do not inherently possess these strengths and can benefit from selection and development.

References

Albrecht, Anne-Grit et al. (2018a): Design, Implementation, and Analysis of the iGOES Project. In: Wiernik, Brenton M.; Rüger, Heiko; Ones, Deniz S. (Eds.): Managing Expatriates: Success Factors in Private and Public Domains, Series on Population Studies 50. Opladen, Germany: Barbara Budrich Publishers.

Albrecht, Anne-Grit et al. (2018b): Success among Self-Initiated versus Assigned Expatriates. In: Wiernik, Brenton M.; Rüger, Heiko; Ones, Deniz S. (Eds.): Managing Expatriates: Success Factors in Private and Public Domains, Series on Population Studies 50. Opladen, Germany: Barbara Budrich Publishers.

Albrecht, Anne-Grit; Ones, Deniz S.; Sinangil, Handan Kepir (2018c): Expatriate Management. In: Ones, Deniz S. et al. (Eds.): The SAGE Handbook of Industrial, Work and Organizational Psychology. Volume 3: Managerial Psychology and Organizational Approaches. 2nd ed. London, United Kingdom: Sage: 429–468.

Albrecht, Anne-Grit et al. (2008): European Big Five Findings of the iGOES Project. Presented at the International Congress of Psychology. Berlin, Germany.

Biemann, Torsten; Andresen, Maike (2010): Self-Initiated Foreign Expatriates versus Assigned Expatriates: Two Distinct Types of International Careers? In: *Journal of Managerial Psychology* 25: 430–448. [https://doi.org/10.1108/02683941011035313].

Borkenau, Peter; Ostendorf, Fritz (1993): NEO-Fünf-Faktoren Inventar (NEO-FFI) nach Costa und McCrae. Handanweisung. Göttingen, Germany: Hogrefe.

Connelly, Brian S. et al. (2014): Opening up Openness: A Theoretical Sort Following Critical Incidents Methodology and Meta-Analytic Investigation of the Trait Family Measures. In: *Journal of Personality Assessment*, Special Section: Openness to Experience 96,1: 17–28. [https://doi.org/10/bc5f].

Costa, Paul T.; McCrae, Robert R. (1992): Professional Manual for the NEO Personality Inventory (NEO PI-R) and NEO Five Factor Inventory (NEO-FFI). Technical Manual. Odessa, FL: Psychological Assessment Resources.

Deller, Jürgen (1997): Expatriate Selection: Possibilities and Limitations of Using Personality Scales. In: Aycan, Zeynep (Ed.): Expatriate Management: Theory and Research, New Approaches to Employee Management 4. Greenwich, CT: JAI Press: 93–116.

Deller, Jürgen; Albrecht, Anne-Grit (2006a): The Big Five and Expatriate Adjustment. Presented at the Congress of the International Association of Applied Psychology. Athens, Greece.

Deller, Jürgen; Albrecht, Anne-Grit (2006b): The Big Five and Expatriate Job Performance. Presented at the Congress of the International Association of Applied Psychology. Athens, Greece.

DeYoung, Colin G.; Quilty, Lena C.; Peterson, Jordan B. (2007): Between Facets and Domains: 10 Aspects of the Big Five. In: *Journal of Personality and Social Psychology* 93,5: 880–896. [https://doi.org/10/b4xsvz].

Dilchert, Stephan; Ones, Deniz S.; Krueger, Robert F. (2014): Maladaptive Personality Constructs, Measures, and Work Behaviors. In: *Industrial and Organizational Psychology* 7,1: 98–110. [https://doi.org/10.1111/iops.12115].

Doherty, Noeleen; Dickmann, Michael; Mills, Timothy (2011): Exploring the Motives of Company-Backed and Self-Initiated Expatriates. In: *International Journal of Human Resource Management* 22,3: 595–611. [https://doi.org/10.1080/09585192.2011.543637].

Fuller, Jerry Bryan, Jr.; Marler, Laura E. (2009): Change Driven by Nature: A Meta-Analytic Review of the Proactive Personality Literature. In: *Journal of Vocational Behavior* 75,3: 329–345. [https://doi.org/10.1016/j.jvb.2009.05.008].

Harris, Hilary; Brewster, Chris (1999): The Coffee-Machine System: How International Selection Really Works. In: *International Journal of Human Resource Management* 10,3: 488–500. [https://doi.org/10.1080/095851999340440].

Hechanova, Regina; Beehr, Terry A.; Christiansen, Neil D. (2003): Antecedents and Consequences of Employees' Adjustment to Overseas Assignment: A Meta-Analytic Review. In: *Applied Psychology* 52,2: 213–236. [https://doi.org/10/d4f4xv].

Hedges, Larry V.; Friedman, Lynn (1993): Gender Differences in Variability in Intellectual Abilities: A Reanalysis of Feingold's Results. In: *Review of Educational Research* 63,1: 94–105. [https://doi.org/10.3102/00346543063001094].

Hogan, Robert T.; Hogan, Joyce C. (1992): Hogan Personality Inventory Manual. 2nd ed. Tulsa, OK: Hogan Assessment Systems.

Hough, Leaetta M.; Ones, Deniz S. (2001): The Structure, Measurement, Validity, and Use of Personality Variables in Industrial, Work, and Organizational Psychology. In: Anderson, Neil et al. (Eds.): Handbook of Industrial, Work and Organizational Psychology. Volume 1: Personnel Psychology. Thousand Oaks, CA: Sage: 233–277. [https://doi.org/10/bc67].

Judge, Timothy A. et al. (2013): Hierarchical Representations of the Five-Factor Model of Personality in Predicting Job Performance: Integrating Three Organizing Frameworks with Two Theoretical Perspectives. In: *Journal of Applied Psychology* 98,6: 875–925. [https://doi.org/10/bdbb].

Kaiser, Robert B.; Hogan, Joyce (2011): Personality, Leader Behavior, and Overdoing It. In: *Consulting Psychology Journal* 63,4: 219–242. [https://doi.org/10.1037/a0026795].

Kostal, Jack W. et al. (2014): Developing Cross-Cultural Personality Norms: Which Grouping Method Is Appropriate? Presented at the Society for Industrial and Organizational Psychology Conference. Honolulu, HI.

Mol, Stefan T. et al. (2009): When Selection Ratios Are High: Predicting the Expatriation Willingness of Prospective Domestic Entry-Level Job Applicants. In: *Human Performance* 22,1: 1–22. [https://doi.org/10.1080/08959280802540437].

Ones, Deniz S. et al. (2012): Cross-Cultural Generalization: Using Meta-Analysis to Test Hypotheses about Cultural Variability. In: Ryan, Ann Marie; Leong, Frederick T.L.; Oswald, Frederick L. (Eds.): Conducting Multinational Research Projects in Organizational Psychology: Challenges and Opportunities, APA/MSU Series on Multicultural Psychology 1. Washington, DC: American Psychological Association: 91–122. [https://doi.org/10/5kz].

Ones, Deniz S.; Dilchert, Stephan (2009): How Special Are Executives? How Special Should Executive Selection Be? Observations and Recommendations. In: *Industrial and Organizational Psychology* 2,2: 163–170. [https://doi.org/10.1111/j.1754-9434.2009.01127.x].

Ones, Deniz S.; Sinangil, Handan Kepir; Wiernik, Brenton M. (2018): Validity of Big Five Traits for Expatriate Success: Results from Turkey. In: Wiernik, Brenton M.; Rüger, Heiko; Ones, Deniz S. (Eds.): Managing Expatriates: Success Factors in Private and Public Domains, Series on Population Studies 50. Opladen, Germany: Barbara Budrich Publishers.

Ones, Deniz S.; Viswesvaran, Chockalingam (1997): Personality Determinants in the Prediction of Aspects of Expatriate Job Success. In: Aycan, Zeynep (Ed.): Expatriate Management: Theory and Research, New Approaches to Employee Management 4. Greenwich, CT: JAI Press: 63–92.

Schmidt, Frank L.; Hunter, John E. (2015): Methods of Meta-Analysis: Correcting Error and Bias in Research Findings. 3rd ed. Thousand Oaks, CA: Sage. [https://doi.org/10/b6mg].

Schmit, Mark J.; Kihm, Jenifer A.; Robie, Chet (2000): Development of a Global Measure of Personality. In: *Personnel Psychology* 53,1: 153–193. [https://doi.org/10.1111/j.1744-6570.2000.tb00198.x].

Sinangil, Handan Kepir; Ones, Deniz S. (2003): Gender Differences in Expatriate Job Performance. In: *Applied Psychology* 52,3: 461–475. [https://doi.org/10/c36tw5].

Stanek, Kevin C.; Ones, Deniz S. (2018): Taxonomies and Compendia of Cognitive Ability and Personality Measures Relevant to Industrial, Work, and Organizational Psychology. In: Ones, Deniz S. et al. (Eds.): The SAGE Handbook of Industrial, Work and Organizational Psychology. Volume 1: Personnel Psychology and Employee Performance. 2nd ed. London, United Kingdom: Sage: 366–407.

Steel, Piers D. (2013): Converting between Meta-Analytic Variance Estimates Based on Correlations and Fisher z. Presented at the Society for Research Synthesis Methodology Annual Meeting. Providence, RI.

Wiernik, Brenton M.; Dilchert, Stephan; Ones, Deniz S. (2016): Creative Interests and Personality: Scientific versus Artistic Creativity. In: *Zeitschrift für Arbeits- und Organisationspsychologie*, Special Issue: Assessment of Vocational Interests 60,2: 65–78. [https://doi.org/10.1026/0932-4089/a000211].

Woo, Sang Eun et al. (2014): Openness to Experience: Its Lower Level Structure, Measurement, and Cross-Cultural Equivalence. In: *Journal of Personality Assessment*, Openness to Experience 96,1: 29–45. [https://doi.org/10/33v].

Antecedents and Consequences of Mobility Self-Efficacy

Stine Waibel, Heiko Rüger, and Brenton M. Wiernik

Abstract

This chapter explores the role of mobility self-efficacy (MSE; individuals' beliefs about their capacity to move and adapt to new places and cultures) in expatriation. Using a sample of 1,771 German Foreign Service (GFS) diplomats on post abroad, we study potential antecedents of MSE as well as its consequences for diplomats' well-being (locational adjustment, job satisfaction, satisfaction with relocation, health-related quality of life, work–life balance, and perceived stress). We find that language proficiency, international mobility experience acquired before entering the GFS, social and organizational support, and job recognition are associated with higher MSE. Mobility self-efficacy is related to expatriate well-being, especially for outcomes that are closely tied to the underlying mobility process (locational adjustment, satisfaction with the rotation process, and perceived work–life balance). Post-hoc sensitivity analyses suggested that the benefits of MSE may be limited in locations where general living conditions are exceedingly difficult. These results suggest that policies and interventions might focus on developing and maintaining individual mobility self-efficacy to promote positive outcomes for expatriate employees, their families, and their organizations.

1 Introduction

Physical mobility, whether moving to a new organization, a new city, or to a new country, is at once a source of potential threats and opportunities. Moving to a new location can cause feelings of social isolation, loss of resources available in one's current location, and, depending on the destination, even physical harm. These risks are likely to be greater the further and more dissimilar the destination is from one's current location. At the same time, moving to a new location can create opportunities to improve one's work and life situations, to have exciting experiences, and to meet new people. Overcoming the challenges associated with mobility can also be a source of psychological fulfillment and creativity. This mix of potential positive and negative outcomes is a core feature of the experience of novelty (Peterson 1999). Individuals vary widely in their responses to the uncertainty of mobility, with some individuals focusing on potential negative outcomes, some focusing on the potential benefits, and most approaching the experience with some ambivalence. In this chapter, we explore individual differences in attitudes toward international mobility and how they may impact expatriate outcomes.

1.1 Mobility and the German Foreign Service

Employees in the German Foreign Service (GFS) must face the dual potentialities of mobility throughout their careers. Most GFS employees rotate from one country to another every three to four years, so they must constantly grapple with the demands and promises of mobility. Rotation can appeal to employees' curiosity about foreign cultures and desires for new experiences, but it can also create fresh experiences of "uprooting" and "abandonment" (Niedner-Kalthoff 2006). Identifying candidates who will respond positively to such intensive mobility and providing sufficient support and resources to enable them to overcome the ensuing adaptation challenges are critical challenges for managing diplomats and other GFS employees.

While professionals in the field are aware of the unique challenges associated with frequent rotation and that unsuccessful coping with frequent relocation is a common experience for diplomats (Rüger et al. 2013), investigations of the specific personal characteristics that contribute to more successful outcomes have been rarely investigated. It is unknown what factors contribute to "mobility competence" among diplomats. Research from the broader expatriate literature is potentially informative (cf. Albrecht et al. 2018; Bhaskar-Shrinivas et al. 2005; Hechanova et al. 2003), but most expatriates must contend with only one international move; it is unclear whether the same personal characteristics will contribute to the well-being of diplomats and other public and private sector expatriates faced with intensive mobility requirements (cf. Fenner/Selmer 2008; Rehg et al. 2012).

1.2   *Psychological Factors Supporting Mobility Success*

Traditional approaches to addressing the so-called "material and immaterial strains" of international mobility have involved compensations via mobility allowances added to basic salaries (e.g., §29 Law of the German Foreign Service). However, a complementary and potentially more effective approach may be to recruit, select, and develop in diplomats the personal aptitudes, attitudes, resources, interpersonal skills, and personality traits that enable them to productively evaluate and respond to these stressors (Kliesow et al. 2005). Such personal capacities are widely regarded to be important for GFS diplomats. For example, "curiosity as well as the ability to quickly navigate in unfamiliar surroundings, and, time and time again, the willingness to engage with people and other cultures" (Paschke et al. 2005: 340) are considered indispensable characteristics for diplomats. Conversely, a "predisposition towards continuance and the familiar" is assumed to have a "destabilizing effect in the case of the Foreign Service" (Kliesow et al. 2005: 255).

The descriptions cited above by leading international diplomacy management practitioners suggest that positive attitudes toward the changes inherent in international mobility and one's capacity to handle them are important for diplomat success. In psychosocial research, these positive beliefs about one's capabilities are referred to as *self-efficacy beliefs*, defined as individuals' beliefs that they "can produce desired results and forestall detrimental ones by their actions" (Bandura 2001: 10). People with strong self-efficacy beliefs put greater and more persistent effort into managing taxing situations, and they also adopt more positive evaluations of situations and their capacity to cope (Bandura 1977). Thus, "efficacy beliefs are concerned not only with the exercise of control over action but also with the self-regulation of thought processes, motivations, and affective and physiological states" (Bandura 1997: 36). Importantly, self-efficacy beliefs influence outcomes not only because they are related to individuals' objective levels of competence, but also because positive self-beliefs are themselves powerful motivational resources for goal selection, goal pursuit, persistence, and evaluations (Lubinski 2010; Vancouver et al. 2010).

The construct of self-efficacy originated in social cognitive theory (Bandura 1977) and has since been widely adopted in psychological theories (e.g., the theory of planned behavior, Ajzen 1991; the job demands-resources model, Bakker/Demerouti 2007; the conservation of resources model, Hobfoll 1989; social cognitive career theory, Lent 2013; models of goal pursuit and motivation, Locke/Latham 2002; and broad models connecting dispositional characteristics to attitudes and behaviors, Judge/Bono 2001), as well as practice addressing such diverse phenomena as health behaviors, career choice, education and training, romantic relationships, and many others (for a review, see Seltzer 2013). Research on domestic employees (Avey et al. 2011; Jimmieson et al. 2004; Judge/Bono 2001; Pulakos et al. 2002; Seltzer 2013; Tornau/Frese 2013) has found that individuals' self-efficacy beliefs are strong predictors of job performance, job satisfaction, adaptation to challenging work environments, and other critical criteria. These findings have been replicated both in Western societies and in a diverse range of other cultural contexts (Bandura 2002).

Originally, self-efficacy was described as being specific to particular tasks (Bandura 1977; e.g., self-efficacy to quit smoking, Gwaltney et al. 2009). This approach remains dominant in most self-efficacy research and practice. However, more recently, scholars have proposed that domain-general self-efficacy (belief in one's capabilities for tasks in general across domains), is both an important enduring personality trait and may account for most of the predictive power of more specific self-efficacy beliefs (Judge/Bono 2001). Studies in numerous domains have compared the relative predictive power of general and domain-specific forms of self-efficacy (e.g., Lindley/Borgen 2002). Meta-analytic evidence has shown that domain-specific self-efficacy measures generally show stronger relations with conceptually-aligned criteria than do domain-general measures (Seltzer 2013).

Expatriate self-efficacy research has primarily focused on general self-efficacy. For example, Black et al.'s (1991) model of expatriate international adjustment presents general self-efficacy beliefs as an important psychological resource that enables expatriates to exhibit newly-learned culturally-appropriate behaviors that enhance their adjustment. Meta-analyses of private-sector expatriate research has confirmed substantial relations (ρs $\approx$ .20) of general self-efficacy with international adjustment, cultural competence, and job performance (Bhaskar-Shrinivas et al. 2005; Hechanova et al. 2003; Mol et al. 2005a; see also Fliege/Wiernik 2018, Chapter 6, this volume). Self-efficacy contextualized to the unique challenges of expatriation has rarely been considered (see Mak/Tran 2001; Osman-Gani/Rockstuhl 2009; Rehg et al. 2012, for exceptions).

1.3   The Present Study

Considering domestic employee findings that contextualized self-efficacy measures are stronger predictors of criteria, in this chapter, we propose that domain-specific self-efficacy reflecting diplomats' beliefs in their ability to effectively handle the challenge of frequent mobility will show stronger relations with expatriate outcomes than the general self-efficacy measures more widely applied in the expatriate literature. We focus on *mobility self-efficacy* (MSE; i.e., expectations of personal mastery when it comes to moving and adapting to new places and cultures). Using a sample of German Foreign Service (GFS) diplomats, we examine potential antecedents of MSE and its associations with subjective well-being outcomes.

Due to processes of attraction, selection, and attrition (Schneider 1987), diplomats' levels of mobility self-efficacy are likely to be higher than the general population. High-MSE individuals are more likely to apply to be diplomats, to be selected for rotation by the GFS, and to remain in the organization through multiple rotations. Nevertheless, diplomats do vary in the strength of their efficacy beliefs (cf. Fliege et al. 2016). Therefore, we first examine whether these individual differences in mobility self-efficacy are associated with previous mobility experiences, past accomplishments, and outside support and environmental factors, as well as socio-demographic characteristics. We investigate these potential antecedents based on general findings from social cognitive research that self-efficacy beliefs develop in part due to positive experiences with a task and perceptions that the tasks is supported by important members of one's social network (cf. Bandura 1977; Sheu et al. 2010).

Next, we examine the association of mobility self-efficacy to expatriate well-being outcomes, including locational adjustment, job and rotation satisfaction, work–life balance, health-related quality of life, and perceived stress. High self-efficacy leads individuals to make more positive evaluations of ambiguous or potentially threatening situations and to engage in more effective coping and adaptation behaviors in changing environments (Van Dyne et al. 2012), so we expect mobility self-efficacy to be positively associated with each well-being outcome. We also compare the relative strength of outcome relations with mobility self-efficacy to those with decontextualized general self-efficacy to examine the benefits of considering self-efficacy beliefs that are specific to the diplomat mobility context.

2   Methods

2.1   *Participants*

The current analyses used the GFS sample of diplomats on post abroad (see Wiernik et al. 2018b, Chapter 1, and Rüger et al. 2018, Appendix B, this volume, for more details). Participants were 47% female (53% male) and had an average age of 45 years. Participants reflect all levels of the GFS civil service (20% higher (top-level) civil service [CS], 37% higher intermediate CS, 25% intermediate CS, 4% ordinary CS, 15% secretarial pool). Participants were posted in a range of international locations, including posts characterized as low-difficulty/high-comfort (e.g., Brussels; 39%), posts characterized as moderate difficulty/comfort (e.g., Sofia; 29%), and posts characterized as high-difficulty/low-comfort (e.g., Kabul; 32%) in terms of their living conditions and popularity.

2.2   *Self-Efficacy Measures*

Mobility self-efficacy (MSE). Mobility self-efficacy beliefs were measured using four items developed for this study. These items measure self-efficacy for moving and adapting to new places and cultures. The four items were "I can easily find my way in new surroundings", "I quickly feel at home in new places", "I think it's exciting to better get to know a foreign country", and "I feel confident in dealing with people of other cultures". Cronbach's α was .72.

General self-efficacy (GSE). General (non-specific) self-efficacy was measured using four items from the General Self-Efficacy Scale (Schwarzer/Jerusalem 1995) assessing self-efficacy toward broadly defined goals and situations (e.g., "I can always manage to solve difficult problems if I try hard enough"). Cronbach's α was .71.

2.3   *Socio-Demographic Variables*

We examined relations between several demographic characteristics and MSE, including age (measured continuously in years), gender (female = 0, male = 1), and civil service grade (treated as a continuous variable ranging from secretarial pool [low] to higher CS [high]).

2.4   Potential Antecedent Measures

Current post characteristics. We examined several features of expatriates' current assignments that may contribute to current MSE beliefs, including the difficulty grade of the post and the time spent in the current location (measured continuously in months).

Previous mobility and mastery experiences. We examined several mobility and intercultural mastery experiences that may contribute to MSE beliefs. These include various forms of international experience (number of previous rotation posts completed in the GFS, number of international stays of longer than a year completed before entering the GFS, and having parents who also worked for the GFS [dummy-coded]), as well as the number of different languages spoken at business and everyday levels of fluency (cf. Wiernik et al. 2018a, Chapter 12, this volume).

Psychosocial resources. We also measured several psychosocial resources that may be present in expatriates' environments which may contribute to their well-being – social support, organizational support, job autonomy, and job recognition.

Social support. Perceived social support was measured using four items from the Berlin Social-Support Scales (Schulz/Schwarzer 2003) which were developed to assess stress and coping among cancer patients. The item showing the largest factor loading for each subscale was selected for use in this abbreviated measure. An example item is "When I am sad, there are people who cheer me up". This measure had a Cronbach's α = .85.

Organizational support. Perceived organizational support was measured with nine items assessing how helpful expatriates found various GFS services to support adjustment in new locations (e.g., language training, counseling, medical evaluations), as well as one item measuring overall satisfaction with support from the organization ("How satisfied are you with the support of the Federal Foreign Office?"; rated on scale from 1 [very dissatisfied] to 4 [very satisfied]). This combined measure showed a Cronbach's α = .77.

Job recognition. Perceived job recognition was measured with 2 items ("I receive high esteem [on my job from others]", "My job provides little recognition…much recognition [4-point scale]; α = .63).

Job autonomy. Perceived job autonomy was measured using three items on individuals' perceptions of their job as giving them opportunities for autonomy (e.g., "I have little decision-making authority" [reversed]; α = .87).

2.5   Outcome Measures

Locational adjustment. Expatriates' adjustment to their current living situations was measured using eight items developed for this study their comfort with everyday needs and activities (e.g., "I can easily look after everyday errands"; α = .81).

Work–life conflict. Perceived work–life conflict was measured using eleven items asking about the degree to which expatriates felt conflict between their work in the GFS and their personal and family life (e.g., "The frequent moves are a burden to family life"). Demands associated with work capture both general work characteristics as well as the demands associated with the frequent rotation to new countries (α = .82).

Job satisfaction. General job satisfaction was measured using seven items asking individuals about their degree of satisfaction with their working conditions, compensation, and career progress. An example item is "How satisfied are you with the working atmosphere at your current post?" The items of this scale were standardized before being summed to bring variables with different response scales to a comparable metric (α = .67).

Satisfaction with rotation process. We measured diplomats' satisfaction with the rotation process using 9 items, including evaluations of life in rotation in general and the way the rotation system works in specific (e.g., "How satisfied are you with the rotation process?"). Items were standardized before summing ($\alpha = .73$).

Health-related quality of life. Self-reported mental and physical health was measured using 13 items from the German Quality of Life Questionnaire (QLQ; Aaronson et al. 1993) that are applicable to non-clinical populations (e.g., "In the last week, did you feel depressed?", "In the last week, did you feel tired?"; $\alpha = .82$). Items were standardized before being summed ($\alpha = .92$).

Perceived stress. Stress was measured with four items selected from the German version of the Perceived Stress Questionnaire (Fliege et al. 2005). Items assessed general feelings of being overwhelmed and unable to manage demands across life domains (e.g., "Your problems seem to be piling up"; $\alpha = .72$).

2.6   Analyses

We calculated correlations between MSE, socio-demographic variables, and each of MSE's potential antecedents, as well as 95% confidence intervals. We also computed correlations of MSE and GSE with each outcome variable. To assess the degree to which the domain-specific MSE construct accounts for incremental variance in expatriate outcomes over domain-general self-efficacy, we estimated OLS regression models with (1) GSE alone or (2) both GSE and MSE as predictors and computed the change in R^2 when adding MSE to the models. All correlations and regression results were corrected for measurement error in measured variables.

We interpreted the magnitudes of correlations using the empirical benchmarks for corrected correlations established by Paterson et al. (2016; cf. Hemphill 2003). Paterson et al. analyzed 258 meta-analyses published in applied psychology and management and developed empirical distributions for correlations between individual-level variables. Compared to Cohen's (1988) widely-cited guidelines, empirical benchmarks such as Paterson et al.'s or Hemphill's provide a much more accurate characterization of the size of effects. Based on the quartiles of their overall corrected correlations distribution, we interpreted corrected correlations $< .15$ as negligible, $.15–.24$ as small, $.25–.39$ as moderate, and $\geq .40$ as large.

3   Results

3.1   Antecedents of Mobility Self-Efficacy

Table 1 shows correlations among MSE, socio-demographic variables, and proposed antecedents of MSE. Age, gender, and civil service grade were negligibly related to MSE, as were living conditions/difficulty of expatriates' current post and the time they had spent in their current location. Among the previous mobility and mastery experiences, MSE had small correlations with number of languages spoken at business ($r_c = .19$) and everyday ($r_c = .15$) levels of fluency. MSE was also slightly to weakly positively related to previous international mobility experiences in the GFS ($r_c = .10$), pre-GFS international experience ($r_c = .15$), and exposure to mobility through having parents who also worked in the GFS ($r_c = .09$).

Table 1: Correlations of mobility self-efficacy with potential antecedents

	Variable	M	SD	1	2	3	4	5	6	7	8	9	10	11	12	13	14
1	Mobility self-efficacy	3.19	0.46														
2	Gender[a]	0.53	0.50	.04 *1421* *-.01, .09*													
3	Age	45.15	9.86	.05 *1283* *.00, .11*	.27 *1358*												
4	Civil service grade	2.58	1.01	.05 *1433* *.00, .11*	.23 *1495*	.01 *1351*											
5	Time at current post	5.85	3.00	.00 *1466* *-.05, .06*	.00 *1499*	.07 *1352*	-.11 *1589*										
6	Post difficulty	2.59	1.86	.01 *1404* *-.06, .06*	.00 *1457*	-.10 *1306*	-.03 *1545*	-.05 *1630*									
7	GFS intern. exp.[b]	0.92	2.10	.10 *1376* *.05, .15*	.21 *1430*	.78 *1293*	.10 *1509*	-.02 *1610*	-.08 *1600*								
8	Pre-GFS intern. exp.[c]	2.50	0.96	.15 *1456* *.11, .20*	.02 *1510*	.07 *1357*	-.01 *1602*	-.02 *1617*	-.02 *1721*	.02 *1644*							
9	Parents GFS employees	3.80	1.30	.09 *1463* *.04, .14*	.10 *1516*	.04 *1361*	-.01 *1609*	.07 *1622*	.04 *1717*	.00 *1652*	.37 *1725*						

$\rightarrow$

Table 1: Correlations of mobility self-efficacy with potential antecedents – continued

	Variable	M	SD	1	2	3	4	5	6	7	8	9	10	11	12	13	14
1	Mobility self-efficacy	3.19	0.46														
10	Business language fluency[d]	0.05	0.23	.19 1377 .14, .24	-.06 1446	.01 1305	.23 1444	.09 1386	-.01 1451	-.02 1411	.10 1460	.07 1468					
11	Everyday language fluency[d]	2.68	0.61	.15 1419 .09, .20	-.09 1488	-.03 1343	.31 1486	.07 1426	-.03 1493	-.04 1455	.07 1505	.03 1513	.61 1462				
12	Perceived org. support	3.06	0.63	.25 1273 .19, .31	-.04 1395	-.01 1256	.09 1484	.02 1476	.01 1510	-.04 1285	-.02 1523	-.01 1530	.04 1351	.06 1392			
13	Perceived social support	2.52	0.74	.17 1356 .12, .22	-.14 1305	-.21 1196	.04 1319	-.15 1262	.01 1322	-.03 1512	-.02 1334	-.02 1339	.02 1270	.02 1299	.18 1342		
14	Perceived job recognition	2.79	0.91	.17 1334 .17, .30	.16 1381	.07 1250	.45 1448	.09 1381	-.04 1449	.01 1408	-.02 1457	-.01 1463	.10 1343	.09 1374	.35 1245	.34 1362	
15	Perceived job autonomy	1.92	0.84	.11 1427 .07, .18	.29 1479	.19 1332	.68 1564	.21 1497	-.03 1570	.05 1530	-.02 1581	.04 1588	.16 1434	.17 1473	.11 1312	.09 1470	.68 1449

Note: zero-correlations corrected for unreliability in measured variables and sample sizes; correlations with mobility self-efficacy shown with 95% confidence intervals; [a] coded female = 0, male = 1; [b] number of previous posts in the GFS; [c] number of international trips before joining the GFS; [d] number of languages spoken with at least this level of fluency.

Psychosocial resources were more strongly related to MSE, with perceived organizational support ($r_c = .25$), perceived social support ($r_c = .17$), and perceived job recognition ($r_c = .17$) all showing weak to moderate correlations. MSE also showed a smaller association with job autonomy ($r_c = .11$).

We fit an OLS regression model predicting mobility self-efficacy using all potential antecedents showing at least a small correlation with MSE (i.e., $r_c \geq .15$). Together, these 6 predictors accounted for just under 10% of the variance in MSE ($R^2 = .089$; adj. $R^2 = .083$).

3.2   Outcomes of Mobility Self-Efficacy

Turning to the potential benefits of high mobility self-efficacy, Table 2 presents corrected correlations between MSE, GSE, and various expatriate outcomes. MSE showed strong relations with perceived work–life conflict ($r_c = -.39$) and satisfaction with the rotation process ($r_c = .43$). That is, stronger MSE was associated with fewer conflicts between diplomats' work and non-work demands and more positive evaluations of the process for their assignment and transition to their current location. MSE showed only a weak relation with locational adjustment ($r_c = .16$). This value is smaller than expected given the centrality of adjustment to expatriate research (Mol et al. 2005b) and the conceptual alignment of adjustment with mobility self-efficacy. However, it is close to the meta-analytic estimate of relations between self-efficacy and locational adjustment ($\rho = .20$, Bhaskar-Shrinivas et al. 2005). MSE relations were also somewhat smaller for criteria not directly related to life in mobility, such as job satisfaction ($r_c = .26$), health-related quality of life ($r_c = .33$), and perceived stress ($r_c = -.19$).

3.3   Mobility and General Self-Efficacy

Consistent with findings for other forms of domain-specific self-efficacy (Seltzer 2013), mobility-specific self-efficacy was very strongly related to domain-general self-efficacy ($r_c = .69$). This very strong convergence raises the question of whether there is benefit from conceptualizing and measuring self-efficacy focused specifically on international mobility, versus focusing on the broader general self-efficacy construct. Examining zero-order correlations in Table 2, it appears that MSE shows stronger correlations than GSE with outcomes more directly related to diplomats' life in mobility – locational adjustment, satisfaction with rotation, and perceived work–life conflict (which includes items related to conflict between family and rotation). In contrast, MSE and GSE showed essentially equal relations for job satisfaction, health-related quality of life, and perceived stress – criteria not directly addressing mobility. Thus, it appears that MSE has incremental value for explaining expatriate outcomes directly connected with adapting to mobility, but not for other outcomes.

We further tested the incremental validity of MSE using stepwise regression (regressing criteria first onto GSE, then adding MSE as a second step). These results are shown in Table 3. Consistent with the pattern of zero-order correlations, mobility self-efficacy showed substantial incremental validity over general self-efficacy for locational adjustment ($\Delta R^2 = .030$), satisfaction with rotation ($\Delta R^2 = .120$), and work–life conflict ($\Delta R^2 = .085$), but negligible incremental validity for other criteria. These results confirm our conclusion that mobility self-efficacy has incremental value for understanding expatriate outcomes with which it is conceptually aligned.

Table 2: Correlations of mobility and general self-efficacy with expatriate outcomes

	Variable	M	SD	1	2	3	4	5	6	7
1	Mobility self-efficacy	3.19	.46							
2	General self-efficacy	2.98	.41	.69						
				.64, .73						
				1296						
3	Locational adjustment	2.75	.60	.16	.05					
				.10, .22	-.01, .12					
				1345	1234					
4	Job satisfaction	.00	.58	.26	.29	.35				
				.19, .33	.22, .36	.32, .44				
				1166	1096	1218				
5	Satisfaction with rotation	.00	.56	.43	.26	.25	.66			
				.36, .49	.19, .33	.20, .33	.58, .70			
				1064	1017	1074	990			
6	Work–life conflict	2.62	.51	-.39	-.26	-.28	-.42	-.56		
				-.45, -.33	-.33, -.20	-.37, -.24	-.47, -.34	-.61, -.50		
				1014	973	1001	913	856		
7	Health-related QoL	.00	.71	.33	.37	.28	.40	.35	-.50	
				.28, .38	.32, .43	.25, .35	.33, .44	.30, .41	-.55, -.45	
				1350	1254	1318	1148	1046	1015	
8	Perceived stress	2.35	.72	-.19	-.23	-.23	-.35	-.27	.49	-.57
				-.24, -.13	-.29, -.17	-.30, -.19	-.40, -.28	-.33, -.20	.44, .55	-.61, -.53
				1439	1320	1403	1216	1094	1045	1428

Note: zero-correlations, 95% confidence intervals, and sample sizes; correlations corrected for unreliability in measured variables; QoL = quality of life.

Table 3: Incremental validity of mobility self-efficacy over general self-efficacy

Variable	Locational adjustment		Job satisfaction		Satisfaction with rotation		Work–life conflict		Health-related QoL		Perceived stress	
General self-efficacy	.05	-.12	.29	.21	.26	-.07	-.26	.02	.37	.27	-.23	-.19
Mobility self-efficacy		.24		.11		.48		-.40		.14		-.06
R^2	.003	.033	.084	.091	.068	.187	.068	.152	.137	.148	.053	.055
ΔR^2		.030		.007		.120		.085		.011		.002
N	1230		1180		1113		1077		1299		1349	

Note: Standardized regression coefficients, corrected for unreliability in all variables; QoL = quality of life.

4   Discussion

Most Foreign Service professionals spend two-thirds of their career abroad and typically move to a new location every 3–4 years. Thus, the mobility demands placed on these professionals are much greater than the demands on most expatiates, who must navigate only one expatriation and repatriation cycle during their careers (Albrecht et al. 2018). During each rotation, diplomats must reorient themselves to a new work and private environment and rebalance work and non-work demands. In this study, we examined diplomats' personal psychological resources to handle these mobility demands inherent in rotational diplomatic service. We explored factors that may contribute to diplomats' mobility self-efficacy – their judgments of how well they can manage the challenges of frequent mobility – as well as the potential benefits of mobility self-efficacy for well-being.

4.1   Antecedents of Mobility Self-Efficacy

Overall, we find that although diplomats went through a similar recruitment and selection process, they still ranged widely in their perceived mobility-specific self-efficacy. Our findings suggest that several experiential and environmental factors may contribute to development of strong MSE. We found that prior international mobility experiences, language proficiency, and supportive social, organizational, and job environments were all associated with mobility self-efficacy. As a cross-sectional and observational study, we cannot confirm the causal direction of these relations (e.g., it may be that individuals low on mobility self-efficacy leave the GFS, so the positive correlation of MSE with the number of previous posts reflects not a developmental effect of past mobility adaptation accomplishments, but rather an attrition effect). Nevertheless, these relations do suggest potential implications for practice and future intervention research to enhance diplomats' MSE.

Our finding that previous international experiences are associated with MSE is consistent with longitudinal and intervention research in other domains showing that positive learning experiences are key drivers of self-efficacy (Sheu et al. 2010). These relationships were positive, but the magnitudes were small. This may reflect that these variables may include a mix of positive and negative mobility experiences. A more nuanced examination of mobility experience that captures diplomats' emotional responses to their experiences may reveal stronger effects (cf. Bandura 1997). These findings qualify emerging arguments about the strengths of "third-culture kids" (i.e., children who accompany their parents on international assignments and spend a significant portion of their adolescence in foreign cultures) for international mobility and their attractiveness as a recruitment source for multinational organizations (Selmer/Lam 2004). International experience is only likely to contribute to mobility self-efficacy if those experiences are positive, and forms of mobility experience outside the family context (e.g., self-initiated international travel) may be more important for developing these beliefs.

Our finding that foreign language proficiency is associated with MSE is also consistent with previous research finding that language skills are associated with confidence in one's ability to interact with people from foreign cultures. Mastering a foreign language (especially at higher levels of practical proficiency) requires engaging deeply with a culture, which can provide positive mastery experiences that carry over to other intercultural settings (Thomas/Lazarova 2014). Language proficiency also provides objective skills that can grant access to informational and social networks and strengthen one's control over events in one's local environment (Peltokorpi 2010). Language skill also makes interactions with host country nationals less intimidating, providing enhanced personal and motivational resources for adaptation (Yamao/Sekiguchi 2015).

We observed positive relations of supportive social, organizational, and job environments with mobility self-efficacy. Given the cross-sectional nature of our data, we cannot firmly establish the causal direction of these relationships – high MSE may, for example, lead diplomats to evaluate ambiguous social or work environments more positively. However, our results align with broader research on social cognitive theory (Sheu et al. 2010) and the theory of planned behavior (Armitage/Conner 2001) on the causal role of social supports and barriers for driving self-efficacy beliefs. Support can provide individuals with emotional reassurance, verbal persuasion, relevant information, and practical aid (Fisher 1985) which, in turn, can strengthen control and mastery beliefs (Fontaine 1986; Gist/Mitchell 1992). Enriched job characteristics, such as receiving acknowledgement of one's efforts from others and having the opportunity to make decisions about one's work, can similarly enhance employees' confidence in their work, motivation, and performance (Fernet et al. 2012; Humphrey et al. 2007). In the case of diplomats, job characteristics and established social relationships can change dramatically when they rotate to new locations every few years (Kliesow et al. 2005). Sending organizations should ensure that diplomats receive sufficient organizational support and job enrichment so that their confidence in their capacity to handle the transitions is not negatively impacted (see also Bellinger et al. 2018, Chapter 14, this volume). Of note, we found that post difficulty was unrelated to MSE mean levels, suggesting that diplomats' feelings of confidence in their mobility competence are not impacted by adverse situational pressures that are largely outside of organizational and individual control.

Finally, it is notable that MSE is not related to socio-demographic characteristics (gender, age, civil service grade). This is in line with other research finding weak and inconsistent relations between demographic characteristics and self-efficacy (e.g., Huang 2013). These nil relations are heartening, as they suggest that the potential benefits of mobility self-efficacy are not limited to specific demographic groups. For example, women have equal mobility self-efficacy as men, despite their possibly greater family responsibilities interfering with mobility (Tharenou 2008; see also Waibel/Rüger 2018, Chapter 18, this volume). Socio-demographic influence on mobility self-efficacy may be stronger in groups that are heterogonous in terms of socioeconomic resources, disability, or other forms of disadvantage (cf. Clark/Nothwehr 1999), but this is unlikely to be a major concern for the diplomat population.

4.2   Benefits of Mobility Self-Efficacy

We found that high feelings of confidence in one's ability to handle mobility challenges were associated with a variety of expatriate well-being outcomes, including locational adjustment, job and rotation satisfaction, work–life conflict, subjective health, and stress perceptions. These relationships were particularly strong for those outcomes that were most closely tied to the challenges of the mobility process (locational adjustment, satisfaction with the rotation process, and perceived work–life balance). Although mobility self-efficacy and domain-general self-efficacy are highly correlated (indeed, general self-efficacy beliefs likely have a causal influence on the development of domain-specific mobility self-efficacy, cf. Betz/Klein 1996; Seltzer 2013), the domain-specific conceptualization of self-efficacy provides unique and incremental insights for understanding responses to the unique challenges of international mobility (cf. Kaiser et al. 2007; Ones/Viswesvaran 1996). In contrast, for outcomes that are more detached from the mobility context (subjective health, job satisfaction, stress), mobility self-efficacy offered no additional explanatory power over general self-efficacy perceptions. This pattern of results shows that while constructs tailored specifically to the expatriation context, such as mobility self-efficacy, have value, they should be considered as part of a broader array of context-general and context-specific individual differences if researchers and practitioners aim to address the full array of important expatriate outcomes (Albrecht et al. 2018)

We found that MSE is related to locational adjustment to local living conditions, but that this correlation was much smaller than observed for other outcomes, particularly other mobility-related outcomes. It is possible that the comparatively weak relation of mobility self-efficacy with locational adjustment stems from differences within our sample on the relative comforts and challenges afforded by diplomats' host country environments. MSE may be more strongly related to adjustment in difficult environments, as the greater adaptation challenges in these contexts may mean that only expatriates with very high mobility self-efficacy are able to cope effectively. Conversely, it is possible that high-difficulty host environments may attenuate MSE-adjustment relations if the greater challenges make it difficult for any expatriate, no matter how confident in their mobility skills, to adapt effectively. We explored these possibilities in a post hoc analysis computing MSE-adjustment correlations separately for diplomats posted in high (e.g., Kabul), moderate (e.g., Sofia), and low (e.g., Brussels) difficulty/discomfort locations. We found that relations of MSE with locational adjustment were much stronger in low ($r_c = .25$ [95% CI .14, .35]) and moderate ($r_c = .31$ [.19, .43]) difficulty posts and weaker in high difficulty posts ($r_c = .11$ [-.01, .23]). Thus, the results of these sensitivity analyses suggest that MSE is beneficial for adjustment, but that this benefit is much diminished in contexts where adapting to local living conditions is very challenging. Future research should examine adjustment processes in such highly challenging environments more thoroughly. Correlations of MSE with other outcomes did not differ substantially across post difficulty levels.

5   Conclusion

Self-reported quality of life tends to be significantly lower among diplomats than in the general population (Fliege et al. 2016). Much of this gap likely stems from the intangible costs of mobility, such as disruptions to social relationships and the loss of support networks. Identifying factors that contribute to better coping and well-being for diplomats and expatriates in general is therefore a critical task for international human resource management. Future research should look more closely at the psychosocial pathways that contribute to success and failure of the mobility process, particularly the social and environmental factors that facilitate positive attitudes toward rotation. Understanding how positive attitudes such as mobility self-efficacy develop and impact the mobility process can enhance the well-being not only of diplomats and other expatriates, but also other employee populations who increasingly must manage diverse forms of job-related spatial mobility (e.g., long-distance commuting, overnight business travel). These emerging forms of short-term or "cyclical" mobility are partly substituting traditional mobility patterns, such as permanent family relocation (Schneider/Collet 2010; Schneider/Meil Landwerlin 2008). Research on factors that support mobility success for expatriates can inform similar research on domestic cyclical mobility, and vice versa. We suggest that mobility self-efficacy may be a factor whose benefits could be realized across these diverse forms of physical mobility.

References

Aaronson, Neil K. et al. (1993): The European Organization for Research and Treatment of Cancer QLQ-C30: A Quality-of-Life Instrument for Use in International Clinical Trials in Oncology. In: *Journal of the National Cancer Institute* 85,5: 365–376. [https://doi.org/10/d9d26h].

Ajzen, Icek (1991): The Theory of Planned Behavior. In: *Organizational Behavior and Human Decision Processes*, Theories of Cognitive Self-Regulation 50,2: 179–211. [https://doi.org/10.1016/0749-5978(91)90020-T].

Albrecht, Anne-Grit; Ones, Deniz S.; Sinangil, Handan Kepir (2018): Expatriate Management. In: Ones, Deniz S. et al. (Eds.): The SAGE Handbook of Industrial, Work and Organizational Psychology. Volume 3: Managerial Psychology and Organizational Approaches. 2nd ed. London, United Kingdom: Sage: 429–468.

Armitage, Christopher J.; Conner, Mark (2001): Efficacy of the Theory of Planned Behaviour: A Meta-Analytic Review. In: *British Journal of Social Psychology* 40,4: 471–499. [https://doi.org/10/gbn].

Avey, James B. et al. (2011): Meta-Analysis of the Impact of Positive Psychological Capital on Employee Attitudes, Behaviors, and Performance. In: *Human Resource Development Quarterly* 22,2: 127–152. [https://doi.org/10.1002/hrdq.20070].

Bakker, Arnold B.; Demerouti, Evangelia (2007): The Job Demands-Resources Model: State of the Art. In: *Journal of Managerial Psychology* 22,3: 309–328. [https://doi.org/10.1108/02683940710733115].

Bandura, Albert (2002): Social Cognitive Theory in Cultural Context. In: *Applied Psychology* 51,2: 269–290. [https://doi.org/10.1111/1464-0597.00092].

Bandura, Albert (2001): Social Cognitive Theory: An Agentic Perspective. In: *Annual Review of Psychology* 52: 1–26. [https://doi.org/10/dqmktz].

Bandura, Albert (1997): Self-Efficacy: The Exercise of Control. New York: Freeman.

Bandura, Albert (1977): Self-Efficacy: Toward a Unifying Theory of Behavioral Change. In: *Psychological Review* 84,2: 191–215. [https://doi.org/10.1037/0033-295X.84.2.191].

Bellinger, Maria M.; Wiernik, Brenton M.; Fliege, Herbert (2018): Organizational and Social Support among Foreign Service Diplomats. In: Wiernik, Brenton M.; Rüger, Heiko; Ones, Deniz S. (Eds.): Managing Expatriates: Success Factors in Private and Public Domains, Series on Population Studies 50. Opladen, Germany: Barbara Budrich Publishers.

Betz, Nancy E.; Klein, Karla L. (1996): Relationships among Measures of Career Self-Efficacy, Generalized Self-Efficacy, and Global Self-Esteem. In: *Journal of Career Assessment* 4,3: 285–298. [https://doi.org/10.1177/106907279600400304].

Bhaskar-Shrinivas, Purnima et al. (2005): Input-Based and Time-Based Models of International Adjustment: Meta-Analytic Evidence and Theoretical Extensions. In: *Academy of Management Journal* 48,2: 257-281. [https://doi.org/10.5465/AMJ.2005.16928400].

Black, J. Stewart; Mendenhall, Mark E.; Oddou, Gary R. (1991): Toward a Comprehensive Model of International Adjustment: An Integration of Multiple Theoretical Perspectives. In: *Academy of Management Review* 16,2: 291–317. [https://doi.org/10/fn7m8b].

Clark, Daniel O.; Nothwehr, Faryle (1999): Exercise Self-Efficacy and Its Correlates among Socio-economically Disadvantaged Older Adults. In: *Health Education & Behavior* 26,4: 535–546. [https://doi.org/10.1177/109019819902600410].

Cohen, Jacob (1988): Statistical Power Analysis for the Behavioral Sciences. 2nd ed. Mahwah, NJ: Erlbaum. [https://doi.org/10/vv3].

Fenner, Charles R., Jr.; Selmer, Jan (2008): Public Sector Expatriate Managers: Psychological Adjustment, Personal Characteristics and Job Factors. In: *International Journal of Human Resource Management* 19,7: 1237–1252. [https://doi.org/10.1080/09585190802110026].

Fernet, Claude; Austin, Stéphanie; Vallerand, Robert J. (2012): The Effects of Work Motivation on Employee Exhaustion and Commitment: An Extension of the JD-R Model. In: *Work & Stress* 26,3: 213–229. [https://doi.org/10.1080/02678373.2012.713202].

Fisher, Cynthia D. (1985): Social Support and Adjustment to Work: A Longitudinal Study. In: *Journal of Management* 11,3: 39–53. [https://doi.org/10.1177/014920638501100304].

Fliege, Herbert et al. (2016): Diplomats' Quality of Life: The Role of Risk Factors and Coping Resources. In: *International Journal of Intercultural Relations* 51: 14–28. [https://doi.org/10.1016/j.ijintrel.2016.01.001].

Fliege, Herbert et al. (2005): The Perceived Stress Questionnaire (PSQ) Reconsidered: Validation and Reference Values from Different Clinical and Healthy Adult Samples. In: *Psychosomatic Medicine* 67,1: 78–88. [https://doi.org/10.1097/01.psy.0000151491.80178.78].

Fliege, Herbert; Wiernik, Brenton M. (2018): Core Self-Evaluative Traits: Self-Efficacy, Locus of Control, Optimism, and Diplomat Success. In: Wiernik, Brenton M.; Rüger, Heiko; Ones, Deniz S. (Eds.): Managing Expatriates: Success Factors in Private and Public Domains, Series on Population Studies 50. Opladen, Germany: Barbara Budrich Publishers.

Fontaine, Gary (1986): Roles of Social Support Systems in Overseas Relocation: Implications for Intercultural Training. In: *International Journal of Intercultural Relations* 10,3: 361–378. [https://doi.org/10.1016/0147-1767(86)90018-0].

Gist, Marilyn E.; Mitchell, Terence R. (1992): Self-Efficacy: A Theoretical Analysis of Its Determinants and Malleability. In: *Academy of Management Review* 17,2: 183-211. [https://doi.org/10.2307/258770].

Gwaltney, Chad J. et al. (2009): Self-Efficacy and Smoking Cessation: A Meta-Analysis. In: *Psychology of Addictive Behaviors* 23,1: 56–66. [https://doi.org/10.1037/a0013529].

Hechanova, Regina; Beehr, Terry A.; Christiansen, Neil D. (2003): Antecedents and Consequences of Employees' Adjustment to Overseas Assignment: A Meta-Analytic Review. In: *Applied Psychology* 52,2: 213–236. [https://doi.org/10/d4f4xv].

Hemphill, James F. (2003): Interpreting the Magnitudes of Correlation Coefficients. In: *American Psychologist* 58,1: 78–79. [https://doi.org/10/fb38g8].

Hobfoll, Stevan E. (1989): Conservation of Resources: A New Attempt at Conceptualizing Stress. In: *American Psychologist* 44,3: 513–524. [https://doi.org/10.1037/0003-066X.44.3.513].

Huang, Chiungjung (2013): Gender Differences in Academic Self-Efficacy: A Meta-Analysis. In: *European Journal of Psychology of Education* 28,1: 1–35. [https://doi.org/10/fzcwwd].

Humphrey, Stephen E.; Nahrgang, Jennifer D.; Morgeson, Frederick P. (2007): Integrating Motivational, Social, and Contextual Work Design Features: A Meta-Analytic Summary and Theoretical Extension of the Work Design Literature. In: *Journal of Applied Psychology* 92,5: 1332–1356. [https://doi.org/10.1037/0021-9010.92.5.1332].

Jimmieson, Nerina L.; Terry, Deborah J.; Callan, Victor J. (2004): A Longitudinal Study of Employee Adaptation to Organizational Change: The Role of Change-Related Information and Change-Related Self-Efficacy. In: *Journal of Occupational Health Psychology* 9,1: 11–27. [https://doi.org/10.1037/1076-8998.9.1.11].

Judge, Timothy A.; Bono, Joyce E. (2001): Relationship of Core Self-Evaluation Traits – Self-Esteem, Generalized Self-Efficacy, Locus of Control, and Emotional Stability – with Job Satisfaction and Job Performance: A Meta-Analysis. In: *Journal of Applied Psychology* 86,1: 80–92. [https://doi.org/10.1037/0021-9010.86.1.80].

Kaiser, Florian G.; Schultz, P. Wesley; Scheuthle, Hannah (2007): The Theory of Planned Behavior without Compatibility? Beyond Method Bias and Past Trivial Associations. In: *Journal of Applied Social Psychology* 37,7: 1522–1544. [https://doi.org/10/d98wfc].

Kliesow, Roland et al. (2005): Bewerbung, Ausbildung und Laufbahnen: Wer soll sich auf den Auswärtigen Dienst bewerben? In: Brandt, Enrico; Buck, Christian (Eds.): Auswärtiges Amt: Diplomatie als Beruf. 4th ed. Wiesbaden, Germany: VS Verlag für Sozialwissenschaften: 253–262. [https://doi.org/10/b6nm].

Lent, Robert W. (2013): Social Cognitive Career Theory. In: Brown, Steven D.; Lent, Robert W. (Eds.): Career Development and Counseling: Putting Theory and Research to Work. 2nd ed. Hoboken, NJ: Wiley: 115–146.

Lindley, Lori D.; Borgen, Fred H. (2002): Generalized Self-Efficacy, Holland Theme Self-Efficacy, and Academic Performance. In: *Journal of Career Assessment* 10,3: 301-314. [https://doi.org/10.1177/10672702010003002].

Locke, Edwin A.; Latham, Gary P. (2002): Building a Practically Useful Theory of Goal Setting and Task Motivation: A 35-Year Odyssey. In: *American Psychologist* 57,9: 705-717. [https://doi.org/10.1037/0003-066X.57.9.705].

Lubinski, David John (2010): Neglected Aspects and Truncated Appraisals in Vocational Counseling: Interpreting the Interest-Efficacy Association from a Broader Perspective: Comment on Armstrong and Vogel (2009). In: *Journal of Counseling Psychology* 57,2: 226–238. [https://doi.org/10.1037/a0019163].

Mak, Anita S.; Tran, Catherine (2001): Big Five Personality and Cultural Relocation Factors in Vietnamese Australian Students' Intercultural Social Self-Efficacy. In: *International Journal of Intercultural Relations* 25,2: 181–201. [https://doi.org/10.1016/S0147-1767(00)00050-X].

Mol, Stefan T. et al. (2005a): Predicting Expatriate Job Performance for Selection Purposes: A Quantitative Review. In: *Journal of Cross-Cultural Psychology* 36,5: 590–620. [https://doi.org/10.1177/0022022105278544].

Mol, Stefan T.; Born, Marise Ph.; van der Molen, Henk T. (2005b): Developing Criteria for Expatriate Effectiveness: Time to Jump off the Adjustment Bandwagon. In: *International Journal of Intercultural Relations* 29,3: 339–353. [https://doi.org/10/dk2vzk].

Niedner-Kalthoff, Ulrike (2006): Rotation und Objektivität: Diplomaten als transnationale Migranten. In: Kreutzer, Florian; Roth, Silke (Eds.): Transnationale Karrieren: Biografien, Lebensführung und Mobilität. Wiesbaden, Germany: VS Verlag für Sozialwissenschaften: 83–99. [https://doi.org/10.1007/978-3-531-90283-8_4].

Ones, Deniz S.; Viswesvaran, Chockalingam (1996): Bandwidth-Fidelity Dilemma in Personality Measurement for Personnel Selection. In: *Journal of Organizational Behavior* 17,6: 609–626. [https://doi.org/10/btr3mt].

Osman-Gani, Aahad M.; Rockstuhl, Thomas (2009): Cross-Cultural Training, Expatriate Self-Efficacy, and Adjustments to Overseas Assignments: An Empirical Investigation of Managers in Asia. In: *International Journal of Intercultural Relations* 33,4: 277–290. [https://doi.org/10.1016/j.ijintrel.2009.02.003].

Paschke, Karl Th.; Schiff, Hans-Peter; Koch, Michael (2005): Die Zukunft der Diplomatie. In: Brandt, Enrico; Buck, Christian (Eds.): Auswärtiges Amt: Diplomatie als Beruf. 4th ed. Wiesbaden, Germany: VS Verlag für Sozialwissenschaften: 339–359. [https://doi.org/10.1007/978-3-531-90050-6_10].

Paterson, Ted A. et al. (2016): An Assessment of the Magnitude of Effect Sizes: Evidence from 30 Years of Meta-Analysis in Management. In: *Journal of Leadership & Organizational Studies* 23,1: 66–81. [https://doi.org/10/bjz9].

Peltokorpi, Vesa (2010): Intercultural Communication in Foreign Subsidiaries: The Influence of Expatriates' Language and Cultural Competencies. In: *Scandinavian Journal of Management* 26,2: 176–188. [https://doi.org/10.1016/j.scaman.2010.02.003].

Peterson, Jordan B. (1999): Maps of Meaning: The Architecture of Belief. New York, NY: Routledge. [https://doi.org/10.4324/9780203902851].

Pulakos, Elaine D. et al. (2002): Predicting Adaptive Performance: Further Tests of a Model of Adaptability. In: *Human Performance* 15,4: 299–323. [https://doi.org/10.1207/S15327043HUP1504_01].

Rehg, Michael T.; Gundlach, Michael J.; Grigorian, Reza A. (2012): Examining the Influence of Cross-cultural Training on Cultural Intelligence and Specific Self-efficacy. In: *Cross Cultural Management* 19,2: 215–232. [https://doi.org/10.1108/13527601211219892].

Rüger, Heiko et al. (2013): Mobilitätskompetenzen im Auswärtigen Dienst: Risiken und protektive Faktoren bei der Bewältigung der Auslandsrotation. Beiträge zur Bevölkerungswissenschaft 44. Würzburg, Germany: Ergon.

Rüger, Heiko et al. (2018): Sampling and Procedures for the Mobility Skills in the German Foreign Service Study. In: Wiernik, Brenton M.; Rüger, Heiko; Ones, Deniz S. (Eds.): Managing Expatriates: Success Factors in Private and Public Domains, Series on Population Studies 50. Opladen, Germany: Barbara Budrich Publishers.

Schneider, Benjamin (1987): The People Make the Place. In: *Personnel Psychology* 40,3: 437–453. [https://doi.org/10.1111/j.1744-6570.1987.tb00609.x].

Schneider, Norbert F.; Collet, Beate (Eds.) (2010): Mobile Living across Europe II: Causes and Consequences of Job-Related Spatial Mobility in Cross-National Comparison. Opladen, Germany: Budrich.

Schneider, Norbert F.; Meil Landwerlin, Gerardo (Eds.) (2008): Mobile Living across Europe I: Relevance and Diversity of Job-Related Spatial Mobility in Six European Countries. Opladen, Germany: Budrich.

Schulz, Ute; Schwarzer, Ralf (2003): Soziale Unterstützung bei der Krankheitsbewältigung: Die Berliner Social Support Skalen (BSSS). In: *Diagnostica* 49,2: 73–82. [https://doi.org/10.1026//0012-1924.49.2.73].

Schwarzer, Ralf; Jerusalem, Matthias (1995): Generalized Self-Efficacy Scale. In: Weinman, John; Wright, Stephen C.; Johnston, Marie (Eds.): Measures in Health Psychology: A User's Portfolio. Volume 3. Windsor, United Kingdom: NFER-NELSON: 35–37. [http://userpage.fu-berlin.de/~health/selfscal.htm].

Selmer, Jan; Lam, Hon (2004): "Third-Culture Kids": Future Business Expatriates? In: *Personnel Review* 33,4: 430–445. [https://doi.org/10.1108/00483480410539506].

Seltzer, Benjamin K. (2013): The Nomological Network of Self-Efficacy and Psychometric Properties of Its General and Specific Measures. Doctoral Dissertation. Minneapolis, MN: University of Minnesota. [http://hdl.handle.net/11299/148904].

Sheu, Hung-Bin et al. (2010): Testing the Choice Model of Social Cognitive Career Theory across Holland Themes: A Meta-Analytic Path Analysis. In: *Journal of Vocational Behavior* 76,2: 252–264. [https://doi.org/10.1016/j.jvb.2009.10.015].

Tharenou, Phyllis (2008): Disruptive Decisions to Leave Home: Gender and Family Differences in Expatriation Choices. In: *Organizational Behavior and Human Decision Processes* 105,2: 183–200. [https://doi.org/10.1016/j.obhdp.2007.08.004].

Thomas, David C.; Lazarova, Mila B. (2014): Essentials of International Human Resource Management: Managing People Globally. Los Angeles, CA: Sage. [https://doi.org/10/b6np].

Tornau, Katharina; Frese, Michael (2013): Construct Clean-up in Proactivity Research: A Meta-Analysis on the Nomological Net of Work-Related Proactivity Concepts and Their Incremental Validities. In: *Applied Psychology* 62,1: 44–96. [https://doi.org/10.1111/j.1464-0597.2012.00514.x].

Van Dyne, Linn et al. (2012): Sub-Dimensions of the Four Factor Model of Cultural Intelligence: Expanding the Conceptualization and Measurement of Cultural Intelligence. In: *Social and Personality Psychology Compass* 6,4: 295–313. [https://doi.org/10.1111/j.1751-9004.2012.00429.x].

Vancouver, Jeffrey B.; Weinhardt, Justin M.; Schmidt, Aaron M. (2010): A Formal, Computational Theory of Multiple-Goal Pursuit: Integrating Goal-Choice and Goal-Striving Processes. In: *Journal of Applied Psychology* 95,6: 985–1008. [https://doi.org/10.1037/a0020628].

Waibel, Stine; Rüger, Heiko (2018): Influence of Gender and Family Status on Expatriate Well-Being. In: Wiernik, Brenton M.; Rüger, Heiko; Ones, Deniz S. (Eds.): Managing Expatriates: Success Factors in Private and Public Domains, Series on Population Studies 50. Opladen, Germany: Barbara Budrich Publishers.

Wiernik, Brenton M. et al. (2018a): Lingua Necessaria? Language Proficiency and Expatriate Success. In: Wiernik, Brenton M.; Rüger, Heiko; Ones, Deniz S. (Eds.): Managing Expatriates: Success Factors in Private and Public Domains, Series on Population Studies 50. Opladen, Germany: Barbara Budrich Publishers.

Wiernik, Brenton M.; Rüger, Heiko; Ones, Deniz S. (2018b): Advancing Expatriate Research in Public and Private Sectors. In: Wiernik, Brenton M.; Rüger, Heiko; Ones, Deniz S. (Eds.): Managing Expatriates: Success Factors in Private and Public Domains, Series on Population Studies 50. Opladen, Germany: Barbara Budrich Publishers.

Yamao, Sachiko; Sekiguchi, Tomoki (2015): Employee Commitment to Corporate Globalization: The Role of English Language Proficiency and Human Resource Practices. In: *Journal of World Business* 50,1: 168–179. [https://doi.org/10.1016/j.jwb.2014.03.001].

Tolerance of Ambiguity: Relations with Expatriate Adjustment and Job Performance

Anne-Grit Albrecht, Deniz S. Ones, Stephan Dilchert, Jürgen Deller, and Frieder M. Paulus

Abstract

International assignments are strongly characterized novelty, complexity, insolubility, and unpredictability. In such environments, dispositional tolerance of (or even attraction to) ambiguity may be an important contributing factor to expatriate success. We use data from the iGOES project to examine the contributions of tolerance of ambiguity to expatriate outcomes. Results show that tolerance for ambiguity has only small positive benefits for expatriate locational and work adjustment, as well as for contextual and management/supervision performance. Tolerance of ambiguity-criterion relationships showed negligible variability across samples, suggesting that these weak relations are stable across differences in cultural distance and time on assignment. Results indicate that organizations selecting expatriates may realize better utility with constructs other than tolerance of ambiguity.

1 Introduction

Ambiguous situations are characterized by novelty, complexity, insolubility, and unpredictability (Budner 1962; McLain 1993) with information that could aid understanding the situation either lacking or being contradictory, incomplete, fragmented, unclear, unstructured, or vague (Norton 1975). In previous research on responses to ambiguous situations, dispositional tolerance of ambiguity has been defined as "the tendency to perceive ambiguous situations as desirable" (Budner 1962: 29). Although there is disagreement in how far individuals with high tolerance of ambiguity actively seek out ambiguous situations, there is agreement among researchers that those low in tolerance of ambiguity perceive ambiguous situations as aversive or threatening (Norton 1975).

On international assignments, one is frequently faced with ambiguous situations, especially when just arriving in a new country. Due to cultural differences in values, norms, and behaviors, expatriates are often unable to interpret social cues or orient themselves in day-to-day life. Without established routines for interactions, expatriates' ability to understand social expectations (Beehr/Glazer 2005) and predict the responses of others (Van Maanen/ Schein 1979) is hampered, causing uncertainty and anxiety. It therefore seems self-evident that expatriates who feel comfortable facing ambiguous situations will have an easier time living and working abroad. Unsurprisingly, this hypothesis has been made by numerous researchers studying the benefits of tolerance of ambiguity for cross-cultural adjustment and job performance (e.g., Arthur/Bennett 1997; Caligiuri/Tarique 2012; Deller 2000; Gregersen et al. 1998; Hannigan 1990; Herman et al. 2010; Mumford et al. 2000; Ronen 1989; Ruben/Kealey 1979). Most of these papers, however, are theoretical; empirical evidence regarding tolerance of ambiguity's relationships with expatriate outcomes is scarce.

For example, the (only) meta-analytic estimate of the relationship between tolerance of ambiguity and expatriate job performance is based on only two studies ($\rho = .35$, total $N = 122$; Mol et al. 2005). The goal this chapter is therefore to empirically investigate the relationship between tolerance of ambiguity and expatriate adjustment and job performance.

1.1   Tolerance of Ambiguity as an Expatriate Success Factor

Early research on tolerance of ambiguity described the construct as a personality trait influencing emotion, motivation, perception, and attitudes (Frenkel-Brunswik 1949). Grenier et al. (2005) also characterized tolerance of ambiguity as consisting of patterns of cognitive, emotional, and behavioral responses to ambiguous situations. We similarly consider the cognitive and emotional impacts ambiguity tolerance may have on expatriate outcomes.

1.1.1   Cognitive Consequences of Tolerance of Ambiguity

Tolerance of ambiguity is associated with a diverse range of cognitive responses to ambiguous stimuli that may be either beneficial or detrimental to expatriate performance. On the one hand, when individuals are high on tolerance of ambiguity, they are more comfortable with uncertainty, so they are less likely to seek out new information to clarify the meaning of ambiguous stimuli (Litman 2010). For example, individuals high on tolerance of ambiguity seek feedback on their performance less frequently than individuals less tolerant of ambiguity (Bennett et al. 1990). Expatriates often arrive on cross-cultural assignments with lower ability to respond to social and environmental cues and with less organizational and job-specific tacit knowledge, compared to their home contexts (Beaverstock 1996; Black 1988). In such contexts, tolerance of ambiguity may lead to overconfidence in one's abilities and inhibit information-seeking behaviors when they are critically necessary for effective performance (Ashford/Cummings 1985; Schmidt/DeShon 2010).

On the other hand, tolerance of ambiguity is also associated with more effective information processing. When they do seek out new information, individuals low on tolerance of ambiguity tend to look for information that supports their preconceptions, while individuals high on tolerance of ambiguity tend to seek out objective information that can potentially disconfirm they prior beliefs (Campbell/Tesser 1983). Similarly, individuals low on tolerance of ambiguity are more likely to oversimply multidimensional information, thus reducing ambiguity through overgeneralization (Domangue 1978). Sweeny et al. (2010) also suggested that individuals with low tolerance of ambiguity tend to avoid information that is threatening. Thus, tolerance of ambiguity may contribute to more effective expatriate performance by enabling expatriates to more effectively learn and adapt their beliefs and behaviors in their new cultural contexts.

Findings of a connection between tolerance of ambiguity and oversimplification are in line with the theoretical origins of the tolerance of ambiguity construct from research grounded on authoritarianism and prejudice, where researchers argued that intolerance of complexity and ambiguity was a contributing factor to adoption of black-and-white authoritarian worldviews (Adorno et al. 1950; Allport 1954). Research in this tradition has found that low tolerance of ambiguity is associated with ethnocentrism (Block/Block 1951), dogmatism (MacDonald 1970), and tendency to stereotype (Friedland et al. 1999). These attitudes are likely to hinder expatriates' ability to adjust to new cultural contexts and interact effectively with host country nationals, especially if they are in a culture that this strongly different from their home country.

1.1.2   Emotional Consequences of Tolerance of Ambiguity

Ambiguity and unpredictability are central constructs in many models of stress (Beehr/ Glazer 2005). Ambiguity is hypothesized to be a powerful stressor across a broad range of situations (e.g., unemployment, De Cuyper et al. 2010; organizational change, Judge et al. 1999). Tolerance of ambiguity is hypothesized to influence affective responses to stressors in two ways. First, individuals intolerant of ambiguity tend to appraise uncertain situations as threatening (Bardi et al. 2009) rather than as a source of opportunity (cf. DeYoung 2015). Accordingly, expatriates low on tolerance of ambiguity are more likely to negatively interpret ambiguous events and to have negative affective responses to everyday challenges of their international assignments.

Second, tolerance of ambiguity can help expatriates to better cope with stressors and avoid adverse outcomes. For example, in his meta-analysis, Frone (1990) found that role ambiguity was more likely to lead to strain reactions for individuals less tolerant of ambiguity. When individuals are tolerant of ambiguity, they are better able to rationally consider negative events and identify potential explanations. In contrast, when individuals are intolerant of ambiguity, they are prone to engage in perseveration, excessive worrying, magical thinking, and other maladaptive coping behaviors (Dugas et al. 2001; Keinan 1994). Without tolerance of amguity, expatriates may lack the psychological resources to adaptively respond to uncertain events in their new contexts.

1.2   *Tolerance of Ambiguity and Expatriate Outcomes*

Expatriate adjustment is often defined as comfort with living and working in the foreign country (e.g., Bhaskar-Shrinivas et al. 2005; Sinangil/Ones 2001). Tolerance of ambiguity enables more positive appraisals of uncertain situations and more adaptive coping with adverse events (both common occurrences on international assignments), and tolerance of ambiguity has been previously associated with adjustment to other major life transitions, such as to college (Bardi et al. 2009) and to new organizations (Friedel/Dalbert 2003). Accordingly, we expect a positive relationship between tolerance of ambiguity and expatriate adjustment.

Hypothesis 1a: Tolerance of ambiguity is positively related to expatriate adjustment, including locational[1], interaction, and work adjustment.

Individuals high on tolerance of ambiguity are better able to respond to potentially threatening ambiguous stimuli, leaving them with more attentional and emotional resources available to respond to work demands and challenges (cf. Demerouti et al. 2001). Individuals tolerant of ambiguity also tend to adopt more effective information processing strategies, allowing them to make better use of job-relevant information available in their work environments. These emotional and cognitive benefits of tolerance of ambiguity are likely to lead expatriates high on this trait to perform more effectively. Although tolerance of ambiguity may potentially keep expatriates from gathering appropriate information based on the belief that they do not need to resolve environmental uncertainty (Ashford/Cummings

---

[1]   In the expatriate literature, locational adjustment (expatriates' comfort handling everyday non-work demands, such as obtaining food, healthcare, safety, and transportation) is commonly referred to as "general" or "cultural" adjustment (Bhaskar-Shrinivas et al. 2005). We prefer the term "locational adjustment", as it captures that this construct refers to the management of the everyday challenges of living in one's current location (cf. Schlunze 2002) better than these more commonly used alternatives.

1985; Schmidt/DeShon 2010), we expect that, overall, the cognitive and emotional consequences of tolerance of ambiguity will have a net benefit for expatriate job performance.

Hypothesis 1b: *Tolerance of ambiguity is positively related to overall expatriate job performance and expatriate job performance dimensions.*

1.2.1   Moderation by Cultural Distance

International assignments are ambiguous because expatriates may be unfamiliar with local cultural, social, and environmental cues. However, some cultures are more similar to each other than others; when cultures are relatively similar to each other (when they are "culturally close"), expatriates may be less likely to experience challenging ambiguous situations when moving between them (Shenkar et al. 2008). When cultures are highly divergent (when they are "culturally distant"), social and environmental uncertainty will be very common, and expatriates are likely to have a stronger sense of "being foreign". Adjustment challenges are more common for expatriates in culturally distant locations. Van Vianen et al. (2004), for example, found expatriates who experienced a large amount of easily visible, "surface-level" differences to report lower levels of locational adjustment (work and interaction adjustment were more influenced by perceived deep-level differences). Because uncertainties are likely to increase as a function of greater cultural distance, we expect that tolerance of ambiguity may be even more relevant for expatriate success when cultural differences between home and host country are greater.

Hypothesis 2:   *The relationships of tolerance of ambiguity with expatriate adjustment and job performance are moderated by cultural distance, such that the relationships are stronger in countries that are more culturally distant.*

1.2.2   Moderation by Time on Assignment

Tolerance of ambiguity may be a relevant predictor of expatriate success only in the beginning of an international assignment. As expatriates become more familiar with their foreign environment, ambiguity abates and experiences of uncertainty become less frequent. Thus, over time, tolerance of ambiguity may become less relevant.

Hypothesis 3:   *The relationships of tolerance of ambiguity with expatriate adjustment and job performance are moderated by time on assignment, such that the relationships are weaker the longer the expatriates have been abroad.*

2   Methods

2.1   Samples

Data for this chapter came from the iGOES project. This project simultaneously gathered data from German-speaking expatriates employed in a variety of jobs, organizations, and countries. Participants in each country were administered the same assessments to allow for examination of the international generalizability of expatriate success factors. Tolerance of ambiguity was measured only in the 15 countries sampled in Wave 1 (Argentina, China, Costa Rica, Czech Republic, Egypt, Ghana, India, Ireland, Italy, the Netherlands, Russia, South Korea, Sweden, Turkey, and the United States). Additional details about the iGOES project are available in Albrecht et al. (2018b, Appendix A, this volume).

2.2   Measures

Tolerance of ambiguity. Tolerance of ambiguity was assessed using the AT-14, a German scale developed by Kischkel (1984). Items of the scale are predominantly work-related, including statements such as "Working on a task, I don't like it when there is confusion about who in particular is responsible for what" ("Ich habe es nicht gern, wenn bei einer Arbeit Unklarheit darüber herrscht, wer im Einzelnen wofür verantwortlich ist") or "For everything there is a right and wrong" ("Für alles gibt es ein Richtig und ein Falsch"). Participants were asked to answer to the items on a scale ranging from 1 = *does not apply at all* to 5 = *fully applies*. The average internal consistency estimate of the scale across countries was α = .70. The overall sample showed a mean of 3.17 (SD = .48).

Adjustment. Self-ratings of adjustment were assessed using Black and Stephens' (1989) 14-item scale in Costa Rica, Czech Republic, Ghana, India, Ireland, the Netherlands, Sweden, and Turkey. For those countries, scores were computed for locational (average α = .72), interaction (average α = .83), and work (average α = .71) adjustment, as well as for total overall expatriate adjustment (average α = .81). In China, Egypt, Russia, South Korea, and the United States, adjustment was assessed using the 3-item measure from Albrecht (2005). For these countries, only total overall expatriate adjustment could be computed (average α = .63).

Job performance. Supervisors, coworkers, or subordinates rated expatriates' job performance using a short job performance survey completed by one rater for each expatriate covering the following dimensions of job performance: technical performance (α = .66), contextual performance (support for organizational goals, extra-role engagement, local cultural knowledge; α = .45), management and supervision (α = .58), and effort and initiative (α = .59). An overall job performance score was computed combining all 17 items of the measure (α = .86).

2.3   Analyses

Correlations of tolerance of ambiguity with each criterion were meta-analytically pooled using psychometric meta-analysis, weighting each correlation by sample size (Schmidt/ Hunter 2015). Both true correlations (correcting for measurement error in both variables) and operational validities (correcting for measurement error only in the criterion) were computed. Job performance correlations were corrected by combining interrater reliability estimates for each performance dimension from a subset of the current sample (see Albrecht et al. 2018b, Appendix A of this volume) with the meta-analytic supervisor interrater reliability distribution reported by Salgado et al. (2003; cf. Viswesvaran et al. 1996).

3 Results

3.1 *Adjustment*

Results for expatriate adjustment are shown in Table 1. Small positive relationships emerged for overall (ρ_{true} = .19), locational (ρ_{true} = .16), and work (ρ_{true} = .22) adjustment, but the relationship between tolerance of ambiguity and interaction adjustment was negligible (ρ_{true} = .06). These results are surprising, as interacting with host country nationals is where cultural differences in behavioral norms may be expected to matter most. True variability (SD_ρ) for tolerance of ambiguity observed correlations were zero for all adjustment dimensions (locational, interaction, and work adjustment), For overall adjustment, there was residual variability (SD_ρ = .12), but this value reduced to zero when analyzing only samples using the longer, more reliable, and more construct-valid 14-item adjustment scale by Black and Stephens (1989). Thus, all between-country variance in the relationship between tolerance of ambiguity and adjustment could be explained by sampling error or measurement error artefacts. The absence of variability in relations across samples precludes any potential for moderation of these relations by cultural distance or time on assignment.

3.2 *Job Performance*

Results for expatriate job performance are shown in Table 2. Small positive relationships emerged for contextual performance (ρ_{true} = .17) and management/supervision (ρ_{true} = .17). Technical performance (ρ_{true} = .04) and effort/initiative (ρ_{true} = .04) were negligibly related to tolerance of ambiguity. The small positive relationship between tolerance of ambiguity and overall job performance (ρ_{true} =.12) thus primarily reflects relations of tolerance of ambiguity with contextual and management performance. As was the case for adjustment, tolerance of ambiguity ‒ performance relations showed zero true variability across countries (except for management, SD_ρ = .12). Accordingly, the impacts of tolerance of ambiguity on most dimensions of job performance cannot be moderated by cultural distance or time on assignment. Correlations between supervisory performance and tolerance of ambiguity (the only relationship with a non-zero residual standard deviation) showed no clear pattern in terms of cultural distance – correlations varied largely independently of the host countries' cultural distance from Germany (e.g., culturally distant countries ranged from r_{Egypt} = -.33 to r_{China} = .07; culturally closer countries ranged from $r_{Netherlands}$ = -.22 to $r_{Czech\ Republic}$ = .17). Thus, our Hypothesis 2 stating that tolerance of ambiguity will be more strongly related to expatriate success in culturally distant locations was not supported. The degree to which tolerance of ambiguity contributes to performance is thus likely relatively stable across cultural contexts. Technical performance reflects performance in the core aspects of one's job (e.g., accounting, engineering) which likely do not differ greatly no matter where a given job is performed (Shin et al. 2007). Similarly, effort/initiative reflects more motivational aspects of job performance, which may also not differ greatly across cultural contexts. Management and supervision and contextual performance, in contrast, involve interactions with host country nationals, including colleagues, supervisors, subordinates, and customers , and engagement with the local culture; for these performance dimensions, adaptation to novel social and environmental cues is likely to be very important. When these cues differ greatly from what one is used to at home, willingness to embrace uncertainty and adapt one's behavior is likely to be critical for effective performance.

Table 1: Relationships between Tolerance of Ambiguity and Expatriate Adjustment

Variable	N	k	r_{obs}	SD_{obs}	ρ_{op}	SD_{op}	90% CI	80% CV	ρ_{true}	SD_ρ
Overall adjustment	1,201	15	.12	.13	.16	.10	.06, .18	.03, .29	.19	.12
Locational adjustment	518	8	.12	.10	.13	.00	.06, .18	.13, .13	.16	.00
Interaction adjustment	518	8	.04	.06	.05	.00	.01, .07	.05, .05	.06	.00
Work adjustment	512	8	.14	.06	.18	.00	.11, .17	.18, .18	.22	.00

Note: N = sample size, k = number of samples included in the analyses, r_{obs} = sample-size weighted mean observed correlation, SD_{obs} = standard deviation of observed correlations, ρ_{op} = operational validity (correlation corrected for criterion unreliability), SD_{op} = standard deviation of operation validities, 90% CI = 90% confidence interval around ρ_{op}, 80% CV = 80% credibility interval around ρ_{op}, ρ_{true} = true score correlation (correlation corrected for predictor and criterion unreliability), SD_ρ = true standard deviation.

Table 2: Relationships between Tolerance of Ambiguity and Expatriate Job Performance

Variable	N	k	r_{obs}	SD_{obs}	ρ_{op}	SD_{op}	90% CI	80% CV	ρ_{true}	SD_ρ
Overall job performance	513	13	.08	.13	.10	.00	.02, .14	.10, .10	.12	.00
Technical performance	517	13	.03	.15	.04	.00	-.04, .10	.04, .04	.04	.00
Contextual performance	515	13	.11	.10	.14	.00	.06, .16	.14, .14	.17	.00
Management/supervision	508	13	.11	.18	.15	.11	.03, .19	.01, .29	.17	.12
Effort/initiative	514	13	.03	.12	.03	.00	-.02, .08	.03, .03	.04	.00

Note: N = sample size, k = number of samples included in the analyses, r_{obs} = sample-size weighted mean observed correlation, SD_{obs} = standard deviation of observed correlations, ρ_{op} = operational validity (correlation corrected for criterion unreliability), SD_{op} = standard deviation of operation validities, 90% CI = 90% confidence interval around ρ_{op}, 80% CV = 80% credibility interval around ρ_{op}, ρ_{true} = true score correlation (correlation corrected for predictor and criterion unreliability), SD_ρ = true standard deviation.

Consistent with results for adjustment and given the zero or small true residual variance, relations between tolerance of ambiguity and job performance were not moderated by time on the assignment. Tolerance of ambiguity appears to be relevant for expatriate job performance independent of how long the expatriate has been abroad. Fully understanding a foreign culture and being able to anticipate the behavior of host country nationals might take quite a long time; expatriates may continue to face ambiguous and uncertain situations throughout their tenure abroad. Moreover, it might take some time for expatriates to become sensitive to subtler cultural differences, which may create new ambiguities in later phases of international assignments (Osland/Osland 2006).

4　Discussion

In the present study, we found small positive relationships between tolerance of ambiguity and expatriate adjustment and job performance. Relationships varied somewhat across specific dimensions of adjustment and performance. Correlations between tolerance of ambiguity and most criteria showed no true variability across countries after accounting for statistical artefacts, indicating that impacts of ambiguity tolerance on adjustment and performance were not moderated by cultural distance or time abroad. Effect sizes were small, indicating that while tolerance of ambiguity contributes to expatriate success, its impact is relatively minor, especially compared to other dispositional characteristics (see, e.g., the other chapters in Section A: Psychological Individual Differences of this volume).

4.1　Potential Limitations

These results question the widespread notion that tolerance of ambiguity is a vital competency for international assignments and suggest that theoretical models emphasizing this construct are misguided. That said, several factors may have contributed to the small relationships observed in this study. First, the attraction-selection-attrition model (Schneider 1987) posits that individuals are more likely to enter and remain in work environments that fit their personal characteristics. It is plausible that individuals intolerant of ambiguity may not be interested in international assignments in the first place and may return home early if their employers do send them abroad. These processes may lead to range restriction in tolerance of ambiguity among expatriates, attenuating potential relations with criteria (Schmidt/ Hunter 2015). Unfortunately, there was no norm information available which we could use to test for differences between a comparable domestic managerial sample and the participants of this study.

Second, the measure of tolerance of ambiguity used in this study may have been deficient. Many of the items are somewhat vague, and they do not specifically assess tolerance of ambiguity in cross-cultural settings. Consequentially, the measure showed weak psychometric properties (e.g., a single latent factor extracted from the items accounted for only 21% of the variance, with a mean factor loading of only .39). While the current analyses corrected for unreliability, they could not correct for potentially poor construct coverage of the tolerance of ambiguity measure. Recently, Herman et al. (2010) developed a tolerance of ambiguity measure specifically for applications in cross-cultural settings. This scales distinguishes four dimensions: (1) valuing diverse others, (2) change, (3) challenging perspectives, and (4) unfamiliarity. Importantly, the "valuing diverse others" dimensions concerns interpersonal interaction. Studies using this scale may be better able to examine the impact of tolerance of ambiguity on interaction adjustment than was possible with the more general measure used in this study.

4.2   *Future Research*

In addition to examining the above potential explanations for the current results, future research should also explore additional avenues for understanding the potential value of ambiguity tolerance in cross-cultural settings. First, future studies should more carefully examine specific events and experiences in expatriates' lives and the specific ways expatriates respond to them. Vignette/factorial survey (Wallander 2009) and experience sampling (Beal 2015) studies may help to identify what kinds of uncertainties expatriates face and what specific compentencies can be selected or trained for to promote effective adaptation. Second, future studies should attend to the changing nature of the expatriate context and job demands over time. For example, while ambiguity may generally decrease over time, it may not do so in a linear fashion; near the end of an international assignment, uncertainties about employment renewal or impending repatriation may pose new challenges for expatriates. Future studies should explore the impact of ambiguity tolerance on these specific expatriate adaptation challenges. Regarding changing job demands over time, expatriate assignments are often associated not only with changes in location, but also changes in job role (e.g., new technical tasks, increased managerial responsibilities). Does tolerance of ambiguity affect the rate at which expatriates' learn their new responsibilities and reach peak performance? Does tolerance for ambiguity help expatriates to respond to continuing changes in job demands over time?

From a practical perspective, the results of this study suggest that organizations need not attend to candidates' tolerance of ambiguity when choosing employees for international assignments. When selecting expatriates, other dispositional characteristics, such as the Big Five personality traits (Albrecht et al. 2018a; Caligiuri 2000; Ones/Viswesvaran 1997) and other dispositional characteristics (see the other chapters in Section A: Psychological Individual Differences of this volume) are likely to have higher utility for decision-making.

References

Adorno, Theodor W. et al. (1950): The Authoritarian Personality. Oxford, United Kingdom: Harpers.

Albrecht, Anne-Grit (2005): Untangling the Laundry List: General Mental Ability, the Big Five, and Context Related Variables as Predictors for Expatriate Success. Master's Thesis. Lüneburg, Germany: Leuphana Universität. [http://opus.uni-lueneburg.de/opus/volltexte/2006/344/].

Albrecht, Anne-Grit; Ones, Deniz S.; Sinangil, Handan Kepir (2018a): Expatriate Management. In: Ones, Deniz S. et al. (Eds.): The SAGE Handbook of Industrial, Work and Organizational Psychology. Volume 3: Managerial Psychology and Organizational Approaches. 2nd ed. London, United Kingdom: Sage: 429–468.

Albrecht, Anne-Grit et al. (2018b): Design, Implementation, and Analysis of the iGOES Project. In: Wiernik, Brenton M.; Rüger, Heiko; Ones, Deniz S. (Eds.): Managing Expatriates: Success Factors in Private and Public Domains, Series on Population Studies 50. Opladen, Germany: Barbara Budrich Publishers.

Allport, Gordon W. (1954): The Nature of Prejudice. Oxford, England: Addison-Wesley.

Arthur, Winfred, Jr.; Bennett, Winston, Jr. (1997): A Comparative Test of Alternative Models of International Assignee Job Performance. In: Aycan, Zeynep (Ed.): Expatriate Management: Theory and Research. New Approaches to Employee Management 4. Greenwich, CT: JAI Press: 141–172.

Ashford, Susan J.; Cummings, L.L. (1985): Proactive Feedback Seeking: The Instrumental Use of the Information Environment. In: *Journal of Occupational Psychology* 58,1: 67–79. [https://doi.org/10.1111/j.2044-8325.1985.tb00181.x].

Bardi, Anat; Guerra, Valeschka M.; Ramdeny, G. Sharadeh D. (2009): Openness and Ambiguity Intolerance: Their Differential Relations to Well-Being in the Context of an Academic Life Transition. In: *Personality and Individual Differences* 47,3: 219–223. [https://doi.org/10/cdsvpr].

Beal, Daniel J. (2015): ESM 2.0: State of the Art and Future Potential of Experience Sampling Methods in Organizational Research. In: *Annual Review of Organizational Psychology and Organizational Behavior* 2: 383–407. [https://doi.org/10.1146/annurev-orgpsych-032414-111335].

Beaverstock, Jonathan V. (1996): Migration, Knowledge and Social Interaction: Expatriate Labour within Investment Banks. In: *Area* 28,4: 459–470. [http://www.jstor.org/stable/20003731].

Beehr, T.A.; Glazer, Sharon (2005): Organizational Role Stress. In: Barling, J.; Kelloway, E. Kevin; Frone, Michael R. (Eds.): Handbook of Work Stress. Thousand Oaks, CA: Sage: 7–34. [https://doi.org/10.4135/9781412975995.n2].

Bennett, Nathan; Herold, David M.; Ashford, Susan J. (1990): The Effects of Tolerance for Ambiguity on Feedback-Seeking Behaviour. In: *Journal of Occupational Psychology* 63,4: 343–348. [https://doi.org/10.1111/j.2044-8325.1990.tb00535.x].

Bhaskar-Shrinivas, Purnima et al. (2005): Input-Based and Time-Based Models of International Adjustment: Meta-Analytic Evidence and Theoretical Extensions. In: *Academy of Management Journal* 48,2: 257–281. [https://doi.org/10.5465/AMJ.2005.16928400].

Black, J. Stewart (1988): Work Role Transitions: A Study of American Expatriate Managers in Japan. In: *Journal of International Business Studies* 19,2: 277–294. [https://doi.org/10.1057/palgrave.jibs.8490383].

Black, J. Stewart; Stephens, Gregory K. (1989): The Influence of the Spouse on American Expatriate Adjustment and Intent to Stay in Pacific Rim Overseas Assignments. In: *Journal of Management* 15,4: 529–544. [https://doi.org/10.1177/014920638901500403].

Block, Jack; Block, Jeanne (1951): An Investigation of the Relationship between Intolerance of Ambiguity and Ethnocentrism. In: *Journal of Personality* 19,3: 303–311. [https://doi.org/10.1111/j.1467-6494.1951.tb01104.x].

Budner, Stanley (1962): Intolerance of Ambiguity as a Personality Variable. In: *Journal of Personality* 30,1: 29–50. [https://doi.org/10.1111/j.1467-6494.1962.tb02303.x].

Caligiuri, Paula M. (2000): Selecting Expatriates for Personality Characteristics: A Moderating Effect of Personality on the Relationship between Host National Contact and Cross-Cultural Adjustment. In: *MIR: Management International Review* 40,1: 61–80. [http://www.jstor.org/stable/40835867].

Caligiuri, Paula; Tarique, Ibraiz (2012): Dynamic Cross-Cultural Competencies and Global Leadership Effectiveness. In: *Journal of World Business*, Special Issue: Leadership in a Global Context 47,4: 612–622. [https://doi.org/10.1016/j.jwb.2012.01.014].

Campbell, Jennifer D.; Tesser, Abraham (1983): Motivational Interpretations of Hindsight Bias: An Individual Difference Analysis. In: *Journal of Personality* 51,4: 605–620. [https://doi.org/10.1111/j.1467-6494.1983.tb00868.x].

De Cuyper, Nele et al. (2010): Objective Threat of Unemployment and Situational Uncertainty during a Restructuring: Associations with Perceived Job Insecurity and Strain. In: *Journal of Business and Psychology* 25,1: 75–85. [https://doi.org/10.1007/s10869-009-9128-y].

Deller, Jürgen (2000): Interkulturelle Eignungsdiagnostik. Zur Verwendbarkeit von Persönlichkeitsskalen. Waldsteinberg, Germany: Heidrun Popp Verlag.

Demerouti, Evangelia et al. (2001): The Job Demands-Resources Model of Burnout. In: *Journal of Applied Psychology* 86,3: 499–512. [https://doi.org/10.1037/0021-9010.86.3.499].

DeYoung, Colin G. (2015): Cybernetic Big Five Theory. In: *Journal of Research in Personality*, Integrative Theories of Personality 56: 33–58. [https://doi.org/10/33h].

Domangue, Barbara B. (1978): Decoding Effects of Cognitive Complexity, Tolerance of Ambiguity, and Verbal-Nonverbal Inconsistency. In: *Journal of Personality* 46,3: 519–535. [https://doi.org/10.1111/j.1467-6494.1978.tb01015.x].

Dugas, M.J.; Gosselin, P.; Ladouceur, R. (2001): Intolerance of Uncertainty and Worry: Investigating Specificity in a Nonclinical Sample. In: *Cognitive Therapy and Research* 25,5: 551–558. [https://doi.org/10.1023/A:1005553414688].

Frenkel-Brunswik, Else (1949): Intolerance of Ambiguity as an Emotional and Perceptual Personality Variable. In: *Journal of Personality* 18,1: 108–143. [https://doi.org/10.1111/j.1467-6494.1949.tb01236.x].

Friedel, Anja; Dalbert, Claudia (2003): Belastung und Bewältigung bei Grundschullehrerinnen: Die Auswirkungen einer Versetzung an die Förderstufe und der Einfluss der Ungewissheitstoleranz. In: *Zeitschrift für Pädagogische Psychologie* 17,1: 55–68. [https://doi.org/10.1024//1010-0652.17.1.55].

Friedland, Nehemia; Keinan, Giora; Tytiun, Talia (1999): The Effect of Psychological Stress and Tolerance of Ambiguity on Stereotypic Attributions. In: *Anxiety, Stress & Coping* 12,4: 397–410. [https://doi.org/10.1080/10615809908249318].

Frone, Michael R. (1990): Intolerance of Ambiguity as a Moderator of the Occupational Role Stress-Strain Relationship: A Meta-Analysis. In: *Journal of Organizational Behavior* 11,4: 309–320. [https://doi.org/10.1002/job.4030110406].

Gregersen, Hal B.; Morrison, Allen J.; Black, J. Stewart (1998): Developing Leaders for the Global Frontier. In: *Sloan Management Review* 40,1: 21–32.

Grenier, S.; Barrette, A.M.; Ladouceur, R. (2005): Intolerance of Uncertainty and Intolerance of Ambiguity: Similarities and Differences. In: *Personality and Individual Differences* 39: 593–600. [https://doi.org/10.1016/j.paid.2005.02.014].

Hannigan, Terence P. (1990): Traits, Attitudes, and Skills That Are Related to Intercultural Effectiveness and Their Implications for Cross-Cultural Training: A Review of the Literature. In: *International Journal of Intercultural Relations* 14,1: 89–111. [https://doi.org/10.1016/0147-1767(90)90049-3].

Herman, Jeffrey L. et al. (2010): The Tolerance for Ambiguity Scale: Towards a More Refined Measure for International Management Research. In: *International Journal of Intercultural Relations* 34,1: 58–65. [https://doi.org/10.1016/j.ijintrel.2009.09.004].

Judge, Timothy A. et al. (1999): Managerial Coping with Organizational Change: A Dispositional Perspective. In: *Journal of Applied Psychology* 84,1: 107–122. [https://doi.org/10.1037/0021-9010.84.1.107].

Keinan, Giora (1994): Effects of Stress and Tolerance of Ambiguity on Magical Thinking. In: *Journal of Personality and Social Psychology* 67,1: 48–55. [https://doi.org/10.1037/0022-3514.67.1.48].

Kischkel, Karl-Heinz (1984): Eine Skala zur Erfassung von Ambiguitätstoleranz. In: *Diagnostica* 30,2: 144–154.

Litman, Jordan A. (2010): Relationships between Measures of I- and D-Type Curiosity, Ambiguity Tolerance, and Need for Closure: An Initial Test of the Wanting-Liking Model of Information-Seeking. In: *Personality and Individual Differences* 48,4: 397–402. [https://doi.org/10.1016/j.paid.2009.11.005].

MacDonald, A.P. (1970): Revised Scale for Ambiguity Tolerance: Reliability and Validity. In: *Psychological Reports* 26,3: 791–798. [https://doi.org/10.2466/pr0.1970.26.3.791].

McLain, David L. (1993): The MSTAT-I: A New Measures of Infividual's Tolerance for Ambiguity. In: *Educational and Psychological Measurement* 53,1: 183–189. [https://doi.org/10.1177/0013164493053001020].

Mol, Stefan T. et al. (2005): Predicting Expatriate Job Performance for Selection Purposes: A Quantitative Review. In: *Journal of Cross-Cultural Psychology* 36,5: 590–620. [https://doi.org/10.1177/0022022105278544].

Mumford, Michael D. et al. (2000): Development of Leadership Skills: Experience and Timing. In: *The Leadership Quarterly* 11,1: 87–114. [https://doi.org/10.1016/S1048-9843(99)00044-2].

Norton, Robert W. (1975): Measurement of Ambiguity Tolerance. In: *Journal of Personality Assessment* 39,6: 607–619. [https://doi.org/10.1207/s15327752jpa3906_11].

Ones, Deniz S.; Viswesvaran, Chockalingam (1997): Personality Determinants in the Prediction of Aspects of Expatriate Job Success. In: Aycan, Zeynep (Ed.): Expatriate Management: Theory and Research, New Approaches to Employee Management 4. Greenwich, CT: JAI Press: 63–92.

Osland, Joyce S.; Osland, Asbjorn (2006): Expatriate Paradoxes and Cultural Involvement. In: *International Studies of Management & Organization* 35,4: 93–116. [https://doi.org/10.1080%2F00208825.2005.11043740].

Ronen, Simcha (1989): Training the International Assignee. In: *Training and Development in Organizations., Frontiers of Industrial and Organizational Psychology*, The Jossey-Bass Management Series and The Jossey-Bass Social and Behavioral Science Series. San Francisco, CA US: Jossey-Bass: 417–453.

Ruben, Brent D.; Kealey, Daniel J. (1979): Behavioral Assessment of Communication Competency and the Prediction of Cross-Cultural Adaptation. In: *International Journal of Intercultural Relations* 3,1: 15–47. [https://doi.org/10.1016/0147-1767(79)90045-2].

Salgado, Jesús F. et al. (2003): A Meta-Analytic Study of General Mental Ability Validity for Different Occupations in the European Community. In: *Journal of Applied Psychology* 88,6: 1068–1081. [https://doi.org/10.1037/0021-9010.88.6.1068].

Schlunze, Rolf D. (2002): Locational Adjustment of Japanese Management in Europe. In: *Asian Business & Management* 1,2: 267–283. [https://doi.org/10.1057/palgrave.abm.9200014].

Schmidt, Aaron M.; DeShon, Richard P. (2010): The Moderating Effects of Performance Ambiguity on the Relationship between Self-Efficacy and Performance. In: *Journal of Applied Psychology* 95,3: 572–581. [https://doi.org/10.1037/a0018289].

Schmidt, Frank L.; Hunter, John E. (2015): Methods of Meta-Analysis: Correcting Error and Bias in Research Findings. 3rd ed. Thousand Oaks, CA: Sage. [https://doi.org/10/b6mg].

Schneider, Benjamin (1987): The People Make the Place. In: *Personnel Psychology* 40,3: 437–453. [https://doi.org/10.1111/j.1744-6570.1987.tb00609.x].

Shenkar, Oded; Luo, Yadong; Yeheskel, Orly (2008): From "Distance" to "Friction": Substituting Metaphors and Redirecting Intercultural Research. In: *Academy of Management Review* 33,4: 905–923. [https://doi.org/10.5465/AMR.2008.34421999].

Shin, Shung J.; Morgeson, Frederick P.; Campion, Michael A. (2007): What You Do Depends on Where You Are: Understanding How Domestic and Expatriate Work Requirements Depend upon the Cultural Context. In: *Journal of International Business Studies* 38: 64–83. [https://doi.org/10.1057/palgrave.jibs.8400247].

Sinangil, Handan Kepir; Ones, Deniz S. (2001): Expatriate Management. In: Anderson, Neil et al. (Eds.): Handbook of Industrial, Work and Organizational Psychology. Volume 1: Personnel Psychology. Thousand Oaks, CA: Sage: 424–443. [https://doi.org/10.4135/9781848608320.n21].

Sweeny, Kate et al. (2010): Information Avoidance: Who, What, When, and Why. In: *Review of General Psychology* 14,4: 340–353. [https://doi.org/10.1037/a0021288].

Van Maanen, John; Schein, Edgar H. (1979): Toward a Theory of Organizational Socialization. In: *Research in Organizational Behavior* 1: 209–264. [http://hdl.handle.net/1721.1/1934].

van Vianen, A.E.M. et al. (2004): Fitting In: Surface- and Deep-Level Cultural Differences and Expatriates' Adjustment. In: *Academy of Management Journal* 47,5: 697–709. [https://doi.org/10.2307/20159612].

Viswesvaran, Chockalingam; Ones, Deniz S.; Schmidt, Frank L. (1996): Comparative Analysis of the Reliability of Job Performance Ratings. In: *Journal of Applied Psychology* 81,5: 557–574. [https://doi.org/10/c8f68f].

Wallander, Lisa (2009): 25 Years of Factorial Surveys in Sociology: A Review. In: *Social Science Research* 38,3: 505–520. [https://doi.org/10.1016/j.ssresearch.2009.03.004].

Validity of Big Five Personality Traits for Expatriate Success: Results from Turkey

Deniz S. Ones, Handan Kepir Sinangil, and Brenton M. Wiernik

Abstract

Despite decades of research on individual and environmental factors that support expatriate success, knowledge of the validity of personality traits for expatriate adjustment and job performance remains nascent. In this study, we report validity results for broad Big Five and compound personality traits for a sample of 220 expatriates working in Turkey. We examine personality relations with both international adjustment and host country national-rated job performance. We find patterns of validity similar to those observed for domestic managers. We discuss implications for expatriate selection and theories of international job performance.

1   Introduction

Since Barrick and Mount's (1991) seminal meta-analysis of relations between overall job performance and the Big Five traits, personality traits have emerged as predictors of performance that are among the most widely-researched and widely-applied in practice (Connelly et al. 2018; Ones et al. 2007). In addition to their substantial predictive validity for overall job performance (Barrick et al. 2001; Ones et al. 2005), measures of the Big Five personality traits are also powerful predictors of specific performance criteria (e.g., counterproductive behaviors; Berry et al. 2007; leadership; DeRue et al. 2011; contextual performance; Chiaburu et al. 2011), as well as of performance in specific occupations (e.g., interpersonal occupations, Mount et al. 1998; including managers, Hough et al. 1998; and salespeople, Vinchur et al. 1998; as well as military occupations, Salgado 1998; and law enforcement, Ones et al. 2011; cf. Salgado et al. 2015). While personality–performance relations are moderated by criterion dimension and occupation and, to a lesser extent, by measurement and situational factors (Judge/Zapata 2015), the results of these meta-analyses have shown remarkable consistency across studies and contexts.

Meta-analyses of Big Five–job performance relations have also established personality trait validities across cultures (Ones et al. 2012). In addition to research conducted in the United States and Canada (Barrick et al. 2001), meta-analyses have estimated Big Five–performance validities in Western Europe (Salgado 1997, 1998), East Asia (Oh 2009; Schmidt/Oh 2013), and South Africa (van Aarde et al. 2017). These meta-analyses have also found that the relations of personality traits to job performance are remarkably consistent across cultures (though the validities of interpersonal traits tend to be somewhat larger in contexts with strong workplace social demands, such as East Asia). Recent authors (Ones et al. 2012; van Aarde et al. 2017) posited that some contributions of personality traits to effective job performance behaviors, like the structure of personality itself (DeYoung 2010, 2015; Markon et al. 2005; McCrae/Costa 1997), reflect cultural universals.

Compared to the substantial evidence of validity of personality traits for job performance in domestic settings, research on personality traits in expatriate contexts is much less developed (Albrecht et al. 2018a). Several meta-analyses have found trait self-efficacy to be substantially related to international adjustment (Bhaskar-Shrinivas et al. 2005; Hechanova et al. 2003). Mol et al. (2005) conducted a preliminary meta-analysis of relations between the Big Five traits and expatriate performance. Consistent with domestic research on employees with managerial responsibility (which most expatriates have), they found that Conscientiousness ($\rho = .21$) and Extraversion ($\rho = .18$) showed substantial relations with otherrated overall performance. Other traits showed smaller relations with performance ($\rho = .13$, Emotional Stability; $\rho = .13$, Openness; $\rho = .14$, Agreeableness). However, these meta-analytic estimates are based only a very small number of studies ($k = 8$–9; total $N = 621$–786). Additional studies conducted after Mol et al. (2005) have found similar results (e.g., Dalton/Wilson 2000; Johnson et al. 2003; Kusch et al. 2008; Muhammad Awais Bhatti et al. 2014; Ramalu et al. 2010; Rose et al. 2010), but the total number of samples and unique expatriates reported in this literature remains small. Thus, there is need for more primary studies to inform expatriate practice, theories of international job performance, and as input for further meta-analytic investigations. Primary studies examining personality traits' influence on international adjustment have found that Emotional Stability, Openness, and Conscientiousness show the strongest relations, with correlations typically around $r = .20$ to $.30$ (Albrecht et al. 2008, 2014; Caligiuri 2000a; Freeman/Olson-Buchanan 2013; Huang et al. 2005; Muhammad Awais Bhatti et al. 2014; Peltokorpi/Froese 2012, 2014). To our knowledge, no meta-analysis has yet examined personality trait relations with expatriate adjustment. In this study, we examine relations of personality traits based on the Big Five/ Five Factor Model (Goldberg 1993; John et al. 2008; McCrae/Costa 1997) with expatriate international adjustment and job performance. We consider trait relations with both overall job performance and more specific performance dimensions that are likely to have divergent nomological networks and differential implications for organizational practice (Campbell/Wiernik 2015; Viswesvaran/Ones 2000).

1.1   *Personality Traits and Expatriate Success*

From a theoretical perspective, job performance (for any employee, in all jobs) has three direct determinants – declarative job knowledge, procedural job knowledge and skill, and motivation (i.e., personal decisions about where, how much, and how long to spend effort at work; Campbell et al. 1993; Campbell/Wiernik 2015; Viswesvaran/Ones 2017). Personality traits are generally argued to primarily influence the third determinant, motivation (Barrick/ Mount 1991; Borman/Motowidlo 1997; Hough/Connelly 2013). Whereas objective abilities, training, education, and other preparatory factors more strongly influence acquisition of job knowledge and skill, personality traits and other "non-cognitive" dispositional characteristics are thought to more strongly impact the types of tasks employees are motivated to perform, how hard they choose to work on those tasks, and how willing (and able) they are to persist at the tasks through difficulties and over long periods of time.

Research on personality traits using a variety of methods, including cross-cultural lexical and questionnaire analyses, scale development and theoretical elaboration, genetic and heritability studies, and brain imaging, neuroscientific, and other biological and computational methods, has converged on the Hierarchical Big Five model as a consensus structure (DeYoung 2015; Goldberg 1993; John et al. 2008; Krueger et al. 2008; Markon et al. 2005; McCrae/Costa 1997). The Big Five traits – Openness, Emotional Stability, Conscientiousness, Extraversion, and Agreeableness – occupy a central level of the taxonomy and represent the major divisions among personality traits. Below the Big Five level, there are multiple personality aspects and facets – narrower traits that capture more specific patterns of thinking, feeling, and acting (Connelly et al. 2014b; DeYoung et al. 2007; Hough/Ones 2001). Above the Big Five are higher-order "metatraits" that represent very broad patterns of behavioral engagement and restraint (Chang et al. 2012; Davies et al. 2015; DeYoung 2015). There are also "compound personality traits", which combine variance from multiple Big Five domains and reflect the unique emergent effects of particular trait configurations or patterns occurring in tandem (Ones et al. 2005, 2016). Below, we organize our discussion of likely personality effects for expatriates according to the Big Five model.

Openness. The most often-cited personality traits believed to promote expatriate success are related to the domain of Openness, an individual's tendency to be curious, flexible, and open to new ideas and experiences (Connelly et al. 2014b, 2014a; Ones/ Viswesvaran 1997; Van der Zee/van Oudenhoven 2000). International human resource managers particularly emphasize Openness when predicting which employees are likely to be able to adjust to living in a new international environment (Ones/Viswesvaran 1999). Individuals high on Openness are likely to be better able to adjust to their new surroundings because they are more willing to engage in new activities, visit new places, try new foods, and, generally, to have new experiences (Albrecht et al. 2014). Conversely, individuals low on Openness tend to be rigid and dogmatic. When confronted with people with values, habits, beliefs, and behaviors unlike their own, expatriates with low Openness may become uncomfortable and may also display inappropriate or insensitive negative responses. Openness may also be related to acquisition of new job knowledge, especially knowledge of culture-specific practices in a new environment. We also note that Openness is moderately related to cognitive ability (Connelly et al. 2014b, 2018; Stanek/Ones 2018). Thus, we expect Openness to be substantially related to both expatriate adjustment and job performance, particularly those dimensions related to adapting to changing contexts and interacting with host country nationals.

Emotional Stability. Emotional Stability (and related traits, such as stress tolerance and emotional control) is also commonly cited as an important factor for expatriate success (Albrecht 2010; Ones/Viswesvaran 1997; Van der Zee/van Oudenhoven 2000; Young 2011). Expatriation is a highly-stressful environment, and expatriates are often separated from resources, comforts, and social networks that would support them and mitigate stressors if they were at home (Johnson et al. 2003). Individuals low on Emotional Stability are thus likely to be unable to adjust properly and may terminate their assignments early. In terms of job performance, Ones and Viswesvaran (1997) argued that Emotional Stability helps expatriates to inhibit negative impulses and cope with stressors, helping them to avoid careless and deviant acts (cf. Bowling/Eschleman 2010). Thus, we expect Emotional Stability to be related to international adjustment and avoiding counterproductive work behaviors.

Conscientiousness. Conscientiousness is a tendency to prioritize long-term goals over short-term goals and to protect one's goal pursuits from disruptions (e.g., distractions, impulses) – it encompasses traits related to dependability, responsibility, dutifulness, perseverance, industriousness, orderliness, and cautiousness (DeYoung 2015; Hough/Ones 2001; Roberts et al. 2005; Stanek/Ones 2018). Compared to Emotional Stability and Openness, Conscientiousness is less often-cited as an important driver of expatriate success (Ones/Viswesvaran 1997; Van der Zee/van Oudenhoven 2000; Young 2011), though there is some empirical support for its validity for performance constructs (Albrecht et al. 2008; Caligiuri 2000b; Mol et al. 2005). Domestic employee meta-analyses have consistently identified Conscientiousness as the strongest Big Five trait predictor of job performance

(Barrick et al. 2001). Conscientiousness helps employees to better prioritize their tasks, maintain on-task attention, set higher, more-motivating goals, better focus during training (enhancing job knowledge), avoid negative impulses, and be more motivated to engage in extra-role discretionary behaviors (Dilchert/Ones 2013). All these factors are as likely to enhance expatriate job performance as domestic employee job performance. Thus, we expect Conscientiousness (and compound traits incorporating it) to be substantially related to all performance dimensions.

Extraversion. Extraversion is a tendency toward behavioral engagement and active pursuit of opportunities and rewards, particularly opportunities for interpersonal contact (DeYoung 2015); it incorporates traits related to assertiveness, dominance, energy, sociability, positive emotions, enthusiasm, and sensation seeking (Hough/Ones 2001; Stanek/Ones 2018). Extraversion is strongly associated with interpersonal and leadership performance (Bono/Judge 2004; DeRue et al. 2011; Mount et al. 1998). As most expatriate jobs are managerial in nature, we expect Extraversion to be substantially related to these aspects of expatriate job performance.

Agreeableness. Agreeableness is a tendency to have positive interactions with others; it is related to politeness, respect for social norms, empathy, consideration for others, trust, and cooperation (Davies 2013; Stanek/Ones 2018). Individuals low on Agreeableness tend to be inconsiderate, rude, aggressive, suspicious, and manipulative. Agreeableness is likely to help expatriates to foster positive connections with host country nationals (Ones/ Viswesvaran 1997). These connections will enhance interpersonal and leadership behaviors (Ones/Dilchert 2009), lead expatriates to be more willing to help their new coworkers, and help expatriates to avoid interpersonally insensitive counterproductive behaviors. Additionally, by helping expatriates to establish a social network and new ties with HCNs, Agreeableness is also likely to enhance international adjustment (Black et al. 1991; Johnson et al. 2003).

Compound personality traits. While each of the Big Five traits individually is likely to impact important expatriate outcomes, we expect that the strongest relations may be observed for compound personality traits that combine variance from multiple Big Five domains (Ones et al. 2005). Compound trait scales often show stronger predictive validity for relevant behaviors than do simple sums of their component parts (Judge/Erez 2007; Ones et al. 2005; Ones/Viswesvaran 2001a, 2001b). This is because compound trait scales tap not only the co-occurrence of traits, but also the unique tendencies and strengths that emerge when an individual possesses certain levels of multiple traits at once (Ones et al. 2016). For example, proactive personality, the tendency to take personal initiative and create change in one's environment (Fuller/Marler 2009), reflects the unique proactive behavioral tendencies that emerge when an individual is simultaneously high on Conscientiousness, Extraversion, *and* Openness. Applied psychology practitioners have developed a variety of compound scales designed to predict specific work criteria. These scales, called COPS ("criterion-focused occupational personality scales"; Ones/Viswesvaran 2001a), assess specific configurations of traits that are uniquely predictive of specific critical workplace criteria (e.g., leadership, counterproductive work behaviors). COPS and other compound trait scales typically show stronger predictive validity than do combinations of basic trait scales (Connelly et al. 2018; Ones/Viswesvaran 2001a; Schmidt et al. 2016)

2   Methods

2.1   Procedure

Data were drawn from Sample 1 of the studies of expatriate success in Turkey (see Wiernik et al. 2018, Chapter 1 of this volume, for more details). Data were collected from expatriates currently working on an international assignment in Turkey and one host country national (HCN) coworker of each expatriate. Participants were volunteers recruited by the third author and a team of senior industrial-organizational psychology student research assistants. A broad range of industries was represented among the organizations from which data were gathered. These included finance/banking, tourism, education, marketing, and engineering. In most organizations, data were collected with the cooperation of the Human Resources department. Researchers administered questionnaires to expatriates and host country nationals separately; expatriates and HCNs did not have access to each other's responses. Expatriates completed a survey assessing demographics, details on their expatriate assignment, and a personality questionnaire. Host country national (HCN) coworkers provided confidential job performance ratings for the expatriate with whom they were working.

Expatriate Sample. We gathered data from 220 expatriates. Expatriates were mostly male (165 males, 29 females, 26 did not report gender) and had a mean age of 40.7 years ($SD = 10.04$), an average of 16.7 years of full-time work experience, and an average of 10 years of organizational tenure. Expatriates had spent an average of 3.08 years ($SD = 5.26$) abroad on previous international assignments and a varying amount of time on their current assignment in Turkey (mean 3.32 months, $SD = 48.14$). Expatriates included executive, mid- and lower-level managers, and as non-managerial (primarily service and educational) employees.

Expatriates were citizens of 25 countries. For those expatriate providing citizenship information, citizenship frequencies were: Australia (2), Austria (1), Belgium (5), Brazil (1), Bulgaria (1), Canada (8), Cyprus (1), Denmark (4), Finland (3), France (27), Germany (23), Greece (1), Hungary (1), Iran (2), Ireland (5), Italy (5), Japan (9), the Netherlands (3), Norway (3), South Africa (2), Spain (2), Sweden (3), Switzerland (5), the United Kingdom (36), and the United States (38). For more information on this sample, see Sinangil and Ones (1997, 2003).

Host Country National Coworker Sample. HCNs had a mean age of 34.68 years ($SD = 8.41$). HCNs were 122 males and 90 females (8 did not report their gender). HCNs had an average of 9.43 years ($SD = 7.70$) of experience in their current occupation and had worked with the expatriates they were rating for an average of 12.98 months ($SD = 24.13$). Raters were recruited based on their experience working closely with the expatriates. Most raters were expatriates' subordinates ($N = 137$), with smaller numbers being expatriates' peers ($N = 55$) or supervisors ($N = 8$); 20 raters did not report their position.

2.2   Measures

Hogan Personality Inventory. Participants' personality traits were measured using the 1992 Hogan Personality Inventory (Hogan/Hogan 1992). The HPI reports seven primary scales that map to the Big Five dimensions of personality (listed in Table 4). The scales are Adjustment (Emotional Stability), Ambition (Extraversion), Sociability (Extraversion), Intellectance (Openness), School Success (Openness), Likeability (Agreeableness), and

Prudence (Conscientiousness). It is important to note some unique features of the HPI relative to other measures based on the Big Five. The HPI Ambition scale combines elements of assertiveness (Extraversion) and industriousness (Conscientiousness); it measures an eponymous compound personality trait and has similarities to the compound assessed by proactive personality scales (Fuller/Marler 2009). The Sociability scale focuses on the sociability and positive emotionality facets of Extraversion (the Enthusiasm aspect; DeYoung et al. 2007). The Prudence scale focuses on the cautiousness and order facets of Conscientiousness (the Orderliness aspect; DeYoung et al. 2007) and traditionalism (Connelly et al. 2014a; Stanek/Ones 2018). The Intellectance scale is more focused on the Intellect aspect of Openness than on the Experiencing aspect (which dominates the NEO PI-R Openness scale; Connelly et al. 2014b; Wiernik et al. 2016; Woo et al. 2014). The School Success scale consists primarily of self-ratings of cognitive ability (particularly acquired science and math knowledge) and interest in formal learning settings. In addition to the 7 primary scales corresponding to the Big Five, the HPI also reports scores for several occupationally-focused compound scales. We examined results for two of these scales likely to be highly-relevant for expatriates. The Stress Tolerance scale measures the degree to which respondents are likely to remain calm and composed under pressure, particularly long-lasting and persistent stressors; it is a compound trait combining (in order) Emotional Stability, Conscientiousness, and Agreeableness (Ones/Viswesvaran 2001b). The Managerial Potential scale measures the degree to which respondents are likely to demonstrate strong leadership abilities and effective planning and decision-making skills; it is a compound trait combining (in order) Emotional Stability, Extraversion, and Conscientiousness (Viswesvaran et al. 1998).

Adjustment to local conditions. Expatriate locational adjustment (comfort living abroad) was measured using 9 items adapted from Black and Stephens (1989). Expatriates rated the conditions and environment they faced in Turkey on a 10-point scale, with higher scores indicating greater adjustment. The 9 items included adjustment to health care facilities, shopping, entertainment, housing conditions, food, cost of living, living conditions in general, daily interactions with Turks, and socialization with Turks ($\alpha = .82$).

Job performance. HCNs completed a 45-item job performance measure evaluating expatriates on 10 dimensions of job performance. The instrument was constructed directly in Turkish (i.e., was not a translated measure) based on existing models of job performance (Campbell et al. 1990; Hough/Dunnette 1992; Viswesvaran et al. 1996) and extensive interviews with Turkish HCNs and expatriates (see Sinangil/Ones 1997). HCNs rated expatriates on 10 performance dimensions (see Table 1). An overall performance index was created using a unit-weighted composite of the 10 subscales. HCNs rated each item on a 9-point scale for its accuracy describing the expatriate's on-the-job behavior (1 = extremely inaccurate, 9 = extremely accurate). Correlations among dimensions are shown in the lower triangle of Table 2.

HCNs are uniquely positioned to provide culturally-contextualized and relevant evaluations expatriate job performance behaviors (Sinangil/Ones 1997, 2003), and HCN reactions to expatriate behavior have an important impact on expatriates' adjustment and effectiveness (Templer 2010). HCNs are thus the ideal source for expatriate job performance information. Our use of data from the HCN perspective also supports recent calls for further consideration of multiple stakeholders in expatriate research (Caligiuri 2000b; Takeuchi 2010).

Table 1: Job performance dimensions assessed

Performance Dimension	Description *(Sample Item)*	Source for Description/Measure	Item	α	IRR
Adjustment to foreign business practices	Knowledge and application of appropriate foreign business practices *(Has knowledge about Turkish work life applications)*	Hough & Dunnette (1992)	4	.84	.58
Establishing and maintaining business contacts	Identifying, developing, using, and maintaining business contacts to achieve goals *(Can develop a communication net with people that he/she encounters at work)*	Hough & Dunnette (1992)	5	.91	.58
Technical competence	Measure of the knowledge required to carry out the tasks of the job *(Uses technical knowledge in solving difficult problems and in helping reach high quality decisions)*	Hough & Dunnette (1992); Viswesvaran (1993)	3	.84	.63
Working with others	Proficiency in working with others, assisting others in the organization *(Has planful and effective work relations with superiors and coworkers)*	Hough & Dunnette (1992)	4	.89	.47
Communicating and persuading	Oral and written proficiency in gathering and transmitting information; persuading others *(Is effective in oral and written communication)*	Hough & Dunnette (1992)	3	.88	.45
Initiative and effort	Dedication to one's job; amount of work expended in striving to do a good job *(Has initiative and takes on extra responsibility)*	Hough & Dunnette (1992)	4	.87	.55
Personal discipline	The extent to which counterproductive behaviors at work are avoided *(Follows rules and regulations and respects authority)*	Campbell et al. (1990); Viswesvaran (1993)	6	.90	.56
Interpersonal relations (avoiding CWB)	The degree to which the expatriate facilitates team performance; supports and champions others in the organization and unit *(Cooperates with others at work)*	Campbell et al. (1990); Viswesvaran (1993)	8	.90	.47
Management and supervision	Proficiency in the coordination of different roles in the organization *(Provides supervision to subordinates)*	Campbell et al. (1990); Viswesvaran (1993)	3	.91	.53
Productivity	Volume of work produced by the expatriate *(Is productive)*	Viswesvaran (1993)	5	.92	.57
Overall expatriate job performance	A unit-weighted composite of the 10 scales; reliability computed as a Mosier reliability (stratified alpha)	Campbell et al. (1990); Hough & Dunnette (1992); Viswesvaran (1993)	45	.96	.89 *.52*

Note: IRR = estimated interrater reliability using meta-analytic values reported by Viswesvaran et al. (1996). For overall job performance, the first value is the estimated criterion interrater reliability for the overall job performance *composite* using the method by Wilmot et al. (2014). The second value (in italics) is the meta-analytic estimate for overall job performance *measures* reported by Viswesvaran et al. (1996).

Table 2: Correlations among performance dimensions

	1	2	3	4	5	6	7	8	9	10
Adjustment to foreign business practices	(.58)	*.58*	*.22*	*.22*	*.22*	*.31*	*.29*	*.22*	*.20*	*.34*
Establishing and maintaining business contacts	.77	(.58)	*.22*	*.22*	*.22*	*.31*	*.29*	*.22*	*.20*	*.34*
Technical competence	.61	.55	(.63)	*.10*	*.10*	*.30*	*.18*	*.10*	*.29*	*.27*
Working with others	.81	.81	.72	(.47)	*.46*	*.24*	*.33*	*.46*	*.21*	*.29*
Communicating and persuading	.71	.73	.62	.81	(.45)	*.24*	*.33*	*.46*	*.21*	*.29*
Initiative and effort	.62	.58	.51	.70	.71	(.55)	*.34*	*.24*	*.29*	*.28*
Personal discipline	.67	.57	.43	.59	.58	.54	(.56)	*.33*	*.22*	*.31*
Interpersonal relations	.50	.50	.41	.56	.50	.45	.59	(.47)	*.21*	*.29*
Management and supervision	.61	.61	.53	.68	.64	.64	.60	.53	(.53)	*.26*
Productivity	.74	.67	.66	.81	.78	.66	.59	.51	.74	(.57)

Note: Values below the diagonal are observed within-rater correlations for the current sample. Values on the diagonal are estimated interrater reliabilities from Viswesvaran et al. (1996). Values above the diagonal are estimated between-raters correlations from Viswesvaran et al. (2005).

We corrected for unreliability in job performance ratings using interrater reliability. We estimated reliabilities for performance dimensions using meta-analytic values from Viswesvaran et al. (1996).[1] For overall job performance, we estimated interrater reliability for the overall performance *composite* using the method described by Wilmot et al. (2014); we used dimension interrater reliabilities from Viswesvaran et al. (1996) and dimension between-raters intercorrelations from Viswesvaran et al. (2005) to estimate a Mosier reliability coefficient for the composite performance measure (r_{yy} = .89). For interested readers, as a comparison, we also report correlations corrected using Viswesvaran et al.'s (1996) meta-analytic mean interrater reliability value for overall job performance *measures* (r_{yy} = .52). We did not correct for unreliability in personality test scores, as we were interested in the validity of personality trait *measures*, rather than the personality trait of the latent integrity *constructs*. We did not correct for range restriction because appropriate applicant or general reference population standard deviation estimates were not available (Ones/Viswesvaran 2003; cf. Kostal et al. 2018, Chapter 2, this volume).

3   Results

Personality criterion-related validity results are shown in Table 3. Locational adjustment showed small positive relations with Managerial Potential (r_c = .18), Ambition (r_c = .17), Sociability (r_c = .15), Prudence (r_c = .14), and Stress Tolerance (r_c = .14), and moderate relations with School Success (r_c = .25). Overall job performance showed its strongest relations with Managerial Potential (r_c = .22) and Ambition r_c = .21) and smaller, but nonetheless noteworthy relations with Intellect (r_c = .17), Prudence (r_c = .17), and Sociability (r_c = .13).

Beyond overall job performance, personality scales also showed substantial relations with several specific performance dimensions. We expected that Emotional Stability would be substantially related to avoiding counterproductive work behaviors; indeed, the HPI Adjustment scale showed a moderate positive relation with personal discipline (r_c = .19). The Adjustment scale also showed small to moderate relations with interpersonal performance, including working with others, interpersonal relations, and management/ supervision (r_c = .12, .20, .24, respectively). This result is likely due to the HPI Adjustment scale including many items related to empathy, a facet more typically associated with the Agreeableness domain (Davies 2013; Hough/Ones 2001).

---

[1]   Adjustment to Foreign Business Practices and Establishing and Maintaining Business Contacts were treated as measures of "Administrative Competence". Technical Competence was treated as a measure of "Quality". Working with Others was treated as a measure of "Interpersonal Competence". Personal Discipline was treated as a measure of "Compliance and Acceptance of Authority". For performance dimension intercorrelations, Communicating and Persuading was treated as a measure of "Interpersonal Competence". Other performance dimension scale labels match construct labels used by Viswesvaran et al. (1996, 2005).

Table 3: Criterion-related validities for personality traits

	Adj	Amb	Soc	Int	Sch	Lik	Pru	StrTol	ManPot
Locational adjustment	.11 (.10)	.17 (.15)	.15 (.14)	.07 (.06)	.25 (.23)	.09 (.08)	.14 (.13)	.14 (.13)	.18 (.16)
	[-.01, .23]	[.05, .29]	[.03, .27]	[-.06, .19]	[.14, .37]	[-.03, .21]	[.02, .26]	[.02, .26]	[.06, .30]
Adjustment to foreign business practices	.08 (.06)	.13 (.10)	.17 (.13)	.03 (.02)	.21 (.16)	.13 (.10)	.07 (.05)	.13 (.10)	.21 (.16)
	[-.07, .22]	[-.01, .28]	[.03, .31]	[-.12, .17]	[.07, .35]	[-.01, .28]	[-.08, .21]	[-.01, .28]	[.07, .35]
Establishing and maintaining business contacts	.07 (.05)	.04 (.03)	.14 (.11)	.17 (.13)	.37 (.28)	.11 (.08)	.08 (.06)	.11 (.08)	.13 (.10)
	[-.08, .21]	[-.11, .18]	[.00, .29]	[.03, .31]	[.23, .50]	[-.04, .25]	[-.07, .22]	[-.04, .25]	[-.01, .28]
Technical competence	-.05 (-.04)	.15 (.12)	-.01 (-.01)	-.09 (-.07)	.09 (.07)	.10 (.08)	.08 (.06)	-.06 (-.05)	.14 (.11)
	[-.19, .09]	[.01, .29]	[-.15, .13]	[-.23, .05]	[-.05, .23]	[-.04, .24]	[-.06, .21]	[-.20, .08]	[.00, .28]
Working with others	.12 (.08)	.13 (.09)	.16 (.11)	-.03 (-.02)	.29 (.20)	.31 (.21)	.06 (.04)	.18 (.12)	.26 (.18)
	[-.04, .28]	[-.03, .29]	[.00, .32]	[-.19, .13]	[.14, .45]	[.15, .46]	[-.10, .22]	[.02, .33]	[.11, .42]
Communicating and persuading	.03 (.02)	.21 (.14)	.21 (.14)	.16 (.11)	.19 (.13)	.15 (.10)	.04 (.03)	.07 (.05)	.28 (.19)
	[-.14, .19]	[.05, .37]	[.05, .37]	[.00, .33]	[.03, .36]	[-.01, .31]	[-.12, .21]	[-.09, .24]	[.12, .44]
Initiative and effort	.01 (.01)	.32 (.24)	.26 (.19)	.12 (.09)	.24 (.18)	.15 (.11)	.04 (.03)	.11 (.08)	.26 (.19)
	[-.14, .16]	[.18, .46]	[.11, .40]	[-.03, .27]	[.10, .39]	[.00, .30]	[-.11, .19]	[-.04, .26]	[.11, .40]
Personal discipline	.19 (.14)	.13 (.10)	.11 (.08)	-.16 (-.12)	.19 (.14)	.39 (.29)	-.07 (-.05)	.19 (.14)	.21 (.16)
	[.04, .33]	[-.01, .28]	[-.04, .25]	[-.31, -.01]	[.04, .33]	[.25, .52]	[-.21, .08]	[.04, .33]	[.07, .36]
Interpersonal relations	.20 (.14)	.29 (.20)	.23 (.16)	-.01 (-.01)	.45 (.31)	.29 (.20)	.10 (.07)	.25 (.17)	.38 (.26)
	[.05, .36]	[.14, .45]	[.08, .39]	[-.18, .15]	[.31, .60]	[.14, .45]	[-.06, .26]	[.09, .40]	[.23, .53]
Management and supervision	.24 (.17)	.56 (.41)	-.02 (-.01)	.09 (.06)	.14 (.10)	-.01 (-.01)	-.33 (-.24)	-.09 (-.07)	.26 (.19)
	[.09, .38]	[.43, .69]	[-.17, .13]	[-.07, .24]	[-.02, .29]	[-.16, .14]	[-.47, -.18]	[-.25, .06]	[.11, .41]
Productivity	.03 (.02)	.26 (.20)	.11 (.08)	-.05 (-.04)	.09 (.07)	.09 (.07)	.13 (.10)	.04 (.03)	.23 (.17)
	[-.12, .17]	[.12, .41]	[-.04, .25]	[-.20, .09]	[-.05, .24]	[-.05, .24]	[-.01, .28]	[-.11, .19]	[.08, .37]
Overall job performance	.08 (.08)	.21 (.20)	.13 (.12)	.17 (.16)	.06 (.06)	.01 (.01)	.17 (.16)	.08 (.08)	.22 (.21)
	[-.03, .20]	[.10, .32]	[.01, .24]	[.06, .28]	[-.05, .18]	[-.11, .13]	[.06, .28]	[-.03, .20]	[.11, .33]
	.11	*.28*	*.17*	*.22*	*.08*	*.01*	*.22*	*.11*	*.29*
	[-.04, .26]	*[.13, .42]*	*[.01, .32]*	*[.07, .37]*	*[-.07, .24]*	*[-.14, .17]*	*[.07, .37]*	*[-.04, .26]*	*[.14, .44]*

Note: $N = 220$, Adj = Adjustment, Amb = Ambition, Soc = Sociability, Int = Intellectance, Sch = School Success, Lik = Likeability, Pru = Prudence, StrTol = Stress Tolerance, ManPot = Managerial Potential. Correlations corrected for criterion interrater unreliability (observed correlations in parentheses), values in brackets are 90% confidence intervals. For overall job performance, values in the first row are the correlation and confidence interval corrected using an estimated criterion interrater reliability of $r_{yy} = .89$ for the overall job performance *composite* (estimated using the method by Wilmot et al. 2014). Values in italics in the second row are the correlation and confidence interval corrected using an estimated criterion interrater reliability of $r_{yy} = .52$ (the meta-analytic estimate for overall job performance measures reported by Viswesvaran et al. 1996).

We predicted that the Assertiveness-related aspect of Extraversion would be related with interpersonal performance, particularly effective leadership. This prediction was supported; Ambition was strongly related to management performance (r_c = .56), as well as interpersonal relations (r_c = .29), communication (r_c = .21), and working with others (r_c = .13). Consistent with the HPI Ambition scale containing variance related to the Industriousness aspect of Conscientiousness, Ambition was also strongly related to initiative and effort (r_c = .32) and productivity (r_c = .26), with small relations with most other performance dimensions. We predicted that Enthusiasm-related Extraversion traits (gregariousness, positive emotions) would also be related to interpersonal performance; this prediction was also supported (Sociability relations with interpersonal performance r_c ranged .14 to .23). Sociability also showed substantial relations with initiative (r_c = .26) and with performance related to adapting to new international work contexts (r_c = .17 with adjustment to foreign business practices, .14 with establishing business contacts).

We posited that Openness would be associated with a wide range of expatriate performance behaviors because curious, open-minded expatriates may regard novel experiences in a foreign country as potentially exhilarating, rather than as a threat. However, we found only negligible to small relations between HPI Intellectance and most criteria; Intellectance was even somewhat *negatively* related to personal discipline (r_c = -.16). These weak relations may reflect that HPI Intellectance is more focused on the Intellect aspect of Openness (openness to new ideas, intellectual efficiency), which may be less relevant for expatriates than the Experiencing aspect (openness to new aesthetic, sensory, and emotional experiences). It may, however, also reflect that Openness (and related constructs, such as tolerance for ambiguity, cf. Albrecht et al. 2018b, Chapter 14, this volume) is less critical for expatriates than commonly thought (cf. Albrecht et al. 2014).

The HPI School Success scale showed very strong relations with many performance dimensions. This may reflect the content on this scale related to self-ratings of cognitive ability. Cognitive ability is the single strongest predictor of performance across occupations and settings (Schmidt et al. 2016; Schmidt/Hunter 2004); self-rated ability as measured by HPI School Success may (albeit imperfectly) capture some of this predictive power (Freund/Kasten 2012). School Success may also capture some of the predictive power of general self-efficacy (cf. Bubany/Hansen 2010; Judge/Bono 2001).

We expected Agreeableness to be related to how effectively expatriates can learn new social customs, understand host country nationals' needs and concerns, and generally interact with their colleagues in a new country. We observed strong relations of Likeability with working with others (r_c = .31) and interpersonal relations (r_c = .29). We also observed very strong relations of Likeability with personal discipline (r_c = .39, note that this measure includes items related to abuse and other forms of interpersonal deviance).

Consistent with its generalizable relations with job performance across industries, occupations, and international contexts, we expected Conscientiousness to show substantial relations with many performance dimensions. HPI Prudence showed the most variable relations with performance dimensions (for example, a moderately large *negative* relation with management and supervision, r_c = -.33). However, its relation with overall job performance (r_c = .17) was on par with relations reported in the European literature (e.g., Salgado 1997). As discussed above, the HPI Ambition scale, which includes Industriousness-related Conscientiousness variance, also showed substantial relations with many performance dimensions, thus generally supporting the predictive power of the Conscientiousness for job performance in expatriate settings.

Finally, we posited that compound personality trait scales, which combine multiple job-relevant personality traits, would be especially strongly related to expatriate success. We found that Stress Tolerance showed very similar patterns of performance validities as Adjustment. Managerial Potential, however, showed moderate to strong positive relations with nearly all performance dimensions. These results indicate that this specific combination of traits measured by the Managerial Potential scale (simultaneously high Assertiveness/Extraversion, Emotional Stability, and Industriousness/Conscientiousness) is particularly relevant as a driver of expatriate success. The only performance dimensions that showed weaker relations with Managerial Potential are technical competence and establishing/maintaining business contacts. These more technical performance dimensions are likely to be more strongly related to cognitive ability, job knowledge, and objective skills, rather than more motivational dispositional traits (Schmidt et al. 2016; Schmidt/Hunter 2004) – that is, these dimensions are more "maximal performance", determined by one's ability, rather than "typical performance", driven more by motivational choices (Ones et al. 2017).

4 Discussion

This study found that personality traits have substantial validity for both expatriate adjustment and job performance. These validities are similar in pattern and magnitude to previous meta-analyses of both expatriate job performance (Mol et al. 2005) and domestic employee job performance across cultural contexts (Barrick et al. 2001; Oh 2009; Ones et al. 2007, 2012; Salgado 1997; van Aarde et al. 2017). Like domestic employees, scales assessing Conscientiousness and Emotional Stability (and compound scales drawing variance from these traits) showed strong relations with multiple performance dimensions. Conscientiousness was related to overall job performance. Also consistent with research on domestic managers and leaders (Bono/Judge 2004; Conway et al. 2001; Hough et al. 1998; Mount et al. 1998), Extraversion and Agreeableness also showed substantial relations with performance, particularly interpersonal performance, among expatriates (most of whom have managerial responsibility). Contrary to common beliefs among laypeople and practitioners, Openness showed negligible to weak relations with expatriate performance. Together, these findings suggest that expatriates and domestic employees are more alike than different in terms of the psychological characteristics that drive effective performance and success.

These results show that expatriate management practice can be enhanced by incorporating personality traits into international human resource management processes. Personality assessment can be incorporated into expatriate HRM in two main ways. First, personality assessments can be added to selection systems for choosing employees to send on international assignments. Expatriate selection is often haphazard and informal (Deller 1997; Harris/Brewster 1999). Informal selection practices can lead both to suboptimal choices for organizational goals as well as introduce unintentional biases into the process (Kuncel et al. 2013). Selecting expatriates using a standardized system, one which ideally incorporates standardized assessments of relevant personality traits, objective measures of abilities, and considerations of individual employee career goals and development needs, can dramatically increase the fairness and effectiveness of international assignments.

Personality trait assessments can also be incorporated into expatriate support, management, and development systems before expatriates depart and once employees arrive in their new locations. Standardized personality assessments can help organizations to identify each expatriate's unique strengths and weaknesses. Managers can then provide expatriates with task assignments that capitalize on each employees' unique personal strengths and provide tailored support to mitigate or compensate for their personal weaknesses and liabilities.

Such practices might be particularly useful if, in addition to self-ratings, personality trait ratings are also obtained from expatriates' host country subordinates, peers, and supervisors (Connelly/Ones 2010; Sinangil/Ones 1997; Takeuchi 2010).

Overall, the current study supports general conclusions that personality traits and other psychological characteristics have substantial value for understanding and enhancing workplace effectiveness and success. Expatriate research and practice should attend more to the impact of general broad (i.e., not only expatriation-specific) factors that drive international assignment success. Relations with Ambition and Managerial Potential scales notwithstanding, the relatively weak validity observed for some areas of technical performance suggests that future expatriate research and practice may also strongly benefit from objectively measuring expatriate cognitive ability and using these results to inform expatriate selection decisions.

References

Albrecht, Anne-Grit (2010): Core Self-Evaluations and Expatriate Functioning: A Multi-National, Multi-Source, Multi-Criterion Study. Doctoral Dissertation. Lüneburg, Germany: Leuphana Universität.

Albrecht, Anne-Grit; Ones, Deniz S.; Sinangil, Handan Kepir (2018a): Expatriate Management. In: Ones, Deniz S. et al. (Eds.): The SAGE Handbook of Industrial, Work and Organizational Psychology. Volume 3: Managerial Psychology and Organizational Approaches. 2nd ed. London, United Kingdom: Sage: 429–468.

Albrecht, Anne-Grit et al. (2018b): Tolerance of Ambiguity: Relations with Expatriate Adjustment and Job Performance. In: Wiernik, Brenton M.; Rüger, Heiko; Ones, Deniz S. (Eds.): Managing Expatriates: Success Factors in Private and Public Domains, Series on Population Studies 50. Opladen, Germany: Barbara Budrich Publishers.

Albrecht, Anne-Grit et al. (2014): Openness in Cross-Cultural Work Settings: A Multicountry Study of Expatriates. In: *Journal of Personality Assessment*, Special Section: Openness to Experience 96,1: 64–75. [https://doi.org/10.1080/00223891.2013.821074].

Albrecht, Anne-Grit et al. (2008): European Big Five Findings of the iGOES Project. Presented at the International Congress of Psychology. Berlin, Germany.

Barrick, Murray R.; Mount, Michael K. (1991): The Big Five Personality Dimensions and Job Performance: A Meta-Analysis. In: *Personnel Psychology* 44,1: 1–26. [https://doi.org/10.1111/j.1744-6570.1991.tb00688.x].

Barrick, Murray R.; Mount, Michael K.; Judge, Timothy A. (2001): Personality and Performance at the Beginning of the New Millennium: What Do We Know and Where Do We Go Next? In: *International Journal of Selection and Assessment* 9,1/2: 9–30. [https://doi.org/10/frqhf2].

Berry, Christopher M.; Ones, Deniz S.; Sackett, Paul R. (2007): Interpersonal Deviance, Organizational Deviance, and Their Common Correlates: A Review and Meta-Analysis. In: *Journal of Applied Psychology* 92,2: 410–424. [https://doi.org/10.1037/0021-9010.92.2.410].

Bhaskar-Shrinivas, Purnima et al. (2005): Input-Based and Time-Based Models of International Adjustment: Meta-Analytic Evidence and Theoretical Extensions. In: *Academy of Management Journal* 48,2: 257–281. [https://doi.org/10.5465/AMJ.2005.16928400].

Black, J. Stewart; Mendenhall, Mark E.; Oddou, Gary R. (1991): Toward a Comprehensive Model of International Adjustment: An Integration of Multiple Theoretical Perspectives. In: *Academy of Management Review* 16,2: 291–317. [https://doi.org/10/fn7m8b].

Black, J. Stewart; Stephens, Gregory K. (1989): The Influence of the Spouse on American Expatriate Adjustment and Intent to Stay in Pacific Rim Overseas Assignments. In: *Journal of Management* 15,4: 529–544. [https://doi.org/10.1177/014920638901500403].

Bono, Joyce E.; Judge, Timothy A. (2004): Personality and Transformational and Transactional Leadership: A Meta-Analysis. In: *Journal of Applied Psychology* 89,5: 901–910. [https://doi.org/10.1037/0021-9010.89.5.901].

Borman, Walter C.; Motowidlo, Stephan J. (1997): Task Performance and Contextual Performance: The Meaning for Personnel Selection Research. In: *Human Performance* 10,2: 99–109. [https://doi.org/10/dp8jh4].

Bowling, Nathan A.; Eschleman, Kevin J. (2010): Employee Personality as a Moderator of the Relationships between Work Stressors and Counterproductive Work Behavior. In: *Journal of Occupational Health Psychology* 15,1: 91–103. [https://doi.org/10.1037/a0017326].

Bubany, Shawn T.; Hansen, Jo-Ida C. (2010): Ability Self-Estimates and Self-Efficacy: Meaningfully Distinct? In: *Measurement and Evaluation in Counseling and Development* 43,3: 168–187. [https://doi.org/10.1177/0748175610384809].

Caligiuri, Paula M. (2000a): Selecting Expatriates for Personality Characteristics: A Moderating Effect of Personality on the Relationship between Host National Contact and Cross-Cultural Adjustment. In: *MIR: Management International Review* 40,1: 61–80. [https://www.researchgate.net/publication/234021408].

Caligiuri, Paula M. (2000b): The Big Five Personality Characteristics as Predictors of Expatriate's Desire to Terminate the Assignment and Supervisor-Rated Performance. In: *Personnel Psychology* 53,1: 67–88. [https://doi.org/10.1111/j.1744-6570.2000.tb00194.x].

Campbell, Charlotte H. et al. (1990): Development of Multiple Job Performance Measures in a Representative Sample of Jobs. In: *Personnel Psychology* 43,2: 277–300. [https://doi.org/10.1111/j.1744-6570.1990.tb01559.x].

Campbell, John P. et al. (1993): A Theory of Performance. In: Schmitt, Neal; Borman, Walter C. (Eds.): Personnel Selection in Organizations. San Francisco, CA: Jossey-Bass: 35–70.

Campbell, John P.; Wiernik, Brenton M. (2015): The Modeling and Assessment of Work Performance. In: *Annual Review of Organizational Psychology and Organizational Behavior* 2: 47–74. [https://doi.org/10/bc4k].

Chang, Luye; Connelly, Brian S.; Geeza, Alexis A. (2012): Separating Method Factors and Higher Order Traits of the Big Five: A Meta-Analytic Multitrait-Multimethod Approach. In: *Journal of Personality and Social Psychology* 102,2: 408–426. [https://doi.org/10/bz9mkz].

Chiaburu, Dan S. et al. (2011): The Five-Factor Model of Personality Traits and Organizational Citizenship Behaviors: A Meta-Analysis. In: *Journal of Applied Psychology* 96,6: 1140–1166. [https://doi.org/10.1037/a0024004].

Connelly, Brian S.; Ones, Deniz S. (2010): An Other Perspective on Personality: Meta-Analytic Integration of Observers' Accuracy and Predictive Validity. In: *Psychological Bulletin* 136,6: 1092–1122. [https://doi.org/10.1037/a0021212].

Connelly, Brian S. et al. (2014a): Opening up Openness: A Theoretical Sort Following Critical Incidents Methodology and Meta-Analytic Investigation of the Trait Family Measures. In: *Journal of Personality Assessment*, Special Section: Openness to Experience 96,1: 17–28. [https://doi.org/10/bc5f].

Connelly, Brian S.; Ones, Deniz S.; Chernyshenko, Oleksandr S. (2014b): Introducing the Special Section on Openness to Experience: Review of Openness Taxonomies, Measurement, and Nomological Net. In: *Journal of Personality Assessment*, Special Section: Openness to Experience 96,1: 1–16. [https://doi.org/10/33f].

Connelly, Brian S.; Ones, Deniz S.; Hülsheger, Ute R. (2018): Personality in Industrial, Work, and Organizational Psychology: Theory, Measurement and Application. In: Ones, Deniz S. et al. (Eds.): The SAGE Handbook of Industrial, Work and Organizational Psychology. Volume 1: Personnel Psychology and Employee Performance. 2nd ed. London, United Kingdom: Sage: 320–365.

Conway, James M.; Lombardo, Kristie; Sanders, Kelley C. (2001): A Meta-Analysis of Incremental Validity and Nomological Networks for Subordinate and Peer Ratings. In: *Human Performance* 14,4: 267–303. [https://doi.org/10.1207/S15327043HUP1404_1].

Dalton, Maxine; Wilson, Meena (2000): The Relationship the Five-Factor Model of Personality to Job Performance for a Group of Middle Eastern Expatriate Managers. In: *Journal of Cross-Cultural Psychology* 31,2: 250–258. [https://doi.org/10.1177/0022022100031002007].

Davies, Stacy E. et al. (2015): The General Factor of Personality: The "Big One," a Self-Evaluative Trait, or a Methodological Gnat That Won't Go Away? In: *Personality and Individual Differences*, Special Issue: Dr. Sybil Eysenck Young Researcher Award 2014 81: 13–22. [https://doi.org/10/bc98].

Davies, Stacy E. (2013): Lower and Higher Order Facets and Factors of the Interpersonal Traits among the Big Five: Specifying, Measuring, and Understanding Extraversion and Agreeableness. Doctoral Dissertation. Minneapolis, MN: University of Minnesota. [http://hdl.handle.net/11299/164781].

Deller, Jürgen (1997): Expatriate Selection: Possibilities and Limitations of Using Personality Scales. In: Aycan, Zeynep (Ed.): Expatriate Management: Theory and Research, New Approaches to Employee Management 4. Greenwich, CT: JAI Press: 93–116.

DeRue, D. Scott et al. (2011): Trait and Behavioral Theories of Leadership: An Integration and Meta-Analytic Test of Their Relative Validity. In: *Personnel Psychology* 64,1: 7–52. [https://doi.org/10.1111/j.1744-6570.2010.01201.x].

DeYoung, Colin G. (2015): Cybernetic Big Five Theory. In: *Journal of Research in Personality*, Special Issue: Integrative Theories of Personality 56: 33–58. [https://doi.org/10/33h].

DeYoung, Colin G. (2010): Personality Neuroscience and the Biology of Traits. In: *Social and Personality Psychology Compass* 4,12: 1165–1180. [https://doi.org/10/bvgnww].

DeYoung, Colin G.; Quilty, Lena C.; Peterson, Jordan B. (2007): Between Facets and Domains: 10 Aspects of the Big Five. In: *Journal of Personality and Social Psychology* 93,5: 880–896. [https://doi.org/10/b4xsvz].

Dilchert, Stephan; Ones, Deniz S. (2013): Gewissenhaftigkeit [Conscientiousness]. In: Sarges, Werner (Ed.): Management-Diagnostik. 4th ed. Göttingen, Germany: Hogrefe: 323–331.

Freeman, Melissa M.; Olson-Buchanan, Julie B. (2013): The Relations between Expatriate Personality and Language Fluency and Its Effect on Host Country Adjustment: An Empirical Study. In: *International Journal of Management* 30,2: 393. [https://www.researchgate.net/publication/297279178].

Freund, Philipp Alexander; Kasten, Nadine (2012): How Smart Do You Think You Are? A Meta-Analysis on the Validity of Self-Estimates of Cognitive Ability. In: *Psychological Bulletin* 138,2: 296–321. [https://doi.org/10.1037/a0026556].

Fuller, Jerry Bryan, Jr.; Marler, Laura E. (2009): Change Driven by Nature: A Meta-Analytic Review of the Proactive Personality Literature. In: *Journal of Vocational Behavior* 75,3: 329–345. [https://doi.org/10.1016/j.jvb.2009.05.008].

Goldberg, Lewis R. (1993): The Structure of Phenotypic Personality Traits. In: *American Psychologist* 48,1: 26–34. [https://doi.org/10/c6tzrk].

Harris, Hilary; Brewster, Chris (1999): The Coffee-Machine System: How International Selection Really Works. In: *International Journal of Human Resource Management* 10,3: 488–500. [https://doi.org/10.1080/095851999340440].

Hechanova, Regina; Beehr, Terry A.; Christiansen, Neil D. (2003): Antecedents and Consequences of Employees' Adjustment to Overseas Assignment: A Meta-Analytic Review. In: *Applied Psychology* 52,2: 213–236. [https://doi.org/10/d4f4xv].

Hogan, Robert T.; Hogan, Joyce C. (1992): Hogan Personality Inventory Manual. 2nd ed. Tulsa, OK: Hogan Assessment Systems.

Hough, Leaetta M.; Connelly, Brian S. (2013): Personality Measurement and Use in Industrial and Organizational Psychology. In: Geisinger, Kurt F. et al. (Eds.): APA Handbook of Testing and Assessment in Psychology. Volume 1, APA Handbooks in Psychology. Washington, DC: American Psychological Association: 501–531. [https://doi.org/10.1037/14047-028].

Hough, Leaetta M.; Dunnette, Marvin D. (1992): US Managers Abroad: What It Takes to Succeed. Presented at the Academy of Management Conference. Las Vegas, NV.

Hough, Leaetta M.; Ones, Deniz S. (2001): The Structure, Measurement, Validity, and Use of Personality Variables in Industrial, Work, and Organizational Psychology. In: Anderson, Neil et al. (Eds.): Handbook of Industrial, Work and Organizational Psychology. Volume 1: Personnel Psychology. Thousand Oaks, CA: Sage: 233–277. [https://doi.org/10/bc67].

Hough, Leaetta M.; Ones, Deniz S.; Viswesvaran, Chockalingam (1998b): Personality Correlates of Managerial Performance Constructs. In: Page, Ron C. (Chair): Personality Determinants of Managerial Potential, Performance, Progression, and Ascendancy. Symposium presented at the Society of Industrial and Organizational Psychology Annual Meeting. Dallas, TX.

Huang, Tsai-Jung; Chi, Shu-Cheng; Lawler, John J. (2005): The Relationship between Expatriates' Personality Traits and Their Adjustment to International Assignments. In: *International Journal of Human Resource Management* 16,9: 1656–1670. [https://doi.org/10.1080/09585190500239325].

John, Oliver P.; Naumann, Laura P.; Soto, Christopher J. (2008): Paradigm Shift to the Integrative Big Five Trait Taxonomy: History, Measurement, and Conceptual Issues. In: John, Oliver P.; Robins, Richard W.; Pervin, Lawrence A. (Eds.): Handbook of Personality: Theory and Research. 3rd ed. New York: Guilford Press: 114–158.

Johnson, Erin C. et al. (2003): Expatriate Social Ties: Personality Antecedents and Consequences for Adjustment. In: *International Journal of Selection and Assessment* 11,4: 277–288. [https://doi.org/10.1111/j.0965-075X.2003.00251.x].

Judge, Timothy A.; Bono, Joyce E. (2001): Relationship of Core Self-Evaluation Traits – Self-Esteem, Generalized Self-Efficacy, Locus of Control, and Emotional Stability – with Job Satisfaction and Job Performance: A Meta-Analysis. In: *Journal of Applied Psychology* 86,1: 80–92. [https://doi.org/10.1037/0021-9010.86.1.80].

Judge, Timothy A.; Erez, Amir (2007): Interaction and Intersection: The Constellation of Emotional Stability and Extraversion in Predicting Performance. In: *Personnel Psychology* 60,3: 573–596. [https://doi.org/10.1111/j.1744-6570.2007.00084.x].

Judge, Timothy A.; Zapata, Cindy (2015): The Person-Situation Debate Revisited: Effect of Situation Strength and Trait Activation on the Validity of the Big Five Personality Traits in Predicting Job Performance. In: *Academy of Management Journal* 58,4: 1149–1179. [https://doi.org/10.5465/amj.2010.0837].

Kostal, Jack W. et al. (2018): Expatriate Personality: Facet-Level Comparisons with Domestic Counterparts. In: Wiernik, Brenton M.; Rüger, Heiko; Ones, Deniz S. (Eds.): Managing Expatriates: Success Factors in Private and Public Domains, Series on Population Studies 50. Opladen, Germany: Barbara Budrich Publishers.

Krueger, Robert F. et al. (2008): Behavioral Genetics and Personality: A New Look at the Integration of Nature and Nurture. In: John, Oliver P.; Robins, Richard W.; Pervin, Lawrence A. (Eds.): Handbook of Personality Psychology: Theory and Research. 3rd ed. New York, NY: Guilford: 287–310.

Kuncel, Nathan R. et al. (2013): Mechanical versus Clinical Data Combination in Selection and Admissions Decisions: A Meta-Analysis. In: *Journal of Applied Psychology* 98,6: 1060–1072. [https://doi.org/10/33p].

Kusch, Réné; Deller, Jürgen; Albrecht, Anne-Grit (2008): Predicting Expatriate Job Performance: Using the Normative NEO-PI-R or the Ipsative OPQ32i? In: *International Journal of Psychology* 43,3–4: 57. [https://doi.org/ 10.1080/00207594.2008.10108483].

Markon, Kristian E.; Krueger, Robert F.; Watson, David (2005): Delineating the Structure of Normal and Abnormal Personality: An Integrative Hierarchical Approach. In: *Journal of Personality and Social Psychology* 88,1: 139–157. [https://doi.org/10.1037/0022-3514.88.1.139].

McCrae, Robert R.; Costa, Paul T. (1997): Personality Trait Structure as a Human Universal. In: *American Psychologist* 52,5: 509–516. [https://doi.org/10.1037/0003-066X.52.5.509].

Mol, Stefan T. et al. (2005): Predicting Expatriate Job Performance for Selection Purposes: A Quantitative Review. In: *Journal of Cross-Cultural Psychology* 36,5: 590–620. [https://doi.org/10.1177/0022022105278544].

Mount, Michael K.; Barrick, Murray R.; Stewart, Greg L. (1998): Five-Factor Model of Personality and Performance in Jobs Involving Interpersonal Interactions. In: *Human Performance* 11,2–3: 145–165. [https://doi.org/10.1080/08959285.1998.9668029].

Muhammad Awais Bhatti et al. (2014): Effects of Personality Traits (Big Five) on Expatriates Adjustment and Job Performance. In: *Equality, Diversity and Inclusion* 33,1: 73–96. [https://doi.org/10.1108/EDI-01-2013-0001].

Oh, In-Sue (2009): The Five Factor Model of Personality and Job Performance in East Asia: A Cross-Cultural Validity Generalization Study. Doctoral Dissertation. Iowa City, IA: University of Iowa. [http://search.proquest.com/dissertations/docview/304903943/].

Ones, Deniz S. et al. (2017): Cognitive Ability: Measurement and Validity for Employee Selection. In: Farr, James L.; Tippins, Nancy Thomas (Eds.): Handbook of Employee Selection. 2nd ed. New York, NY: Routledge: 251–276.

Ones, Deniz S. et al. (2016): Conceptual and Methodological Complexity of Narrow Trait Measures in Personality-Outcome Research: Better Knowledge by Partitioning Variance from Multiple Latent Traits and Measurement Artifacts. In: *European Journal of Personality* 30,4: 319–321. [https://doi.org/10/bp27].

Ones, Deniz S. et al. (2012): Cross-Cultural Generalization: Using Meta-Analysis to Test Hypotheses about Cultural Variability. In: Ryan, Ann Marie; Leong, Frederick T.L.; Oswald, Frederick L. (Eds.): Conducting Multinational Research Projects in Organizational Psychology: Challenges and Opportunities, APA/MSU Series on Multicultural Psychology 1. Washington, DC: American Psychological Association: 91–122. [https://doi.org/10/5kz].

Ones, Deniz S. et al. (2011): Meta-Analyses of Integrity and Personality Measures for Law Enforcement. Paper. Presented at the Society for Industrial and Organizational Psychology Conference. Chicago, IL. [https://doi.org/10.1037/e518362013-217].

Ones, Deniz S. et al. (2007): In Support of Personality Assessment in Organizational Settings. In: *Personnel Psychology* 60,4: 995–1027. [https://doi.org/10.1111/j.1744-6570.2007.00099.x].

Ones, Deniz S.; Dilchert, Stephan (2009): How Special Are *Executives? How Special Should Executive Selection Be? Observations and Recommendations. In: Industrial and Organizational Psychology* 2,2: 163–170. [https://doi.org/10.1111/j.1754-9434.2009.01127.x].

Ones, Deniz S.; Viswesvaran, Chockalingam (2003): Job-Specific Applicant Pools and National Norms for Personality Scales: Implications for Range-Restriction Corrections in Validation Research. In: *Journal of Applied Psychology* 88,3: 570–577. [https://doi.org/10.1037/0021-9010.88.3.570].

Ones, Deniz S.; Viswesvaran, Chockalingam (2001a): Integrity Tests and Other Criterion-Focused Occupational Personality Scales (COPS) Used in Personnel Selection. In: *International Journal of Selection and Assessment* 9,1/2: 31–39. [https://doi.org/10.1111/1468-2389.00161].

Ones, Deniz S.; Viswesvaran, Chockalingam (2001b): Personality at Work: Criterion-Focused Occupational Personality Scales Used in Personnel Selection. In: Roberts, Brent W.; Hogan, Robert T. (Eds.): Personality Psychology in the Workplace, Decade of Behavior. Washington, DC: American Psychological Association: 63–92. [https://doi.org/10.1037/10434-003].

Ones, Deniz S.; Viswesvaran, Chockalingam (1999): Relative Importance of Personality Dimensions for Expatriate Selection: A Policy Capturing Study. In: *Human Performance* 12,3/4: 275–294. [https://doi.org/10.1080/08959289909539872].

Ones, Deniz S.; Viswesvaran, Chockalingam (1997): Personality Determinants in the Prediction of Aspects of Expatriate Job Success. In: Aycan, Zeynep (Ed.): Expatriate Management: Theory and Research, New Approaches to Employee Management 4. Greenwich, CT: JAI Press: 63–92.

Ones, Deniz S.; Viswesvaran, Chockalingam; Dilchert, Stephan (2005): Personality at Work: Raising Awareness and Correcting Misconceptions. In: *Human Performance* 18,4: 389–404. [https://doi.org/10.1207/s15327043hup1804_5].

Peltokorpi, Vesa; Froese, Fabian J. (2014): Expatriate Personality and Cultural Fit: The Moderating Role of Host Country Context on Job Satisfaction. In: *International Business Review* 23,1: 293–302. [https://doi.org/10.1016/j.ibusrev.2013.05.004].

Peltokorpi, Vesa; Froese, Fabian J. (2012): The Impact of Expatriate Personality Traits on Cross-Cultural Adjustment: A Study with Expatriates in Japan. In: *International Business Review* 21,4: 734–746. [https://doi.org/10.1016/j.ibusrev.2011.08.006].

Ramalu, Subramaniarn Sri et al. (2010): Personality and Expatriate Performance: The Mediating Role of Expatriate Adjustment. In: *Journal of Applied Business Research* 26,6: 113–122. [https://doi.org/10.19030/jabr.v26i6.334].

Roberts, Brent W. et al. (2005): The Structure of Conscientiousness: An Empirical Investigation Based on Seven Major Personality Questionnaires. In: *Personnel Psychology* 58,1: 103–139. [https://doi.org/10.1111/j.1744-6570.2005.00301.x].

Rose, Raduan Che et al. (2010): Expatriate Performance in Overseas Assignments: The Role of Big Five Personality. In: *Asian Social Science* 6,9: 104. [https://doi.org/10/b6p2].

Salgado, Jesús F. (1998): Big Five Personality Dimensions and Job Performance in Army and Civil Occupations: A European Perspective. In: *Human Performance* 11,2–3: 271–288. [https://doi.org/10.1080/08959285.1998.9668034].

Salgado, Jesús F. (1997): The Five Factor Model of Personality and Job Performance in the European Community. In: *Journal of Applied Psychology* 82,1: 30–43. [https://doi.org/10/fbdhdn].

Salgado, Jesús F.; Anderson, Neil; Táuriz, Gabriel (2015): The Validity of Ipsative and Quasi-Ipsative Forced-Choice Personality Inventories for Different Occupational Groups: A Comprehensive Meta-Analysis. In: *Journal of Occupational and Organizational Psychology* 88,4: 797–834. [https://doi.org/10.1111/joop.12098].

Schmidt, Frank L.; Hunter, John E. (2004): General Mental Ability in the World of Work: Occupational Attainment and Job Performance. In: *Journal of Personality and Social Psychology* 86,1: 162–173. [https://doi.org/10.1037/0022-3514.86.1.162].

Schmidt, Frank L.; Oh, In-Sue (2013): Methods for Second Order Meta-Analysis and Illustrative Applications. In: *Organizational Behavior and Human Decision Processes* 121,2: 204–218. [https://doi.org/10.1016/j.obhdp.2013.03.002].

Schmidt, Frank L.; Oh, In-Sue; Shaffer, Jonathan Andrew (2016): The Validity and Utility of Selection Methods in Personnel Psychology: Practical and Theoretical Implications of 100 Years of Research Findings. Fox School of Business Research Paper. Philadelphia, PA: Temple University. [https://doi.org/10.13140/RG.2.2.18843.26400].

Sinangil, Handan Kepir; Ones, Deniz S. (2003): Gender Differences in Expatriate Job Performance. In: *Applied Psychology* 52,3: 461–475. [https://doi.org/10/c36tw5].

Sinangil, Handan Kepir; Ones, Deniz S. (1997): Empirical Investigations of the Host Country Perspective in Expatriate Management. In: Aycan, Zeynep (Ed.): Expatriate Management: Theory and Research, New Approaches to Employee Management 4. Greenwich, CT: JAI Press: 173–205.

Stanek, Kevin C.; Ones, Deniz S. (2018): Taxonomies and Compendia of Cognitive Ability and Personality Measures Relevant to Industrial, Work, and Organizational Psychology. In: Ones, Deniz S. et al. (Eds.): The SAGE Handbook of Industrial, Work and Organizational Psychology. Volume 1: Personnel Psychology and Employee Performance. 2nd ed. London, United Kingdom: Sage: 366–407.

Takeuchi, Riki (2010): A Critical Review of Expatriate Adjustment Research through a Multiple Stakeholder View: Progress, Emerging Trends, and Prospects. In: *Journal of Management* 36,4: 1040–1064. [https://doi.org/10.1177/0149206309349308].

Templer, Klaus J. (2010): Personal Attributes of Expatriate Managers, Subordinate Ethnocentrism, and Expatriate Success: A Host-Country Perspective. In: *International Journal of Human Resource Management* 21,10: 1754–1768. [https://doi.org/10.1080/09585192.2010.500493].

van Aarde, Ninette; Meiring, Deon; Wiernik, Brenton M. (2017): The Validity of the Big Five Personality Traits for Job Performance: Meta-Analyses of South African Studies. In: *International Journal of Selection and Assessment* 25,3: 223–239. [https://doi.org/10.1111/ijsa.12175].

Van der Zee, Karen I.; van Oudenhoven, Jan Pieter (2000): The Multicultural Personality Questionnaire: A Multidimensional Instrument of Multicultural Effectiveness. In: *European Journal of Personality* 14,4: 291–309. [https://doi.org/10/b7jfj8].

Vinchur, Andrew J. et al. (1998): A Meta-Analytic Review of Predictors of Job Performance for Salespeople. In: *Journal of Applied Psychology* 83,4: 586–597. [https://doi.org/10.1037/0021-9010.83.4.586].

Viswesvaran, Chockalingam (1993): Modeling Job Performance: Is There a General Factor? Doctoral Dissertation. Iowa City, IA: The University of Iowa. [http://www.dtic.mil/dtic/tr/fulltext/u2/a294282.pdf].

Viswesvaran, Chockalingam; Ones, Deniz S. (2017): Job Performance Models. In: Rogelberg, Steven G. (Ed.): The SAGE Encyclopedia of Industrial and Organizational Psychology. 2nd ed. Thousand Oaks, CA: Sage: 797–801. [https://doi.org/10.4135/9781483386874.n275].

Viswesvaran, Chockalingam; Ones, Deniz S. (2000): Perspectives on Models of Job Performance. In: *International Journal of Selection and Assessment* 8,4: 216–226. [https://doi.org/10/ctcc82].

Viswesvaran, Chockalingam; Ones, Deniz S.; Hough, Leaetta M. (1998): Construct Validity of Managerial Potential Scales. Presented at the Society for Industrial and Organizational Psychology Annual Meeting. Dallas, TX.

Viswesvaran, Chockalingam; Ones, Deniz S.; Schmidt, Frank L. (1996): Comparative Analysis of the Reliability of Job Performance Ratings. In: *Journal of Applied Psychology* 81,5: 557–574. [https://doi.org/10/c8f68f].

Viswesvaran, Chockalingam; Schmidt, Frank L.; Ones, Deniz S. (2005): Is There a General Factor in Job Performance Ratings? A Meta-Analytic Framework for Disentangling Substantive and Error Influences. In: *Journal of Applied Psychology* 90,1: 108–131. [https://doi.org/10.1037/0021-9010.90.1.108].

Wiernik, Brenton M.; Dilchert, Stephan; Ones, Deniz S. (2016): Creative Interests and Personality: Scientific versus Artistic Creativity. In: *Zeitschrift für Arbeits- und Organisationspsychologie*, Special Issue: Assessment of Vocational Interests 60,2: 65–78. [https://doi.org/10.1026/0932-4089/a000211].

Wiernik, Brenton M.; Rüger, Heiko; Ones, Deniz S. (2018): Advancing Expatriate Research in Public and Private Sectors. In: Wiernik, Brenton M.; Rüger, Heiko; Ones, Deniz S. (Eds.): Managing Expatriates: Success Factors in Private and Public Domains, Series on Population Studies 50. Opladen, Germany: Barbara Budrich Publishers.

Wilmot, Michael P.; Wiernik, Brenton M.; Kostal, Jack W. (2014): Increasing Interrater Reliability Using Composite Performance Measures. In: *Industrial and Organizational Psychology* 7,4: 539–542. [https://doi.org/10/38v].

Woo, Sang Eun et al. (2014): Openness to Experience: Its Lower Level Structure, Measurement, and Cross-Cultural Equivalence. In: *Journal of Personality Assessment*, Openness to Experience 96,1: 29–45. [https://doi.org/10/33v].

Young, Rudolph (2011): Is There a Perfect Personality for Expatriates? The Chronicle of Higher Education. [http://www.chronicle.com/article/Is-There-a-Perfect-Personality/126964/].

Core Self-Evaluative Traits: Self-Efficacy, Locus of Control, Optimism and Diplomat Success

Herbert Fliege and Brenton M. Wiernik

Abstract

Work-related international assignments create a need for adjustment which may cause stress, diminish work satisfaction, and affect health which, in turn, may result in assignment failure. Foreign Service assignments, unlike most business assignments, follow a rotational pattern with postings to another country every few years, involving a regularly recurring need for adjustment. The study examines psychological factors that could facilitate adjustment and protect from negative outcomes. The focus is on three core self-evaluations (CSE) – self-efficacy, internal locus of control (LOC), and dispositional optimism. We test the hypothesis that each of these core self-evaluations is associated with better expatriate well-being in Foreign Service personnel. Employees of the German Federal Foreign Office in rotation were surveyed using online questionnaires on stress, physical and mental health, locational adjustment, job satisfaction, and work-family conflict as outcomes, and core self-evaluations as predictors. Each self-evaluative trait individually, as well as a composite CSE measure, showed strong relations with satisfaction, work–family reconciliation, health, and (low) stress. Relations were weaker with locational adjustment. Correlational patterns for the CSE facets were very similar, and all positive criterion relations were accounted for by the general CSE factor. Core self-evaluations play an important role for expatriate well-being in terms of health, work, and adjustment outcomes. Sending organizations can draw on these findings with respect to personnel recruitment, selection, and pre-departure training.

1   Introduction

Overseas relocations involve various challenges related to cultural, environmental, work role, partnership, and family adjustment (Gregersen/Black 1990). When these challenges become overly stressful, negative health outcomes, maladjustment and dissatisfaction, and expatriate turnover may result (Black 1990; Hechanova et al. 2003; Mendenhall/Oddou 1985). The variety and intensities of stressors associated with international assignments leads many expatriates to experience mental health problems (Foyle et al. 1998). Compared to domestic employees, expatriates show increased levels of psychosocial distress and worse mental and work-related well-being (Anderzén/Arnetz 1999; Nicholson/Imaizumi 1993).

However, personal characteristics are likely to lead expatriates to have differing responses to the challenges of international assignments. While some expatriates may view learning new cultural customs, moving one's family, and adapting to changing work roles as insurmountable challenges, others may see them as opportunities to learn, grow, and demonstrate their capabilities. The transactional model of stress (Lazarus/Folkman 1984) posits that differences in appraisal of stressful events (i.e., as positive, neutral, or negative) and in evaluation of one's capacity to manage them can dramatically change the degree to which individuals' coping resources are taxed and to which they experience negative strain outcomes. A variety of traits have been linked with individual differences in expatriate outcomes. For example, the personality trait Openness (Albrecht et al. 2014), tolerance for ambiguity (Albrecht et al. 2018a, Chapter 4, this volume), and interpersonal skills (Bhaskar-Shrinivas et al. 2005) have all been shown to positively contribute (with varying magnitudes) to effective adjustment of expatriates to their new international contexts.

Self-efficacy, a generalized belief that one is capable of overcoming challenges and achieving goals (Bandura 1997), is among the most frequently studied individual differences in expatriate research and shows a moderate positive relationship with adjustment (Bhaskar-Shrinivas et al. 2005; Hechanova et al. 2003). Self-efficacy is a broad evaluative trait that reflects a fundamental attitude individuals hold about themselves. Judge et al. (1997) referred to these broad self-evaluative traits as "core self-evaluations (CSE)" and identified general self-esteem and internal locus of control as additional traits within this cluster. Emotional Stability is also typically included as a CSE trait, but this may reflect an overly narrow conceptualization of the Emotional Stability construct (e.g., as simply the inverse of self-esteem; Judge et al. 2004; cf. DeYoung 2015) and Emotional Stability items show divergent patterns of factor loadings from other CSE traits (Albrecht et al. 2013). Judge et al. (1997) also included positive affectivity, negative affectivity, and optimism/pessimism as CSE traits, but these have been infrequently included in subsequent CSE research. However, meta-analytic evidence supports including optimism within this domain (Judge/Bono 2001a). Subsequent research has supported "core self-evaluations" as a higher-order factor subsuming these evaluative traits (Judge et al. 2002, 2003; but there is controversy over what traits meet both conceptual and empirical criteria to be included in this domain; Chen 2012; Johnson et al. 2011, 2012). Substantial research has connected core self-evaluations to work attitudes, job performance, motivation, and stress management, among other criteria (see Chang et al. 2012 for a comprehensive review and meta-analysis). Interestingly, in many studies, the higher-order CSE accounts for all the predictive power of the individual CSE traits and shows stronger criterion relations than any individual CSE trait (that is, the predictive power of self-efficacy, locus of control, etc. appears to stem from their shared variance in the higher-order factor rather than from the individual traits per se).

While self-efficacy has been frequently studied in expatriate research, other core self-evaluative traits have received comparatively less attention (e.g., Lazarova et al. 2010, included optimism among their list of resources for expatriate success, but, to our knowledge, no expatriate studies have explicitly measured this trait). In this study, we examine the role of several CSE traits for coping with the demands of international job-related mobility. We measure three self-evaluations in this study – generalized self-efficacy, internal locus of control, and dispositional optimism/lack of pessimism. These three variables were chosen because they play key roles in psychological research on stress and coping (Carver et al. 2010; Jerusalem/Schwarzer 2014; Krause/Stryker 1984) and because each has at various times been conceptualized as part of the core self-evaluations domain (Judge/Bono 2001a). Each of these traits is a broadly-defined positive self-evaluation, but they have some important distinctions. Optimism reflects the extent to which people hold generalized favorable expectancies of good outcomes (Carver/Scheier 2014). Optimism is self-evaluative as it concerns one's own future and beliefs in one's competence are a key source of optimism (Judge/Bono 2001a). However, the concept does not preclude external agents as the source of positive outcomes. For optimists, a good outcome may occur independently of their actions. This stands in contrast to internal locus of control (LOC; Krause/Stryker 1984), which refers to a general belief that events in one's life are the result of one's own actions, as opposed to external forces. Locus of control beliefs reflect the agent to which outcomes are attributed, but they do not specify what outcomes are likely (i.e., individuals with internal LOC may anticipate negative outcomes because of a perceived lack of competence). These conceptual distinctions acknowledged, empirically, these traits are strongly related (Judge et al. 2002; Scheier et al. 1994), and it is easy to understand their strong relations (i.e., someone who believes they are capable and in control of their lives would presumably feel optimistic about the future).

1.1   Study Aims

This study examines associations between diplomats' core self-evaluations and their *health, work*, and *adjustment outcomes*. Expatriate research has mainly focused on work and adjustment outcomes, such as locational adjustment, job satisfaction, job performance, organizational commitment, and turnover, as indicators of expatriate success (Lazarova/ Thomas 2012), with adjustment dominating research (Albrecht et al. 2018b). We hope to widen this perspective to include expatriate well-being, including personal, family, and health outcomes.

In terms of health outcomes, we examine the relations of self-evaluations to perceived stress and subjective health. Because of the stressful nature of expatriation, health problems are among the major causes of early return from international assignments (Burkholder et al. 2010; Patel et al. 2006), and models of stress management for expatriates have been frequently studied (Brown 2008). However, evidence on strain and health outcomes, including physical and mental health, of expatriates is very limited. Protective factors, other than mere medical parameters, which could mitigate expatriates' health risks have not been sufficiently identified.

In terms of personal and family outcomes, we explore the role of self-evaluations in determining expatriates' perceptions of reconcilability between work and family life. Work–family balance is an important contributor to work and life satisfaction, relationship satisfaction, and other positive life outcomes (Mesmer-Magnus/Viswesvaran 2005). Work–family balance can be easily impaired by the challenges that international relocations involve for expatriate families (Caligiuri/Lazarova 2005). Reconcilability issues are a prominent reason for the failure of international assignments (Black/Stephens 1989; Caligiuri et al. 1998; Shaffer/Harrison 1998; Stephens/Black 1991). Both expatriate employees and their accompanying partners are exposed to the demands of international adjustment (Brown 2008; Shaffer/Harrison 2001), and expatriates' and spouses' adjustment mutually influence each other (Bhaskar-Shrinivas et al. 2005; Takeuchi et al. 2002; Van der Zee et al. 2005), so understanding factors that contribute to work–family reconciliation among expatriates is vital to ensure international assignment success.

Each of the core self-evaluations included in this study have been examined in previous research and associated with better adjustment to life stress and better health and well-being (Carver et al. 2010; Schwarzer 2014; Steptoe/Wardle 2001), and self-efficacy and LOC have additionally also been associated with expatriate well-being, adjustment, and success (Anderzén/Arnetz 1999; Bhaskar-Shrinivas et al. 2005; Black 1990; Harrison et al. 1996; Hechanova et al. 2003; Osman-Gani/Rockstuhl 2009; Shaffer et al. 1999; Ward/Kennedy 1992). Accordingly, in this study, we expected to find moderate positive relations between expatriate self-evaluations and all health and work-related outcomes.

Heretofore, no studies on self-evaluations in expatriates have examined Foreign Service personnel. Although many of the demands and stressors faced by diplomats are comparable to those faced by private sector expatriates, there are also some important differences. Most importantly, unlike business expatriates, Foreign Service employees are exposed to a form of mobility that follows a rotational pattern of moves to a new host country every three to five years (for the German Foreign Service; Brandt/Buck 2005). This continuous rotation pattern is quite different from the once-off, often developmental nature of most private sector international assignments (Stahl et al. 2002; Wiernik/Wille 2018). Although frequent relocation is part of the occupational routine for Foreign Service employees and takes place within a highly institutionalized setting (Brandt/Buck 2005; Holland 1984), it can nevertheless cause serious psychological distress in individuals as it repeatedly generates uncertainty, reduces control, and increases ambiguity (Wilkinson/Singh 2010). As this unique population has been rarely studied in expatriate research, an additional contribution of this research is to examine the role of self-evaluations in supporting well-being in diplomatic expatriates experiencing repeated international relocation.

2   Methods

2.1   Data Collection and Sample

The data used for this study originate from a cross-sectional survey among employees of the German Federal Foreign Office in rotation (Rüger et al. 2013). Participants were diplomats and other rotating employees of the Foreign Office working in a variety of roles and at various hierarchical levels. Data were collected in late 2011 using online questionnaires. All employees were invited to participate in the study. $N = 2,598$ employees responded (response rate = 35.5%), of whom $N = 1,777$ were on post abroad (not in Germany). The sample comprised 41% female and 59% male employees with a mean age of 45.7 years ($SD = 9.7$; range 20 to 67 years). Participating diplomats had an average record of 5 international assignments ($SD = 2.5$). Self-rated questionnaires concerning stress, health, locational adjustment, job satisfaction, work-family conflict and personal resources were administered electronically as part of a larger survey on experiences working in the Foreign Office (see Wiernik et al. 2018, Chapter 1, and Rüger et al. 2018, Appendix B, this volume, for more details).

2.2   Outcome Measures

Stress. Experienced stress was measured with items from the German version of the Perceived Stress Questionnaire (PSQ; Fliege et al. 2005). The PSQ measures subjectively experienced stress independent of a specific source, objective situation, or stage in the coping process. We included the four items with the highest discriminatory power (corrected item-scale correlation) from the four subscales (*worries, tension, joy* [reversed], *demands*). Internal consistency of the stress measure was Cronbach's $\alpha = .72$.

    Health. Health was measured using subscales from the German version of the Quality of Life Questionnaire (QLQ; Aaronson et al. 1993). This measure has been used in a variety of medical and non-medical populations. The subscales selected for the present study were those that were most relevant to non-infirmed individuals. The QLQ physical health subscale consisted of 8 items assessing various physical symptoms (e.g., "Have you had trouble sleeping?", "Did you need to rest?"). The QLQ mental health subscale consisted of three items assessing emotional functioning ("Were you worried?", "Were you irritable?", "Did you feel low?"). These subscales were summed and combined with two items that were global assessments of health and quality of life to form an overall health score (13 items total). Reliabilities for these scales were α = .88 (Physical), .83 (Mental), and .92 (Overall).

Locational adjustment. Adjustment is the most commonly studied outcome in expatriate research (Black et al. 1991). In this study, adjustment was measured using eight items assessing the degree of comfort an individual feels living in their new location, including physical conditions (e.g., climate, safety, housing conditions), completing everyday tasks, and meeting psychological needs (e.g., finding social contact and recreation, living in accordance with one's values). Black et al. referred to this form of adjustment as "general adjustment" (in contrast to comfort interacting with host country nationals [interaction adjustment] and fulfilling new work responsibilities [work adjustment]). Schlunze (2002) proposed "locational adjustment" as an alternative label for this construct, as it specifically refers to expatriates' ability to function effectively in their new countries. We agree with Schlunze's reasoning and adopt this terminology in preference to the less descriptive "general adjustment" (which might be confused with the construct representing the shared variance among each facet of adjustment; Wiernik et al. 2015) or "cultural adjustment" (cf. Bhaskar-Shrinivas et al. 2005; as this outcome includes a broader set of challenges than merely adapting to a new culture). The locational adjustment scale had a reliability of α = .84.

Job satisfaction. Expatriates' satisfaction with various qualities of their job was measured with 13 items developed for this study (α = .77). Items specified satisfaction with the level of workplace cooperation, pay, recognition, meaningfulness, autonomy, task variety, and job security (e.g., "How satisfied are you with the working atmosphere at your current post?").

Satisfaction with the rotation process. Diplomats' satisfaction with the rotation process was assessed with four items developed for this study. One item assessed global satisfaction with the rotation process. The second item asked respondents to indicate if they perceived living in a rotational scheme as an opportunity, a simple necessity, or as a hindrance. The third and fourth items asked whether the frequent rotation interfered with expatriates' ability to perform effectively or retain organizational knowledge. Cronbach's α was .63.

Work–family conflict. Perceptions of conflict between working in the Foreign Service and other life responsibilities were measured with 12 items developed for this study. Items included perceptions of conflict between family life and both general work demands as well as the specific process of frequent international moves (e.g., "To what extent do you consider working in Foreign Service to be reconcilable with having a family?"). Cronbach's α was .81.

2.3   Predictor Measures

Scales assessing three core self-evaluative traits were used as predictors of health- and work-related expatriate outcomes – general self-efficacy, internal locus of control, and dispositional pessimism/optimism.

Self-efficacy. Self-efficacy was measured using a short form of the General Self-Efficacy Scale (Schwarzer/Jerusalem 1995) comprising five items that assess individuals' self-efficacy toward broadly defined goals and situations (e.g., "I can always manage to solve difficult problems if I try hard enough"; Scholler et al. 1999). Cronbach's α was .72.

Internal Locus of Control (LOC). The degree to which the expatriates feel they are in control of the outcomes in their life was assessed with four items that were derived from an inspection of the research and existing LOC instruments. The items were adapted for the study with a view to keeping them short and comprehensive (e.g., "I am in charge of my own life's destiny."). Cronbach's α was .51.

Pessimism/Optimism. Optimism was assessed using a short form of the Life Orientation Test (Scheier/Carver 1985). The scale included 4 items intended to measure dispositional optimistic outcome expectancies (e.g., "I'm always optimistic about my future.") with two items focusing on optimism and two items focusing on pessimism (e.g., "I almost never expect things to work out the way I want them to."; Scholler et al. 1999). The pessimism items were reverse-scored to compute an overall optimism score. Cronbach's α was .61.

Core self-evaluations. In addition to examining outcome relations for each of the evaluative traits separately, we also examined relations with the general core self-evaluations construct (Judge/Bono 2001b) by computing a unit-weighted composite of the self-efficacy, internal LOC, and optimism scales.

2.4   Analyses

We computed bivariate correlations between the three core self-evaluations and all outcome variables. For each relation, we report the sample size, observed correlation (r), and the correlation corrected for attenuation due to measurement error in both variables (r_c). Measurement error has a systematic downward biasing effect on observed correlations, leading to reduced statistical power, increased Type II error, and overly pessimistic estimates of construct relations. Disattenuation corrects this bias and provides more accurate estimates of relations (Schmidt/Hunter 1996). Additionally, disattenuation allows us to compare correlations across predictors and criteria; some constructs (e.g., stress) could only be measured with a small number of items and thus have relatively low internal consistency, making them more affected by measurement error than constructs assessed with more robust measures. As a measure of the precision of the estimated relations, we report 95% confidence intervals around the corrected correlation coefficients. We examined the magnitude of the corrected correlations. Based on the empirical distributions of effect sizes for general psychological and clinical research reported by Hemphill (2003), we interpreted values less than .10 as negligible, .10–.19 as small, .20–.29 as moderate, .30–.44 as large and values from .45 as very large.

In addition to zero-order correlations, we were also interested in examining the relative contribution of each of these core self-evaluative traits independent of the contribution of the general CSE factor. To estimate these incremental contributions, we computed semipartial (part) correlations between each of the core self-evaluative scales and the criteria after controlling for the other two scales.

3   Results

3.1   Overall Core Self-Evaluations Relations

Proponents on the core self-evaluations construct posit that specific self-evaluative traits are facets of a broader tendency to hold positive self-views. Facets of core self-evaluations typically show very strong correlations, indicating the presence of a dominant general factor that accounts for the majority of the reliable variance in these traits (Ree et al. 2015). The results of this study support regarding the three self-evaluative traits examined as facets of a dominant general CSE factor. Self-efficacy showed a correlation of $r = .20$ ($r_c = .48$) with internal LOC and of $r = .44$ ($r_c = .66$) with optimism. Internal LOC correlated $r = .37$

(r_c = .66) with optimism. These strong correlations lead to a single general factor accounting for 63% of the reliable variance in the three scales.

Bivariate correlations between the core self-evaluations composite and outcomes are shown in Table 1. All bivariate associations emerged are in the expected direction. The core self-evaluations composite correlated positively with all health outcomes (overall, mental, physical), locational adjustment, job satisfaction, and satisfaction with the rotation, and negatively with stress and work–family conflict. As could be expected given the large sample size, confidence intervals were relatively narrow (and thus, all correlations are statistically significant). Correlations were very strong for health outcomes (mean absolute r_c = .49), for satisfaction with one's job (r_c = .51) and with life in rotation (r_c = .48), and with perceived work–family conflict (r_c = -.41). CSE was only weakly related to locational adjustment (r_c = .14). These correlations are in line with previous primary studies and meta-analyses of relations between core self-evaluations and stress perceptions (Chang et al. 2012), subjective health (Kammeyer-Mueller et al. 2009; Tsaousis et al. 2007), job satisfaction (Chang et al. 2012), work–family conflict (Boyar/Mosley 2007), and expatriate adjustment (Bhaskar-Shrinivas et al. 2005).

Table 1: Relations of Core Self-Evaluations Composite with Diplomat Outcomes

Outcome	N	r	r_c	95% CI
Health outcomes				
Stress	1,514	-.37	-.49	-.28, -.40
Subjective health: Overall	1,424	.41	.48	.43, .54
Subjective health: Mental	1,424	.43	.53	.48, .59
Subjective health: Physical	1,424	.35	.42	.37, .48
Work and adjustment outcomes				
Locational adjustment	1,551	.11	.14	.08, .20
Job satisfaction	1,540	.40	.51	.46, .57
Satisfaction with rotation	1,358	.33	.48	.41, .54
Work–family conflict	1,275	-.33	-.41	-.47, -.36

Note: r_c = correlation corrected for attenuation due to measurement error in both variables; 95% CI = 95% confidence interval for the corrected correlations.

3.2   *CSE Facet Relations*

After examining criterion relations with the CSE composite, we also examined relations with individual core self-evaluation facets. Bivariate and semipartial correlations for the three CSE facets (self-efficacy, LOC, pessimism/optimism) are shown in Tables 2–4, respectively. Again, all bivariate criterion relationships were in the expected direction. Self-efficacy, internal locus of control, and optimism each showed strong to very strong relations with stress, subjective health, job and rotation satisfaction, and work–family conflict. CSE facets also again showed weak to moderate relations (negligible in the case of self-efficacy) with locational adjustment.

Table 2: Relations of Self-Efficacy with Diplomat Outcomes

Outcome	N	r	r_c	95% CI	r_{part}
Health outcomes					
Stress	1,257	-.25	-.34	-.15, -.29	-.02
Subjective health: Overall	1,201	.29	.36	.29, .42	-.05
Subjective health: Mental	1,201	.32	.41	.35, .48	-.10
Subjective health: Physical	1,201	.24	.30	.23, .37	-.02
Work and adjustment outcomes					
Locational adjustment	1,277	.05	.06	-.01, .13	.09
Job satisfaction	1,272	.27	.37	.30, .44	-.02
Satisfaction with rotation	1,145	.24	.36	.28, .44	-.10
Work–family conflict	1,275	-.22	-.29	-.22, -.35	.02

Note: r_c = correlation corrected for attenuation due to measurement error in both variables; 95% CI = 95% confidence interval for the corrected correlations; r_{part} = part (semi-partial) correlation, controlling for internal locus of control and optimism.

Table 3: Relations of Internal Locus of Control (LOC) to Diplomat Outcomes

Outcome	N	r	r_c	95% CI	r_{part}
Health outcomes					
Stress	1,339	-.28	-.46	-.26, -.42	.22
Subjective health: Overall	1,273	.31	.45	.38, .53	-.22
Subjective health: Mental	1,273	.32	.49	.42, .57	-.26
Subjective health: Physical	1,273	.27	.40	.33, .48	-.20
Work and adjustment outcomes					
Locational adjustment	1,357	.08	.13	.05, .21	-.01
Job satisfaction	1,349	.30	.48	.41, .56	-.25
Satisfaction with rotation	1,211	.24	.42	.33, .52	-.21
Work–family conflict	1,354	-.27	-.41	-.34, -.49	.24

Note: r_c = correlation corrected for attenuation due to measurement error in both variables; 95% CI = 95% confidence interval for the corrected correlations; r_{part} = part (semi-partial) correlation, controlling for self-efficacy and optimism.

Table 4: Relations of Self-Efficacy with Diplomat Outcomes

Outcome	N	r	r_c	95% CI	r_{part}
Health outcomes					
Stress	1,352	-.35	-.52	-.28, -.43	.36
Subjective health: Overall	1,286	.37	.49	.43, .56	-.27
Subjective health: Mental	1,286	.38	.53	.47, .60	-.29
Subjective health: Physical	1,286	.31	.42	.36, .49	-.21
Work and adjustment outcomes					
Locational adjustment	1,374	.14	.19	.12, .26	-.17
Job satisfaction	1,368	.36	.53	.47, .60	-.34
Satisfaction with rotation	1,226	.27	.44	.35, .52	-.18
Work–family conflict	1,372	-.28	-.40	-.33, -.47	.17

Note: r_c = correlation corrected for attenuation due measurement error in both variables; 95% CI = 95% confidence interval for the corrected correlations; r_{part} = part (semi-partial) correlation, controlling for self-efficacy and internal locus of control.

It is likely that much of these criterion relations are attributable to the shared self-evaluative nature of these traits (i.e., they both reflect the general core self-evaluations factor), rather than due to the specific content of the facets (i.e., self-efficacy vs. locus of control vs. optimism). To test this possibility, we examined the semipartial correlations between each of the CSE facets and the expatriate outcomes, controlling for the other two CSE facet scales. These values reflect the relation between each criterion and the part of the CSE facet that is unique to that trait (not shared with the other facets). These values are shown in last columns of Tables 2–4. Results show that all of the positive relations between CSE facets and expatriate outcomes are attributable to the common CSE general factor. After controlling for shared variance with other CSE facets, self-efficacy showed essentially negligible relations with all criteria. For LOC and optimism, all semipartial correlations substantially decreased in magnitude, but also reversed in direction. This indicates that the unique part of these facets is associated with *worse* expatriate outcomes. For example, after controlling for the general CSE factor, optimism is weakly to moderately associated with negative outcomes, increased stress and work–family conflict, dissatisfaction, and poor locational adjustment. These results are similar to studies examining other multidimensional constructs with dominant general factors. For example, while overall job satisfaction is positively related to job performance, the specific variance of some satisfaction facets is negatively related to performance (Wiernik et al. 2015), and facets of Extraversion correlate in opposite directions with health and subjective well-being after controlling for the common trait variance (Chen et al. 2012). These reversed correlations should not be over-interpreted. After removing general factor variance, reliability of the specific factors is likely to be very small (Gignac/Watkins 2013), so there is substantial measurement and sampling error in our estimates of the specific factor correlations. From a practical perspective, the best conclusion to draw is that self-efficacy, internal locus of control, and optimism are all positively related to subjective health, stress, satisfaction, and work-family balance, but that all of their positive relations are attributable to individuals' overall positive self-regard (Judge/ Bono 2001a).

4   Discussion

The findings confirm the hypothesis that expatriates who possess more confident self-evaluations in terms of self-efficacy beliefs, internal locus of control, and optimism tend to experience less stress and work–family conflict and better satisfaction and subjective health outcomes. Applying a stress research perspective to the context of international job assignments, these results endorse the major role of positive self-evaluations for successfully coping with the stressfulness of expatriation. Individuals with high levels of positive self-regard approach the challenges of expatriation more confidently, enabling them to better manage the plethora of stressors associated with international assignments.

The wide range of outcomes associated with positive core self-evaluations is of note. Previous meta-analytic has shown strong relations between CSE and job satisfaction in a wide variety of job contexts (Chang et al. 2012); this study confirms the important role of CSE for supporting work satisfaction in the context of international assignments. This study also found that CSE was a strong contributor to satisfaction with the process of recurring international job assignments, a form of satisfaction that is unique to the specific job context of international diplomacy (Brandt/Buck 2005). Research on Foreign Service personnel is scarce and, to our knowledge, satisfaction with the rotation process has not been examined as an outcome in other research. Rotation is a central feature of the work situation in diplomacy. Thus, satisfaction with this scheme is important not just for the success of the current diplomatic assignment, but also for the ongoing process of repeated assignments. As a result, knowing the important role CSE plays in driving satisfaction with this process can help the Foreign Office and other employers of expatriates in similar contexts support satisfaction during long international careers.

CSE also contributed to reduced perceptions of work–family conflict. While balance between work and non-work roles is important in any context, expatriate research has explicitly pointed to the importance of accompanying partners' and families' adjustment in supporting or detracting from expatriate success (Black/Stephens 1989; Caligiuri et al. 1998; Shaffer/Harrison 1998). The recurring nature of international assignments for the expatriates in the current sample, as opposed to once-in-a-lifetime assignments, renders even more difficult the challenges faced by accompanying partners (e.g., difficulty pursuing their own careers, discontinuity in social and educational environments for children). Accordingly, the present results highlight core self-evaluations as a key factor that can help Foreign Service expatriates to balance their competing life demands and thus contribute to the success of their international assignments.

Finally, core self-evaluations were strongly related to both mental and physical health outcomes. Health problems are one of the most common factors leading to the failure of international assignments (Patel et al. 2006), so these results again emphasize the role of positive self-evaluations as a protective factor contributing to sustained expatriate success.

The one criterion examined that shows a weaker relation with core self-evaluations is locational adjustment. CSE was only weakly related to expatriates' ability to effectively manage daily tasks and feel comfortable in their new location ($r_c = .14$). This value is similar to meta-analytic estimates of the relationship between self-efficacy and locational (i.e., not interaction or work) adjustment (Bhaskar-Shrinivas et al. 2005). Two factors may contribute to this relatively low criterion relationship. First, locational adjustment may be more strongly influenced by external factors than by individuals' attitudes. While the self-confidence associated with high CSE make expatriates more willing to face these challenges, it is likely that other factors, such as cognitive ability, interpersonal skills, and social support structures, will have a stronger impact on whether or not expatriates can actually overcome them (Hechanova et al. 2003). If this is the case, it behooves sending organizations to proactively train, prepare, and support employees before sending them on international assignments, as general self-confidence will not be adequate to ensure successful adjustment and performance. Alternatively, the weak relationship may stem from the nature of the core self-evaluations measures used. Self-efficacy, internal locus of control, and optimism were each measured in a context-neutral manner without reference to expatriates' international situations. Locational adjustment is an outcome which is uniquely specific to expatriation, so its weak relations with self-evaluations may be the result of bandwidth misalignment (Hogan/Roberts 1996) – while core self-evaluations may predict context-general outcomes (such as health or job satisfaction, which were measured using context-general scales developed in the broader psychological and health literatures) well, more context-specific outcomes may require self-evaluation measures that are contextualized to the specific international context. Personality research (Shaffer/Postlethwaite 2012), especially research on self-efficacy (Seltzer 2013), has found that contextualized measures often show stronger criterion relations than general measures. It is likely that CSE measures that directly assessed self-evaluations with regard to the challenges of expatriation, such as interacting with individuals from other cultures (cf. Bhaskar-Shrinivas et al. 2004; Osman-Gani/ Rockstuhl 2009) or adapting to new situations (see Waibel et al. 2018, Chapter 3, this volume), would show stronger relations with locational adjustment. Future research should explore this possibility.

4.1   Overall CSE versus CSE Facets

We examined three different self-evaluations in this study – generalized self-efficacy, internal locus of control, and dispositional optimism. These traits can be conceptually distinguished and, indeed, correlations among these traits showed that substantial unique variance was present even after accounting for the general CSE factor (mean r_c = .60; 37% reliable variance not accounted for by the general factor). However, despite this empirical distinctiveness, all of the positive relations between the individual CSE facets and expatriate outcomes were accounted for by the general factor. After removing the shared variance, CSE facets showed negligible or even negative relationships with expatriate well-being. These results suggest that future expatriate research could benefit from use of shorter measures directly assessing the CSE general factor (e.g., Judge et al. 2003; see Albrecht et al. 2013, for a well-validated German translation). Shorter measures would help to reduce respondent fatigue and allow for measures of other important constructs to be included. Our results suggest that little will be lost by use of such general measures.

4.2   Implications for Expatriate Selection and Management

Core self-evaluations are often regarded as some of the most important traits for determining workplace success (Judge/Bono 2001b). The present study supports this conclusion for attitudinal and well-being outcomes of expatriates. Sending organizations can apply these findings by tailoring recruitment strategies for expatriates toward individuals who express not only an interest in but also appropriate confidence in dealing with the challenges of international work assignments (Deller 1997; Phillips et al. 2014). These individuals are likely to demonstrate the highest levels of enduring well-being through their international assignments. Moreover, employers should also help their employees to develop and strengthen their optimism, internal control, self-efficacy and other self-evaluative beliefs

(Chen 2012) before starting on an overseas assignment and throughout their tenure (Deshpande/ Viswesvaran 1992). Such prevention strategies could help maintain health and work satisfaction and thus contribute to expatriate success (Hechanova et al. 2003).

References

Aaronson, Neil K. et al. (1993): The European Organization for Research and Treatment of Cancer QLQ-C30: A Quality-of-Life Instrument for Use in International Clinical Trials in Oncology. In: *Journal of the National Cancer Institute* 85,5: 365–376. [https://doi.org/10/d9d26h].

Albrecht, Anne-Grit et al. (2014): Openness in Cross-Cultural Work Settings: A Multicountry Study of Expatriates. In: *Journal of Personality Assessment*, Openness to Experience 96,1: 64–75. [https://doi.org/10.1080/00223891.2013.821074].

Albrecht, Anne-Grit et al. (2013): Construct- and Criterion-Related Validity of the German Core Self-Evaluations Scale: A Multi-Study Investigation. In: *Journal of Personnel Psychology* 12,2: 85–91. [https://doi.org/10.1027/1866-5888/a000070].

Albrecht, Anne-Grit et al. (2018a): Tolerance of Ambiguity: Relations with Expatriate Adjustment and Job Performance. In: Wiernik, Brenton M.; Rüger, Heiko; Ones, Deniz S. (Eds.): Managing Expatriates: Success Factors in Private and Public Domains, Series on Population Studies 50. Opladen, Germany: Barbara Budrich Publishers.

Albrecht, Anne-Grit; Ones, Deniz S.; Sinangil, Handan Kepir (2018b): Expatriate Management. In: Ones, Deniz S. et al. (Eds.): The SAGE Handbook of Industrial, Work and Organizational Psychology. Volume 3: Managerial Psychology and Organizational Approaches. 2nd ed. London, United Kingdom: Sage: 429–468.

Anderzén, Ingrid; Arnetz, Bengt B. (1999): Psychophysiological Reactions to International Adjustment: Results from a Controlled, Longitudinal Study. In: *Psychotherapy and Psychosomatics* 68,2: 67–75. [https://doi.org/10.1159/000012315].

Bandura, Albert (1997): Self-Efficacy: The Exercise of Control. New York: Freeman.

Bhaskar-Shrinivas, Purnima et al. (2005): Input-Based and Time-Based Models of International Adjustment: Meta-Analytic Evidence and Theoretical Extensions. In: *Academy of Management Journal* 48,2: 257–281. [https://doi.org/10.5465/AMJ.2005.16928400].

Bhaskar-Shrinivas, Purnima et al. (2004): What Have We Learned about Expatriate Adjustment?: Answers Accumulated from 23 Years of Research. In: *Academy of Management Proceedings* 2004,1: A1–A6. [https://doi.org/10.5465/AMBPP.2004.13863144].

Black, J. Stewart (1990): Locus of Control, Social Support, Stress, and Adjustment in International Transfers. In: *Asia Pacific Journal of Management* 7,1: 1–29. [https://doi.org/10/b8nrr6].

Black, J. Stewart; Mendenhall, Mark E.; Oddou, Gary R. (1991): Toward a Comprehensive Model of International Adjustment: An Integration of Multiple Theoretical Perspectives. In: *Academy of Management Review* 16,2: 291–317. [https://doi.org/10/fn7m8b].

Black, J. Stewart; Stephens, Gregory K. (1989): The Influence of the Spouse on American Expatriate Adjustment and Intent to Stay in Pacific Rim Overseas Assignments. In: *Journal of Management* 15,4: 529–544. [https://doi.org/10.1177/014920638901500403].

Boyar, Scott L.; Mosley, Donald C., Jr. (2007): The Relationship between Core Self-Evaluations and Work and Family Satisfaction: The Mediating Role of Work-family Conflict and Facilitation. In: *Journal of Vocational Behavior* 71,2: 265–281. [https://doi.org/10.1016/j.jvb.2007.06.001].

Brandt, Enrico; Buck, Christian (2005): Auswärtiges Amt: Diplomatie als Beruf. 4th ed. Wiesbaden, Germany: VS Verlag für Sozialwissenschaften. [https://doi.org/10/b6k9].

Brown, Robert J. (2008): Dominant Stressors on Expatriate Couples during International Assignments. In: *International Journal of Human Resource Management* 19,6: 1018–1034. [https://doi.org/10.1080/09585190802051303].

Burkholder, Justin D. et al. (2010): Health and Well-Being Factors Associated with International Business Travel. In: *Journal of Travel Medicine* 17,5: 329–333. [https://doi.org/10.1111/j.1708-8305.2010.00441.x].

Caligiuri, Paula M. et al. (1998): Testing a Theoretical Model for Examining the Relationship between Family Adjustment and Expatriates' Work Adjustment. In: *Journal of Applied Psychology* 83,4: 598–614. [https://doi.org/10.1037/0021-9010.83.4.598].

Caligiuri, Paula M.; Lazarova, Mila B. (2005): Expatriate Assignments and Work-Family Conflict. In: Poelmans, Steven A.Y. (Ed.): International Research in Work and Family. Mahwah, NJ: Erlbaum: 121–146.

Carver, Charles S.; Scheier, Michael F. (2014): Dispositional Optimism. In: *Trends in Cognitive Sciences* 18,6: 293–299. [https://doi.org/10.1016/j.tics.2014.02.003].

Carver, Charles S.; Scheier, Michael F.; Segerstrom, Suzanne C. (2010): Optimism. In: *Clinical Psychology Review*, Special Issue: Positive Clinical Psychology 30,7: 879–889. [https://doi.org/10.1016/ j.cpr.2010.01.006].

Chang, Chu-Hsiang (Daisy) et al. (2012): Core Self-Evaluations: A Review and Evaluation of the Literature. In: *Journal of Management* 38,1: 81–128. [https://doi.org/10/dbd9nb].

Chen, Fang Fang et al. (2012): Modeling General and Specific Variance in Multifaceted Constructs: A Comparison of the Bifactor Model to Other Approaches. In: *Journal of Personality* 80,1: 219–251. [https://doi.org/10/d6ht4b].

Chen, Gilad (2012): Evaluating the Core: Critical Assessment of Core Self-Evaluations Theory. In: *Journal of Organizational Behavior* 33,2: 153–160. [https://doi.org/10.1002/job.761].

Deller, Jürgen (1997): Expatriate Selection: Possibilities and Limitations of Using Personality Scales. In: Aycan, Zeynep (Ed.): Expatriate Management: Theory and Research, New Approaches to Employee Management 4. Greenwich, CT: JAI Press: 93–116.

Deshpande, Satish P.; Viswesvaran, Chockalingam (1992): Is Cross-Cultural Training of Expatriate Managers Effective: A Meta Analysis. In: *International Journal of Intercultural Relations* 16,3: 295–310. [https://doi.org/10.1016/0147-1767(92)90054-X].

DeYoung, Colin G. (2015): Cybernetic Big Five Theory. In: *Journal of Research in Personality*, Integrative Theories of Personality 56: 33–58. [https://doi.org/10/33h].

Fliege, Herbert et al. (2005): The Perceived Stress Questionnaire (PSQ) Reconsidered: Validation and Reference Values from Different Clinical and Healthy Adult Samples. In: *Psychosomatic Medicine* 67,1: 78–88. [https://doi.org/10.1097/01.psy.0000151491.80178.78].

Foyle, M.F.; Beer, M.D.; Watson, J.P. (1998): Expatriate Mental Health. In: *Acta Psychiatrica Scandinavica* 97,4: 278–283. [https://doi.org/10.1111/j.1600-0447.1998.tb10000.x].

Gignac, Gilles E.; Watkins, Marley W. (2013): Bifactor Modeling and the Estimation of Model-Based Reliability in the WAIS-IV. In: *Multivariate Behavioral Research* 48,5: 639–662. [https://doi.org/10.1080/00273171.2013.804398].

Gregersen, Hal B.; Black, J. Stewart (1990): A Multifaceted Approach to Expatriate Retention in International Assignments. In: *Group & Organization Studies* 15,4: 461–485. [https://doi.org/10.1177/105960119001500409].

Harrison, J. Klin.; Chadwick, M.; Scales, Maria (1996): The Relationship between Cross-Cultural Adjustment and the Personality Variables of Self-Efficacy and Self-Monitoring. In: *International Journal of Intercultural Relations* 20,2: 167–188. [https://doi.org/10/c6wnz9].

Hechanova, Regina; Beehr, Terry A.; Christiansen, Neil D. (2003): Antecedents and Consequences of Employees' Adjustment to Overseas Assignment: A Meta-Analytic Review. In: *Applied Psychology* 52,2: 213–236. [https://doi.org/10/d4f4xv].

Hemphill, James F. (2003): Interpreting the Magnitudes of Correlation Coefficients. In: *American Psychologist* 58,1: 78–79. [https://doi.org/10/fb38g8].

Hogan, Joyce; Roberts, Brent W. (1996): Issues and Non-Issues in the Fidelity-Bandwidth Trade-Off. In: *Journal of Organizational Behavior* 17,6: 627–637. [https://doi.org/10.1002/(SICI)1099-1379(199611)17:6<627::AID-JOB2828>3.0.CO;2-F].

Holland, H.M. (1984): Managing Diplomacy: The United States and Japan. Stanford, CA: Hoover Press.

Jerusalem, Matthias; Schwarzer, Ralf (2014): Self-Efficacy as a Resource Factor in Stress Appraisal Processes. In: Schwarzer, Ralf (Ed.): Self-Efficacy: Thought Control of Action. London: Routledge, Taylor and Francis: 195–213.

Johnson, Russell E. et al. (2012): Recommendations for Improving the Construct Clarity of Higher-Order Multidimensional Constructs. In: *Human Resource Management Review*, Construct Clarity in Human Resource Management Research 22,2: 62–72. [https://doi.org/10.1016/j.hrmr.2011.11.006].

Johnson, Russell E.; Rosen, Christopher C.; Chang, Chu-Hsiang (2011): To Aggregate or Not to Aggregate: Steps for Developing and Validating Higher-Order Multidimensional Constructs. In: *Journal of Business and Psychology* 26,3: 241–248. [https://doi.org/10.1007/s10869-011-9238-1].

Judge, Timothy A. et al. (2003): The Core Self-Evaluations Scale: Development of a Measure. In: *Personnel Psychology* 56,2: 303–331. [https://doi.org/10.1111/j.1744-6570.2003.tb00152.x].

Judge, Timothy A. et al. (2002): Are Measures of Self-Esteem, Locus of Control, Neuroticism, Generalized Self-Efficacy Indicators of a Common Construct? In: *Journal of Personality and Social Psychology* 83,3: 693–710. [https://doi.org/10.1037//0022-3514.83.3.693].

Judge, Timothy A.; Bono, Joyce E. (2001a): A Rose by Any Other Name: Are Self-Esteem, Generalized Self-Efficacy, Neuroticism, and Locus of Control Indicators of a Common Construct? In: Roberts, Brent W.; Hogan, Robert T. (Eds.): Personality Psychology in the Workplace, Decade of Behavior. Washington, DC: American Psychological Association: 93–118. [https://doi.org/10.1037/10434-004].

Judge, Timothy A.; Bono, Joyce E. (2001b): Relationship of Core Self-Evaluation Traits – Self-Esteem, Generalized Self-Efficacy, Locus of Control, and Emotional Stability – with Job Satisfaction and Job Performance: A Meta-Analysis. In: *Journal of Applied Psychology* 86,1: 80–92. [https://doi.org/10.1037/0021-9010.86.1.80].

Judge, Timothy A.; Locke, Edwin A.; Durham, Cathy C. (1997): The Dispositional Causes of Job Satisfaction: A Core Evaluations Approach. In: *Research in Organizational Behavior* 19: 151–188.

Judge, Timothy A.; van Vianen, Annelies E.M.; de Pater, Irene E. (2004): Emotional Stability, Core Self-Evaluations, and Job Outcomes: A Review of the Evidence and an Agenda for Future Research. In: *Human Performance* 17,3: 325–346. [https://doi.org/10/bk2gjb].

Kammeyer-Mueller, John D.; Judge, Timothy A.; Scott, Brent A. (2009): The Role of Core Self-Evaluations in the Coping Process. In: *Journal of Applied Psychology* 94,1: 177–195. [https://doi.org/10/d767bb].

Krause, Neal; Stryker, Sheldon (1984): Stress and Well-Being: The Buffering Role of Locus of Control Beliefs. In: *Social Science & Medicine* 18,9: 783–790. [https://doi.org/10.1016/0277-9536(84)90105-9].

Lazarova, Mila B.; Thomas, David C. (2012): Expatriate Adjustment and Performance Revisited. In: Stahl, Günter K.; Björkman, Ingmar; Morris, Shad (Eds.): Handbook of Research in International Human Resource Management. 2nd ed. Cheltenham, United Kingdom: Edward Elgar: 271–292. [https://doi.org/10/b6mm].

Lazarova, Mila B.; Westman, Mina; Shaffer, Margaret A. (2010): Elucidating the Positive Side of the Work-Family Interface on International Assigments: A Model of Expatriate Work and Family Performance. In: *Academy of Management Review* 35,1: 93–117. [https://doi.org/10.1057/9781137006004_14].

Lazarus, Richard S.; Folkman, Susan (1984): Stress, Appraisal, and Coping. New York: Springer. [http://site.ebrary.com/id/10265641].

Mendenhall, Mark E.; Oddou, Gary R. (1985): The Dimensions of Expatriate Acculturation: A Review. In: *Academy of Management Review* 10,1: 39–47. [https://doi.org/10/bnxd7m].

Mesmer-Magnus, Jessica R.; Viswesvaran, Chockalingam (2005): Convergence between Measures of Work-to-Family and Family-to-Work Conflict: A Meta-Analytic Examination. In: *Journal of Vocational Behavior* 67,2: 215–232. [https://doi.org/10.1016/j.jvb.2004.05.004].

Nicholson, Nigel; Imaizumi, Ayako (1993): The Adjustment of Japanese Expatriates to Living and Working in Britain. In: *British Journal of Management* 4: 119–134. [https://doi.org/10/c38jjn].

Osman-Gani, Aahad M.; Rockstuhl, Thomas (2009): Cross-Cultural Training, Expatriate Self-Efficacy, and Adjustments to Overseas Assignments: An Empirical Investigation of Managers in Asia. In: *International Journal of Intercultural Relations* 33,4: 277–290. [https://doi.org/10.1016/ j.ijintrel.2009.02.003].

Patel, Dipti et al. (2006): Morbidity in Expatriates: A Prospective Cohort Study. In: *Occupational Medicine* 56,5: 345–352. [https://doi.org/10.1093/occmed/kql026].

Phillips, Jean M. et al. (2014): Recruiting Global Travelers: The Role of Global Travel Recruitment Messages and Individual Differences in Perceived Fit, Attraction, and Job Pursuit Intentions. In: *Personnel Psychology* 67,1: 153–201. [https://doi.org/10.1111/peps.12043].

Ree, Malcolm James; Carretta, Thomas R.; Teachout, Mark S. (2015): Pervasiveness of Dominant General Factors in Organizational Measurement. In: *Industrial and Organizational Psychology* 8,3: 409–427. [https://doi.org/10.1017/iop.2015.16].

Rüger, Heiko et al. (2013): Mobilitätskompetenzen im Auswärtigen Dienst: Risiken und protektive Faktoren bei der Bewältigung der Auslandsrotation. Beiträge zur Bevölkerungswissenschaft 44. Würzburg, Germany: Ergon.

Rüger, Heiko et al. (2018): Sampling and Procedures for the Mobility Skills in the German Foreign Service Study. In: Wiernik, Brenton M.; Rüger, Heiko; Ones, Deniz S. (Eds.): Managing Expatriates: Success Factors in Private and Public Domains, Series on Population Studies 50. Opladen, Germany: Barbara Budrich Publishers.

Scheier, Michael F.; Carver, Charles S. (1985): Optimism, Coping, and Health: Assessment and Implications of Generalized Outcome Expectancies. In: *Health Psychology* 4,3: 219–247. [https://doi.org/10.1037/0278-6133.4.3.219].

Scheier, Michael F.; Carver, Charles S.; Bridges, Michael W. (1994): Distinguishing Optimism from Neuroticism (and Trait Anxiety, Self-Mastery, and Self-Esteem): A Reevaluation of the Life Orientation Test. In: *Journal of Personality and Social Psychology* 67,6: 1063–1078. [https://doi.org/10.1037/0022-3514.67.6.1063].

Schlunze, Rolf D. (2002): Locational Adjustment of Japanese Management in Europe. In: *Asian Business & Management* 1,2: 267–283. [https://doi.org/10.1057/palgrave.abm.9200014].

Schmidt, Frank L.; Hunter, John E. (1996): Measurement Error in Psychological Research: Lessons from 26 Research Scenarios. In: *Psychological Methods* 1,2: 199–223. [https://doi.org/10/fww5q4].

Scholler, Gudrun; Fliege, Herbert; Klapp, Burghard Friedrich (1999): Fragebogen zu Selbstwirksamkeit, Optimismus und Pessimismus: Restrukturierung, Itemselektion und Validierung eines Instruments an Untersuchungen klinischer Stichproben. In: *Psychotherapie, Psychosomatik, Medizinische Psychologie* 49,8: 275–283. [http://europepmc.org/abstract/med/10488648].

Schwarzer, Ralf (Ed.) (2014): Self-Efficacy: Thought Control of Action. London, United Kingdom: Routledge. [https://doi.org/10.4324/9781315800820].

Schwarzer, Ralf; Jerusalem, Matthias (1995): Generalized Self-Efficacy Scale. In: Weinman, John; Wright, Stephen C.; Johnston, Marie (Eds.): Measures in Health Psychology: A User's Portfolio. Volume 3. Windsor, United Kingdom: NFER-NELSON: 35–37. [http://userpage.fu-berlin.de/ ~health/selfscal.htm].

Seltzer, Benjamin K. (2013): The Nomological Network of Self-Efficacy and Psychometric Properties of Its General and Specific Measures. Doctoral Dissertation. Minneapolis, MN: University of Minnesota. [http://hdl.handle.net/11299/148904].

Shaffer, Jonathan A.; Postlethwaite, Bennett E. (2012): A Matter of Context: A Meta-Analytic Investigation of the Relative Validity of Contextualized and Noncontextualized Personality Measures. In: *Personnel Psychology* 65,3: 445–494. [https://doi.org/10.1111/j.1744-6570.2012.01250.x].

Shaffer, Margaret A.; Harrison, David A. (2001): Forgotten Partners of International Assignments: Development and Test of a Model of Spouse Adjustment. In: *Journal of Applied Psychology* 86,2: 238–254. [https://doi.org/10.1037/0021-9010.86.2.238].

Shaffer, Margaret A.; Harrison, David A. (1998): Expatriates' Psychological Withdrawal from International Assignments: Work, Nonwork, and Family Influences. In: *Personnel Psychology* 51,1: 87–118. [https://doi.org/10.1111/j.1744-6570.1998.tb00717.x].

Shaffer, Margaret A.; Harrison, David A.; Gilley, K. Matthew (1999): Dimensions, Determinants, and Differences in the Expatriate Assignment Process. In: *Journal of International Business Studies* 30,3: 557–581. [https://doi.org/10.1057/palgrave.jibs.8490083].

Stahl, Günter K.; Miller, Edwin L.; Tung, Rosalie L. (2002): Toward the Boundaryless Career: A Closer Look at the Expatriate Career Concept and the Perceived Implications of an International Assignment. In: *Journal of World Business* 37,3: 216–227. [https://doi.org/10/ddttgr].

Stephens, Gregory K.; Black, J. Stewart (1991): The Impact of Spouse's Career Orientation on Managers during International Assignments. In: *Journal of Management Studies* 28,4: 17–428. [https://doi.org/10.1111/j.1467-6486.1991.tb00289.x].

Steptoe, Andrew; Wardle, Jane (2001): Locus of Control and Health Behaviour Revisited: A Multivariate Analysis of Young Adults from 18 Countries. In: *British Journal of Psychology* 92,4: 659–672. [https://doi.org/10.1348/000712601162400].

Takeuchi, Riki; Yun, Seokhwa; Tesluk, Paul E. (2002): An Examination of Crossover and Spillover Effects of Spousal and Expatriate Cross-Cultural Adjustment on Expatriate Outcomes. In: *Journal of Applied Psychology* 87,4: 655–666. [https://doi.org/10/d2ddkj].

Tsaousis, Ioannis et al. (2007): Do the Core Self-Evaluations Moderate the Relationship between Subjective Well-Being and Physical and Psychological Health? In: *Personality and Individual Differences* 42,8: 1441–1452. [https://doi.org/10.1016/j.paid.2006.10.025].

Van der Zee, Karen I.; Ali, Anees J.; Salomé, Esther (2005): Role Interference and Subjective Well-Being among Expatriate Families. In: *European Journal of Work and Organizational Psychology* 14,3: 239–262. [https://doi.org/10.1080/13594320500146250].

Waibel, Stine; Rüger, Heiko; Wiernik, Brenton M. (2018): Antecedents and Consequences of Mobility Self-Efficacy. In: Wiernik, Brenton M.; Rüger, Heiko; Ones, Deniz S. (Eds.): Managing Expatriates: Success Factors in Private and Public Domains, Series on Population Studies 50. Opladen, Germany: Barbara Budrich Publishers.

Ward, Colleen; Kennedy, Antony (1992): Locus of Control, Mood Disturbance, and Social Difficulty during Cross-Cultural Transitions. In: *International Journal of Intercultural Relations* 16,2: 175–194. [https://doi.org/10.1016/0147-1767(92)90017-O].

Wiernik, Brenton M.; Rüger, Heiko; Ones, Deniz S. (2018): Advancing Expatriate Research in Public and Private Sectors. In: Wiernik, Brenton M.; Rüger, Heiko; Ones, Deniz S. (Eds.): Managing Expatriates: Success Factors in Private and Public Domains, Series on Population Studies 50. Opladen, Germany: Barbara Budrich Publishers.

Wiernik, Brenton M.; Wille, Bart (2018): Careers, Career Development, and Career Management. In: Ones, Deniz S. et al. (Eds.): The SAGE Handbook of Industrial, Work and Organizational Psychology. Volume 3: Managerial Psychology and Organizational Approaches. 2nd ed. London, United Kingdom: Sage: 547–585.

Wiernik, Brenton M.; Wilmot, Michael P.; Kostal, Jack W. (2015): How Data Analysis Can Dominate Interpretations of Dominant General Factors. In: *Industrial and Organizational Psychology* 8,03: 438–445. [https://doi.org/10/895].

Wilkinson, Amanda; Singh, Gangaram (2010): Managing Stress in the Expatriate Family: A Case Study of the State Department of the United States of America. In: *Public Personnel Management* 39,2: 169–181. [https://doi.org/10.1177/009102601003900206].

Integrity: Generalizing Findings from Domestic to Expatriate Contexts

Handan Kepir Sinangil, Deniz S. Ones, and Brenton M. Wiernik

Abstract

Integrity tests have been established as strong predictors of both counterproductive work behaviors and productive job performance. However, heretofore no studies have examined integrity measures in expatriate contexts. In this study, we use a sample of 220 expatriates working in Turkey to examine integrity's validity for both international adjustment and host country national ratings of ten dimensions of job performance. Consistent with domestic research, a measure of integrity provided substantial validity for counterproductive work behaviors and other job performance dimensions. However, there were negligible relations with international adjustment. We recommend that integrity measures be incorporated into expatriate employee selection and assessment systems that aim to minimize expatriate counterproductivity and maximize job performance.

1   Introduction

Integrity is a compound personality trait that reflects individuals' tendencies to be responsible, trustworthy, dependable, and reliable (Ones 1993; Viswesvaran/Ones 2016). In the scientific consensus structure of personality traits – the Hierarchical Big Five model (DeYoung 2015; Dilchert et al. 2014; Goldberg 1993; John et al. 2008; Krueger et al. 2008; Markon et al. 2005; McCrae/Costa 1997; Ones et al. 2005; 2016) – trait integrity reflects a combination of variance from Conscientiousness, Agreeableness, and Emotional Stability (Hough/Ones 2001; Ones 1993; Ones/Viswesvaran 2001a, 2001b). Integrity occupies a similar position in the personality construct space as the higher-order metatrait Factor Alpha (tendency toward restraint of destructive negative emotional, social, and motivational impulses, also called Stability or Socialization; Davies et al. 2015; DeYoung 2015; Digman 1997), though more heavily-focused on Conscientiousness (whereas the strongest indicator of metatrait Factor Alpha is Emotional Stability; Chang et al. 2012).

Historically, integrity tests were originally developed to screen employees prone to deviant or counterproductive work behaviors, such as theft, sabotage, malingering, abuse, or withdrawal (Ones/Dilchert 2013; Ones/Viswesvaran 2001a). Psychometric integrity tests have very large predictive validity both for counterproductive work behaviors ($\rho = -.30$ for predictive studies of job applicants) and productive job performance ($\rho = .41$ for predictive studies of job applicants; Ones et al. 1993), as well as for absenteeism ($\rho = -.33$; Ones et al. 2003) and drug and alcohol abuse ($\rho = .21–.51$; Schmidt et al.

1997).[1] Validities are even higher for studies conducted outside the United States and Canada, such as in Europe, Asia, or South Africa (Giordano et al. 2017; Ones et al. 2014). Compared to dozens of other potential tools that could be used to inform personnel selection decisions (e.g., interviews, job experience, work samples, assessment centers), integrity tests provide the single greatest incremental validity over general cognitive ability (mean combined validity $\rho = .78$, $\Delta R = .13$; cf. $\Delta R = .117$ for structured interviews and $< .10$ for other predictors; Schmidt et al. 2016; Schmidt/Hunter 1998). Personality-based integrity tests (versus overt integrity tests assessing attitudes toward deviant acts and, rarely, admissions of past deviant behavior; Blonigen et al. 2011) tend to show more generalizable and stronger validity for productive job performance. Importantly, the most productive application of integrity tests is not to attempt to screen out high-risk employees or to label applicants as "dishonest", but rather to use integrity tests in the same way as other employee personality measures – to identify applicants who are likely to perform their duties responsibly and well, to be good organizational citizens, *and* to avoid counterproductive or detrimental behaviors.

However, despite the voluminous and robust evidence supporting use of integrity tests for personnel selection, use of integrity tests for expatriate selection remains rare (Bártolo-Ribeiro/Andrade 2015; cf. Myors et al. 2008; Ryan/Sackett 1987; Steiner 2012). This may stem in part from a lack of research examining the validity of integrity tests for job performance specifically in expatriate contexts. International assignments tend to require similar personal characteristics and competencies as domestic assignments (Shaffer et al. 2006; Shin et al. 2007), meaning that validity evidence for domestic employees is likely to generalize to expatriates (Albrecht et al. 2018). Nevertheless, empirical demonstrations of the validity of integrity tests for expatriate success can usefully inform international HRM practice, as well as theoretical accounts of the nature and determinants of expatriate job performance. Such evidence is particularly important given the high value HR professionals ascribe to expatriate responsibility and ethical conduct (Tye/Chen 2005) and growing societal attention to global ethical leadership (Connelly/Ones 2008; Morrison 2001). In this study, we provide, to our knowledge, the first empirical investigation of the validity of a psychometric integrity test for international adjustment and job performance in a sample of professional expatriates.

2   Methods

2.1   Procedure

Data were drawn from Sample 1 of the studies of expatriate success in Turkey (see Ones et al. 2018, Chapter 5, this volume, for more details). Data were collected from expatriates currently working on an international assignment in Turkey and one host country national (HCN) coworker of each expatriate. Participants were volunteers and worked in a wide range of industries, including banking, tourism, education, marketing, and engineering. Expatriates completed a survey assessing demographics, details on their expatriate assignment, and a personality questionnaire. Host country national coworkers provided confidential job performance ratings for the expatriate with whom they were working.

---

[1]   Recently, some researchers have proposed that integrity test research may be biased if conducted by self-interested test publishers (Van Iddekinge et al. 2012). However, meta-analytic evidence shows that these concerns are unfounded; integrity test validity does not differ across peer-reviewed/published versus unpublished reports or when comparing research conducted by independent researchers and test publishers (Harris et al. 2012; Ones et al. 1995, 1996, 2012).

2.2   Expatriate Sample

We gathered data from 220 expatriates (165 male, 29 female, 26 did not report gender) with a mean age of 40.7 years ($SD = 10.04$), an average of 16.7 years of full-time work experience, and an average of 10 years of organizational tenure. Expatriates had spent an average of 3.08 years ($SD = 5.26$) abroad on previous international assignments and a varying amount of time on their current assignment in Turkey (mean 3.32 months, $SD = 48.14$). Expatriates included primarily mid-level managers, with smaller numbers of executives, lower-level managers, and non-managerial employees.

Expatriates were citizens of 25 countries. For those expatriate providing citizenship information, citizenship frequencies were: Australia (2), Austria (1), Belgium (5), Brazil (1), Bulgaria (1), Canada (8), Cyprus (1), Denmark (4), Finland (3), France (27), Germany (23), Greece (1), Hungary (1), Iran (2), Ireland (5), Italy (5), Japan (9), the Netherlands (3), Norway (3), South Africa (2), Spain (2), Sweden (3), Switzerland (5), the United Kingdom (36), and the United States (38).

2.3   Host Country National Coworker Sample

HCNs (122 male, 90 female, 8 did not report their gender) who were working with each of the expatriates described above participated in the study to provide criterion ratings. The HCN coworkers had a mean age of 34.68 years ($SD = 8.41$), an average of 9.43 years ($SD = 7.70$) of experience in their current occupation, and an average of 12.98 months ($SD = 24.13$) working with the expatriates they were rating. Most raters were expatriates' subordinates ($N = 137$), with smaller numbers being expatriates' peers ($N = 55$) or supervisors ($N = 8$); 20 raters did not report their position.

2.4   Measures

Integrity. Integrity was assessed using the Reliability scale of the Hogan Personality Inventory (HPI; Hogan/Hogan 1992). The 1992 HPI Reliability scale is an 18-item personality-based "occupational" or compound personality scale designed "to identify individuals who are honest, dependable, and responsive to supervision" (p. 67). Items on the Reliability scale are drawn from the HPI Adjustment (Emotional Stability), Likeability (Agreeableness), and Prudence (Conscientiousness) scales. The Reliability scale was originally developed to predict counterproductive work behaviors, and its construct- and criterion-related validity have been supported in hundreds of samples (Hogan/Hogan 1989, 1992, 2007)

Adjustment to local conditions. Expatriate locational adjustment (comfort living abroad) was measured using 9 items adapted from Black and Stephens (1989). Expatriates rated the conditions and environment they faced in Turkey on a 10-point scale, with higher scores indicating greater adjustment. The 9 items included adjustment to health care facilities, shopping, entertainment, housing conditions, food, cost of living, living conditions in general, daily interactions with Turks, and socialization with Turks ($\alpha = .82$).

Job performance. HCNs completed a 45-item job performance measure evaluating expatriates on 10 dimensions of job performance. The instrument was constructed directly in Turkish (i.e., was not a translated measure) based on existing models of job performance (Campbell et al. 1990; Hough/Dunnette 1992; Viswesvaran et al. 1996) and extensive interviews with Turkish HCNs and expatriates (see Sinangil/Ones 1997). HCNs rated expatriates on 10 performance dimensions (Table 1; for intercorrelations among dimensions, see

Ones et al. 2018, Chapter 5, this volume, for more details). An overall performance index was created using a composite of the 10 subscales. HCNs rated each item on a 9-point scale for its accuracy describing expatriates' on-the-job behavior (1 = extremely inaccurate, 9 = extremely accurate).

HCNs are uniquely positioned to provide culturally-contextualized and relevant evaluations expatriate job performance behaviors (Sinangil/Ones 1997, 2003), and HCN reactions to expatriate behavior have an important impact on expatriates' adjustment and effectiveness (Templer 2010). HCNs are thus the ideal source for expatriate job performance information. Our use of data from the HCN perspective also supports recent calls for further consideration of multiple stakeholders in expatriate research (Caligiuri 2000; Takeuchi 2010).

We corrected for unreliability in job performance ratings using interrater reliability. We estimated reliabilities for performance dimensions from the meta-analytic values reported by Viswesvaran et al. (1996). For overall job performance, we estimated interrater reliability for the overall performance *composite* using the method by Wilmot et al. (2014; estimated r_{yy} = .89; see Ones et al. 2018, Chapter 5, this volume, for more details). For interested readers, as a comparison, we also report correlations corrected using Viswesvaran et al.'s (1996) meta-analytic mean interrater reliability value for overall job performance *measures* (r_{yy} = .52). We did not correct for unreliability in integrity test scores, as we were interested in the validity of integrity *measures*, rather than the validity of the latent integrity *construct*.

3   Results

Results are shown in Table 2. Integrity scale scores were unrelated to expatriate international adjustment (r_c = .02 [90% confidence interval -.10, .14]). However, consistent with meta-analytic findings for domestic employees, we found that integrity was strongly positively related to personal discipline (avoiding counterproductive work behaviors; r_c = .41 [.28, .55]). Integrity showed only a weak positive relation with overall job performance (r_c = .12 [.00, .23] if corrected using a criterion reliability of r_{yy} = .89; .15 [.00, .30] if corrected using a criterion reliability of r_{yy} = .52; see above); this value is close to the lower end of the 80% credibility interval of true operational validity coefficients for overall job performance of domestic employees in medium complexity jobs ($\rho_{CV.L}$ = .14; Ones et al. 1993). However, integrity showed stronger relations with some dimensions of expatriate job performance. In addition to personal discipline, integrity was also moderately to strongly related to interpersonal relations (r_c = .31 [.15, .46]) and working with others (r_c = .26 [.11, .42]). Interestingly, integrity showed a moderate *negative* relation with management and supervision (r_c = -.25 [-.39, -.10]). This finding is somewhat surprising, but it is consistent with recent research suggesting that similar personality profiles may underlie both leadership and counterproductive work behaviors (Wiernik/Wilmot 2016). Little research has examined relations of integrity tests with leadership performance, but available studies have found positive relations (van Aswegen/Engelbrecht 2009; studies of other-rated integrity have also found positive relations with leader effectiveness, e.g., Hooijberg et al. 2010; Kaiser/Hogan 2010; see also Wilmot 2017 for a meta-analytic review of leadership relations with metatrait Factor Alpha, with which integrity is strongly related). Moreover, integrity is widely regarded as a critical competency for leaders (Birkland 2008; Hogan/Kaiser 2005; Jackson/Ones 2007), so we caution against over-interpreting the negative relation observed in this study.

Table 1: Job performance dimensions assessed

Performance Dimension	Description (*Sample Item*)	Source for Description/Measure	Item	α	IRR
Adjustment to foreign business practices	Knowledge and application of appropriate foreign business practices *(Has knowledge about Turkish work life applications)*	Hough & Dunnette (1992)	4	.84	.58
Establishing and maintaining business contacts	Identifying, developing, using, and maintaining business contacts to achieve goals *(Can develop a communication net with people that he/she encounters at work)*	Hough & Dunnette (1992)	5	.91	.58
Technical competence	Measure of the knowledge required to carry out the tasks of the job *(Uses technical knowledge in solving difficult problems and in helping reach high quality decisions)*	Hough & Dunnette (1992); Viswesvaran (1993)	3	.84	.63
Working with others	Proficiency in working with others, assisting others in the organization *(Has planful and effective work relations with superiors and coworkers)*	Hough & Dunnette (1992)	4	.89	.47
Communicating and persuading	Oral and written proficiency in gathering and transmitting information; persuading others *(Is effective in oral and written communication)*	Hough & Dunnette (1992)	3	.88	.45
Initiative and effort	Dedication to one's job; amount of work expended in striving to do a good job *(Has initiative and takes on extra responsibility)*	Hough & Dunnette (1992)	4	.87	.55
Personal discipline	The extent to which counterproductive behaviors at work are avoided *(Follows rules and regulations and respects authority)*	Campbell et al. (1990); Viswesvaran (1993)	6	.90	.56
Interpersonal relations (avoiding CWB)	The degree to which the expatriate facilitates team performance; supports and champions others in the organization and unit *(Cooperates with others at work)*	Campbell et al. (1990); Viswesvaran (1993)	8	.90	.47
Management and supervision	Proficiency in the coordination of different roles in the organization *(Provides supervision to subordinates)*	Campbell et al. (1990); Viswesvaran (1993)	3	.91	.53
Productivity	Volume of work produced by the expatriate *(Is productive)*	Viswesvaran (1993)	5	.92	.57
Overall expatriate job performance	A unit-weighted composite of the 10 scales; reliability computed as a Mosier reliability (stratified alpha)	Campbell et al. (1990); Hough & Dunnette (1992); Viswesvaran (1993)	45	.96	.89 .52

Note: IRR = estimated interrater reliability using meta-analytic values reported by Viswesvaran et al. (1996). For overall job performance, the first value is the estimated criterion interrater reliability for the overall job performance *composite* using the method by Wilmot et al. (2014). The second value (in italics) is the meta-analytic estimate for overall job performance *measures* reported by Viswesvaran et al. (1996).

Investigating the connection between leadership and deviance and the personality traits that predict these critical performance domains is an important area for ongoing research. Overall, the findings of the current study show that integrity tests have substantial validity for components of expatriate job performance, particularly for counterproductive work behaviors (the criteria integrity tests were originally designed to measure) and contextual and interpersonal performance (criteria that may be especially important for expatriates learning to interact with coworkers in new cultural contexts).

Table 2: Relations of integrity measure to international adjustment and job performance

Criterion	r	r_c	90% confidence interval	
Adjustment to local conditions	.02	.02	-.10	.14
Adjustment to foreign business practices	.03	.04	-.11	.18
Establishing and maintaining business	.03	.04	-.11	.18
Technical competence	.09	.11	-.03	.25
Working with others	.18	.26	.11	.42
Communicating and persuading	.07	.10	-.06	.27
Initiative and effort	.09	.12	-.03	.27
Interpersonal relations	.21	.31	.15	.46
Management and supervision	-.18	-.25	-.39	-.10
Productivity	.07	.09	-.05	.24
Personal discipline (avoiding CWB)	.31	.41	.28	.55
Overall job performance	.11	.12	.00	.23
		.15	*.00*	*.30*

Note: N = 220, r = observed correlation, r_c = correlation corrected for interrater unreliability in the criterion. For overall job performance, values in the first row are the correlation and confidence interval corrected using an estimated criterion interrater reliability of r_{yy} = .89 for the overall job performance *composite* (estimated using the method by Wilmot et al. 2014). Values in italics in the second row are the correlation and confidence interval corrected using an estimated criterion interrater reliability of r_{yy} = .52 (the meta-analytic estimate for overall job performance *measures* reported by Viswesvaran et al. 1996)

4 Discussion

This study found substantial validity of integrity tests for other-rated counterproductive work behaviors and other dimensions of job performance for professional/managerial expatriates working in Turkey. The very strong relations between integrity and counterproductive work behaviors is consistent with recent meta-analytic evidence that integrity test validities for counterproductive behaviors may be higher in international settings (Ones et al. 2014). To our knowledge, this is the first study of integrity test validity for expatriate job performance. Future research should continue to examine integrity relations with expatriate success, both as input for future meta-analyses and to examine potential moderation of validities by cross-cultural differences in perceptions of and importance ascribed to leadership ethics (cf. Birkland 2008).

The current results suggest that multinational organizations may realize substantial value by incorporating integrity tests into expatriate selection and assessment procedures (Fine 2012; Ones et al. 2018), particularly in a global business environment that increasingly emphasizes leader ethical conduct (Morrison 2001). Importantly, we observed negligible to weak relations of integrity with international adjustment and technical performance dimensions (e.g., productivity, technical competence, establishing/maintaining business contacts, adjustment to foreign business practices). Other individual factors, such as cognitive ability and Openness (particularly the Experiencing aspect; Connelly et al. 2014b, 2014a) may be more relevant for these performance domains (Albrecht et al. 2014). Thus, the value of integrity tests can best be realized as a part of a broader selection and assessment system incorporating integrity tests alongside standardized measures of ability and other dispositional competencies critical for expatriate success.

References

Albrecht, Anne-Grit et al. (2014): Openness in Cross-Cultural Work Settings: A Multicountry Study of Expatriates. In: *Journal of Personality Assessment*, Special Section: Openness to Experience 96,1: 64–75. [https://doi.org/10.1080/00223891.2013.821074].

Albrecht, Anne-Grit; Ones, Deniz S.; Sinangil, Handan Kepir (2018): Expatriate Management. In: Ones, Deniz S. et al. (Eds.): The SAGE Handbook of Industrial, Work and Organizational Psychology. Volume 3: Managerial Psychology and Organizational Approaches. 2nd ed. London, United Kingdom: Sage: 429–468.

Bártolo-Ribeiro, Rui; Andrade, Luís José (2015): Expatriates Selection: An Essay of Model Analysis. In: *Journal of Spatial and Organizational Dynamics*, Multiculturality in Organizational and Social Space: New Challenges 3,1: 47–57. [http://www.cieo.pt/journal/2015/JSD_1_2015.pdf#page=48].

Birkland, Adib Samadani (2008): A Cross-Cultural Comparison Senior Leader Misbehavior Perceptions. Doctoral Dissertation. Minneapolis, MN: University of Minnesota. [http://search.proquest.com/docview/760104900].

Black, J. Stewart; Stephens, Gregory K. (1989): The Influence of the Spouse on American Expatriate Adjustment and Intent to Stay in Pacific Rim Overseas Assignments. In: *Journal of Management* 15,4: 529–544. [https://doi.org/10.1177/014920638901500403].

Blonigen, Daniel M. et al. (2011): Delineating the Construct Network of the Personnel Reaction Blank: Associations with Externalizing Tendencies and Normal Personality. In: *Psychological Assessment* 23,1: 18–30. [https://doi.org/10.1037/a0021048].

Caligiuri, Paula M. (2000): The Big Five Personality Characteristics as Predictors of Expatriate's Desire to Terminate the Assignment and Supervisor-Rated Performance. In: *Personnel Psychology* 53,1: 67–88. [https://doi.org/10.1111/j.1744-6570.2000.tb00194.x].

Campbell, Charlotte H. et al. (1990): Development of Multiple Job Performance Measures in a Representative Sample of Jobs. In: *Personnel Psychology* 43,2: 277–300. [https://doi.org/10.1111/j.1744-6570.1990.tb01559.x].

Chang, Luye; Connelly, Brian S.; Geeza, Alexis A. (2012): Separating Method Factors and Higher Order Traits of the Big Five: A Meta-Analytic Multitrait-Multimethod Approach. In: *Journal of Personality and Social Psychology* 102,2: 408–426. [https://doi.org/10/bz9mkz].

Connelly, Brian S. et al. (2014a): Opening up Openness: A Theoretical Sort Following Critical Incidents Methodology and Meta-Analytic Investigation of the Trait Family Measures. In: *Journal of Personality Assessment*, Special Section: Openness to Experience 96,1: 17–28. [https://doi.org/10/bc5f].

Connelly, Brian S.; Ones, Deniz S. (2008): The Personality of Corruption: A National-Level Analysis. In: *Cross-Cultural Research* 42,4: 353–385. [https://doi.org/10.1177/1069397108321904].

Connelly, Brian S.; Ones, Deniz S.; Chernyshenko, Oleksandr S. 2014b: Introducing the Special Section on Openness to Experience: Review of Openness Taxonomies, Measurement, and Nomological Net. In: *Journal of Personality Assessment*, Special Section: Openness to Experience 96,1: 1–16. [https://doi.org/10/33f].

Davies, Stacy E. et al. (2015): The General Factor of Personality: The "Big One," a Self-Evaluative Trait, or a Methodological Gnat That Won't Go Away? In: *Personality and Individual Differences*, Dr. Sybil Eysenck Young Researcher Award 2014 81: 13–22. [https://doi.org/10/bc98].

DeYoung, Colin G. (2015): Cybernetic Big Five Theory. In: *Journal of Research in Personality*, Special Issue: Integrative Theories of Personality 56: 33–58. [https://doi.org/10/33h].

Digman, John M. (1997): Higher-Order Factors of the Big Five. In: *Journal of Personality and Social Psychology* 73,6: 1246–1256. [https://doi.org/10.1037/0022-3514.73.6.1246].

Dilchert, Stephan; Ones, Deniz S.; Krueger, Robert F. (2014): Maladaptive Personality Constructs, Measures, and Work Behaviors. In: *Industrial and Organizational Psychology* 7,1: 98–110. [https://doi.org/10.1111/iops.12115].

Fine, Saul (2012): Estimating the Economic Impact of Personnel Selection Tools on Counterproductive Work Behaviors. In: *Economics and Business Leaders* 1,4: 1–9. [https://doi.org/10.17811/ebl.1.4.2012.1-9].

Giordano, Casey A.; Ones, Deniz S.; Viswesvaran, Chockalingam (2017): Integrity Testing and Antisocial Work Behavior. In: Carducci, Bernardo J. (Ed.): The Wiley Encyclopedia of Personality and Individual Differences. Volume 4. Hoboken, NJ: Wiley.

Goldberg, Lewis R. (1993): The Structure of Phenotypic Personality Traits. In: *American Psychologist* 48,1: 26–34. [https://doi.org/10/c6tzrk].

Harris, William G. et al. (2012): Test Publishers' Perspective on "An Updated Meta-Analysis": Comment on Van Iddekinge, Roth, Raymark, and Odle-Dusseau (2012). In: *Journal of Applied Psychology* 97,3: 531–536. [https://doi.org/10.1037/a0024767].

Hogan, Joyce C.; Hogan, Robert T. (1989): How to Measure Employee Reliability. In: *Journal of Applied Psychology* 74,2: 273–279. [https://doi.org/10.1037/0021-9101.74.2.273].

Hogan, Robert T.; Hogan, Joyce C. (2007): Hogan Personality Inventory Manual. 3rd ed. Tulsa, OK: Hogan Assessment Systems.

Hogan, Robert T.; Hogan, Joyce C. (1992): Hogan Personality Inventory Manual. 2nd ed. Tulsa, OK: Hogan Assessment Systems.

Hogan, Robert T.; Kaiser, Robert B. (2005): What We Know about Leadership. In: *Review of General Psychology* 9,2: 169–180. [https://doi.org/10.1037/1089-2680.9.2.169].

Hooijberg, Robert; Lane, Nancy; Diversé, Albert (2010): Leader Effectiveness and Integrity: Wishful Thinking? In: *International Journal of Organizational Analysis* 18,1: 59–75. [https://doi.org/10.1108/19348831011033212].

Hough, Leaetta M.; Dunnette, Marvin D. (1992): US Managers Abroad: What It Takes to Succeed. Presented at the Academy of Management Conference. Las Vegas, NV.

Hough, Leaetta M.; Ones, Deniz S. (2001): The Structure, Measurement, Validity, and Use of Personality Variables in Industrial, Work, and Organizational Psychology. In: Anderson, Neil et al. (Eds.): Handbook of Industrial, Work and Organizational Psychology. Volume 1: Personnel Psychology. Thousand Oaks, CA: Sage: 233–277. [https://doi.org/10/bc67].

Jackson, Hannah L.; Ones, Deniz S. (2007): Counterproductive Leader Behavior. In: Werner, Steve (Ed.): Managing Human Resources in North America: Current Issues and Perspectives. New York, NY: Routledge: 114–126. [https://doi.org/10/b6p3].

John, Oliver P.; Naumann, Laura P.; Soto, Christopher J. (2008): Paradigm Shift to the Integrative Big Five Trait Taxonomy: History, Measurement, and Conceptual Issues. In: John, Oliver P.; Robins, Richard W.; Pervin, Lawrence A. (Eds.): Handbook of Personality: Theory and Research. 3rd ed. New York: Guilford Press: 114–158.

Kaiser, Robert B.; Hogan, Robert T. (2010): How to (and How Not to) Assess the Integrity of Managers. In: *Consulting Psychology Journal* 62,4: 216–234. [https://doi.org/10.1037/a0022265].

Krueger, Robert F. et al. (2008): Behavioral Genetics and Personality: A New Look at the Integration of Nature and Nurture. In: John, Oliver P.; Robins, Richard W.; Pervin, Lawrence A. (Eds.): Handbook of Personality Psychology: Theory and Research. 3rd ed. New York, NY: Guilford: 287–310.

Markon, Kristian E.; Krueger, Robert F.; Watson, David (2005): Delineating the Structure of Normal and Abnormal Personality: An Integrative Hierarchical Approach. In: *Journal of Personality and Social Psychology* 88,1: 139–157. [https://doi.org/10.1037/0022-3514.88.1.139].

McCrae, Robert R.; Costa, Paul T. (1997): Personality Trait Structure as a Human Universal. In: *American Psychologist* 52,5: 509–516. [https://doi.org/10.1037/0003-066X.52.5.509].

Morrison, Allen (2001): Integrity and Global Leadership. In: *Journal of Business Ethics* 31,1: 65–76. [https://doi.org/10.1023/A:1010789324414].

Myors, Brett et al. (2008): International Perspectives on the Legal Environment for Selection. In: *Industrial and Organizational Psychology* 1,2: 206–246. [https://doi.org/10.1111/j.1754-9434.2008.00040.x].

Ones, Deniz S. et al. (2018): Personality and Counterproductive Work Behaviors. In: Zeigler-Hill, Virgil; Shackelford, Todd K. (Eds.): Encyclopedia of Personality and Individual Differences. Berlin, Germany: Springer.

Ones, Deniz S. et al. (2014): Cross-Cultural Validity of Pre-Employment Integrity Tests: A Transcultural Meta-Analytic Investigation. Presented at the Society for Industrial and Organizational Psychology Conference. Honolulu, HI.

Ones, Deniz S. et al. (1996): Controversies over Integrity Testing: Two Viewpoints. In: *Journal of Business and Psychology* 10,4: 487–501. [https://doi.org/10.1007/BF02251783].

Ones, Deniz S. (1993): Establishing Construct Validity for Integrity Tests. Doctoral Dissertation. Iowa City, IA: University of Iowa. [http://www.dtic.mil/dtic/tr/fulltext/u2/a293940.pdf].

Ones, Deniz S.; Dilchert, Stephan (2013): Counterproductive Work Behaviors: Concepts, Measurement, and Nomological Network. In: Geisinger, Kurt F. et al. (Eds.): APA Handbook of Testing and Assessment in Psychology. Volume 1, APA Handbooks in Psychology. Washington, DC: American Psychological Association: 643–659. [https://doi.org/10.1037/14047-035].

Ones, Deniz S.; Sinangil, Handan Kepir; Wiernik, Brenton M. (2018): Validity of Big Five Personality Traits for Expatriate Success: Results from Turkey. In: Wiernik, Brenton M.; Rüger, Heiko; Ones, Deniz S. (Eds.): Managing Expatriates: Success Factors in Private and Public Domains, Series on Population Studies 50. Opladen, Germany: Barbara Budrich Publishers.

Ones, Deniz S.; Viswesvaran, Chockalingam (2001a): Integrity Tests and Other Criterion-Focused Occupational Personality Scales (COPS) Used in Personnel Selection. In: *International Journal of Selection and Assessment* 9,1/2: 31–39. [https://doi.org/10.1111/1468-2389.00161].

Ones, Deniz S.; Viswesvaran, Chockalingam (2001b): Personality at Work: Criterion-Focused Occupational Personality Scales Used in Personnel Selection. In: Roberts, Brent W.; Hogan, Robert T. (Eds.): Personality Psychology in the Workplace, Decade of Behavior. Washington, DC: American Psychological Association: 63–92. [https://doi.org/10.1037/10434-003].

Ones, Deniz S.; Viswesvaran, Chockalingam; Dilchert, Stephan (2005): Personality at Work: Raising Awareness and Correcting Misconceptions. In: *Human Performance* 18,4: 389–404. [https://doi.org/10.1207/s15327043hup1804_5].

Ones, Deniz S.; Viswesvaran, Chockalingam; Schmidt, Frank L. (2012): Integrity Tests Predict Counterproductive Work Behaviors and Job Performance Well: Comment on Van Iddekinge, Roth, Raymark, and Odle-Dusseau (2012). In: *Journal of Applied Psychology* 97,3: 537–542. [https://doi.org/10.1037/a0024825].

Ones, Deniz S.; Viswesvaran, Chockalingam; Schmidt, Frank L. (2003): Personality and Absenteeism: A Meta-Analysis of Integrity Tests. In: *European Journal of Personality* 17,S1: S19–S38. [https://doi.org/10.1002/per.487].

Ones, Deniz S.; Viswesvaran, Chockalingam; Schmidt, Frank L. (1995): Integrity Tests: Overlooked Facts, Resolved Issues, and Remaining Questions. In: *American Psychologist* 50,6: 456–457. [https://doi.org/10.1037/0003-066X.50.6.456].

Ones, Deniz S.; Viswesvaran, Chockalingam; Schmidt, Frank L. (1993): Comprehensive Meta-Analysis of Integrity Test Validities: Findings and Implications for Personnel Selection and Theories of Job Performance. In: *Journal of Applied Psychology* 78,4: 679–703. [https://doi.org/10/c48t8j].

Ones, Deniz S. et al. (2016): Conceptual and Methodological Complexity of Narrow Trait Measures in Personality-Outcome Research: Better Knowledge by Partitioning Variance from Multiple Latent Traits and Measurement Artifacts. In: *European Journal of Personality* 30,4: 319–321. [https://doi.org/10/bp27].

Ryan, Ann Marie; Sackett, Paul R. (1987): A Survey of Individual Assessment Practices by I/O Psychologists. In: *Personnel Psychology* 40,3: 455–488. [https://doi.org/10.1111/j.1744-6570.1987.tb00610.x].

Schmidt, Frank L.; Hunter, John E. (1998): The Validity and Utility of Selection Methods in Personnel Psychology: Practical and Theoretical Implications of 85 Years of Research Findings. In: *Psychological Bulletin* 124,2: 262–274. [https://doi.org/10.1037/0033-2909.124.2.262].

Schmidt, Frank L.; Oh, In-Sue; Shaffer, Jonathan Andrew (2016): The Validity and Utility of Selection Methods in Personnel Psychology: Practical and Theoretical Implications of 100 Years of Research Findings. Fox School of Business Research Paper. Philadelphia, PA: Temple University. [https://doi.org/10.13140/RG.2.2.18843.26400].

Schmidt, Frank L.; Viswesvaran, Vish; Ones, Deniz S. (1997): Validity of Integrity Tests for Predicting Drug and Alcohol Abuse: A Meta-Analysis. In: Bukoski, William J. (Ed.): Meta-Analysis of Drug Abuse Prevention Programs, NIDA Research Monograph Series 170. NIH Publication 97–4146. Rockville, MD: National Institutes of Health, National Institute on Drug Abuse: 69–95. [https://archives.drugabuse.gov/pdf/monographs/monograph170/monograph170.pdf].

Shaffer, Margaret A. et al. (2006): You Can Take It with You: Individual Differences and Expatriate Effectiveness. In: *Journal of Applied Psychology* 91,1: 109–125. [https://doi.org/10.1037/0021-9010.91.1.109].

Shin, Shung J.; Morgeson, Frederick P.; Campion, Michael A. (2007): What You Do Depends on Where You Are: Understanding How Domestic and Expatriate Work Requirements Depend upon the Cultural Context. In: *Journal of International Business Studies* 38: 64–83. [https://doi.org/10.1057/palgrave.jibs.8400247].

Sinangil, Handan Kepir; Ones, Deniz S. (2003): Gender Differences in Expatriate Job Performance. In: *Applied Psychology* 52,3: 461–475. [https://doi.org/10/c36tw5].

Sinangil, Handan Kepir; Ones, Deniz S. (1997): Empirical Investigations of the Host Country Perspective in Expatriate Management. In: Aycan, Zeynep (Ed.): Expatriate Management: Theory and Research, New Approaches to Employee Management 4. Greenwich, CT: JAI Press: 173–205.

Steiner, Dirk D. (2012): Personnel Selection across the Globe. In: Schmitt, Neal (Ed.): The Oxford Handbook of Personnel Assessment and Selection. Oxford University Press: 740–767. [https://doi.org/10/b6p4].

Takeuchi, Riki (2010): A Critical Review of Expatriate Adjustment Research through a Multiple Stakeholder View: Progress, Emerging Trends, and Prospects. In: *Journal of Management* 36,4: 1040–1064. [https://doi.org/10.1177/0149206309349308].

Templer, Klaus J. (2010): Personal Attributes of Expatriate Managers, Subordinate Ethnocentrism, and Expatriate Success: A Host-Country Perspective. In: *International Journal of Human Resource Management* 21,10: 1754–1768. [https://doi.org/10.1080/09585192.2010.500493].

Tye, Mary G.; Chen, Peter Y. (2005): Selection of Expatriates: Decision-Making Models Used by HR Professionals. In: *Human Resource Planning* 28,4: 15–21.

van Aswegen, Anja S.; Engelbrecht, Amos S. (2009): The Relationship between Transformational Leadership, Integrity, and an Ethical Climate in Organisations. In: *SA Journal of Human Resource Management* 7,1: 175. [https://doi.org/10.4102/sajhrm.v7i1.175].

Van Iddekinge, Chad H. et al. (2012): The Criterion-Related Validity of Integrity Tests: An Updated Meta-Analysis. In: *Journal of Applied Psychology* 97,3: 499–530. [https://doi.org/10.1037/a0021196].

Viswesvaran, Chockalingam (1993): Modeling Job Performance: Is There a General Factor? Doctoral Dissertation. Iowa City, IA: The University of Iowa. [http://www.dtic.mil/dtic/tr/fulltext/u2/a294282.pdf].

Viswesvaran, Chockalingam; Ones, Deniz S. (2016): Integrity Tests: A Review of Alternate Conceptualizations and Some Measurement and Practical Issues. In: Kumar, Updesh (Ed.): The Wiley Handbook of Personality Assessment. Hoboken, NJ: Wiley: 59–73. [https://doi.org/10.1002/9781119173489.ch5].

Viswesvaran, Chockalingam; Ones, Deniz S.; Schmidt, Frank L. (1996): Comparative Analysis of the Reliability of Job Performance Ratings. In: *Journal of Applied Psychology* 81,5: 557–574. [https://doi.org/10/c8f68f].

Wiernik, Brenton M.; Wilmot, Michael P. (2016): Prone to Lead, Prone to Misdeeds? Shared Personality Profiles of CWB and Leadership. Presented at the Academy of Management Conference. Anaheim, CA.

Wilmot, Michael P. (2017): Personality and Its Impacts across the Behavioral Sciences: A Quantitative Review of Meta-Analytic Findings. Doctoral Dissertation. Minneapolis, MN: University of Minnesota.

Wilmot, Michael P.; Wiernik, Brenton M.; Kostal, Jack W. (2014): Increasing Interrater Reliability Using Composite Performance Measures. In: *Industrial and Organizational Psychology* 7,4: 539–542. [https://doi.org/10/38v].

The Impact of Age and Experience on Expatriate Outcomes

Anne-Grit Albrecht, Brenton M. Wiernik, Jürgen Deller, Stephan Dilchert, Deniz S. Ones, and Frieder M. Paulus

Abstract

Age and international experience are widely believed to importantly impact expatriate success. These variables are believed to be proxies for variables such as job knowledge, adaptability, and trainability and have a strong influence on organizational expatriation decisions. In this chapter, we examine age and experience relations with expatriate success in the iGOES samples. We find that age and experience have weak relations with most criteria and suggest more fruitful avenues for future expatriate research and practice.

1 Introduction

There is a strong need for identifying variables that facilitate expatriate success, both to inform expatriate selection and to tailor training and management practices to individual needs (Albrecht et al. 2018b; Deller 2007). In practice, demographic and background characteristics, such as employee age, job experience, and organizational tenure, are frequently used by organizational decision-makers as easily obtainable proxies for other constructs, such as job knowledge, organizational socialization, adaptability, trainability, and physical skills (Sturman 2003). As such, these variables have a strong influence on organizational decisions, including selection, promotion, and training (Perry/Finkelstein 1999; Tesluk/Jacobs 1998), particularly in expatriate settings where formal selection systems that can reduce reliance on such heuristics are rare (Anderson 2005; Deller 1997; Harris/Brewster 1999). This practice is potentially troubling, as empirical findings indicate that these variables have little impact on performance and other work outcomes (Ng/Feldman 2008, 2010; Sturman 2003; Wiernik et al. 2013, 2016). It may be that these factors are more relevant in the unique context of international assignments, but the expatriate literature provides little data to address this possibility. For instance, Mol et al.'s (2005) meta-analysis of predictors of expatriate job performance included only 3 studies on age (total $N = 490$). Previous international experience, the background variable for which they could locate the largest number of studies, similarly included only 6 studies ($N = 938$). Given the large influence age and experience have on international assignment decisions, evaluating whether these variables are demonstrably relevant is of paramount importance. These questions are particularly important in light of global demographic shifts leading to increasingly older workforces (WHO 2011), particularly among expatriates, whose average age and career tenure has shifted from younger to older employees (BGRS 2016; Cartus 2016). We address these questions in this chapter.

1.1 Age and Expatriate Success

Increasingly, organizations select older employees for international assignments, reasoning that expatriate assignments are "most easily rationalized when [applied] to older, presumably more experienced employees" (Brookfield GRS 2015: 17). Given that older employees tend to have higher salaries and hierarchical levels (the meta-analytic correlation of age and salary is $\rho = .26$, $k = 52$, $N = 40,192$, Ng et al. 2005), this trend potentially adds to the already high costs of expatriate assignments to organizations. In parallel, many individuals remain active in the workforce well into retirement age (Fasbender et al. 2014); several consultancies have emerged that offer services from formally retired senior experts, frequently sending them to work on temporary projects in other countries (Deller/Pundt 2014). From these practices, it is apparent that many organizations regard older employees' greater experience as an asset to be leveraged on an international assignment, especially when expatriates are sent abroad to manage critical organizational functions.

However, despite widespread belief in the advantages of experience during expatriation, there is also a pervasive view that job performance declines with age (Ng/Feldman 2008). These beliefs may stem from observable age-related declines in some speed, learning, and processing-related cognitive abilities (Klein et al. 2015; Salthouse 2004). Specifically for expatriation, many individuals believe that older expatriates will be less flexible, willing, and able to adapt to changing cultural norms in a foreign context (Olsen/Martins 2009; older expatriates may also have more family responsibilities, further increasing the difficulty of international mobility, Haslberger/Brewster 2008). Negligible to weak relations of age with performance in domestic settings suggest that these negative beliefs are likely unfounded (Ng/Feldman 2008; Sturman 2003). Moreover, domestic research also shows that older individuals tend to appraise everyday hassles as less stressful (Aldwin et al. 1996) and are better able to cope with negative events and emotions (Gross et al. 1997). In an expatriate context, these findings suggest that older expatriates may find international adjustment *easier* because they have more effective appraisal and coping mechanisms to respond to challenges they encounter abroad. However, whether older expatriates are more or less able to adjust, perform, and persist on expatriate assignments remains to be empirically demonstrated.

Age is generally unrelated to performance in Western contexts. However, cultures around the world vary in their degree of reverence for older individuals. For example, in many Asian cultures, age is associated with wisdom, expertise, and competence (Löckenhoff et al. 2009; Sung 2001). These evaluations may result in stereotypes differentially affecting performance evaluations at work (Posthuma/Campion 2009). For example, relationships between age and performance ratings may be larger in cultures with more favorable views of aging. Selmer (2001) also argued that older expatriates may find it easier to adjust when they are afforded more respect by host country nationals. Selmer observed much stronger age-adjustment relations ($r_{obs} = .21$) among Western expatriates in China than the near zero effects reported in Hechanova et al.'s (2003) meta-analysis. Cultural attitudes toward aging, therefore, are likely important moderators of age relations with expatriate success.

1.2 Work Experience and Expatriate Success

The concepts of job tenure, work experience, organizational tenure, and seniority are often used interchangeably (Hofmann et al. 1992) and together are one of the most frequently encountered concepts in human resources management practice (Quiñones et al. 1995). Individuals are frequently dispatched on international assignments based on their experience and supposed technical expertise. As shown Table 1, however, the empirical evidence suggests that different types of experience are relatively useless predictors of expatriate success. All operationalizations of experience are unrelated to expatriate job performance and at most weakly related to expatriate adjustment.

Table 1: Previous meta-analyses of experience and expatriate success

	N	k	ρ	SD_ρ	80% CV
Overall job performance					
Previous international experience[M]	938	6	.02	.20	-.24, .28
Number of international assignments[M]	310	2	.06	.00	.06, .06
Job-relevant experience[M]	259	2	.09	.00	.09, .09
Locational adjustment					
Previous international experience[H]	1,635	8	.08	.10	-.05, .21
Previous international experience[B]	4,073	19	.04	.08	-.06, .14
Total work experience[H]	340	3	.05	.02	.02, .08
Organizational tenure[H]	1,297	5	-.01	.07	-.10, .08
Time in current location[H]	1,792	8	.14	.14	-.04, .32
Interaction adjustment					
Previous international experience[H]	1,348	7	.11	.03	.07, .15
Previous international experience[B]	2,762	10	.13	.05	.06, .20
Organizational tenure[H]	1,181	5	.05	.03	.01, .09
Time in current location[H]	768	4	.17	.00	.17, .17
Work adjustment					
Previous international experience[H]	1,240	7	.08	.00	.08, .08
Previous international experience	2,736	12	.06	.06	-.02, .14
Organizational tenure[H]	1,110	5	.06	.00	.06, .06
Time in current location[H]	937	5	.15	.00	.15, .15

Note: N = total sample size, k = number of samples included in meta-analysis, ρ = mean correlation corrected for unreliability in the criterion, SD_ρ = true standard deviation of ρ, 80% CV = 80% credibility interval around ρ (all intervals computed by current authors), [M] Mol et al. (2005), [H] Hechanova et al. (2003), [B] Bhaskar-Shrinivas et al. (2005).

Meta-analytic results suggest negligible relations of experience with expatriate success, but these estimates are based on relatively small total samples, and there are reasons to believe that experience could play a role in the adjustment and job performance of expatriates. Previous international experience can help expatriates to form more realistic expectations and reduce the uncertainty associated with moving abroad (Black et al. 1991; Caligiuri et al. 2001). Expatriates with prior international experience may also have established coping strategies for handling adjustment challenges (e.g., dealing with home sickness, handling everyday tasks without speaking the host country language, Berry/Sam 1997). More generally, both human capital theory (Ehrenberg/Smith 2012) and learning theory

(Weiss 1990) posit that individuals accumulate job knowledge over time which enhances job performance. It is possible that negligible relations observed between experience and success in previous expatriate research stems from suboptimal operationalization of the experience construct (typically previous international experience, rather than job-specific work experience). Therefore, in this chapter, we test a broad range of experience variables and their relationships with expatriate success.

2   Methods

2.1   Sample

The current analyses are based on 2,168 German-speaking expatriates who took part in the iGOES project. This project assessed expatriates working in a variety of roles and industries in 28 countries (for more details, see Wiernik et al. 2018, Chapter 1 of this volume). As can be seen in Table 2, our sample covered a large range of ages (min = 19, max = 71), was highly educated (average of 17.4 years of formal education), and was roughly 30% female. These distributions resemble the general global expatriate population (BGRS 2016; Cartus 2016). Analyses are based on both waves of data collection in the iGOES project (see Albrecht et al. 2018a, Appendix A, this volume). Wave 1 includes samples from Argentina, China, Costa Rica, Czech Republic, Egypt, Ghana, India, Ireland, Italy, the Netherlands, Russia, South Korea, Sweden, Turkey, and the USA. Wave 2 includes samples from Austria, Denmark, Finland, France, Ireland, Italy, Malaysia, Morocco, the Netherlands, Poland, Singapore, Spain, Switzerland, Thailand, Turkey, and the UK.

Table 2: Sample characteristics across all countries

Variable	*N*	*M*	*SD*	Min	Max
Age (years)	2,167	36.78	8.88	19	71
Gender (male = 0, female = 1)	685	.316	.465	0	1
Marital status (% in stable relationship)	1,466	.676	.468	0	1
Years of formal education	2,096	17.40	2.45	9	21
Total work experience (months)	958	138.89	101.73	2	588
Organizational tenure (months)	2,132	77.30	83.98	0	648
Time in current location (months)	2,126	33.57	32.40	0	144
Number of previous expatriate assignments	2,116	1.00	1.34	0	10
Total time on expatriate assignments (months)	1,029	23.28	42.04	0	342
Number of assignments in same cultural cluster	1,134	.57	.75	0	4

Note: Zero values for organizational tenure/time in current location indicate that the expatriate had begun working for the organization/had arrived in the current location fewer than four weeks before the time of the survey.

2.2   Measures

Age and experience. In this chapter, we analyze a broad range of variables related to expatriate age and experience. These include overall work experience (in any job and context, with any organization), tenure with current employer, tenure on current assignment, number of previous expatriate assignments in general, number of previous expatriate assignments in the same cultural cluster as the current one, and total time spent on previous expatriate assignments. As shown in Table 2, the sample covers a broad range of levels on all tenure-related variables ranging from zero (those expatriates that had started their current assignment or job with their current employer less than a month before the time of the interview) to 12 years on the assignment and 54 years of tenure with the current employer. Roughly half of the sample (47.4%) had not been on a prior expatriate assignment, 28% had had one prior international assignment, 13% had had two prior stints as an expatriate, and only very few more (three assignments: 6%, four assignments: 4% individuals, > 4 assignments: 6%). The large majority (77%) had not previously worked in the same cultural cluster as their current location. Total time spent on previous assignments again varied widely, ranging from one month to 29 years on four different assignments.

Adjustment. Self-ratings of adjustment were assessed using Black and Stephens' (1989) 14-item scale in Wave 2 of the data collection. For these samples, scores were computed for locational (comfort with everyday tasks, such as obtaining food, entertainment, and transportation; average $\alpha = .72$), interaction (comfort communicating and interacting with host country nationals; average $\alpha = .83$), and work (comfort with one's work role; average $\alpha = .71$) adjustment, as well as for total overall expatriate adjustment (average $\alpha = .81$). In Wave 1, adjustment was assessed using the 3-item measure from Albrecht (2005). For these samples, only total overall expatriate adjustment could be computed (average $\alpha = .63$).

Satisfaction. Job satisfaction was assessed using Judge et al.'s (1998) five-item scale. This scale assesses overall job satisfaction through a series of general judgments about the overall quality of the work experience (example item: "I feel fairly well satisfied with my present job"; average $\alpha = .80$). Life satisfaction was assessed using Diener et al.'s (1985) short-form Satisfaction with Life Scale, consisting of four items such as "In most ways my life is close to ideal" and "The conditions of my life are excellent". The average internal consistency of this scale in this study was $\alpha = .74$; values ranged from .70 (Finland and Turkey) to .88 (Mexico) in individual country samples.

Job performance. Supervisors, coworkers, or subordinates rated expatriates' job performance using a short job performance survey completed by one rater for each expatriate covering the following dimensions of job performance: technical performance ($\alpha = .66$ for Wave 1, .90 for Wave 2), management and supervision ($\alpha = .58$ for Wave 1, .86 for Wave 2), effort and initiative ($\alpha = .59$ for Wave 1, .84 for Wave 2), contextual performance (support for organizational goals, extra-role engagement, cultural knowledge; $\alpha = .45$, only in Wave 1), interpersonal relations (e.g., communication effectiveness, cooperation, getting along with others; $\alpha = .88$, only in Wave 2), and personal discipline (avoiding counterproductive work behaviors; $\alpha = .85$, only in Wave 2). An overall job performance score was computed combining all items of the measure ($\alpha = .86$ for Wave 1, .96 for Wave 2).

2.3   Analyses

Correlations for each sample were pooled using psychometric meta-analysis (Schmidt/Hunter 2015), correcting for sampling error and criterion unreliability. Adjustment and satisfaction were corrected using alpha coefficients from the current samples. Job performance was corrected using the supervisor meta-analytic interrater reliability distribution for each performance dimension from Viswesvaran et al. (1996). Age and experience were assumed to be measured without error.

3   Results

3.1   Age

Age relations with performance are shown in Table 3; relations with adjustment and satisfaction are shown in Table 4. Relations between age and expatriate job performance were negligible to small, with magnitudes ranging from $|\rho| = .02$ (effort and initiative, personal discipline) to .14 (management and supervision). Apart from contextual performance, where the residual standard deviation was zero, small to moderate amounts of between-country variance could not be explained by sampling error or unreliability in the criterion measures. A closer look at country-level correlations, however, revealed no pattern supporting our hypothesis that the relationship between age and job performance should be stronger in countries having a more positive view of the elderly. In fact, China, India, and Korea – countries often cited as associating age with positive attributes such as wisdom and experience – were in the middle of the observed effect size distribution (overall job performance: China $r_{obs} = .09$, India $r_{obs} = .17$, Korea $r_{obs} = .14$). Outliers on both ends were countries that do not have a strong reputation as holding negative (Egypt $r_{obs} = -.59$, France $r_{obs} = -.53$) or positive (Ireland $r_{obs} = .54$, Italy $r_{obs} = .45$) views of the elderly. We therefore expect that the remaining residual variation in age–performance relations to be caused primarily by second-order sampling error.

Relations of age with adjustment and satisfaction were slightly stronger than those for job performance but still generally small, ranging from $|\rho| = .03$ (interaction adjustment) to .19 (locational adjustment). Nearly all the variance in age relations with work and overall adjustment was explained by sampling error and criterion unreliability, indicating that these relations are generalizable and do not vary across a broad range of host countries. For locational and interaction adjustment and for job and life satisfaction, small to moderate amounts of variance remained unexplained; again, no clear picture emerged suggesting older expatriates to having an easier time adjusting in Asian countries.

3.2   Experience

Results for experience variables are also shown in Tables 3 and 4. Total work experience was negligibly related to all performance dimensions, as was organizational tenure (excluding a small negative relation with interpersonal performance). Previous international experience was similarly unrelated to most performance dimensions. Previous experience in the same cultural cluster was positively associated with contextual performance ($\rho = .13$); this is likely because this performance scale includes an item related to accommodation of local cultural customs. International experience was also weakly negative related to personal discipline, but these relations were highly variable across samples and may be attributable to second-order sampling error.

Table 3: Associations between expatriate age and experience and expatriate job performance

Criterion	Age/experience	k	N	$\bar{r}$	SD_r	SD_{res}	$SE_{\bar{r}}$	ρ	SD_ρ	90% CI	80% CV
Overall performance	Age	31	944	.05	.21	.11	.04	**.06**	.15	-.02, .15	-.12, .25
	Total work experience	17	419	-.03	.19	.00	.05	**-.04**	.00	-.15, .06	-.04, -.04
	Organizational tenure	31	933	.01	.22	.12	.04	**.02**	.16	-.07, .11	-.19, .23
	Time in current location	31	929	.08	.20	.07	.04	**.11**	.10	.02, .19	-.02, .24
	Number of previous expatriate assignments	30	833	.02	.22	.10	.04	**.03**	.14	-.06, .12	-.15, .21
	Total time on expatriate assignments	17	406	-.02	.25	.14	.06	**-.02**	.20	-.16, .12	-.27, .23
	Number of assignments in same cultural cluster	30	919	.01	.21	.09	.04	**.02**	.13	-.07, .10	-.15, .18
Technical performance	Age	31	948	.04	.22	.12	.04	**.05**	.16	-.04, .14	-.16, .26
	Total work experience	17	419	.01	.18	.00	.04	**.01**	.00	-.09, .11	.01, .01
	Organizational tenure	31	936	.02	.21	.09	.04	**.03**	.12	-.05, .12	-.12, .19
	Time in current location	31	933	.09	.23	.13	.04	**.13**	.18	.04, .22	-.10, .36
	Number of previous expatriate assignments	30	837	.00	.24	.14	.04	**-.01**	.19	-.10, .09	-.25, .24
	Total time on expatriate assignments	17	406	-.02	.25	.13	.06	**-.03**	.18	-.16, .11	-.26, .21
	Number of assignments in same cultural cluster	30	924	.00	.21	.11	.04	**.00**	.15	-.09, .09	-.19, .20
Contextual performance	Age	14	520	.07	.16	.00	.04	**.09**	.00	.00, .19	.09, .09
	Organizational tenure	14	510	.07	.17	.04	.05	**.09**	.05	-.01, .20	.03, .15
	Time in current location	14	519	.16	.11	.00	.03	**.23**	.00	.16, .29	.23, .23
	Number of previous expatriate assignments	13	412	.06	.16	.00	.04	**.08**	.00	-.02, .19	.08, .08
	Number of assignments in same cultural cluster	13	494	.10	.17	.06	.05	**.13**	.08	.02, .24	.03, .23

$\downarrow$

Table 3: Associations between expatriate age and experience and expatriate job performance – continued

Criterion	Age/experience	k	N	$\bar{r}$	SD_r	SD_{res}	$SE_{\bar{r}}$	ρ	SD_ρ	90% CI	80% CV
Interpersonal performance	Age	17	425	-.07	.24	.12	.06	**-.11**	.17	-.25, .03	-.33, .11
	Total work experience	17	419	-.06	.21	.00	.05	**-.08**	.00	-.20, .04	-.08, -.08
	Organizational tenure	17	424	-.10	.20	.00	.05	**-.15**	.00	-.26, -.03	-.15, -.15
	Time in current location	17	411	-.02	.23	.10	.06	**-.03**	.15	-.16, .11	-.22, .16
	Number of previous expatriate assignments	17	423	-.08	.26	.15	.06	**-.12**	.23	-.27, .03	-.41, .17
	Total time on expatriate assignments	17	406	-.05	.27	.16	.06	**-.07**	.24	-.22, .09	-.37, .24
	Number of assignments in same cultural cluster	17	426	-.04	.24	.13	.06	**-.06**	.18	-.20, .09	-.29, .18
Management/ supervision	Age	31	936	.10	.23	.14	.04	**.14**	.19	.04, .23	-.11, .38
	Total work experience	17	416	.03	.21	.05	.05	**.04**	.07	-.08, .16	-.05, .13
	Organizational tenure	31	925	.04	.19	.01	.03	**.05**	.02	-.03, .13	.03, .07
	Time in current location	31	921	.10	.20	.08	.04	**.14**	.11	.06, .22	.00, .28
	Number of previous expatriate assignments	30	828	.04	.17	.00	.03	**.05**	.00	-.02, .12	.05, .05
	Total time on expatriate assignments	17	403	.06	.22	.06	.05	**.08**	.08	-.04, .20	-.02, .17
	Number of assignments in same cultural cluster	30	911	.02	.18	.00	.03	**.02**	.00	-.05, .10	.02, .02
Effort and initiative	Age	31	937	.02	.23	.13	.04	**.02**	.18	-.07, .11	-.21, .25
	Total work experience	17	411	-.04	.19	.00	.05	**-.05**	.00	-.15, .05	-.05, -.05
	Organizational tenure	31	926	.02	.22	.11	.04	**.02**	.15	-.06, .11	-.17, .22
	Time in current location	31	922	.03	.19	.02	.03	**.04**	.03	-.03, .12	.00, .08
	Number of previous expatriate assignments	30	826	.01	.22	.10	.04	**.01**	.13	-.08, .10	-.15, .18
	Total time on expatriate assignments	17	398	-.02	.23	.08	.05	**-.02**	.10	-.14, .10	-.15, .11
	Number of assignments in same cultural cluster	30	912	-.01	.21	.10	.04	**-.01**	.13	-.09, .08	-.18, .16

$\downarrow$

Table 3: Associations between expatriate age and experience and expatriate job performance – continued

Criterion	Age/experience	k	N	$\bar{r}$	SD_r	SD_{res}	$SE_{\bar{r}}$	ρ	SD_ρ	90% CI	80% CV
Personal discipline	Age	17	423	-.01	.22	.06	.05	**-.02**	.09	-.13, .10	-.12, .09
	Total work experience	17	417	-.01	.18	.00	.04	**-.02**	.00	-.11, .08	-.02, -.02
	Organizational tenure	17	422	-.08	.26	.17	.06	**-.11**	.22	-.25, .04	-.39, .18
	Time in current location	17	409	-.02	.27	.18	.07	**-.03**	.24	-.18, .12	-.33, .28
	Number of previous expatriate assignments	17	421	-.12	.25	.14	.06	**-.16**	.20	-.29, -.02	-.41, .09
	Total time on expatriate assignments	17	404	-.07	.25	.14	.06	**-.10**	.19	-.24, .03	-.34, .14
	Number of assignments in same cultural cluster	17	424	-.07	.20	.00	.05	**-.10**	.00	-.21, .01	-.10, -.10

Note: k = number of samples, N = total sample size, $\bar{r}$ = mean observed correlation, SD_r = observed standard deviation of correlations, SD_{res} = residual standard deviation of correlations after accounting for sampling error and unreliability, $SE_{\bar{r}}$ = standard error of mean observed correlation; ρ = mean correlation corrected for unreliability in criteria, SD_ρ = true distribution standard deviation; 90% CI = 90% confidence interval for ρ; 80% CV = 80% credibility interval for ρ.

Table 4: Associations between expatriate age and experience and expatriate adjustment and satisfaction

Criterion	Age/experience	k	N	$\bar{r}$	SD_r	SD_{res}	$SE_{\bar{r}}$	ρ	SD_ρ	90% CI	80% CV
Overall adjustment	Age	31	2,166	.12	.12	.02	.02	**.16**	.02	.12, .21	.14, .19
	Total work experience	17	957	.13	.16	.08	.04	**.17**	.11	.09, .26	.04, .31
	Organizational tenure	31	2,131	.05	.12	.02	.02	**.06**	.02	.02, .11	.04, .09
	Time in current location	31	2,125	.28	.15	.08	.03	**.38**	.11	.32, .43	.23, .52
	Number of previous expatriate assignments	31	1,852	.00	.15	.08	.03	**.00**	.10	-.06, .06	-.14, .13
	Total time on expatriate assignments	18	1,028	.03	.17	.11	.04	**.04**	.15	-.05, .13	-.15, .23
	Number of *assignments* in same cultural cluster	31	2,167	.04	.11	.00	.02	**.06**	.00	.01, .10	.06, .06
Locational adjustment	Age	22	1,475	.16	.15	.09	.03	**.19**	.12	.13, .26	.04, .34
	Total work experience	17	957	.16	.18	.12	.04	**.20**	.15	.11, .28	.00, .39
	Organizational tenure	22	1,445	.10	.14	.07	.03	**.12**	.09	.06, .18	.01, .24
	Time in current location	22	1,435	.16	.16	.10	.03	**.20**	.12	.13, .27	.04, .35
	Number of previous expatriate assignments	22	1,342	-.01	.14	.06	.03	**-.01**	.08	-.07, .05	-.11, .09
	Total time on expatriate assignments	17	955	.04	.14	.04	.03	**.05**	.05	-.02, .12	-.01, .11
	Number of assignments in same cultural cluster	22	1,476	.00	.10	.00	.02	**.01**	.00	-.04, .05	.01, .01

$\downarrow$

Table 4: Associations between expatriate age and experience and expatriate adjustment and satisfaction – continued

Criterion	Age/experience	k	N	$\bar{r}$	SD_r	SD_{res}	$SE_{\bar{r}}$	ρ	SD_ρ	90% CI	80% CV
Interaction adjustment	Age	22	1,474	.03	.16	.10	.03	**.03**	.11	-.03, .09	-.11, .17
	Organizational tenure	17	956	.05	.16	.09	.04	**.06**	.10	-.01, .13	-.07, .19
	Total work experience	22	1,444	-.05	.12	.00	.03	**-.06**	.00	-.10, -.01	-.06, -.06
	Time in current location	22	1,434	.17	.12	.00	.02	**.19**	.00	.14, .23	.19, .19
	Number of previous expatriate assignments	22	1,341	-.03	.16	.09	.03	**-.03**	.10	-.09, .03	-.16, .10
	Total time on expatriate assignments	17	954	-.03	.17	.10	.04	**-.03**	.11	-.10, .04	-.17, .10
	Number of assignments in same cultural cluster	22	1,475	.03	.13	.05	.03	**.03**	.05	-.02, .09	-.04, .10
Work adjustment	Age	22	1,466	.11	.11	.00	.02	**.14**	.00	.09, .18	.14, .14
	Total work experience	17	954	.10	.10	.00	.02	**.12**	.00	.07, .17	.12, .12
	Organizational tenure	22	1,437	.10	.11	.00	.02	**.13**	.00	.08, .17	.13, .13
	Time in current location	22	1,427	.20	.11	.00	.02	**.24**	.00	.20, .29	.24, .24
	Number of previous expatriate assignments	22	1,335	.06	.12	.00	.02	**.07**	.00	.02, .12	.07, .07
	Total time on expatriate assignments	17	951	.11	.15	.06	.04	**.13**	.08	.06, .20	.03, .23
	Number of assignments in same cultural cluster	22	1,467	.02	.10	.00	.02	**.02**	.00	-.02, .07	.02, .02

Table 4: Associations between expatriate age and experience and expatriate adjustment and satisfaction – continued

Criterion	Age/experience	k	N	$\bar{r}$	SD_r	SD_{res}	$SE_{\bar{r}}$	ρ	SD_ρ	90% CI	80% CV
Job satisfaction	Age	20	1,192	.10	.14	.06	.03	**.12**	.06	.06, .18	.04, .20
	Total work experience	17	956	.08	.12	.00	.03	**.09**	.00	.03, .14	.09, .09
	Organizational tenure	20	1,169	.08	.09	.00	.02	**.09**	.00	.05, .13	.09, .09
	Time in current location	20	1,153	.06	.19	.14	.04	**.07**	.15	-.01, .14	-.13, .26
	Number of previous expatriate assignments	20	1,153	.05	.10	.00	.02	**.06**	.00	.02, .10	.06, .06
	Total time on expatriate assignments	17	930	.10	.09	.00	.02	**.11**	.00	.07, .15	.11, .11
	Number of assignments in same cultural cluster	20	1,193	.05	.11	.00	.02	**.05**	.00	.01, .10	.05, .05
Life satisfaction	Age	17	956	-.07	.16	.09	.04	**-.08**	.10	-.15, .00	-.21, .06
	Total work experience	17	957	-.05	.13	.00	.03	**-.05**	.00	-.11, .01	-.05, -.05
	Organizational tenure	17	949	.00	.11	.00	.03	**.00**	.00	-.05, .05	.00, .00
	Time in current location	17	917	-.05	.14	.04	.03	**-.06**	.05	-.12, .01	-.12, .01
	Number of previous expatriate assignments	17	957	.02	.10	.00	.02	**.02**	.00	-.02, .07	.02, .02
	Total time on expatriate assignments	17	931	.03	.09	.00	.02	**.03**	.00	-.01, .07	.03, .03
	Number of assignments in same cultural cluster	17	957	.01	.14	.04	.03	**.01**	.05	-.05, .08	-.05, .08

Note: k = number of samples, N = total sample size, $\bar{r}$ = mean observed correlation, SD_r = observed standard deviation of correlations, SD_{res} = residual standard deviation of correlations after accounting for sampling error and unreliability, $SE_{\bar{r}}$ = standard error of mean observed correlation; ρ = mean correlation corrected for unreliability in criteria, SD_ρ = true distribution standard deviation; 90% CI = 90% confidence interval for ρ; 80% CV = 80% credibility interval for ρ.

The most relevant experience variable for job performance was time in the current location, which showed small relations with overall performance, technical performance, management and supervision, and, especially, contextual performance (this effect may also reflect the cultural accommodation content on this scale). However, these relations were also somewhat variable across samples, and no pattern for this variation was discernable.

For the attitudinal criteria, total work experience and organizational tenure showed small positive relations with locational and work adjustment. Previous international experience was generally unrelated to these criteria (though total time on previous expatriate assignments appeared to be weakly related to work adjustment and job satisfaction). Tenure on the current assignment was again the most useful experience predictor, showing moderate to strong relations with all adjustment criteria. Time in current location was unrelated to job and life satisfaction.

As supplemental analyses, we compared adjustment outcomes for expatriates who were binational (held citizenship and extensive experience in two countries) to those who were "single-national" (Table 5) or for expatriates who spent their childhoods in their home country versus abroad (Table 6). Binational expatriates showed slightly *lower* locational and work adjustment, but all other comparisons were negligible.

Table 5: Adjustment of binational and "single-national" expatriates

	Binational			Single-national					
	N	*M*	*SD*	*N*	*M*	*SD*	*u*	*d*	95% CI
Overall adjustment	143	3.88	.53	1331	3.95	.49	1.08	**-.14**	-.31, .03
Locational adjustment	143	3.80	.67	1331	3.92	.59	1.14	**-.20**	-.37, -.03
Interaction adjustment	143	3.78	.88	1330	3.75	.81	1.09	**.04**	-.13, .21
Work adjustment	142	4.07	.70	1323	4.19	.62	1.11	**-.18**	-.35, -.01

Note: *N* = sample size, *u* = ratio of standard deviations, *d* = standardized mean difference (Cohen's *d*), 95% CI = 95% CI around *d*, positive *d* values indicate higher adjustment for binational expatriates.

Table 6: Adjustment of expatriates based on childhood location

	Reared abroad			Reared in home					
	N	*M*	*SD*	*N*	*M*	*SD*	*u*	*d*	95% CI
Overall adjustment	127	3.97	.53	1332	3.95	.49	1.09	**.05**	-.13, .23
Locational adjustment	127	3.94	.58	1332	3.91	.60	.97	**.05**	-.13, .23
Interaction adjustment	127	3.78	.83	1331	3.75	.81	1.03	**.04**	-.14, .22
Work adjustment	126	4.20	.69	1325	4.18	.63	1.11	**.03**	-.15, .21

Note: *N* = sample size, *u* = ratio of standard deviations, *d* = standardized mean difference (Cohen's *d*), 95% CI = 95% CI around *d*, positive *d* values indicate higher adjustment for expatriates reared abroad.

4   Discussion

The current analyses revealed that across host countries, relations between age and expatriate job performance and adjustment were negligible to small. For age and performance, the largest correlation emerged with management/supervision ($\rho = .14$, indicating older expatriates perform slightly better on average). For adjustment, the largest age relation was with locational adjustment ($\rho = .19$, again indicating that older expatriates show somewhat more success). We hypothesized that age–success relations would be more strongly positive in countries with more positive views of older adults, but the small variability across countries and lack of systematic pattern of variation in effect sizes across countries provided no support for this hypothesis. On the one hand, one could interpret these findings as indicating that cultural values do not exert strong influence on age—expatriate success relations. On the other hand, findings by Löckenhoff et al. (2009) suggest that the picture might simply be more complex than we expected. In their study comparing perceptions of aging across 26 cultures, Löckenhoff et al. found that in addition to cultural values, many other factors also influence age perceptions within countries, including population age composition, levels of education among older generations, and economic conditions. Despite this possibility, the absence of a systematic pattern of effect size variation across countries suggests that age cannot provide stable utility for making expatriation decisions. Our findings do not support trends toward favoring older employees when the goal is to enhance adjustment and job performance abroad. Expatriate age appears to be consistently unrelated to expatriate success, independent of host country culture.

In interpreting the (non-)relations between age and expatriate success, it is important to remember that age is not a causal factor in itself, but a proxy for other variables (cf. Sturman 2003). Future research may be more informative by assessing the constructs posited to impact expatriate success (e.g., job knowledge, social support, coping behaviors), rather than approximating them using age. To illustrate how researchers might do so, we examined more closely the relation between age and locational adjustment. The items on this scale cover a broad range of living conditions outside of work (food, shopping, health care, leisure time, cost of living, and housing conditions). Those items with the strongest age correlation were housing conditions ($r_{obs} = .15$) and cost of living ($r_{obs} = .14$). Both of these factors are strongly influenced by the generosity of expatriates' compensation packages. Senior expatriates, in our sample often working as CEOs or CFOs of local subsidiaries, are usually provided with much more extensive packages than younger expatriates filling assistant or technical expert positions. Research examining expatriate compensation packages would be more informative than research approximating this variable using age, both for theoretical understanding and for informing organizational practice to reduce costs and provide better support for expatriates.

The current findings of mostly negligible relations of expatriate success with a range of experience variables (total work experience, organizational tenure, time and number of prior international assignments, and number of prior international assignments in the same cultural cluster as the current host country) also have implications for organizational practice. Only tenure on the current assignment showed consistent substantial relations with adjustment and performance, indicating that expatriates tend to become somewhat more successful the longer they are on-location. These findings suggest that there may be a substantial "spin-up" period before expatriates adapt to their new context and can perform at their maximal levels (cf. Black/Mendenhall 1991). Thus, organizations should consider the benefits and drawbacks of short-term international assignments. While these assignments may be useful if the goal is to solve specific technical problems, the time it takes for expatriates to adjust and reach their maximal performance levels may limit the return on the high personal, organizational, and financial costs of the international move. More value may be realized if expatriates are given more time abroad. Similarly, if expatriation is used as a developmental experience, employees will receive the most benefit if they are given sufficient time to adjust and learn their new roles.

4.1   Future Research Directions

Considering the effect of time-on-location on expatriate outcomes, future research could profit by drawing from the organizational socialization literature and the conceptual parallels between newcomer adjustment to an organization and expatriate adjustment to a new country. Future research might also benefit from a stronger focus on the work roles and duties expatriates perform while abroad, rather than merely the international context (cf. Shin et al. 2007). Research examining the impact of job-specific and task-specific experience (Quiñones et al. 1995) can inform research on knowledge acquisition and utilization during expatriation and guide organizational practice on preparation for cross-cultural assignments and individual career development via international rotation. Future research should also examine curvilinear effects of different forms of experience on expatriate outcomes (e.g., are international experiences more beneficial when they occur early in one's career?, is there a set point beyond which additional international experience does not help to ease adjustment and enhance performance abroad?). Finally, future research should examine the impact of other forms of international experience (e.g., leisure travel, study abroad, cf. Takeuchi et al. 2005) and the role of affective valence of prior experience for expatriate success (e.g., what is the impact of prior negative experiences in a specific country on future adjustment in that country?).

References

Albrecht, Anne-Grit (2005): Untangling the Laundry List: General Mental Ability, the Big Five, and Context Related Variables as Predictors for Expatriate Success. Master's Thesis. Lüneburg, Germany: Leuphana Universität. [http://opus.uni-lueneburg.de/opus/volltexte/2006/344/].

Albrecht, Anne-Grit et al. (2018a): Design, Implementation, and Analysis of the iGOES Project. In: Wiernik, Brenton M.; Rüger, Heiko; Ones, Deniz S. (Eds.): Managing Expatriates: Success Factors in Private and Public Domains, Series on Population Studies 50. Opladen, Germany: Barbara Budrich Publishers.

Albrecht, Anne-Grit; Ones, Deniz S.; Sinangil, Handan Kepir (2018b): Expatriate Management. In: Ones, Deniz S. et al. (Eds.): The SAGE Handbook of Industrial, Work and Organizational Psychology. Volume 3: Managerial Psychology and Organizational Approaches. 2nd ed. London, United Kingdom: Sage: 429–468.

Aldwin, Carolyn M. et al. (1996): Age Differences in Stress, Coping, and Appraisal: Findings from the Normative Aging Study. In: *The Journals of Gerontology*: Series B: Psychological Sciences and Social Sciences 51B,4: P179–P188. [https://doi.org/10.1093/geronb/51B.4.P179].

Anderson, Barbara A. (2005): Expatriate Selection: Good Management or Good Luck? In: *International Journal of Human Resource Management* 16,4: 567–583. [https://doi.org/10.1080/09585190500051647]

Berry, J.W.; Sam, D.L. (1997): Acculturation and Adaptation. In: Berry, John W.; Segall, Marshall H.; Kagitçibasi, Cigdem (Eds.): Handbook of Cross-Cultural Psychology. Volume 3: Social Behavior and Applications. 2nd ed. Boston: Allyn and Bacon: 291–326.

BGRS (2016): Breakthrough to the Future of Global Talent Mobility: 2016 Global Mobility Trends Survey Report. Toronto, Canada: Brookfield Global Relocation Services. [http://globalmobilitytrends.brookfieldgrs.com].

BGRS (2015): Mindful Mobility: 2015 Global Mobility Trends Survey Report. Toronto, Canda: Brookfield Global Relocation Services.

Bhaskar-Shrinivas, Purnima et al. (2005): Input-Based and Time-Based Models of International Adjustment: Meta-Analytic Evidence and Theoretical Extensions. In: *Academy of Management Journal* 48,2: 257–281. [https://doi.org/10.5465/AMJ.2005.16928400].

Black, J. Stewart; Mendenhall, Mark E. (1991): The U-Curve Adjustment Hypothesis Revisited: A Review and Theoretical Framework. In: *Journal of International Business Studies* 22,2: 225–247. [https://doi.org/10.1057/palgrave.jibs.8490301].

Black, J. Stewart; Mendenhall, Mark E.; Oddou, Gary R. (1991): Toward a Comprehensive Model of International Adjustment: An Integration of Multiple Theoretical Perspectives. In: *Academy of Management Review* 16,2: 291–317. [https://doi.org/10.5465/AMR.1991.4278938].

Black, J. Stewart; Stephens, Gregory K. (1989): The Influence of the Spouse on American Expatriate Adjustment and Intent to Stay in Pacific Rim Overseas Assignments. In: *Journal of Management* 15,4: 529–544. [https://doi.org/10.1177/014920638901500403].

Caligiuri, Paula M. et al. (2001): The Theory of Met Expectations Applied to Expatriate Adjustment: The Role of Cross-Cultural Training. In: *International Journal of Human Resource Management* 12,3: 357–372. [https://doi.org/10.1080/09585190121711].

Cartus (2016): Trends in Global Relocation: 2016 Global Mobility Policy & Practices Survey. Danburry, CT: Cartus Corporation. [http://guidance.cartusrelocation.com/global-mobility-policy-and-practices-survey-2016.html].

Deller, Jürgen (2007): Internationaler Personaleinsatz. In: Schuler, Heinz; Sonntag, Karlheinz (Eds.): Handbuch der Arbeits- und Organisationspsychologie. Handbuch der Psychologie 6. Göttingen, Germany: Hogrefe: 648–654.

Deller, Jürgen (1997): Expatriate Selection: Possibilities and Limitations of Using Personality Scales. In: Aycan, Zeynep (Ed.): Expatriate Management: Theory and Research, New Approaches to Employee Management 4. Greenwich, CT: JAI Press: 93–116.

Deller, Jürgen; Pundt, Leena (2014): Flexible Transitions from Work to Retirement in Germany. In: Alcover, Carlos-María et al. (Eds.): Bridge Employment: A Research Handbook. New York: Routledge: 167–192.

Diener, Ed et al. (1985): The Satisfaction with Life Scale. In: *Journal of Personality Assessment* 49,1: 71–75. [https://doi.org/10.1207/s15327752jpa4901_13].

Ehrenberg, Ronald G.; Smith, Robert S. (2012): Modern Labor Economics: Theory and Public Policy. Boston, MA: Prentice Hall.

Fasbender, Ulrike et al. (2014): Deciding Whether to Work after Retirement: The Role of the Psychological Experience of Aging. In: *Journal of Vocational Behavior* 84,3: 215–224. [https://doi.org/10/bc4p].

Gross, James J. et al. (1997): Emotion and Aging: Experience, Expression, and Control. In: *Psychology and Aging* 12,4: 590–599. [https://doi.org/10.1037/0882-7974.12.4.590].

Harris, Hilary; Brewster, Chris (1999): The Coffee-Machine System: How International Selection Really Works. In: *International Journal of Human Resource Management* 10,3: 488–500. [https://doi.org/10.1080/095851999340440].

Haslberger, Arno; Brewster, Chris (2008): The Expatriate Family: An International Perspective. In: *Journal of Managerial Psychology* 23,3: 324–346. [https://doi.org/10.1108/02683940810861400].

Hechanova, Regina; Beehr, Terry A.; Christiansen, Neil D. (2003): Antecedents and Consequences of Employees' Adjustment to Overseas Assignment: A Meta-Analytic Review. In: *Applied Psychology* 52,2: 213–236. [https://doi.org/10.1111/1464-0597.00132].

Hofmann, David A.; Jacobs, Rick; Gerras, Steve J. (1992): Mapping Individual Performance over Time. In: *Journal of Applied Psychology* 77,2: 185–195. [https://doi.org/10.1037/0021-9010.77.2.185].

Judge, Timothy A. et al. (1998): Dispositional Effects on Job and Life Satisfaction: The Role of Core Evaluations. In: *Journal of Applied Psychology* 83,1: 17–34. [https://doi.org/10.1037/0021-9010.83.1.17].

Klein, Rachael M. et al. (2015): Cognitive Predictors and Age-Based Adverse Impact among Business Executives. In: *Journal of Applied Psychology* 100,5: 1497–1510. [https://doi.org/10.1037/a0038991].

Löckenhoff, Corinna E. et al. (2009): Perceptions of Aging across 26 Cultures and Their Culture-Level Associates. In: *Psychology and Aging* 24,4: 941–954. [https://doi.org/10.1037/a0016901].

Mol, Stefan T. et al. (2005): Predicting Expatriate Job Performance for Selection Purposes: A Quantitative Review. In: *Journal of Cross-Cultural Psychology* 36,5: 590–620. [https://doi.org/10.1177/0022022105278544].

Ng, Thomas W.H. et al. (2005): Predictors of Objective and Subjective Career Success: A Meta-Analysis. In: *Personnel Psychology* 58,2: 367–408. [https://doi.org/10.1111/j.1744-6570.2005.00515.x].

Ng, Thomas W.H.; Feldman, Daniel C. (2010): The Relationships of Age with Job Attitudes: A Meta-Analysis. In: *Personnel Psychology* 63,3: 677–718. [https://doi.org/10.1111/j.1744-6570.2010.01184.x].

Ng, Thomas W.H.; Feldman, Daniel C. (2008): The Relationship of Age to Ten Dimensions of Job Performance. In: *Journal of Applied Psychology* 93,2: 392–423. [https://doi.org/10.1037/0021-9010.93.2.392].

Olsen, Jesse E.; Martins, Luis L. (2009): The Effects of Expatriate Demographic Characteristics on Adjustment: A Social Identity Approach. In: *Human Resource Management* 48,2: 311–328. [https://doi.org/10.1002/hrm.20281].

Perry, Elissa L.; Finkelstein, Lisa M. (1999): Toward a Broader View of Age Discrimination in Employment-Related Decisions: A Joint Consideration of Organizational Factors and Cognitive Processes. In: *Human Resource Management Review* 9,1: 21–49. [https://doi.org/10.1016/S1053-4822(99)00010-8].

Posthuma, Richard A.; Campion, Michael A. (2009): Age Stereotypes in the Workplace: Common Stereotypes, Moderators, and Future Research Directions. In: *Journal of Management* 35,1: 158–188. [https://doi.org/10.1177/0149206308318617].

Quiñones, Miguel A.; Ford, J. Kevin; Teachout, Mark S. (1995): The Relationship between Work Experience and Job Performance: A Conceptual and Meta-analytic Review. In: *Personnel Psychology* 48,4: 887–910. [https://doi.org/10.1111/j.1744-6570.1995.tb01785.x].

Salthouse, Timothy A. (2004): Localizing Age-Related Individual Differences in a Hierarchical Structure. In: *Intelligence* 32,6: 541–561. [https://doi.org/10.1016/j.intell.2004.07.003].

Schmidt, Frank L.; Hunter, John E. (2015): Methods of Meta-Analysis: Correcting Error and Bias in Research Findings. 3rd ed. Thousand Oaks, CA: Sage. [https://doi.org/10/b6mg].

Selmer, Jan (2001): Expatriate Selection: Back to Basics? In: *The International Journal of Human Resource Management* 12,8: 1219–1233. [https://doi.org/10.1080/09585190110083767].

Shin, Shung J.; Morgeson, Frederick P.; Campion, Michael A. (2007): What You Do Depends on Where You Are: Understanding How Domestic and Expatriate Work Requirements Depend upon the Cultural Context. In: *Journal of International Business Studies* 38: 64–83. [https://doi.org/10.1057/palgrave.jibs.8400247].

Sturman, Michael C. (2003): Searching for the Inverted U-Shaped Relationship between Time and Performance: Meta-Analyses of the Experience/Performance, Tenure/Performance, and Age/Performance Relationships. In: *Journal of Management* 29,5: 609–640. [https://doi.org/10.1016/s0149-2063(03)00028-x].

Sung, Kyu-taik (2001): Elder Respect: Exploration of Ideals and Forms in East Asia. In: *Journal of Aging Studies* 15,1: 13–26. [https://doi.org/10.1016/S0890-4065(00)00014-1].

Takeuchi, Riki et al. (2005): An Integrative View of International Experience. In: *Academy of Management Journal* 48,1: 85–100. [https://doi.org/10.5465/AMJ.2005.15993143].

Tesluk, Paul E.; Jacobs, Rick R. (1998): Toward an Integrated Model of Work Experience. In: *Personnel Psychology* 51,2: 321–355. [https://doi.org/10.1111/j.1744-6570.1998.tb00728.x].

Viswesvaran, Chockalingam; Ones, Deniz S.; Schmidt, Frank L. (1996): Comparative Analysis of the Reliability of Job Performance Ratings. In: *Journal of Applied Psychology* 81,5: 557–574. [https://doi.org/10/c8f68f].

Weiss, Howard M. (1990): Learning Theory and Industrial and Organizational Psychology. In: Dunnette, Marvin D.; Hough, Leaetta M. (Eds.): Handbook of Industrial and Organizational Psychology. Volume 1. 2nd ed. Palo Alto, CA: Consulting Psychologists Press: 171–221.

WHO (2011): Global Health and Aging. Geneva, Switzerland: World Health Organization. [http://www.who.int/ageing/publications/global_health.pdf].

Wiernik, Brenton M.; Dilchert, Stephan; Ones, Deniz S. (2016): Age and Employee Green Behaviors: A Meta-Analysis. In: *Frontiers in Psychology*, Research Topic: Corporate Social Responsibility and Organizational Psychology: Quid pro Quo 7: 194. [https://doi.org/10/bc4f].

Wiernik, Brenton M.; Ones, Deniz S.; Dilchert, Stephan (2013): Age and Environmental Sustainability: A Meta-Analysis. In: *Journal of Managerial Psychology*, Special Issue: Facilitating Age Diversity in Organizations 28,7/8: 826–856. [https://doi.org/10/bc4q].

Wiernik, Brenton M.; Rüger, Heiko; Ones, Deniz S. (2018): Advancing Expatriate Research in Public and Private Sectors. In: Wiernik, Brenton M.; Rüger, Heiko; Ones, Deniz S. (Eds.): Managing Expatriates: Success Factors in Private and Public Domains, Series on Population Studies 50. Opladen, Germany: Barbara Budrich Publishers.

Impacts of Age, Tenure, and Experience on Expatriate Adjustment and Job Satisfaction

Stine Waibel, Heiko Rüger, Brenton M. Wiernik, and Herbert Fliege

Abstract

This chapter analyses how time-related variables such as age and organizational tenure relate to expatriate adjustment and job satisfaction using a sample of 1,771 German Foreign Service (GFS) diplomats, as well as the moderating effects of hierarchical level and job autonomy of these relations. We observed no significant age effects on locational adjustment, supporting meta-analytic findings and theoretical predictions from socioemotional selectivity theory that diverging growth and loss processes may cancel out. We find that, in general, diplomats report similar levels of job satisfaction across career stages, but that that job autonomy moderates relations between tenure and satisfaction among high-level diplomats. When high-ranking civil servants lack job autonomy, their job satisfaction decrease with progressing tenure and age, likely due to increasingly frustrated expectations. The present study adds to a still sparse literature analyzing changes in expatriate outcomes associated with time-related factors.

1   Introduction

The relationship between age and expatriate success has not figured prominently in expatriation research (Olsen/Martins 2009). The demographic composition of the expatriate workforce is changing (Napier et al. 2014), and a reconsideration of demographic characteristics beyond mere treatment as control variables is in order (cf. Wechtler et al. 2015). The average age of expatriate professionals is rising. Currently, almost 60% of expatriates are 40 or older, whereas the historical average was around 54% (BGRS 2016: 17). Brookfield GRS attributed this shift to "companies' desire to maximize and leverage known past performance" by selecting more experienced employees as expatriates (BGRS 2011: 10). Of course, the composition of the international assignee population is prone to annual fluctuations due to changing economic conditions, so a longer time series would be necessary to discern a stable secular trend. The graying of expatriates echoes similar age shifts in general Western populations which have also brought to the fore the need to understand how to retain and motivate older workers (Fasbender et al. 2014; Kooij et al. 2008).

The aging expatriate population raises questions about the impacts these shifts may have expatriate success. This chapter examines the impact of age and two related temporal variables – organizational tenure and experience – on expatriate outcomes. Our analyses draw on lifespan psychology to examine how socioemotional priorities of expatriates of different ages impact adjustment and satisfaction. We contribute to the still scarce knowledge on age effects in expatriation, interpret our results considering existing evidence, and discuss implications for expatriate management practice. Our results are of interest for foreign services as well as multinational organizations that rely on a workforce prepared for frequent international relocation to maintain efficient and integrated organizational functioning.

1.1 Temporal Variables and Organizational Outcomes

From the perspective of the organizational sciences, several theoretical frameworks (e.g., Caspi et al. 2005; Kacmar/Ferris 1989; Kanfer/Ackerman 2004; Ng/Feldman 2010; Rauschenbach et al. 2013; Rhodes 1983; Super 1980), as well as persistent lay stereotypes (Dennis/Thomas 2007), suggest a variety of mechanisms through which employee age may impact organizationally-relevant outcomes (e.g., job performance, motivation, job satisfaction, organizational commitment). However, statistically-powerful meta-analytic and large-sample investigations show that most age effects are negligible to small. Compared to younger employees, older employees tend to more strongly value job autonomy ($\rho = .27$; Kooij et al. 2011) and less value opportunities for promotion/advancement ($\rho = -.23$; Kooij et al. 2011) and career development ($\rho = -.14$, cf. $\rho = -.22$ for career development behavior; Ng/Feldman 2012), but age is largely unrelated to other motives (e.g., job security, altruism). In terms of performance, older employees tend to persist more through challenges ($\rho = .27$), to perform fewer unsafe or counterproductive behaviors ($\rho = -.10$, $-.12$), and to be less tardy/absent ($\rho = -.26$; Ng/Feldman 2008). Age is negligibly to weakly related to other performance domains (e.g., core technical performance, helping, creativity/innovation, pro-environmental behavior; Ng/Feldman 2008, 2012; Wiernik et al. 2016), as well as other important criteria, such as stress, work–family balance, workplace interpersonal relationships, and many health outcomes (Ng/Feldman 2012; Rauschenbach et al. 2013). However, relations of age with most criteria are highly variable across studies, indicating that relations may be stronger in some contexts.

In contrast to generally negligible relations of age with work behaviors, age shows small to moderate relations (ρs around .10–.20) with a variety of positive work attitudes, such as job satisfaction, organizational commitment, job involvement, and (low) perceived stressors (Ng/Feldman 2010, 2012). The size of age–attitude relations appears to be decreasing over time (Ng/Feldman 2010; Teclaw et al. 2014), perhaps in response to improved organizational management practices. Some studies have found U-shaped relations between age and work attitudes (e.g., Clark et al. 1996; Hochwarter et al. 2001); the magnitudes of such curvilinear effects are small (cf. Ng/Feldman 2010). As with behaviors, age–attitude relations are variable across studies; Ng and Feldman (2015) meta-analytically found that age and job autonomy interacted to drive relations with work attitudes.

Beyond age, other temporal variables, such as experience and organizational tenure have also received much attention in organizational research. Organizational tenure and work experience are weakly to moderately positively related with job performance; this effect is strongest at low levels of experience/tenure and decreases over time (Ng/Feldman 2015; Sturman 2003). Tenure and experience appear to be unrelated to satisfaction (Ng et al. 2005).

An important caveat for interpreting relations between temporal variables and work outcomes is that these variables are not posited to impact outcomes *per se*, but rather are regarded as proxy indicators for other time-related variables that have direct effects, such as changes in life, work, and family roles, cognitive and physical abilities, accumulated knowledge and skill, personality traits, and psychological self-concepts (cf. Caspi et al. 2005; Kanfer/Ackerman 2004; Kooij et al. 2008; Lawrence 1987). These underlying processes may be partly conflicting and may cancel out in zero-order relations between temporal variables and outcomes (Hur et al. 2014; Rauschenbach et al. 2013); therefore, analyses of temporal variables must carefully specify the specific theoretical model connecting the temporal variable with the outcome and attempt to control competing factors. Further, researchers must consider whether sample attrition effects can account for observed results; higher levels of satisfaction or performance among older workers may simply reflect that dissatisfied and poorly performing workers have left the workforce (Kirian 2008).

1.2 Expatriate Research on Temporal Variables

In expatriate research, meta-analyses have found expatriate age to be negligibly related to locational, work, and interaction adjustment (ρs range -.03 to .07; Hechanova et al. 2003) and job performance ($\rho = .04$; Mol et al. 2005). Thus, evidence does not support zero-order relations between age and expatriate success, though some researchers have suggested more complex relations (see below). A small number of studies have examined relations between expatriate age and work attitudes, such as job satisfaction and organizational commitment. Parallel to findings from domestic employees, age tends to be associated with more positive attitudes among expatriates (e.g., Black et al. 1992; Gregersen/Black 1992; van Oudenhoven et al. 2003), though negative relations are not uncommon (Bhuian/Mengue 2002). To our knowledge, no meta-analysis has examined the relation between expatriate age/tenure and job attitudes.

Though age is occasionally considered atheoretically in expatriate research (e.g., as a control variable), several frameworks on the relation between expatriate age and attitudinal outcomes have been proposed. First, Selmer (2001) proposed that age may facilitate adjustment in non-Western host societies that culturally revere experience and seniority.[1] Second, Wechtler et al. (2015) applied socioemotional selectivity theory (Carstensen et al. 1999) to argue that age enhances the effects of emotional regulation processes on adjustment. This echoes other findings from expatriates showing age-related growth of socioemotional traits and skills, such as intercultural competence, cultural empathy, and open-mindedness (Froese/ Peltokorpi 2011; Van der Zee/Brinkmann 2004; Van Oudenhoven et al. 2003). Third, research on career development suggests that employees who invest large portions of their careers in a single organization develop strong psychological and social ties to their organization, as well as accumulate tacit knowledge and practical benefits that enhance their embeddedness in the organization (Feldman/Ng 2007). Deeply embedded older expatriates with long tenure may thus be more willing to endure adjustment hardships, be better able to garner organizational and social support, and more likely to maintain positive views of their employer (Banai/Reisel 1993; Gregersen 1992; Gregersen/Black 1992; Gregersen 1992), particularly if they have had much previous international experience in their careers.

---

[1] However, a subsequent inter-contextual meta-analysis of expatriates in a wide range of countries did not replicate these results (Albrecht et al. 2018b, Chapter 8, this volume). This study found no pattern of relations between age–adjustment correlations and cultural age norms. In the current study, we are unable to examine cultural norm effects on age–attitude relations, as geographic information was not gathered to preserve respondent anonymity.

1.3   The Current Study

This study examines the impact of expatriate, tenure, and experience on attitudinal outcomes in a unique population of expatriates – diplomats in the German Foreign Service (GFS). In contrast to private sector expatriates for whom an international assignment may be undertaken only once or twice in their careers (Albrecht et al. 2018a), for diplomats, international assignments are a basic professional requirement. Throughout their careers, diplomats move to a new host country every 3–5 years. Therefore, ability and motivation to lead a professional life as a "permanent expatriate" are important criteria during personnel recruitment. Diplomats typically join the GFS early in their careers and remain until their retirement. A consequence of these frequent rotations and early recruitment is that calendar age, organizational tenure, and international experience are highly correlated among GFS diplomats (see Tables 1 and 2). Below, we consider the impacts of these variables on expatriate outcomes, while acknowledging that we cannot separate their distinct effects. To develop our hypotheses, we draw on both the expatriate literature and relevant findings from domestic employees.

1.4   Locational Adjustment

Socioemotional selectivity theory (Carstensen et al. 1999) posits that employees' priorities change as they age. Younger employees anticipate long future careers, so they focus on developing new skills and securing advancement opportunities. Older employees, by contrast, perceive shorter remaining periods in their careers, so they invest in activities and resources that provide them with more immediate affective satisfaction (e.g., building social ties, increasing comfort). This change in priorities is associated with increased interpersonal and emotional regulatory skill (Caspi et al. 2005), which may facilitate expatriate adjustment (Wechtler et al. 2015). However, becoming older is also associated with loss of social resources (Baltes et al. 1999). Expatriation may accentuate this process as international moves disrupt older expatriates' already weakening social relationships, support systems, and local networks (Caligiuri et al. 1998; Fontaine 1986). This is particularly true for close, intimate relationships that are hard to replace (Lang/Carstensen 1994; versus flexible, more transient relationships; Morgan 1988). Consequently, it is likely that international moves are associated with greater social and emotional costs for older individuals, since they will have more difficulty reconstructing their social environment.

Overall, while diplomats may improve their social and emotional skills over time, they will at the same time be more prone to loss of the social resources that are evidently an important component of cross-cultural adjustment. Therefore, we do not expect to find an effect of age on diplomats' adjustment to the living conditions in the host environment. This proposition is in line with meta-analytic evidence cited above. Similarly and also in line with previous meta-analytic findings (Hechanova et al. 2003), we expect weak relations of expatriate organizational tenure and previous international experience on adjustment.

Table 1: Descriptive statistics and zero-order correlations among study variables

		Mean	SD	Min	Max	1	2	3	4	5	6	7
1	Age	45.14	9.82	23	63							
2	Organizational tenure	18.13	9.73	1	44	.82 (.81, .83)						
3	No. previous assignments	5.85	3	0	19	.78 (.76, .80)	.87 (.86, .88)					
4	General job satisfaction	0.00	.58	-2.84	1.26	.00 (-.06, .06)	.05 (-.01, .11)	.01 (-.04, .07)				
5	Locational adjustment	2.75	.6	1.13	3.88	.01 (-.04, .06)	.02 (-.02, .07)	-.03 (-.08, .01)	.35 (.29, .41)			
6	Perceived social support	3.06	.63	1	4	-.22 (-.26, -.16)	-.16 (-.21, -.11)	-.15 (-.20, -.10)	.31 (.24, .37)	.19 (.14, .25)		
7	Emotional functioning	65.58	26.32	0	100	.08 (.03, .13)	.07 (.02, .11)	.07 (.02, .11)	.43 (.37, .49)	.25 (.19, .30)	.30 (.25, .35)	
8	Job autonomy	2.79	.91	1	4	.19 (.15, .24)	.21 (.17, .26)	.21 (.18, .26)	.49 (.44, .54)	.06 (.01, .12)	.09 (.04, .14)	.17 (.12, .21)

Note: 90% confidence intervals in parentheses; correlations are corrected for measurement error.

1.5   Job Satisfaction

First, in line with Ng and Feldman's (2010) meta-analysis and most expatriate research cited above, we predict age and tenure will be positively related with diplomats' attitudes toward their jobs. This hypothesis is based on the theoretical premise that continuous investment in one's organization and international skillset will produce identification with their work and satisfaction with employment as a highly-mobile diplomat (Becker 1960; Gregersen 1992). In addition, firm-specific investments make alternative employment opportunities become less attractive and available over time, in turn increasing commitment and satisfaction with the current job (Feldman/Ng 2007).

Second, we test if the relation between temporal variables and job satisfaction is moderated by job characteristics. Some work values, particularly values for job autonomy, increase in priority over the lifespan (Kooij et al. 2011). Autonomy (i.e., freedom in scheduling one's work and deciding how to complete tasks; Hackman/Oldham 1976) is associated with job satisfaction (Humphrey et al. 2007). Autonomy may be particularly valuable for expatriates facing international job transitions, as it allows them flexibility to apply their prior work and life experiences and adapt their new roles to be more predictable and controllable (cf. Black 1988). Socioemotional selectivity theory predicts that older individuals prioritize immediate emotional fulfillment, as they have less time remaining in the future for situations to improve (Carstensen et al. 1999); older diplomats may thus respond more negatively to lack of autonomy than younger diplomats, as they are more sensitive to the frustration of these increasingly important needs (Krumm et al. 2013). This effect may be particularly pronounced among high-level civil servants in the GFS, as these employees often expect that advancement in the Foreign Service implies gains in discretion and autonomy (Holland 1984). Frustration of these expectations may enhance senior diplomats' dissatisfaction in jobs that are overly constraining (Wanous et al. 1992).

2   Methods

2.1   Participants

The Foreign Service diplomat sample includes 1,771 diplomats who were posted abroad at the time of data collection (see Wiernik et al. 2018, Chapter 1, and Rüger et al. 2018, Appendix B, this volume, for more details). The sample was 47% female. Diplomats ranged in age from 23 to 63 ($M = 45.14$, $SD = 9.82$). Age, organizational tenure, and rotation experience (number of previous international assignments) were all highly correlated (r ranged .78 to .87; see Table 1). Average organizational tenure and rotation experience for different age groups are presented in Table 2. Diplomats younger than 30 years had completed fewer than two previous assignments on average and spent about four years in the organization, while the oldest group of diplomats ($\geq$ 60 years) had completed more than ten previous assignments on average and had more than 30 years of organizational tenure.

Table 2: Completed rotation posts and organizational tenure by age groups

Age group	Previous international assignments			Organizational tenure		
	N	M	SD	N	M	SD
20-29	108	1.86	.80	106	4.31	2.11
30-39	234	3.09	1.38	238	9.63	5.14
40-49	492	6.07	1.88	493	19.04	5.14
50-59	365	7.67	2.38	371	24.54	7.36
60+	94	10.39	2.47	94	32.85	5.84
Total	1,293	5.94	2.99	1,302	18.50	9.60

Note: own calculations.

2.2   Measures

Time-related variables. Age and organizational tenure were measured continuously in years. Expatriate experience was measured as the number of previous international rotation assignments the employee had completed prior to the current one.

Locational adjustment. Expatriates' adjustment to their current living situations was measured using eight items assessing the degree of comfort individuals felt in their new location regarding everyday needs and activities (e.g., "I can easily look after everyday errands"; $\alpha = .81$).

Job satisfaction. General job satisfaction was measured using seven items assessing individuals' degree of satisfaction with their working conditions, compensation, and career progress. An example item is "How satisfied are you with the working atmosphere at your current post?" The items of this scale were standardized before being summed to bring variables with different response scales to a comparable metric ($\alpha = .67$).

Social support. Perceived social support was measured using four items from the Berlin Social-Support Scales (Schulz/Schwarzer 2003) which were developed to assess stress and coping among cancer patients. The item showing the largest factor loading for each subscale was selected for use in this abbreviated measure. An example item is "When I am sad, there are people who cheer me up". This measure had a Cronbach's $\alpha = .85$.

Emotional functioning. Emotional functioning was measured by selecting three of the four items from the Quality of Life Questionnaire (QLQ; Aaronson et al. 1993) that relate to emotional functioning (e.g., "Did you feel depressed?"; $\alpha = .82$).

Job autonomy. Perceived job autonomy was measured using three items on individuals' perceptions of their job as giving them opportunities for autonomy (e.g., "I have little decision-making authority" [reversed]; $\alpha = .87$).

Control variables. For the regression analyses, we controlled for gender, civil service grade (hierarchical level; categories are secretarial pool, ordinary civil service diplomats [CS], intermediate CS, higher intermediate CS, and higher [upper-level] CS), and years spent on the current assignment. Gender was controlled because of substantial gender relations with age in this sample, as well as with the attitudinal variables under investigation (see Waibel/Rüger 2018, Chapter 18, this volume). Similarly, hierarchical level and time on current assignment were controlled because these variables have been meta-analytically shown to have substantial effects on expatriate adjustment and other attitudinal outcomes.

2.3   Analyses

We first analyzed whether the time-related variables of age, organizational tenure, and expatriate experience were correlated with job satisfaction or general adjustment. Aligned with our proposition derived from socioemotional selectivity theory, we also check (1) if social resources (perceived social support) decrease with age, tenure, and experience, and (2) whether emotional regulation improves over time. We approximate emotional regulation with the emotional functioning subscale of the QLQ. Correlations were corrected for unreliability using coefficient alpha for the psychological and attitudinal measures; age, tenure, and experience were assumed to be measured without error.

We then tested our hypotheses regarding the interaction between organizational tenure and autonomy in predicting job satisfaction using moderated multiple regression. We used tenure instead of age as a predictor because tenure was strongly correlated with age (Table 1), and there were fewer missing values for the tenure measure. Results using age instead showed similar results. We mean-centered age and autonomy in the regressions to enable meaningful interpretation of the interaction effect.

We estimated this model in 3 subsamples. First, we examined the results in the entire sample of GFS employees. Next, we estimated the model separately in subsamples of (1) only upper-level diplomats and (2) lower-level employees (including ordinary, intermediate, and higher intermediate civil servants and the secretarial pool). The higher-level employee subsample is most directly comparable in their qualifications and job roles to the private sector expatriate managers that are the focus of most expatriate research. The lower-level sample reflects an alternative population of employees that is relatively less-studied in expatriate research. Estimating the models across hierarchical levels also allows us to examine whether autonomy is differentially important across different GFS roles. In each sample, models were estimated controlling for gender, time on current assignment, and civil service grade (hierarchical level).

3   Results

Descriptive statistics and correlations are shown in Table 1. As expected, we did not find meaningful association between overall adjustment and age ($r_c = .01$), tenure ($r_c = .02$), or number of previous assignments ($r_c = -.03$). In line with our hypotheses, we found a small decline in perceived social support ($r_c = -.22$) as diplomats become older. As perceived social support is positively related to adjustment ($r_c = .19$), the decrease in social resources associated with age is apparently *not* reflected in lower adjustment for diplomats more advanced in age and organizational tenure, indicative of a compensation process. Contrary to our expectation, emotional functioning increased only slightly with age ($r = .08$); this negligible relation may be due to the available measure, which assesses emotional functioning/mental health, rather than the social and emotional regulatory capacities considered by socioemotional selectivity theory *per se*. Also contrary to our expectations, job satisfaction was not associated with age ($r_c = .00$), tenure ($r_c = .05$), and or number of completed assignments ($r_c = .01$).

Analyses of the moderating effect of job autonomy on the time–satisfaction relation are shown in Table 3. We introduced variables in blocks. The first block included control variables, the second block added main effects of job autonomy and organizational tenure, and the third block added the interaction between autonomy and tenure. Step 1 of the model

Table 3: Regression of job satisfaction onto the interaction between tenure and job autonomy

	All GFS Employees			Upper-level civil servants			Other civil servants		
	Step 1	Step 2	Step 3	Step 1	Step 2	Step 3	Step 1	Step 2	Step 3
Male	.01 (.04)	-.03 (.04)	-.03 (.04)	.03 (.07)	.03 (.07)	.03 (.07)	.01 (.04)	-.04 (.04)	-.04 (.04)
Time on current assignment	.03 (.01)	.02 (.01)	.02 (.01)	.14 (.03)	.18 (.03)	.15 (.03)	.01 (.01)	-.01 (.01)	-.01 (.01)
Civil service grade[A]									
Secretary pool	-.25 (.06)	.00 (.07)	-.01 (.06)				-.16 (.06)	.08 (.07)	.08 (.07)
Ordinary	-.21 (.11)	-.13 (.11)	-.12 (.11)				-.12 (.11)	-.06 (.11)	-.06 (.11)
Intermediate	-.32 (.05)	-.13 (.05)	-.13 (.05)				-.23 (.05)	-.06 (.05)	-.06 (.05)
Higher-intermediate	-.11 (.04)	-.07 (.04)	-.07 (.04)						
Organizational tenure		-.05 (.00)	-.06 (.00)		-.12 (.00)	-.46 (.01)		-.04 (.00)	-.04 (.00)
Job autonomy		.39 (.02)	.38 (.02)		.30 (.06)	.31 (.06)		.41 (.03)	.40 (.03)
Org. tenure × job autonomy			.06 (.00)			.45 (.01)			.02 (.00)
N	1,151	1,151	1,151	240	240	240	911	911	911
R/adj. R	.300/.292	.416/.409	.421/.413	.148/.000	.315/.260	.425/.386	.247/.234	.394/.384	.394/.383
R^2/adj. R^2	.090/.085	.173/.167	.177/.171	.022/-.003	.099/.068	.181/.149	.061/.055	.155/.148	.155/.147
Δ adj. R^2		.082	.003		.068	.081		.093	.000
(90% confidence interval)		(.052, .111)	(.000, .025)		(.015, .121)	(.019, .144)		(.059, .126)	(.000, .021)

Note: Standardized regression coefficients with robust standard errors in parentheses; [A] referenced to upper-level civil service for all GFS employees models and to higher-intermediate civil service for lower-level civil servants models.

for all GFS employees showed that increasing hierarchical level was generally associated with higher job satisfaction (all civil service grade βs were negative, referenced to upper-level CS diplomats); Step 2 shows that much of these effects were accounted for by differences in tenure and autonomy across CS grades. Adding main effects for tenure and autonomy substantially improves model prediction (adjusted ΔR^2 = .082 [90% CI .052, .111]), indicating that these variables are associated with job satisfaction. However, adding the interaction between tenure and autonomy negligibly and non-significantly increased model prediction (adjusted ΔR^2 = .003 [90% CI .000, .025]). This indicates that while job autonomy does promote satisfaction among GFS employees, this effect appears to be relatively constant across tenure levels.

Results for lower-level employees were essentially identical to those for the full GFS sample. However, results for upper-level civil servants were strongly divergent. For these employees, the interaction effect was strong, and adding it substantially increased model prediction (adjusted ΔR^2 = .081 [90% CI .019, .144]). This interaction is depicted in Figure 1.

Figure 1: Job autonomy as moderator in the relationship between job satisfaction and tenure

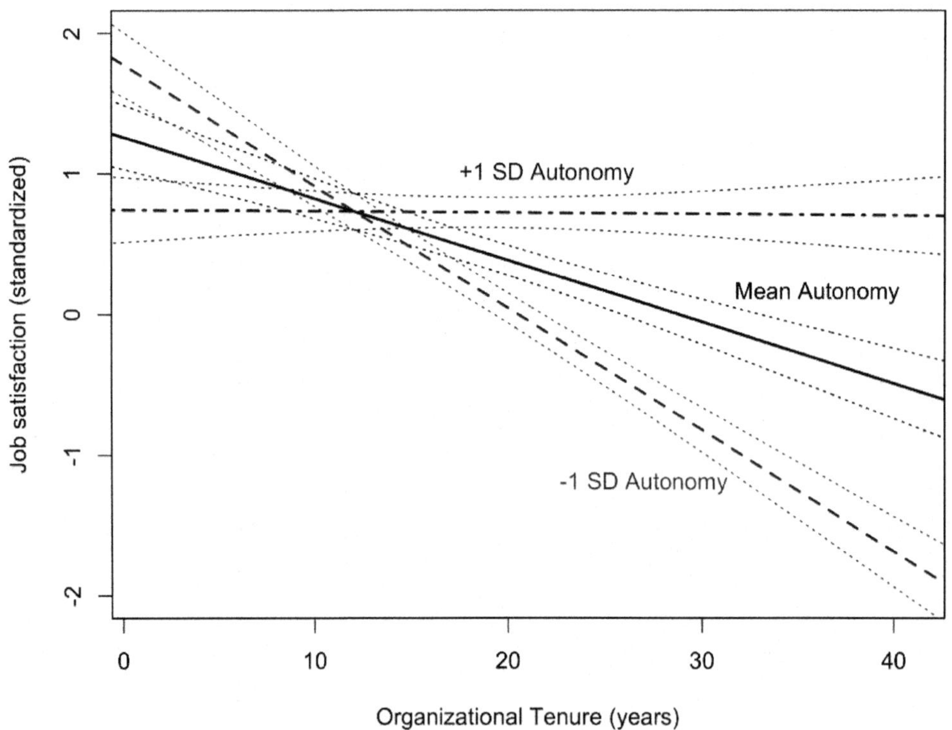

Note: Marginal effect of organizational tenure on job satisfaction for three levels of job autonomy, with 90% confidence interval. Lines based on upper-level civil servants regression model shown in Table 3 (controlling for gender and time on current assignment).

For high-autonomy positions, tenure is unrelated to job satisfaction. However, as job autonomy decreases, the relation between tenure and satisfaction becomes increasingly negative. Supporting our predictions, high-ranking diplomats with long tenure appear to expect a great deal of autonomy in carrying out their duties, and they grow increasingly frustrated if such latitude is not afforded. (One may alternatively interpret this interaction as indicating, while autonomy is strongly associated with satisfaction among long tenure diplomats [β = .76 at +1 SD tenure], for earlier-career diplomats, too much autonomy may be overwhelming [β = -.14 at -1 SD tenure].)

4   Discussion

Using a sample of German Foreign Service (GFS) employees, we tested if temporal variables – age, tenure, experience, and hierarchical level – contributed to expatriates' job satisfaction and adjustment to changing host environments. The present study adds to a growing literature analyzing the role of temporal variables in driving expatriate outcomes.

Overall, we did not observe substantial effects of temporal variables on locational adjustment. These results are in line with current meta-analytic evidence. Supporting our predictions derived from socioemotional selectivity theory, we found that age was associated with losses in social support and (slight) increases in emotional functioning. These factors influence adjustment in the opposite direction. Thus, if they emerge simultaneously, their effects may cancel out, explaining the near-zero overall age effect. While our results indicate that high mobility may particularly threaten the social relations of older employees, the negligible overall age effect on adjustment indicates that they can compensate for this social resource loss by growth in other areas, including emotional competence.

By and large, our results therefore speak against indiscriminate claims that age can serve as a positive personal characteristic in recruiting and selecting "the most costly employees of any business organization" (i.e., expatriates; Selmer 2001: 1220). Rather, it is more useful to consider the differential effects of time-related processes and their concomitant compensation. Employers should consider how to provide age-sensitive social support structures during international assignments while recognizing the benefits older expatriates' experience and personal growth may provide. These compensatory processes should be the subject of further research.

Our second central finding is that diplomats report similar levels of job satisfaction over their career spans. This finding runs counter to our hypothesis that the more expatriate employees advance in terms of age and tenure, the more time and energy they will have invested into international assignments, the more they will have socialized to their international jobs, and the more they will commit to their employing organization. This result is in line with findings from recent studies on domestic employees, which have also contested simplified assumptions about older workers reporting unequivocally higher levels of job satisfaction (cf. Krumm et al. 2013; Ng/Feldman 2010; Teclaw et al. 2014). Our findings should not be taken to mean that these investment factors are unimportant for satisfaction, only that age as a proxy variable is too deficient and contaminated to detect their effects.

Instead, among higher-level civil service diplomats, we found support for our hypothesis derived from socioemotional selectivity theory and the theory of met expectations that job autonomy moderates the relation between time-related variables and general job satisfaction. We found that when jobs lacked autonomy, increased tenure was strongly associated with decreased job satisfaction. This finding contrasts Ng and Feldman's (2015) meta-analytic findings that autonomy is more strongly related to satisfaction among *younger* employees; Ng and Feldman interpreted their finding as supporting socioemotional selectivity theory's prediction that younger workers more strongly value knowledge acquisition (on the basis that high-autonomy jobs allow more opportunities to learn and grow). However, our results do align with socioemotional selectivity theory's prediction that older workers are more sensitive to needs–supply misfit (cf. Krumm et al. 2013) and that older workers' have greater autonomy needs (Kooij et al. 2011). For the current sample, this finding also supports predictions from the theory of met expectations, which posits that high-level employees may expect wide latitude in how they work and grow increasingly dissatisfied if these expectations are unmet (Wanous et al. 1992). Finally, our results also support predictions from selective optimization and compensation theory, which posit that individuals seek to tailor their environments to fit their unique strengths and weaknesses. Older workers are more aware of their personal needs, so autonomy to work as they want is more important to their satisfaction than it is for younger workers, who may need more support and guidance (Truxillo et al. 2012).

Our findings that job autonomy is generally beneficial for satisfaction aligns with meta-analytic findings (Humphrey et al. 2007) and other expatriate research highlighting the negative impacts of low autonomy and poor employment conditions on expatriates in transition (e.g., Bolino/Feldman 2000; Takeuchi et al. 2008). Large bureaucratic organizations sometimes provide limited leeway for employees to tailor their jobs. Future research should explore how organizations can improve expatriate job characteristics and better align expatriates' expectations with their real work experiences, particularly for high performer employees (like the upper-level diplomats in the current sample) who offer great value to their organizations (Black/Gregersen 1990). In managing high-level expatriates, multinational organizations should consider expatriates' qualifications and occupational levels, as well as how the value attributed to autonomy and other job characteristics may change as their careers progress. Lack of renewed stimulation after international job transitions and misfit between valued job characteristics and actual job definitions may lead to a dissatisfied and potentially unproductive workforce.

4.1   Study Strengths and Limitations

Our study is characterized by several important strengths and limitations. Starting with the strengths, we used a large sample diplomats in the German Foreign Service. This sample is both part of an understudied population (public sector expatriates) and permits several important inferences. First, the GFS experiences little early attrition of employees, reducing the likelihood of selective dropout biasing our results (healthy worker effect). Second, this employment stability also permits us to rule out increases in job satisfaction as simply reflecting career advancement, as diplomats typically stay within the same career track throughout their working life (cf. research suggesting that age- and tenure-related increases in job satisfaction may simply be due to employees' occupational mobility; Morrow/McElroy 1987).

A limitation of our study, as mentioned previously, is that, because of the cross-sectional nature of our data, we were not able to distinguish the effects of chronological age, organizational tenure, and accumulated international experience (cf. Sturman 2003). For our sample of German diplomats, these temporal variables are strongly correlated. We considered the implications of this confounding in our theoretical development regarding conflicting developmental effects on adjustment. Additionally, in cross-sectional samples as heterogeneous in age as ours, age–criterion relations may further be confounded by generational cohort effects (Riley 1973). Separating the influences of maturation, experience, tenure, and cohort requires cross-sequential designs involving longitudinal analyses of multiple cohorts; such samples are difficult to realize in expatriate research and are not possible for the current population considering needs to maintain anonymity.

In summary, this chapter provides new insights into the role of temporal variables for expatriate attitudes. We show consistency with previous findings from expatriate and domestic research and highlight the importance of met expectations over the lifespan for driving satisfaction.

References

Aaronson, Neil K. et al. (1993): The European Organization for Research and Treatment of Cancer QLQ-C30: A Quality-of-Life Instrument for Use in International Clinical Trials in Oncology. In: *Journal of the National Cancer Institute* 85,5: 365–376. [https://doi.org/10.1093/jnci/85.5.365].

Albrecht, Anne-Grit; Ones, Deniz S.; Sinangil, Handan Kepir (2018a): Expatriate Management. In: Ones, Deniz S. et al. (Eds.): The SAGE Handbook of Industrial, Work and Organizational Psychology. Volume 3: Managerial Psychology and Organizational Approaches. 2nd ed. London, United Kingdom: Sage: 429–468.

Albrecht, Anne-Grit et al. (2018b): The Impact of Age and Experience on Expatriate Outcomes. In: Wiernik, Brenton M.; Rüger, Heiko; Ones, Deniz S. (Eds.): Managing Expatriates: Success Factors in Private and Public Domains. Leverkusen, Germany: Budrich.

Baillargeon, Jacques (2001): Characteristics of the Healthy Worker Effect. In: *Occupational Medicine* 16,2: 359–366. [http://health.phys.iit.edu/archives/attachments/20070212/b653e956/attachment-0002.pdf].

Baltes, Paul B.; Staudinger, Ursula M.; Lindenberger, Ulman (1999): Lifespan Psychology: Theory and Application to Intellectual Functioning. In: *Annual Review of Psychology* 50: 471–507. [https://doi.org/10.1146/annurev.psych.50.1.471].

Banai, Moshe; Reisel, William D. (1993): Expatriate Managers' Loyalty to the MNC: Myth or Reality? An Exploratory Study. In: *Journal of International Business Studies* 24,2: 233–248. [https://doi.org/10.1057/palgrave.jibs.8490231].

Becker, Howard S. (1960): Notes on the Concept of Commitment. In: *American Journal of Sociology* 66,1: 32–40. [https://doi.org/10.1086/222820].

BGRS (2016): Breakthrough to the Future of Global Talent Mobility: 2016 Global Mobility Trends Survey Report. Toronto, Canada: Brookfield Global Relocation Services. [http://globalmobilitytrends.brookfieldgrs.com].

BGRS (2011): Global Relocation Trends: 2011 Survey Report. Toronto, Canda: Brookfield Global Relocation Services.

Bhuian, Shahid N.; Mengue, Bulent (2002): An Extension and Evaluation of Job Characteristics, Organizational Commitment and Job Satisfaction in an Expatriate, Guest Worker, Sales Setting. In: *Journal of Personal Selling & Sales Management* 22,1: 1–11. [https://doi.org/10.1080/08853134.2002.10754288].

Black, J. Stewart (1988): Work Role Transitions: A Study of American Expatriate Managers in Japan. In: *Journal of International Business Studies* 19,2: 277–294. [https://doi.org/10.1057/palgrave.jibs.8490383].

Black, J. Stewart; Gregersen, Hal B. (1990): Expectations, Satisfaction, and Intention to Leave of American Expatriate Managers in Japan. In: *International Journal of Intercultural Relations* 14,4: 485–506. [https://doi.org/10.1016/0147-1767(90)90032-R].

Black, J. Stewart; Gregersen, Hal B.; Mendenhall, M. E. (1992): Toward a Theoretical Framework of Repatriation Adjustment. In: *Journal of International Business Studies* 23,4: 737–760. [https://doi.org/10.1057/palgrave.jibs.8490286].

Bolino, Mark C.; Feldman, Daniel C. (2000): The Antecedents and Consequences of Underemployment among Expatriates. In: *Journal of Organizational Behavior* 21,8: 889–911. [https://doi.org/10.1002/1099-1379(200012)21:8<889::AID-JOB60>3.0.CO;2-G].

Caligiuri, Paula M. et al. (1998): Testing a Theoretical Model for Examining the Relationship between Family Adjustment and Expatriates' Work Adjustment. In: *Journal of Applied Psychology* 83,4: 598–614. [https://doi.org/10.1037/0021-9010.83.4.598].

Carstensen, Laura L.; Isaacowitz, Derek M.; Charles, Susan T. (1999): Taking Time Seriously: A Theory of Socioemotional Selectivity. In: *American Psychologist* 54,3: 165–181. [https://doi.org/10.1037/0003-066X.54.3.165].

Caspi, Avshalom; Roberts, Brent W.; Shiner, Rebecca L. (2005): Personality Development: Stability and Change. In: *Annual Review of Psychology* 56: 453–484. [https://doi.org/10.1146/annurev.psych.55.090902.141913].

Clark, Andrew; Oswald, Andrew; Warr, Peter (1996): Is Job Satisfaction U-Shaped in Age? In: *Journal of Occupational and Organizational Psychology* 69,1: 57–81. [https://doi.org/10.1111/j.2044-8325.1996.tb00600.x].

Dennis, Helen; Thomas, Kathryn (2007): Ageism in the Workplace. In: *Generations* 31,1: 84–89. [http://www.ingentaconnect.com/content/asag/gen/2007/00000031/00000001/art00014].

Fasbender, Ulrike et al. (2014): Deciding Whether to Work after Retirement: The Role of the Psychological Experience of Aging. In: *Journal of Vocational Behavior* 84,3: 215–224. [https://doi.org/10/bc4p].

Feldman, Daniel C.; Ng, Thomas W.H. (2007): Careers: Mobility, Embeddedness, and Success. In: *Journal of Management* 33,3: 350–377. [https://doi.org/10.1177/0149206307300815].

Fontaine, Gary 1986): Roles of Social Support Systems in Overseas Relocation: Implications for Intercultural Training. In: *International Journal of Intercultural Relations* 10,3: 361–378. [https://doi.org/10.1016/0147-1767(86)90018-0].

Froese, Fabian Jintae; Peltokorpi, Vesa (2011): Cultural Distance and Expatriate Job Satisfaction. In: *International Journal of Intercultural Relations* 35,1: 49–60. [https://doi.org/10.1016/j.ijintrel.2010.10.002].

Gregersen, Hal B.; Black, J. Stewart (1992): Antecedents to Commitment to a Parent Company and a Foreign Operation. In: *Academy of Management Journal* 35,1: 65–90. [https://doi.org/10.2307/256473].

Gregersen, Hal B. (1992): Commitments to a Parent Company and a Local Work Unit during Repatriation. In: *Personnel Psychology* 45: 29–54. [https://doi.org/10.1111/j.1744-6570.1992.tb00843.x]

Hackman, J. Richard; Oldham, Greg R. (1976): Motivation through the Design of Work: Test of a Theory. In: *Organizational Behavior and Human Performance* 16,2: 250–279. [https://doi.org/10.1016/0030-5073(76)90016-7].

Hechanova, Regina; Beehr, Terry A.; Christiansen, Neil D. (2003): Antecedents and Consequences of Employees' Adjustment to Overseas Assignment: A Meta-Analytic Review. In: *Applied Psychology* 52,2: 213–236. [https://doi.org/10.1111/1464-0597.00132].

Hochwarter, Wayne A. et al. (2001): A Note on the Nonlinearity of the Age-Job-Satisfaction Relationship. In: *Journal of Applied Social Psychology* 31,6: 1223–1237. [https://doi.org/10.1111/j.1559-1816.2001.tb02671.x].

Holland, Harrison M. (1984): Managing Diplomacy: The United States and Japan. Hoover Press Publication 300. Stanford, CA: Hoover Institution Press, Stanford University.

Humphrey, Stephen E.; Nahrgang, Jennifer D.; Morgeson, Frederick P. (2007): Integrating Motivational, Social, and Contextual Work Design Features: A Meta-Analytic Summary and Theoretical Extension of the Work Design Literature. In: *Journal of Applied Psychology* 92,5: 1332–1356. [https://doi.org/10.1037/0021-9010.92.5.1332].

Hur, Won-Moo; Moon, Tae-Won; Han, Su-Jin (2014): The Role of Chronological Age and Work Experience on Emotional Labor: The Mediating Effect of Emotional Intelligence. In: *Career Development International* 19,7: 734–754. [https://doi.org/10.1108/CDI-12-2013-0162].

Kacmar, K. Michele (Micki); Ferris, Gerald R. (1989): Theoretical and Methodological Considerations in the Age-Job Satisfaction Relationship. In: *Journal of Applied Psychology* 74,2: 201–207. [https://doi.org/10.1037/0021-9010.74.2.201].

Kanfer, R.; Ackerman, P. L. (2004): Aging, Adult Development, and Work Motivation. In: *Academy of Management Review* 29,3: 440–458. [https://doi.org/10.5465/AMR.2004.13670969]

Kooij, Dorien et al. (2008): Older Workers' Motivation to Continue to Work: Five Meanings of Age: A Conceptual Review. In: *Journal of Managerial Psychology* 23,4: 364–394. [https://doi.org/10.1108/02683940810869015].

Kooij, Dtam et al. (2011): Age and Work-Related Motives: Results of a Meta-Analysis. In: *Journal of Organizational Behavior* 32,2: 197–225. [https://doi.org/10.1002/job.665].

Krumm, Stefan; Grube, Anna; Hertel, Guido (2013): No Time for Compromises: Age as a Moderator of the Relation between Needs-supply Fit and Job Satisfaction. In: *European Journal of Work and Organizational Psychology* 22,5: 547–562. [https://doi.org/10.1080/1359432X.2012.676248].

Lang, Frieder R.; Carstensen, Laura L. (1994): Close Emotional Relationships in Late Life: Further Support for Proactive Aging in the Social Domain. In: *Psychology and Aging* 9,2: 315–324. [https://doi.org/10.1037/0882-7974.9.2.315].

Lawrence, Barbara S. (1987): An Organizational Theory of Age Effects. In: Bacharach, Samuel B.; DiTomaso, Nancy (Eds.): Research in the Sociology of Organizations. Volume 5. Greenwich, CT: JAI Press: 37–71.

Mol, Stefan T. et al. (2005): Predicting Expatriate Job Performance for Selection Purposes: A Quantitative Review. In: *Journal of Cross-Cultural Psychology* 36,5: 590–620. [https://doi.org/10.1177/0022022105278544].

Morgan, David L. (1988): Age Differences in Social Network Participation. In: *Journal of Gerontology* 43,4: 129–137. [https://doi.org/10.1093/geronj/43.4.S129].

Morrow, Paula C.; McElroy, James C. (1987): Work Commitment and Job Satisfaction over Three Career Stages. In: *Journal of Vocational Behavior* 30,3: 330–346. [https://doi.org/10.1016/0001-8791(87)90009-1].

Napier, Nancy K.; Holden, Nigel; Muñiz-Ferrer, Marta (2014): Demographics and Working Abroad: What's Missing, What's next? In: Collings, David G.; Wood, Geoffrey T.; Caligiuri, Paula M. (Eds.): The Routledge Companion to International Human Resource Management. Abingdon, United Kingdom: Routledge: 348–362. [https://doi.org/10.4324/9781315761282.ch21].

Ng, Thomas W. H. et al. (2005): Predictors of Objective and Subjective Career Success: A Meta-Analysis. In: *Personnel Psychology* 58,2: 367–408. [https://doi.org/10.1111/j.1744-6570.2005.00515.x].

Ng, Thomas W. H.; Feldman, Daniel C. (2015): The Moderating Effects of Age in the Relationships of Job Autonomy to Work Outcomes. In: *Work, Aging and Retirement* 1,1: 64–78. [https://doi.org/10.1093/workar/wau003].

Ng, Thomas W. H.; Feldman, Daniel C. (2012): Evaluating Six Common Stereotypes about Older Workers with Meta-Analytical Data. In: *Personnel Psychology* 65,4: 821–858. [https://doi.org/10.1111/peps.12003].

Ng, Thomas W. H.; Feldman, Daniel C. (2010): The Relationships of Age with Job Attitudes: A Meta-Analysis. In: *Personnel Psychology* 63,3: 677–718. [https://doi.org/10.1111/j.1744-6570.2010.01184.x].

Ng, Thomas W. H.; Feldman, Daniel C. (2008): The Relationship of Age to Ten Dimensions of Job Performance. In: *Journal of Applied Psychology* 93,2: 392–423. [https://doi.org/10.1037/0021-9010.93.2.392].

Olsen, Jesse E.; Martins, Luis L. (2009): The Effects of Expatriate Demographic Characteristics on Adjustment: A Social Identity Approach. In: *Human Resource Management* 48,2: 311–328. [https://doi.org/10.1002/hrm.20281].

Rauschenbach, Cornelia et al. (2013): Age and Work-Related Stress: A Review and Meta-Analysis. In: *Journal of Managerial Psychology* 28,7/8: 781–804. [https://doi.org/10.1108/JMP-07-2013-0251].

Rhodes, Susan R. (1983): Age-Related Differences in Work Attitudes and Behavior: A Review and Conceptual Analysis. In: *Psychological Bulletin* 93,2: 328–367. [https://doi.org/10.1037/0033-2909.93.2.328].

Riley, Matilda White (1973): Aging and Cohort Succession: Interpretations and Misinterpretations. In: *Public Opinion Quarterly* 37,1: 35. [https://doi.org/10.1086/268058].

Schulz, Ute; Schwarzer, Ralf (2003): Soziale Unterstützung bei der Krankheitsbewältigung: Die Berliner Social Support Skalen (BSSS). In: *Diagnostica* 49,2: 73–82. [https://doi.org/10.1026//0012-1924.49.2.73].

Selmer, Jan (2001): Expatriate Selection: Back to Basics? In: *The International Journal of Human Resource Management* 12,8: 1219–1233. [https://doi.org/10.1080/09585190110083767].

Sturman, Michael C. (2003): Searching for the Inverted U-Shaped Relationship between Time and Performance: Meta-Analyses of the Experience/Performance, Tenure/Performance, and Age/Performance Relationships. In: *Journal of Management* 29,5: 609–640. [https://doi.org/10.1016/s0149-2063(03)00028-x].

Super, Donald E. (1980): A Life-Span, Life-Space Approach to Career Development. In: *Journal of Vocational Behavior* 16,3: 282–298. [https://doi.org/10.1016/0001-8791(80)90056-1].

Takeuchi, Riki; Shay, Jeffrey P.; Jiatao, Li (2008): When Does Decision Autonomy Increase Expatriate Managers' Adjustment? An Empirical Test. In: *Academy of Management Journal* 51,1: 45–60. [https://doi.org/10.5465/AMJ.2008.30696751].

Teclaw, Robert et al. (2014): Employee Age and Tenure within Organizations: Relationship to Workplace Satisfaction and Workplace Climate Perceptions. In: *The Health Care Manager* 33,1: 4–19. [https://doi.org/10.1097/01.HCM.0000440616.31891.2d].

Truxillo, Donald M. et al. (2012): A Lifespan Perspective on Job Design: Fitting the Job and the Worker to Promote Job Satisfaction, Engagement, and Performance. In: *Organizational Psychology Review* 2,4: 340–360. [https://doi.org/10.1177/2041386612454043].

Van der Zee, Karen I.; Brinkmann, Ursula (2004): Construct Validity Evidence for the Intercultural Readiness Check against the Multicultural Personality Questionnaire. In: *International Journal of Selection and Assessment* 12,3: 285–290. [https://doi.org/10.1111/j.0965-075X.2004.283_1.x].

van Oudenhoven, J. P.; Mol, S.; Van der Zee, Karen I. (2003): Study of the Adjustment of Western Expatriates in Taiwan ROC with the Multicultural Personality Questionnaire. In: *Asian Journal of Social Psychology* 6,2: 159–170. [https://doi.org/10.1111/1467-839X.t01-1-00018]

Wanous, John P. et al. (1992): The Effects of Met Expectations on Newcomer Attitudes and Behaviors: A Review and Meta-Analysis. In: *Journal of Applied Psychology* 77,3: 288–297. [https://doi.org/10.1037/0021-9010.77.3.288].

Wechtler, Heidi; Koveshnikov, Alexei; Dejoux, Cecile (2015): Just like a Fine Wine? Age, Emotional Intelligence, and Cross-Cultural Adjustment. In: *International Business Review* 24,3: 409–418. [https://doi.org/10.1016/j.ibusrev.2014.09.002].

Wiernik, Brenton M.; Dilchert, Stephan; Ones, Deniz S. (2016): Age and Employee Green Behaviors: A Meta-Analysis. In: *Frontiers in Psychology*, Research Topic: Corporate Social Responsibility and Organizational Psychology: Quid pro Quo 7: 194. [https://doi.org/10/bc4f].

Expatriate Leadership Experience: Host Country Burden or Resource?

Jack W. Kostal, Brenton M. Wiernik, and Deniz S. Ones

Abstract

Expatriates have the potential to strongly positively or negatively impact the host country nationals (HCN) with whom they work. Scholarly discussions of expatriation have at times characterized expatriates either as promising high-potentials with substantial knowledge and experience to offer, or else as employees lacking critical experiences, knowledge, and skills needed to successfully navigate challenging managerial situations overseas. This chapter examines the accuracy of these stereotypes as characterizations of the typical level of managerial experience that expatriates possess. We use transcultural meta-analysis of experience data for a total of 728 expatriate managers and 9,995 domestic managers originating from 32 countries and working in 30 countries to examine differences in leadership experience between expatriate and domestic managers. Results show that expatriates tend to have more experience than domestic managers in both their host countries ($\delta = .27$) and their origin countries ($\delta = .29$), with consistent differences across experience dimensions and countries. We describe a theoretical framework linking expatriate experience and actions to HCN outcomes that provides context for results call for further research on the impact of expatriates on their host countries.

1 Introduction

Globalization has resulted in an economic environment where organizations possess many opportunities – and face increasing pressure – to expand internationally. With any international venture, one concern is that poor management of foreign operations will result in monetary losses for the organization. To guard against this possibility, expatriation has become a key means by which organizations ensure success in foreign operations, develop cross-culturally competent managers, and transfer organizational knowledge across work units (Collings et al. 2007). In response to the important role that expatriates play in multinational organizations' international strategies, a sizable psychological literature has developed that explores the unique challenges associated with managing expatriate employees (Albrecht et al. 2018; Sinangil/Ones 2001).

Notably, most of this literature has focused on expatriates themselves, such as identifying antecedents of successful expatriate adjustment (Hechanova et al. 2003) or understanding how expatriates reintegrate into their workgroups when they return home (Burmeister et al. 2015). This focus on expatriate outcomes is understandable given the high costs of failed international assignments, but such a narrow focus ignores other stakeholders in the expatriation process (Takeuchi 2010). In particular, the presence of expatriates can have a substantial impact on the lives of the host country nationals (HCNs) whom they manage. Although prior studies have examined the dynamics of interpersonal exchanges between expatriates and HCNs, most have focused on the impact that such dynamics have on expatriate performance (Takeuchi 2010). Little is known regarding the impact of expatriates on the performance, satisfaction, and career prospects of those whom they manage. On the one hand, expatriates may possess unique organizational knowledge and skills that can provide added value to HCNs beyond what could be expected from local managers (Bonache Pérez/Pla-Barber 2005). On the other hand, expatriates may take opportunities away from HCNs and interfere with the development and advancement of local talent (Bhanugopan/Fish 2007).

In this study, we examine the possibility that expatriates can positively impact HCNs by providing unique organizational knowledge and skills. First, we provide a model that explicates the causal pathways through which expatriate performance, knowledge, and skills can influence the workplace experiences of HCNs whom they manage. We argue that, to the extent that expatriates possess unique levels of knowledge and skill, benefits to HCNs are possible. Next, scholars and mass media have at times suggested that expatriates lack critical experience and competence to handle challenging managerial situations overseas. This stereotype contrasts with the perceptions of practitioners who view expatriate assignments as a means for building the skills of high potential employees while benefitting foreign operations. Accordingly, we test which of these viewpoints is more accurate, using large-scale data provided by an international consulting firm.

1.1 A Model of Causal Pathways between Expatriate Performance and HCN Outcomes

For medium- and high-complexity jobs, of which managerial positions are an example, experience is a moderately strong predictor of overall job performance (Sturman 2003). Experience is an indirect determinant of performance (McCloy et al. 1994). Critical experiences provide individuals with opportunities to gain role-specific knowledge, practice job skills, and develop attitudes and confidence that can increase motivation in challenging work situations. These developmental opportunities thus facilitate performance on related dimensions of job performance.

Campbell and Wiernik (2015) describe a comprehensive model of job performance that includes eight dimensions of performance that are present to some degree in all jobs – technical performance, communication, initiative/effort, counterproductive work behavior, hierarchical leadership, peer leadership, hierarchical management, and peer management. We posit that performance of expatriate managers on each of these dimensions can have important impacts on HCNs through one of four mechanisms:

1. Resource facilitation – The primary role of most expatriate managers is to establish or improve operations in foreign subsidiaries (Collings et al. 2007). The major component of this role is effective procurement and allocation of organizational resources (i.e., hierarchical and peer management performance). These include both tangible resources (e.g., goods, supplies) and intangible resources (e.g., strategies, coordination across units). When expatriates manage effectively by providing their subordinates and peers with the necessary materials, strategies, and coordination, HCNs benefit from increased capacity to perform their own roles.
2. Knowledge sharing – Organizational knowledge transfer is one of the prime reasons for expatriate assignments (Fang et al. 2010). Knowledge is shared through effective communication and a variety of hierarchical and peer leadership behaviors (e.g., initiating structure, training, coaching, mentoring). HCNs will be more likely to benefit

from expatriates' knowledge if expatriates have had previous experience with these kinds of developmental activities.

3. Motivation and support – Beyond knowledge transfer, host country nationals can also benefit from other effective expatriate leadership behaviors (e.g., consideration, goal emphasis, empowerment, role-modeling). These leadership behaviors, like all job performance behaviors, are skills that can be learned and practiced (Campbell/Wiernik 2015). Working with expatriate managers who have had opportunities to practice effective leadership skills can benefit HCNs by helping them to be more engaged (Bono et al. 2007) and perform better (Judge/Piccolo 2004), especially if these previous experiences were similar to the challenging and complex situations that often characterize expatriate assignments.

4. Indirect impacts – When the organization performs well, HCNs often benefit. Most simply, HCNs can only remain employed if the organization survives and prospers. In addition, increased organization success often leads to expansions in operations, which creates new opportunities for HCNs to advance into more senior organizational positions (Bhanugopan/Fish 2007) and increased economic opportunities for other individuals in host country communities. From a psychological perspective, it is stressful to work in a failing organization (Moore et al. 2006), and unit level performance is associated with job satisfaction (Whitman et al. 2010), so increased organizational success fostered by effective expatriate performance can also lead to improved HCN psychological and physical well-being.

To the degree that expatriates have more relevant job experience than local managers, their correspondingly increased job performance can benefit HCNs through each of these four channels. Such differences between expatriate and domestic managers are likely, as expatriates are often chosen from individuals identified as "high potentials" (Harris/ Brewster 1999). However, lack of candidate willingness to accept expatriate assignments (Mol et al. 2009) and reliance on informal recommendations and assessments when making selection decisions (Harris/Brewster 1999) may result in impoverished applicant pools and non-optimal selection. It is plausible that idealized "best practices" (i.e., sending experienced, high-potential managers overseas for further development) are often violated in practice. Stereotypes of incompetent, struggling expatriates would suggest this is the case.

1.2 Competing Stereotypes of Expatriate Managers

Academic scholars and mass media have sometimes suggested that expatriate managers lack critical experience and competence to handle challenging managerial situations overseas (e.g., The Economist 2014). This stereotype seems to have emerged in the 1960s, 1970s, and early 1980s, with the perception that organizations were using expatriate assignments to rid themselves of poorly performing employees (Sinangil/Ones 2001). More recently, however, a competing stereotype has emerged characterizing expatriates as ambitious, flexible, high-quality employees. Frequent movement across national borders has come to be perceived as a form of boundaryless career (Stahl et al. 2002), and international experience is often regarded as a key prerequisite for effective leadership performance in multinational organizations. As a result, ambitious individuals may see gaining international experience as a way to distinguish themselves, and organizations may use expatriate assignments as a way to build key global business competencies in high-potential employees (Harris/ Brewster 1999).

Organizations may also use expatriates as a key strategic resource to develop international subsidiaries. Local leadership experience is often limited in newly emerging economies (Huang 2013). In these contexts, high-potential expatriates who are effective at sharing their knowledge can represent a potential boon to HCNs, as their greater leadership experience can provide benefits both directly through effective management and knowledge sharing and indirectly by ensuring the success of the organization.

In this paper, we examine the accuracy of a key component of these contrasting stereotypes – patterns of expatriate experience – in contemporary organizations. The contrasting stereotypes of expatriate managers described previously suggest two competing hypotheses. First, if organizations send expatriates to locations where local employees lack the necessary competencies to meet organizational management goals (Huang 2013), we would expect organizations to choose expatriates who possess more critical management experiences than managers available in local talent pools. In contrast, if organizations primarily use international assignments to rid themselves of low-quality employees, we would expect expatriates to have a relative lack of relevant experience, compared to HCNs. In this case, expatriates may become a burden on HCNs, as their lack of experience could interfere with organizational success. This suggests competing hypotheses:

Resource hypothesis: *Expatriate managers will have greater levels of leadership experience when compared with host country domestic managers.*

Burden hypothesis: *Expatriate managers will exhibit lower levels of leadership experience when compared with host country domestic managers.*

Contrasting expatriate stereotypes also suggest competing hypotheses regarding comparisons of expatriates with domestic managers in their countries of origin. If individuals seek out international assignments to advance their careers and organizations use expatriation to prepare high-potential employees for promotion, we would expect expatriate managers to exhibit relatively greater levels of experience than their domestic counterparts at home. In contrast, if organizations primarily use expatriate assignments to remove problematic employees to roles where they can cause little harm, we would expect expatriates to have less relevant experience than managers who remain at home. This suggests competing hypotheses:

Development hypothesis: *Expatriate managers will have greater levels of leadership experience when compared with domestic managers in their origin countries.*

Displacement hypothesis: *Expatriate managers will have lower levels of leadership experience when compared with domestic managers in their origin countries.*

To test these competing hypotheses, we used a large dataset provided by an international consulting firm to compare expatriates, host country domestic managers, and origin country domestic managers on several dimensions of key leadership experience (described below). In doing so, we shed light on whether expatriates represent a potential resource or burden for HCNs and whether expatriates represent the best or the worst that their home countries have to offer.

2   Methods

2.1   Participants

Leadership experience data were gathered from 765 expatriate managers and 9,024 domestic managers originating from 64 countries and working in 78 countries as part of assessments conducted by a global executive recruitment and talent management consultancy. Participants were members of many organizations and were assessed for a mix of selection and development purposes. The lead authors of this chapter were given access to primary datasets containing leadership experience data on expatriates and managers. Analyses were conducted on all within-country samples with $N > 4$. This resulted in expatriate-host country national comparisons being conducted with 661 expatriates and 8,905 HCNs in 30 countries. Expatriate–origin country domestic manager comparisons were conducted with 712 expatriates and 8,788 domestic managers from 32 countries.

Expatriate managers were from the following countries[1]: Argentina (0.8%), Australia (5.0%), Austria (0.7%), Belgium (2.1%), Brazil (1.2%), Canada (6.3%), China (0.8%), Colombia (0.9%), Egypt (1.0%), Finland (0.7%), France (11.6%), Germany (6.1%), Greece (0.8%), Hong Kong (1.3%), India (3.9%), Ireland (1.8%), Italy (2.2%), Japan (1.4%), Lebanon (0.7%), Malaysia (1.4%), Mexico (1.4%), the Netherlands (2.4%), New Zealand (1.8%), Norway (1.7%), Philippines (0.7%), Russia (1.0%), Saudi Arabia (0.8%), Singapore (1.3%), South Africa (2.2%), Spain (1.3%), Sweden (1.7%), Switzerland (2.2%), the United Kingdom (12.8%), and the United States (12.3%); small numbers of expatriates also came from Bangladesh, Croatia, Cyprus, Denmark, Guatemala, Hungary, Indonesia, Jordan, Kuwait, Latvia, Malta, Mauritius, Moldova, Nigeria, Oman, Pakistan, Peru, Poland, Portugal, Romania, Senegal, Serbia, Slovenia, South Korea, Syria, Taiwan, Thailand, Turkey, Ukraine, and Zimbabwe. Experience of domestic managers was assessed in the following countries: Argentina (0.8%), Australia (3.6%), Austria (0.3%), Belgium (0.9%), Brazil (0.9%), Canada (6.7%), China (1.6%), the Czech Republic (0.3%), Colombia (0.1%), Egypt (0.2%), France (3.8%), Germany (3.4%), Greece (0.2%), Hong Kong (0.4%), India (1.2%), Indonesia (0.1%), Ireland (0.6%), Italy (1.6%), Japan (0.3%), Kuwait (1.6%), Lebanon (0.1%), Malaysia (0.3%), Mexico (0.8%), the Netherlands (1.1%), New Zealand (0.3%), Norway (0.2%), Russia (0.8%), Saudi Arabia (0.7%), Singapore (0.4%), South Africa (2.1%), South Korea (0.4%), Spain (0.5%) Sweden (0.4%), Switzerland (0.7%), the United Kingdom (5.5%), and the United States (57.3%)[2]. In all, 9 of the 10 GLOBE cultural clusters were represented in the samples.

Participants included managers from all hierarchical levels, ranging from first-line managers to senior executives. Among expatriates, 7% were first-line managers, 19% were mid-level managers, 60% were business unit managers, and 14% were senior executives. Among domestic managers, 15% were first-line managers, 26% were mid-level managers, 44% were business unit managers, and 14% were senior executives. Across all samples, 12% of expatriates and 23% of domestic managers were female. Expatriates reported a mean age of 41.96 years ($SD = 5.88$) and a mean organizational tenure of 11.83 years ($SD = 6.46$). Domestic managers reported a mean age of 43.31 years ($SD = 6.87$) and a mean organizational tenure of 13.11 years ($SD = 7.61$).

---

[1]   Numbers in parentheses indicate the percent of the total expatriate or domestic sample from each country.

[2]   The consultancy providing the data was U.S.-based, so the United States sample of domestic managers is substantially larger than other countries. However, conducting analysis within-countries controls for the potential for oversampling of U.S. managers to influence results.

2.2   Measures

Expatriate status, origin country, and host country. Participants completed a demographic questionnaire as part of an assessment battery used for either selection/promotion or development purposes. As part of this questionnaire, participants indicated their country of citizenship (origin country), current location (host country), and expatriate status (yes or no). Expatriates were identified as those individuals who responded "yes" to the expatriate status question. Domestic managers were identified as those individuals responding "no" to this question and who were also currently located in their country of citizenship.

Leadership experience. Leadership experience was measured using the Leadership Experiences Inventory (LEI). The LEI is a proprietary 105-item scale that assesses the respondent's degree of previous exposure to critical business, management, and leadership experiences. The instrument contains 23 subscales organized into four dimensions which measure exposure to general management experiences (e.g., strategy development, project management), risky or critical experiences (e.g., crisis management, high-risk decision making), overcoming challenges and adversity (e.g., inheriting problems and challenges, interpersonal challenges), and personal and career-related experiences (e.g., self-development, mentoring others). Table 1 presents descriptions of the subscales associated with each dimension. This measure has been found to correlate positively with managerial competencies and career outcomes, and higher level managers report higher mean levels of leadership experience (VanKatwyk et al. 2006). Responses to this instrument were collected at the same time as those for the demographic questionnaire.

2.3   Analyses

To account for unequal sampling and potential mean-level experience differences across countries, all expatriate–domestic comparisons were conducted within-countries and combined using transcultural meta-analysis (Ones et al. 2012). This approach allowed us to examine the cross-national consistency of differences in experience between expatriate and domestic managers. Standardized mean differences (Cohen's d) were computed between expatriate and domestic managers for each host and origin country in the sample for overall leadership experience, for each experience dimension, and for each experience subscale. These effects were pooled using psychometric meta-analysis (Schmidt/Hunter 2015). There was substantial variability across countries in the ratio of expatriates to domestic managers, especially for the United States. Accordingly, we weighted effect sizes by their inverse sampling error variance, rather than by total sample size, to avoid assigning too much weight to the United States sample (Hedges/Olkin 1985). Sampling error variance in the d values was computed using the formula accounting for unequal group sizes (Schmidt/ Hunter 2015: 293). Reliability information for the country samples was unavailable, so corrections for attenuation due to measurement error were made using Mosier composite reliability values reported by Connelly (2008) for a United States managerial sample completing the LEI.

Table 1: Experience Dimensions Assessed by the Leadership Experience Inventory

Scales and subscales

General management experiences

Strategy development
Experience creating policies that set strategic direction for the organization.

Project management and implementation
Experience managing and/or implementing key projects.

Business development and marketing
Experience in business development and/or marketing

Business growth
Experience growing a new or existing business (e.g., new product line, new market).

Product development
Experience developing new or enhanced project.

Start-up business
Experience managing a start-up or new business.

Financial management
Experience involving financial management (e.g., budget management).

Operations management
Experience related to managing core operations of a business (e.g., scheduling production, procuring resources and facilities).

Support functions
Experience in activities where the main responsibilities are to provide functional support (e.g., HR, IT, Marketing) to organizational operations.

External relations
Experience representing the organization to external stakeholders.

Overcoming challenge and adversity

Inherited problems and challenges
Experience taking over a situation with significant problems or challenges to be resolved.

Interpersonally challenging situations
Experiences that are challenging because of strong interpersonal components (e.g., adversarial relations).

Downturns and/or failures
Experience managing through a downturn or responding to a failed initiative or failure in the business.

Difficult financial situations
Experience dealing with difficult, challenging, and/or complex financial issues.

Difficult staffing situations
Experience dealing with staff-related situations that are challenging and/or adversarial in nature (e.g., poor performance, layoffs).

$\downarrow$

Table 1: Experience Dimensions Assessed by the Leadership Experience Inventory – continued

Scales and subscales

Risky and/or critical experiences

High-risk situations
Experience with responsibility for situations that are very risky in terms of potential failure, costs, and/or negative impact on the organization.

Critical negotiations
Experience that includes negotiations in which the outcome is extremely important for the organization's future.

Crisis management
Experience responding to and managing an expected or unexpected business crisis (e.g., key supplier unexpectedly shuts down).

Highly visible/critical assignments
Experience with being responsible for assignments that have the attention of senior leaders and/or the public.

Personal and career-related experience[†]

Self-development
Experience focused on developing oneself (e.g., engaged in structured self-development program).

Developing others
Experience focused on developing others (e.g., mentoring).

Extracurricular activities
Experience gained outside of the job or organizational context (e.g., involvement in professional association or community group).

Note: Adapted from VanKatwyk et al. (2006); [†] The Personal and Career-related Experience scale includes a subscale related to international and cross-cultural experience. However, many expatriates in the present samples included their current assignment as part of their experience in this area. Accordingly, this subscale was excluded from our analyses and was not included in the Personal and Career-related Experience or Total Experience scores.

3　Results

3.1　Comparison of Expatriate Managers to Host Country National Managers

Meta-analytic comparisons between expatriates' leadership experience and that of host country national managers are shown in Table 2.[3] As shown in the table, virtually all the variation in observed d values across countries was due to sampling error; individual country results should not be over-interpreted. There were substantial differences across countries in the representation of expatriates and HCN managers at each hierarchical level, which could result in artificial variability in results across countries. Accordingly, we present results for both the full sample and for samples of only business unit-level managers (the best-represented managerial level in the data).

---

[3]　Individual country results for all analyses are available upon request.

Table 2: Experience of Expatriate vs. HCN Managers: Meta-analytic Comparisons between Expatriates from All Sources and HCNs

Experience dimension	$\bar{d}$	SD_d	δ	SD_δ	90% CI	80% CV
Total leadership experience	.27	.33	.27	.23	.18, .37	-.02, .56
	.25	*.29*	*.25*	*.08*	*.15, .35*	*.14, .36*
General management experiences	.26	.33	.26	.24	.16, .36	-.04, .57
	.22	*.31*	*.22*	*.13*	*.12, .33*	*.05, .39*
Strategy development	.26	.35	.26	.27	.15, .37	-.08, .60
	.25	*.34*	*.25*	*.19*	*.13, .37*	*.01, .50*
Project management and implementation	.26	.31	.26	.20	.17, .36	.01, .52
	.19	*.29*	*.20*	*.08*	*.09, .30*	*.09, .30*
Business development and marketing	.25	.35	.25	.26	.14, .36	-.09, .59
	.21	*.33*	*.21*	*.19*	*.10, .33*	*-.03, .45*
Business growth	.25	.36	.26	.28	.15, .37	-.10, .61
	.22	*.36*	*.22*	*.23*	*.10, .35*	*-.07, .52*
Product development	.25	.29	.25	.16	.17, .34	.04, .46
	.17	*.28*	*.17*	*.05*	*.07, .28*	*.11, .24*
Start-up business	.36	.34	.36	.25	.26, .47	.04, .69
	.28	*.31*	*.28*	*.15*	*.17, .39*	*.09, .47*
Financial management	.24	.33	.24	.24	.14, .34	-.07, .55
	.20	*.29*	*.21*	*.09*	*.10, .31*	*.09, .32*
Operations management	.21	.31	.21	.20	.11, .30	-.05, .47
	.15	*.28*	*.15*	*.03*	*.05, .25*	*.12, .19*
Support functions	.17	.30	.17	.19	.08, .26	-.07, .41
	.13	*.25*	*.14*	*.00*	*.05, .22*	*.14, .14*
External relations	.17	.30	.17	.19	.08, .26	-.07, .41
	.13	*.29*	*.13*	*.09*	*.03, .24*	*.02, .24*
Overcoming challenge and adversity	.30	.34	.30	.24	.20, .41	-.01, .62
	.30	*.29*	*.30*	*.08*	*.20, .40*	*.19, .41*
Inherited problems and challenges	.22	.34	.22	.25	.11, .32	-.10, .54
	.23	*.35*	*.23*	*.21*	*.10, .35*	*-.04, .50*
Interpersonally challenging situations	.40	.32	.40	.22	.30, .50	.11, .69
	.40	*.28*	*.41*	*.05*	*.31, .51*	*.34, .48*
Downturns and/or failures	.19	.32	.19	.22	.09, .29	-.09, .47
	.16	*.31*	*.17*	*.13*	*.06, .28*	*.00, .33*
Difficult financial situations	.20	.32	.20	.22	.11, .30	-.08, .49
	.17	*.29*	*.17*	*.07*	*.07, .27*	*.08, .26*
Difficult staffing situations	.24	.37	.25	.28	.14, .36	-.12, .61
	.24	*.29*	*.24*	*.07*	*.14, .34*	*.16, .33*

↓

Table 2: Experience of Expatriate vs. HCN Managers: Meta-analytic Comparisons between Expatriates from All Sources and HCNs − continued

Experience dimension	$\bar{d}$	SD_d	δ	SD_δ	90% CI	80% CV
Risky and/or critical experiences	.22	.31	.22	.21	.13, .32	-.04, .49
	.19	*.28*	*.19*	*.03*	*.10, .29*	*.16, .23*
High-risk situations	.25	.34	.25	.25	.15, .36	-.07, .57
	.24	*.30*	*.24*	*.11*	*.13, .35*	*.09, .39*
Critical negotiations	.19	.29	.19	.17	.10, .28	-.02, .41
	.13	*.27*	*.14*	*.00*	*.04, .23*	*.14, .14*
Crisis management	.20	.31	.20	.20	.11, .29	-.05, .45
	.17	*.28*	*.17*	*.05*	*.07, .27*	*.11, .23*
Highly visible/critical assignments	.23	.32	.23	.21	.14, .33	-.04, .51
	.21	*.29*	*.21*	*.06*	*.11, .31*	*.13, .29*
Personal and career-related experience	.27	.20	.28	.00	.21, .34	.28, .28
	.22	*.24*	*.22*	*.00*	*.13, .30*	*.22, .22*
Self-development	.33	.19	.34	.00	.28, .40	.34, .34
	.27	*.27*	*.28*	*.00*	*.18, .38*	*.28, .28*
Developing others	.16	.27	.16	.13	.08, .24	-.01, .33
	.13	*.28*	*.14*	*.06*	*.03, .24*	*.06, .21*
Extracurricular activities	.18	.26	.19	.11	.11, .27	.05, .33
	.12	*.30*	*.12*	*.11*	*.02, .23*	*-.01, .26*

Note: $N = 661$ expatriates and 8,905 host country nationals ($N = 365$ and 3,661 for business unit-level only); $k = 30$ (22 for business unit-level only); SD_d = observed standard deviation of d values; δ = mean expatriate-HCN difference corrected for unreliability in the experience measure; SD_δ = true standard deviation of δ after accounting for sampling error; 90% CI = 90% confidence interval around the mean effect size; 80% CV = 80% credibility interval; values in italics are for business unit-level only; positive values indicate expatriates are more experienced.

Overall, results showed that expatriates tended to have more experience than host country national managers across leadership experience dimensions. Compared to HCNs, expatriate managers showed the greatest experiential strengths for overcoming challenge and adversity and for some areas of general management experience. However, within each of the broad experiential dimensions examined, clear strengths and weaknesses were present. We focus our discussion on results controlling for managerial level (i.e., the business unit-level samples). The profile of expatriate leadership experience compared to HCNs for business unit-level managers is shown in Figure 1.

Expatriates showed a small advantage compared to HCNs for general management experience ($\delta = .22$), with this advantage especially pronounced for strategy development ($\delta = .25$) and operating a start-up business ($\delta = .28$). In contrast, expatriates showed no major advantage for operations, support functions, or everyday external relations (δs < .16). Expatriates appear to have the potential to be resources for business experience for HCNs if their assignments involve high-level strategic management, but less so if their duties involve primarily everyday operations.

Figure 1: Experience profile of expatriate managers from all sources compared to host country national managers

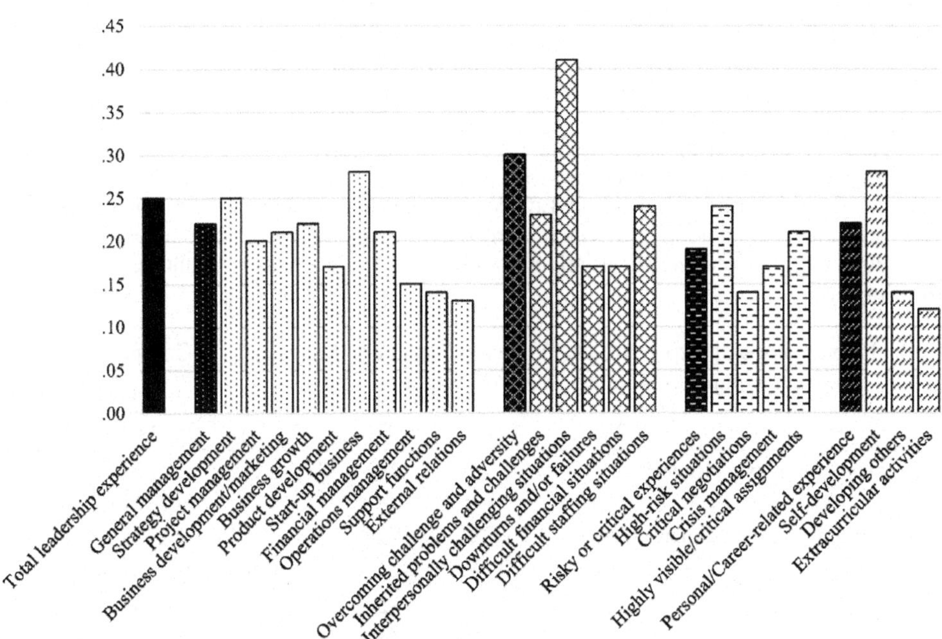

Note: Values are unreliability-corrected d values based on business-unit level managers only. Positive values indicate that expatriates have more experience.

Overcoming challenge and adversity was characterized by substantially more experience for expatriates (δ = .32). Expatriates were especially more experienced at handling challenging interpersonal situations (δ = .41), but they had relatively less experience in managing downturns (δ = .17) and difficult financial situations (δ = .17). This pattern of results suggests an experiential advantage for expatriates in exposure to challenging interpersonal situations, which could provide the opportunity to develop the social skills needed to manage interpersonal relations in a foreign context.

The area of experience where expatriates showed the least experiential advantage compared to HCNs was in handling risky and critical situations (δ = .19). Apart from managing initiatives with a high cost of failure (δ = .24), expatriates tended to have similar levels of experience as HCNs on the dimensions of this factor (e.g., δ = .14 for critical negotiations). In terms of personal and career-related experiences, expatriates were more experienced than HCNs for pursuing self-development opportunities (δ = .28), but they showed no appreciable experiential advantage for developing others (δ = .14) or engaging in professional extracurricular activities (δ = .12).

In general, the profile of expatriate business managers compared to their HCN counterparts shows that expatriates have more experience handling important strategic and business development decisions, especially when these tasks involve interpersonal challenges and high stakes for failure. The implication is that, in providing strategic expertise and vision for successfully transforming an organization, expatriates tend to represent an important resource from which host country nationals can benefit. This benefit would be even greater if they were also more experienced in developing others and passing on their knowledge; however, our results suggested less advantage for expatriates on this facet of experience.

3.2   Comparison of Expatriate Managers to Domestic (Origin Country) Managers

In addition to considering the benefits expatriates may offer to host country nationals, a related question is how expatriates' experiences compare to those of domestic managers in their countries of origin. Meta-analytic comparisons between leadership experiences for countries' managers abroad and at home are shown in Table 3. As was the case for expatriate-HCN comparisons, most variation in observed d values across countries was due to sampling error.

Table 3: Experience of Expatriate vs. Domestic Managers: Meta-analytic Comparisons between Countries' Managers Abroad and at Home

Experience dimension	$\bar{d}$	SD_d	δ	SD_δ	90% CI	80% CV
Total leadership experience	.29	.28	.29	.15	.21, .37	.09, .49
	.27	*.31*	*.27*	*.16*	*.16, .37*	*.06, .47*
General management experiences	.28	.28	.28	.17	.20, .36	.07, .49
	.25	*.31*	*.25*	*.16*	*.14, .35*	*.04, .45*
Strategy development	.27	.32	.27	.22	.18, .36	-.02, .55
	.26	*.32*	*.26*	*.19*	*.15, .37*	*.01, .51*
Project management and implementation	.27	.25	.27	.10	.20, .35	.15, .40
	.19	*.28*	*.19*	*.09*	*.09, .29*	*.07, .31*
Business development and marketing	.26	.30	.26	.19	.18, .35	.02, .51
	.27	*.31*	*.27*	*.17*	*.16, .38*	*.06, .49*
Business growth	.27	.29	.28	.19	.19, .37	.04, .52
	.27	*.31*	*.28*	*.17*	*.17, .38*	*.06, .49*
Product development	.23	.30	.24	.19	.15, .33	-.01, .48
	.14	*.32*	*.15*	*.19*	*.04, .26*	*-.09, .39*
Start-up business	.35	.36	.36	.28	.25, .46	.00, .72
	.34	*.38*	*.35*	*.28*	*.21, .48*	*-.01, .71*
Financial management	.25	.25	.25	.10	.18, .32	.12, .38
	.20	*.29*	*.21*	*.13*	*.10, .31*	*.03, .38*
Operations management	.24	.23	.24	.00	.18, .31	.24, .24
	.18	*.26*	*.18*	*.00*	*.09, .27*	*.18, .18*
Support functions	.22	.23	.22	.01	.15, .29	.21, .23
	.17	*.24*	*.17*	*.00*	*.09, .25*	*.17, .17*
External relations	.19	.29	.20	.17	.11, .28	-.03, .42
	.18	*.29*	*.18*	*.12*	*.08, .28*	*.02, .34*

$\downarrow$

Table 3: Experience of Expatriate vs. Domestic Managers: Meta-analytic Comparisons between Countries' Managers Abroad and at Home − continued

Experience dimension	$\bar{d}$	SD_d	δ	SD_δ	90% CI	80% CV
Overcoming challenge and adversity	.32	.26	.32	.12	.24, .39	.16, .48
	.30	*.32*	*.30*	*.18*	*.19, .41*	*.08, .53*
Inherited problems and challenges	.25	.24	.25	.06	.18, .32	.18, .33
	.25	*.27*	*.25*	*.08*	*.16, .35*	*.15, .35*
Interpersonally challenging situations	.42	.28	.42	.17	.34, .50	.21, .63
	.41	*.34*	*.42*	*.22*	*.30, .54*	*.13, .70*
Downturns and/or failures	.19	.26	.19	.12	.12, .27	.05, .34
	.17	*.32*	*.18*	*.18*	*.07, .29*	*-.06, .41*
Difficult financial situations	.20	.24	.20	.10	.13, .28	.08, .33
	.16	*.27*	*.16*	*.13*	*.06, .26*	*-.01, .33*
Difficult staffing situations	.25	.28	.26	.11	.18, .33	.12, .39
	.23	*.34*	*.24*	*.11*	*.14, .34*	*.10, .38*
Risky and/or critical experiences	.24	.26	.24	.14	.16, .32	.06, .42
	.22	*.32*	*.22*	*.13*	*.12, .32*	*.05, .39*
High-risk situations	.25	.25	.25	.13	.18, .33	.08, .42
	.25	*.29*	*.25*	*.12*	*.15, .35*	*.10, .40*
Critical negotiations	.22	.25	.22	.16	.14, .30	.01, .43
	.19	*.28*	*.19*	*.13*	*.09, .29*	*.02, .36*
Crisis management	.21	.27	.21	.08	.14, .28	.10, .32
	.19	*.29*	*.19*	*.15*	*.09, .30*	*.00, .38*
Highly visible/critical assignments	.24	.26	.25	.14	.17, .32	.07, .42
	.22	*.29*	*.22*	*.13*	*.12, .32*	*.05, .39*
Personal and career-related experience	.25	.29	.26	.18	.17, .34	.03, .48
	.22	*.30*	*.23*	*.15*	*.12, .33*	*.04, .42*
Self-development	.30	.31	.32	.21	.23, .41	.05, .59
	.32	*.35*	*.33*	*.24*	*.21, .46*	*.02, .64*
Developing others	.18	.24	.18	.09	.11, .25	.07, .30
	.14	*.25*	*.14*	*.00*	*.05, .23*	*.14, .14*
Extracurricular activities	.13	.28	.13	.17	.05, .22	-.09, .36
	.07	*.25*	*.07*	*.00*	*-.01, .16*	*.07, .07*

Note: $N = 712$ expatriates and 8,788 domestic managers in origin country ($N = 395$ and 3,714 for business unit-level only); $k = 32$ (23 for business unit-level only); SD_d = observed standard deviation of d values; δ = mean expatriate-domestic difference corrected for unreliability in the experience measure; SD_δ = true standard deviation of δ after accounting for sampling error; 90% CI = 90% confidence interval around the mean effect size; 80% CV = 80% credibility interval; values in italics are for business unit-level only; positive values indicate expatriates are more experienced.

Similar to the expatriate–HCN results, expatriates tended to have more experience than domestic managers in their origin countries across experience dimensions, with the areas of greatest experiential advantage occurring in overcoming adversity and some areas of general management experience. As before, we focus on analyses computed at the business unit level to control for differences in managerial level between expatriates and origin country nationals. The profile of expatriate leadership experience compared to domestic managers in their origin countries for business unit-level managers is shown in Figure 2.

Figure 2: Experience profile of countries' managers abroad versus at home

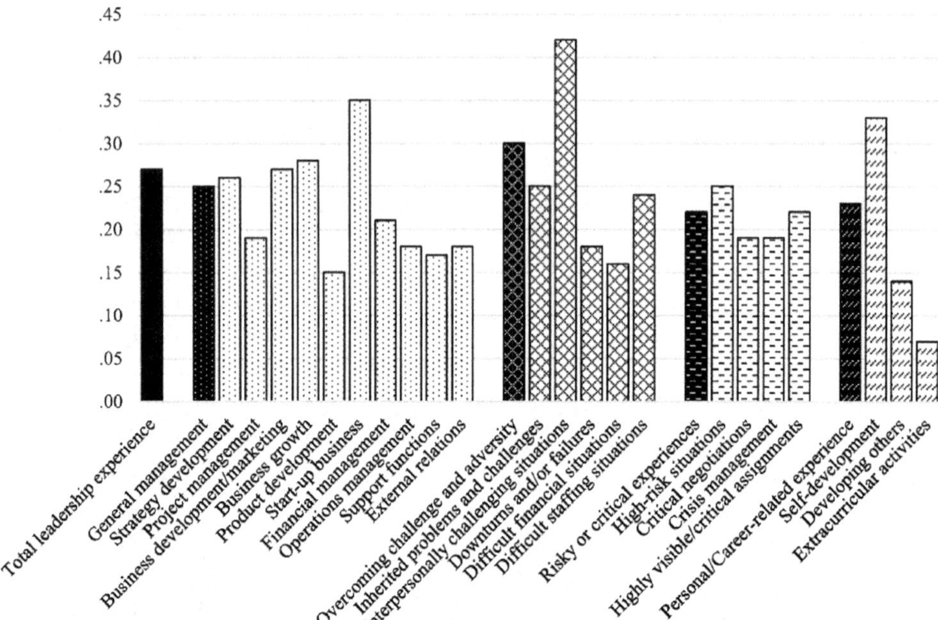

Note: Values are unreliability-corrected *d* values based on business-unit level managers only. Positive values indicate that expatriates have more experience.

For general management experience, expatriates showed small to moderate advantages over their domestic counterparts for strategy development (δ = .26 for business unit-level managers), business development (δ = .27), business growth (δ = .28), and starting a new business (δ = .35). For other areas of general management experience, such as product development and everyday operations and support, expatriates showed little differences from domestic managers. Organizations frequently deploy expatriates to open new operations or rescue foreign subsidiaries (Bonache Pérez/Pla-Barber 2005); these results are consistent with the hypothesis that organizations select employees who are well-prepared to fill these roles. However, we note that it is also possible that some of the differences observed between expatriates and origin country nationals result from experiences gained during the assignment, since the experience questionnaire was completed after expatriates had already been assigned abroad.

Similar to HCNs comparisons, expatriates' greatest area of strength over origin country domestic managers was in overcoming challenge and adversity (δ = .30). Expatriates had substantially more experience than domestic managers for handling interpersonal challenges (δ = .42), difficult staffing situations (δ = .24), and inherited problems (δ = .25). As before, these results are consistent with the hypothesis that organizations effectively select expatriates who have experience handling the challenging interpersonal contexts characteristic of international assignments (Black et al. 1991).

Compared to their domestic counterparts, expatriates had the least experiential advantage in handling critical situations, such as crises ($\delta = .19$) or critical negotiations ($\delta = .19$), though they did show a small experiential advantage for managing high-stakes situations ($\delta = .25$) and assignments under a great deal of public scrutiny ($\delta = .22$). Expatriates were also very similar to domestic managers in terms of experience developing subordinates ($\delta = .14$) and engagement in professional extracurricular activities ($\delta = .07$).

One area where expatriates had substantially more experience than their domestic counterparts was pursuit of professional self-development opportunities ($\delta = .33$). This supports characterizations of expatriates as ambitious, self-directed employees who pursue international assignments as a way of distinguishing themselves and advancing their careers (Stahl et al. 2002). Taken together, the patterns of evidence regarding expatriate experience relative to origin country nationals paints a picture of capable, experienced employees. Far from the stereotype of the struggling expatriate, our evidence is consistent with the hypothesis that individuals who pursue and are selected for international assignments represent the "cream of the crop" each country has to offer in terms of business, management, and leadership experience.

4 Discussion

The current study shows that expatriates tend to possess higher levels of leadership experience than either host country nationals or domestic managers in their countries of origin. This trend is consistent across all types of leadership experiences investigated, but varied in magnitude across experience dimensions. Expatriates had no marked advantage over HCNs or domestic managers for everyday operations and support functions, managing financial crises, negotiation, or developing others. However, expatriates were substantially more experienced than HCNs or domestic managers in areas related to establishing business strategy, developing new and high-risk ventures, interpersonal challenges, and pursuing self-development.

These results are most consistent with the resource and development hypotheses we proposed at the outset of this paper. Greater levels of experience for expatriates compared to HCNs suggest that expatriates can be a substantial resource for HCNs, rather than an undue burden on emerging economies, if their greater experience in managing high-risk, interpersonally challenging situations can be leveraged properly. Expatriates' greater levels of experience compared to domestic managers in their origin countries is consistent with organizational use of international assignments to transfer organizational knowledge and as a developmental technique for high-potentials. Expatriation has become a vital part of global business strategy and career development; contemporary organizations do not use expatriation merely to reassign struggling employees. Moreover, expatriates' higher levels of experience managing high-risk and challenging interpersonal situations may contribute to increased performance that will benefit HCNs through each of the four channels discussed in the framework we presented above.

4.1 Limitations and Future Directions for Research

The study has two important limitations. First, we were unable to explore the processes through which experience impacts expatriate selection. Some organizations may have formal experience requirements for prospective expatriates, while in others experience may be more an implicit indicator of employee potential. Alternative selection processes will not change our overall findings that expatriate experience is likely a HCN resource and that organizations do not tend to send inexperienced employees abroad, but it may impact interpretations of differences between expatriates and their domestic counterparts at home (e.g., do differences indicate that expatriates are more ambitious).

Second, the competing expatriate stereotypes we described concern both expatriate experience *and competence*. In this study, we could examine only the experience component of these stereotypes. While experience and competence are related, they are distinct. Experienced expatriates may nevertheless lack critical job knowledge and skill that makes them a burden for HCNs. Future research should thus extend the current results by directly examining how different dimensions of expatriate managers' job performance impact host country nationals' outcomes. Some previous studies have offered preliminary examinations of the impact of expatriates on HCNs (Takeuchi 2010), but these studies have focused on overall performance or adjustment. Understanding the role of expatriates in facilitating HCN success requires more detailed consideration of how specific domains of effective and ineffective performance behaviors impact the work context and behavior of host country nationals. It is our hope that the framework we present can serve as a guide for how future researchers might investigate the mechanisms through which expatriates can be deployed to promote the well-being of the HCNs they supervise and their host country.

Future research should also expand the breadth of activities that are considered when assessing leadership experience. The Leadership Experience Inventory used in the present study measures experience with some aspects of leadership performance, such as handling interpersonal challenges, developing others, and role modeling. However, most of its scales are focused on technical business and management experience. Leadership and management are distinct, equally important performance domains (Campbell/Wiernik 2015). Experience specifically with performing interpersonal leadership behaviors, such as consideration/support, initiating structure, goal emphasis/motivation, and empowerment/facilitation, may be as relevant for business unit success and the careers of expatriates and domestic managers as technical operations and management experience. Future research on leadership experience should incorporate assessments of experience with performing specific interpersonal leadership tasks.

4.2   *Implications for Expatriate Management and Career Development*

The results of this study have implications effectively managing and developing expatriates. Relative to their host country national counterparts, expatriates tend to have the greatest experiential advantage in terms of strategy, high-risk activities, and interpersonal challenges. However, they tend to have no noticeable advantage for experience in other areas, such as day-to-day business operations and managing crises, failures, and financial problems. When expatriates are sent abroad, HCNs may look to them with the understanding that they have skills and experiences which local managers lack. But this is not uniformly so. In these cases, halo may operate, leading HCNs to believe that the expatriate has superior experience across the board – potentially resulting in overlooking HCN talent in areas where the expatriate experience advantage is not as large. To avoid this problem, organizations should strengthen expatriate employees' experience in areas where they may be weaker (i.e., no better than HCNs), and strategically deploy expatriates to locations where local talent pools lack the specific competencies at which individual expatriate employees excel.

In terms of using international assignments as a developmental opportunity, it is important to recognize how expatriates might benefit from the experience. Expatriation can often be seen as a "baptism by fire" experience that can propel employees to new levels of success (Stahl et al. 2002). Planning expatriate assignments so that they will provide the specific experiences needed to facilitate employees' career goals will ensure that the experience contributes to continued employee career development.

This paper shows that expatriates tend to possess strengths in several key areas of managerial job experience when compared with both origin- and host-country nationals. Expatriate advantages in high-risk, interpersonal, and strategic experience might be leveraged to positively impact the lives of HCNs. This paper contributes to the growing literature that shifts focus in expatriate research from the adjustment and success of expatriates themselves to better understand the impact of international exchanges on all parties involved. As continued globalization leads to higher frequencies of expatriate assignments, understanding not only the difficulties of expatriation for expatriates, but also the difficulties that expatriates may cause for their host country coworkers and communities, will become vitally important.

References

Albrecht, Anne-Grit; Ones, Deniz S.; Sinangil, Handan Kepir (2018): Expatriate Management. In: Ones, Deniz S. et al. (Eds.): The SAGE Handbook of Industrial, Work and Organizational Psychology. Volume 3: Managerial Psychology and Organizational Approaches. 2nd ed. London, United Kingdom: Sage: 429–468.

Bhanugopan, Ramudu; Fish, Alan (2007): Replacing Expatriates with Local Managers: An Exploratory Investigation into Obstacles to Localization in a Developing Country. In: *Human Resource Development International* 10,4: 365–381. [https://doi.org/10/bg3jrc].

Black, J. Stewart; Mendenhall, Mark E.; Oddou, Gary R. (1991): Toward a Comprehensive Model of International Adjustment: An Integration of Multiple Theoretical Perspectives. In: *Academy of Management Review* 16,2: 291–317. [https://doi.org/10/fn7m8b].

Bonache Pérez, Jaime; Pla-Barber, José (2005): When Are International Managers a Cost Effective Solution? The Rationale of Transaction Cost Economics Applied to Staffing Decisions in MNCs. In: *Journal of Business Research* 58,10: 1320–1329. [https://doi.org/10.1016/j.jbusres.2004.05.004].

Bono, Joyce E. et al. (2007): Workplace Emotions: The Role of Supervision and Leadership. In: *Journal of Applied Psychology* 92,5: 1357–1367. [https://doi.org/10.1037/0021-9010.92.5.1357].

Burmeister, Anne et al. (2015): The Micro-Processes during Repatriate Knowledge Transfer: The Repatriates' Perspective. In: *Journal of Knowledge Management* 19,4: 735–755. [https://doi.org/10.1108/JKM-01-2015-0011].

Campbell, John P.; Wiernik, Brenton M. (2015): The Modeling and Assessment of Work Performance. In: *Annual Review of Organizational Psychology and Organizational Behavior* 2: 47–74. [https://doi.org/10/bc4k].

Collings, David G.; Scullion, Hugh; Morley, Michael J. (2007): Changing Patterns of Global Staffing in the Multinational Enterprise: Challenges to the Conventional Expatriate Assignment and Emerging Alternatives. In: *Journal of World Business* 42,2: 198–213. [https://doi.org/10.1016/j.jwb.2007.02.005].

Connelly, Brian S. (2008): Reliability of the Leadership Experience Inventory. White Paper. Minneapolis, MN: Personnel Decisions International.

Fang, Yulin et al. (2010): Multinational Firm Knowledge, Use of Expatriates, and Foreign Subsidiary Performance. In: *Journal of Management Studies* 47,1: 27–54. [https://doi.org/10.1111/j.1467-6486.2009.00850.x].

Harris, Hilary; Brewster, Chris (1999): The Coffee-Machine System: How International Selection Really Works. In: *International Journal of Human Resource Management* 10,3: 488–500. [https://doi.org/10.1080/095851999340440].

Hechanova, Regina; Beehr, Terry A.; Christiansen, Neil D. (2003): Antecedents and Consequences of Employees' Adjustment to Overseas Assignment: A Meta-Analytic Review. In: *Applied Psychology* 52,2: 213–236. [https://doi.org/10/d4f4xv].

Hedges, Larry V.; Olkin, Ingram (1985): Statistical Methods for Meta-Analysis. Orlando, FL: Academic Press.

Huang, Joy (2013): Developing Local Talent for Future Leadership. In: *China Business Review* 40,1: 28–30. [http://www.chinabusinessreview.com/developing-local-talent-for-future-leadership].

Judge, Timothy A.; Piccolo, Ronald F. (2004): Transformational and Transactional Leadership: A Meta-Analytic Test of Their Relative Validity. In: *Journal of Applied Psychology* 89,5: 755–768. [https://doi.org/10.1037/0021-9010.89.5.755].

McCloy, Rodney A.; Campbell, John P.; Cudeck, Robert (1994): A Confirmatory Test of a Model of Performance Determinants. In: *Journal of Applied Psychology* 79,4: 493–505. [https://doi.org/10.1037/0021-9010.79.4.493].

Mol, Stefan T. et al. (2009): When Selection Ratios Are High: Predicting the Expatriation Willingness of Prospective Domestic Entry-Level Job Applicants. In: *Human Performance* 22,1: 1–22. [https://doi.org/10.1080/08959280802540437].

Moore, Sarah; Grunberg, Leon; Greenberg, Edward (2006): Surviving Repeated Waves of Organizational Downsizing: The Recency, Duration, and Order Effects Associated with Different Forms of Layoff Contact. In: *Anxiety, Stress, and Coping* 19,3: 309–329. [https://doi.org/10.1080/10615800600901341].

Ones, Deniz S. et al. (2012): Cross-Cultural Generalization: Using Meta-Analysis to Test Hypotheses about Cultural Variability. In: Ryan, Ann Marie; Leong, Frederick T.L.; Oswald, Frederick L. (Eds.): Conducting Multinational Research Projects in Organizational Psychology: Challenges and Opportunities, APA/MSU Series on Multicultural Psychology 1. Washington, DC: American Psychological Association: 91–122. [https://doi.org/10/5kz].

Schmidt, Frank L.; Hunter, John E. (2015): Methods of Meta-Analysis: Correcting Error and Bias in Research Findings. 3rd ed. Thousand Oaks, CA: Sage. [https://doi.org/10/b6mg].

Sinangil, Handan Kepir; Ones, Deniz S. (2001): Expatriate Management. In: Anderson, Neil et al. (Eds.): Handbook of Industrial, Work and Organizational Psychology. Volume 1: Personnel Psychology. Thousand Oaks, CA: Sage: 424–443. [https://doi.org/10/b6pn].

Stahl, Günter K.; Miller, Edwin L.; Tung, Rosalie L. (2002): Toward the Boundaryless Career: A Closer Look at the Expatriate Career Concept and the Perceived Implications of an International Assignment. In: *Journal of World Business* 37,3: 216–227. [https://doi.org/10/ddttgr].

Sturman, Michael C. (2003): Searching for the Inverted U-Shaped Relationship between Time and Performance: Meta-Analyses of the Experience/Performance, Tenure/Performance, and Age/Performance Relationships. In: *Journal of Management* 29,5: 609–640. [https://doi.org/10.1016/s0149-2063(03)00028-x].

Takeuchi, Riki (2010): A Critical Review of Expatriate Adjustment Research through a Multiple Stakeholder View: Progress, Emerging Trends, and Prospects. In: *Journal of Management* 36,4: 1040–1064. [https://doi.org/10.1177/0149206309349308].

The Economist (2014): Bumpkin Bosses. In: *The Economist* 411,8886: 70. [http://www.economist.com/news/business/21601889-leaders-western-companies-are-less-globally-minded-they-think-they-are-bumpkin-bosses].

VanKatwyk, Paul; Laczo, Roxanne M.; Tuzinski, Kathy (2006): The Leadership Experience Inventory. Technical Manual. Minneapolis, MN: Personnel Decisions International.

Whitman, Daniel S.; Van Rooy, David L.; Viswesvaran, Chockalingam (2010): Satisfaction, Citizenship Behaviors, and Performance in Work Units: A Meta-Analysis of Collective Construct Relations. In: *Personnel Psychology* 63,1: 41–81. [https://doi.org/10/dxcff5].

Success among Self-Initiated versus Assigned Expatriates

*Anne-Grit Albrecht, Stephan Dilchert, Deniz S. Ones, Jürgen Deller,
and Frieder M. Paulus*

Abstract

This chapter compares the success outcomes of self-initiated and employer-initiated expatriates. Results show negligible to small differences between these groups on adjustment, job satisfaction, and job performance, though self-initiated expatriates do show somewhat better interaction adjustment. Results suggest that self-initiation is not a powerful determinant of expatriate success.

1   Introduction

Expatriates reflect a highly heterogeneous population of employees. The common unifying characteristics of all expatriate positions are that employees are living and working for an extended period in a foreign cultural environment (versus mobile international business travelers who merely commute to and from foreign locations) and that the assignments are intended to be temporary (versus immigrants who intend to remain in their new location in perpetuity; Albrecht et al. 2018a). However, within this category, individual expatriates hold jobs ranging from CEO of a local subsidiary of a large multinational corporation, to high-ranking diplomat, to non-managerial technical specialist, to academic researcher, to luxury hotel chef, to opera singer, just to name a few. While these employees are united by the international context of their work, their diverse environmental circumstances and personal characteristics make it likely for the factors that contribute to success to differ across expatriate subgroups.

One key distinction between subgroups of expatriates that has received increasing research attention is whether expatriates initiated their international transfer themselves or whether they were assigned to a foreign position by their employer. Studies comparing these groups have often found strong similarities on many dimensions (e.g., Jokinen et al. 2008), but self-initiated and assigned expatriates are distinguishable in terms of the nature of their assignments, employees' motives and personal characteristics, and some success outcomes (Andresen et al. 2012). In terms of the nature of the assignment, assigned expatriates tend to be higher-level and more senior employees sent abroad to fill critical organizational roles, whereas self-initiated expatriates often enter lower-level positions or even new organizations and have more freedom to pursue their personal goals (Andresen et al. 2015; Inkson et al. 1997). In terms of employee characteristics, self-initiated expatriates tend to be younger and more often female (Andresen et al. 2015; Biemann/Andresen 2010), as well as more adventurous and higher on proactivity-related personality traits (Biemann/ Andresen 2010; Doherty et al. 2011). Self-initiated expatriates are often argued to pursue international experience as a way to build career competencies and distinguish themselves (Al Ariss 2010; Stahl et al. 2002; Suutari/Brewster 2000; Vance 2005); however, self-initiated and assigned expatriates appear to be similarly career-oriented and motivated to pursue (or accept) international assignments to advance their career objectives (Andresen et al. 2015; Doherty et al. 2011). In terms of success outcomes, self-initiated expatriates tend to adjust somewhat better than assigned expatriates, particularly for interaction adjustment (comfort communicating with host country nationals; Peltokorpi/Froese 2009; Selmer et al. 2015). This difference may be because self-initiated expatriates are more deeply invested in engaging with the host country culture. However, research on differences in success between types of expatriates is still nascent. In this chapter, we extend research on differences between self-initiated and assigned expatriates by exploring differences between these groups on several dimensions of expatriate success.

2 Methods

2.1 Samples

Analyses in this chapter are based on data from 2,169 expatriates from both waves of the iGOES project (see Wiernik et al. 2018, Chapter 1, this volume). This project assessed German-speaking expatriates working in numerous countries[1] in private sector organizations. The large majority of participants had managerial responsibilities, and participants worked in a wide variety of industries and functional roles. As can be seen in Table 1, participants include a wide range of ages and educational levels and were roughly 30% female; these values are consistent with most samples in the expatriate literature.

Also shown in Table 1, most participants were self-initiated expatriates, but for a substantial minority, the expatriate assignment was initiated primarily by the employer or expatriates' spouses. More information on the iGOES project is available in Albrecht et al. (2018b, Appendix A, this volume).

2.2 Measures

Source of expatriation initiation. The source of initiation of the expatriate assignment was measured differently in Wave 1 and Wave 2 of the iGOES project. In Wave 1, initiation was measured using a categorial item asking participants to indicate whether their assignment was initiated by themselves, by their employer, or jointly between themselves and their employer. In Wave 2, participants were asked to separately rate the degree to which they themselves, their employer, and their spouse had initiated the assignment with a scale values ranging from 1 = *not at all* to 5 = *exclusively*. In the Mexican sample of Wave 2, initiation was also assessed using qualitative interviews to better understand the behaviors expatriates perceive as reflecting low versus high degrees of initiative. In addition to self-ratings of the degree of self-, employer-, and spouse-initiation of their international moves, these expatriates were asked to verbally describe the specific actions they, their organization, and their spouse took that led to their decision to move abroad. Two independent raters read transcripts of the responses and scored them on the three initiative scales. Example qualitative responses include "I searched for positions abroad and found this job

---

[1] There were not substantial differences across countries in rates of different sources of initiation of expatriation, so data from all countries within each wave were pooled for analysis.

in Mexico" (high self-initiation) and "I wrote my Master's thesis on [a topic relevant to my current employer]. Somehow, [my current employer], a company in Mexico, learned about the thesis and contacted me with a job offer" (high employer-initiation). Agreement between raters, as well between raters and expatriates' self-ratings, was extremely high. The qualitative responses indicate that expatriates perceived a variety of non-mutually-exclusive actions on the part of themselves, their employers, and their spouses as reflective of initiation and support our measurement of these three sources of initiation as separate variables.

Because the measures of expatriation initiation source were not commensurate across waves, data for each wave were analyzed separately.

Job performance. Supervisors, coworkers, or subordinates rated expatriates' job performance using a short job performance survey completed by one rater for each expatriate covering the following dimensions of job performance: technical performance (average Cronbach's $\alpha = .66$ across countries for Wave 1, .90 for Wave 2), contextual performance ($\alpha = .45$, wave 1 only), management and supervision ($\alpha = .58$ for Wave 1, .86 for Wave 2), effort and initiative ($\alpha = .59$ for Wave 1, .84 for Wave 2), interpersonal relations ($\alpha = .88$, wave 2 only) and personal discipline ($\alpha = .85$, wave 2 only). An overall job performance score was computed summing all performance dimension measures ($\alpha = .86$ for wave 1, .96 for wave 2).

Table 1: Sample Characteristics

Variable	*N*	%	*Mean*	*SD*	Min	Max
Demographics						
Age (in years)	2,169	—	36.80	8.87	19	71
Gender (% female)	687	31.5	—	—	—	—
Marital Status (% in stable relationship)	1,472	67.5	—	—	—	—
Years of formal education	2,164	—	17.40	2.45	1	32
Tenure with current employer (in months)	2,135	—	77.34	83.92	1	648
Tenure on current assignment (in months)	2,128	—	33.55	32.35	1	144
Nature of expatriation						
Wave 1						
Self-initiated	701	59.06	—	—	—	—
Organization-initiated	275	23.17	—	—	—	—
Jointly-initiated	200	9.17	—	—	—	—
Wave 2						
Self-initiated	977	—	3.84	1.28	1	5
Organization-initiated	956	—	2.74	1.62	1	5
Spouse-initiated	841	—	2.13	1.43	1	5

Note: Values computed across countries and both waves of the iGOES data collection.

Adjustment. Self-rated adjustment was assessed using Black and Stephens' (1989) 14-item scale in Costa Rica, Czech Republic, Ghana, India, Ireland, the Netherlands, Sweden, and Turkey. This scale produces separate scores for locational, interaction, and work adjustment. Locational adjustment refers to an expatriate's perceived ability to manage everyday life demands (e.g., running errands, moving around, accessing food and healthcare) in their current location. Interaction adjustment refers to expatriates' comfort with communicating with host country nationals in both work and nonwork settings. Work adjustment refers to expatriates' perceived ability to carry out their work assignments in their current location. Total or overall adjustment was computed as the sum of all 14 items on the scale. In these countries, the average internal consistency estimates were $\alpha = .81$ for total overall adjustment, $\alpha = .72$ for locational adjustment, $\alpha = .83$ for interaction adjustment, $\alpha = .71$ for work adjustment.

In China, Egypt, Russia, South Korea, and the United States, adjustment was assessed using Albrecht's (2005) 3-item measure (the item measuring perceived overall adjustment was excluded). Consequently, only one value for total overall adjustment could be estimated for these countries (average $\alpha = .63$).

Job satisfaction. Job satisfaction was assessed using the five-item scale provided by Judge et al. (1998). This scale assesses overall job satisfaction through a series of general judgments about the overall quality of the work experience (example item: "I feel fairly well satisfied with my present job"; average $\alpha = .80$).

Life satisfaction. In Wave 2, life satisfaction was measured using the short version of the Satisfaction with Life Scale developed by Diener et al. (1985), consisting of four items (examples: "In most ways my life is close to ideal", "The conditions of my life are excellent"). The average internal consistency of this scale across countries was $\alpha = .74$.

2.3 Analyses

For Wave 1, success criteria for groups of expatriates reporting each source of initiation (self, employer, joint) were compared using standardized mean differences (Cohen's d) and standard deviation ratios (u values). For Wave 2, correlations were computed between each initiation rating scale and each criterion.

3   Results

3.1   Wave 1

Comparisons of expatriate success outcomes across sources of initiation for Wave 1 are shown in Tables 2–4. Job performance mean differences were negligible for all groups and performance dimensions (absolute d values ranged from .00 to .11; these values are all below the 10th percentile of effects in organizational research; Paterson et al. 2016). Job satisfaction showed similarly negligible differences across groups. Results are more complex for adjustment. While self-initiated and employer-initiated expatriates showed negligible differences for most dimensions of adjustment, self-initiated expatriates were moderately higher on interaction adjustment than employer-initiated expatriates ($d = .44$, see Table 2), indicating that expatriates who sought out international opportunities on their own (versus being assigned abroad by their employers) reported greater comfort interacting with host country nationals. These findings are consistent with previous studies of adjustment differences between self-initiated and assigned expatriates (Froese and Peltokorpi 2013; Selmer et al. 2015). This result is interesting, as interacting with host country nationals is often the most difficult aspect of adjusting to a new international context; finding that individuals who choose their own expatriate experience have fewer problems interacting has implications for how organizations select employees for international assignments, as well as for supporting and managing expatriates on location.

Table 2: Success of Self- versus Employer-Initiated Expatriates: Wave 1

Variable	Self-initiated			Employer-initiated					
	N	M	SD	N	M	SD	u	d	95% CI
Adjustment									
Overall adjustment (3-item)	691	4.00	.64	273	3.84	.60	1.07	**.25**	.13, .37
Overall adjustment (14-item)	316	3.86	.51	103	3.80	.52	.99	**.13**	-.06, .32
Locational adjustment	316	3.77	.64	103	3.79	.62	1.04	**-.03**	-.22, .15
Interaction adjustment	316	3.88	.76	103	3.53	.87	.88	**.44**	.25, .63
Work adjustment	311	4.07	.65	103	4.18	.62	1.05	**-.16**	-.35, .03
Job satisfaction	137	4.04	.71	59	4.12	.60	1.17	**-.11**	-.37, .14
Job performance									
Overall job performance	284	4.32	.42	128	4.29	.45	.94	**.09**	-.09, .26
Technical performance	288	4.47	.52	128	4.43	.50	1.03	**.08**	-.09, .25
Contextual performance	284	4.20	.56	129	4.16	.58	.97	**.07**	-.11, .24
Management and supervision	281	4.14	.57	128	4.13	.63	.90	**.02**	-.16, .19
Effort and initiative	285	4.39	.50	128	4.40	.53	.95	**-.02**	-.19, .16

Note: N = sample size, M = mean, SD = standard deviation, u = ratio of standard deviations, d = observed standardized mean difference (Cohen's d), 95% CI = 95% confidence interval around d. Positive d values indicate self-initiated expatriates score higher.

Table 3: Success of Self- versus Jointly-Initiated Expatriates: Wave 1

Variable	Self-initiated			Jointly-initiated			u	d	95% CI
	N	M	SD	N	M	SD			
Adjustment									
Overall adjustment (3-item)	691	4.00	.64	197	3.93	.61	1.04	**.11**	-.03, .24
Overall adjustment (14-item)	316	3.86	.51	72	3.84	.49	1.04	**.05**	-.16, .27
Locational adjustment	316	3.77	.64	72	3.80	.62	1.03	**-.05**	-.26, .17
Interaction adjustment	316	3.88	.76	72	3.65	.69	1.11	**.31**	.09, .52
Work adjustment	311	4.07	.65	71	4.19	.62	1.05	**-.17**	-.39, .04
Job satisfaction	137	4.04	.71	40	4.12	.50	1.42	**-.12**	-.41, .18
Job performance									
Overall job performance	284	4.32	.42	102	4.30	.39	1.08	**.06**	-.13, .25
Technical performance	288	4.47	.52	102	4.48	.45	1.16	**-.03**	-.22, .16
Contextual performance	284	4.20	.56	102	4.14	.59	.95	**.09**	-.10, .28
Management and supervision	281	4.14	.57	100	4.15	.56	1.02	**-.01**	-.20, .18
Effort and initiative	285	4.39	.50	102	4.37	.47	1.08	**.03**	-.16, .22

Note: N = sample size, M = mean, SD = standard deviation, u = ratio of standard deviations, d = observed standardized mean difference (Cohen's d), 95% CI = 95% confidence interval around d. Positive d values indicate self-initiated expatriates score higher.

Table 4: Success of Employer- versus Jointly-Initiated Expatriates: Wave 1

Variable	Employer-initiated			Jointly-initiated					
	N	M	SD	N	M	SD	u	d	95% CI
Adjustment									
Overall adjustment (3-item)	273	3.84	.60	197	3.93	.61	.97	**-.15**	-.30, .00
Overall adjustment (14-item)	103	3.80	.52	72	3.84	.49	1.06	**-.08**	-.33, .17
Locational adjustment	103	3.79	.62	72	3.80	.62	1.00	**-.01**	-.26, .24
Interaction adjustment	103	3.53	.87	72	3.65	.69	1.26	**-.15**	-.40, .10
Work adjustment	103	4.18	.62	71	4.19	.62	.99	**-.01**	-.27, .24
Job satisfaction	59	4.12	.60	40	4.12	.50	1.21	**.00**	-.34, .34
Job performance									
Overall job performance	128	4.29	.45	102	4.30	.39	1.16	**-.03**	-.25, .19
Technical performance	128	4.43	.50	102	4.48	.45	1.12	**-.11**	-.33, .10
Contextual performance	129	4.16	.58	102	4.14	.59	.98	**.02**	-.19, .24
Management and supervision	128	4.13	.63	100	4.15	.56	1.13	**-.03**	-.25, .19
Effort and initiative	128	4.40	.53	102	4.37	.47	1.13	**.05**	-.17, .26

Note: N = sample size, M = mean, SD = standard deviation, u = ratio of standard deviations, d = observed standardized mean difference (Cohen's d), 95% CI = 95% confidence interval around d. Positive d values indicate self-initiated expatriates score higher.

Comparisons of jointly-initiated expatriates to self-initiated (Table 3) and employer-initiated (Table 4) expatriates indicate that these expatriates display adjustment levels that are intermediary between purely self-initiated and employer-initiated expatriates (mean differences show the same patterns, but are generally attenuated in magnitude). Finally, for all group comparisons and criteria, standard deviation ratios (u values) did not differ substantially from 1, indicating that source of initiation does not have an appreciable homogenizing effect on expatriate outcomes.

3.2   Wave 2

Results for Wave 2 analyses are shown in Table 5. As would be expected, different sources of initiation of the expatriate experience were negatively correlated (e.g., self-initiation correlated $r = -.50$ with employer-initiation). However, these correlations were far from unity, indicating that most expatriates tend to embark on their assignments for a myriad of reasons originating from both their own initiative and the desires of their employers or family. Decisions to go abroad are complex and multiply-determined. The distribution of scores on spouse initiative were extremely skewed and bimodal – 57% of the expatriates indicated their spouse had not initiated the assignment at all, 6% a little, 9% somewhat, 23% strongly, and finally 6% exclusively. Accordingly, linear correlation results should be interpreted cautiously.

The large majority of the correlations between expatriate outcomes and sources of initiation are negligible to small. Degree of self-initiation showed small positive relationships with most job performance dimensions; these relationships are somewhat larger than were observed for Wave 1 (recall that $d \approx 2 \times r$), but not so much larger as to preclude sampling error as an explanation. Consistent with the results from Wave 1, self-initiation also showed a small positive relation with interaction adjustment ($r_c = .11$). The magnitude of the effect size is weaker than in Wave 1; the difference likely reflects a combination of sampling error and differences in measurement method (degree of self-initiation versus a dichotomous self- vs. employer-initiated comparison). Degree of employer-initiation also showed small positive relations with work adjustment and job satisfaction ($r_c = .14, .13$, respectively). This may reflect that organizations may provide greater transitional support to expatriates when the move is employer-initiated (for comparison, though the magnitudes of the differences were smaller in Wave 1, they were in the same direction). The one relationship in Table 5 showing a substantially larger magnitude is between employer-initiation and management performance ($r_c = .24$). This relationship may reflect a selection effect. Employer-initiated expatriates are often sent abroad to manage critical organizational facilities and to prepare employees for future advancement to top-level executive positions. Employees chosen for such assignments are typically high-potential individuals with a record of successful managerial performance. Thus, the stronger relationships could reflect that these employer-chosen expatriates arrived in their new positions with greater capabilities for successful leadership.

Table 5: Relations between Sources of Initiation and Expatriate Success: Wave 2

Variable	Self-initiation				Employer-initiation				Spouse-initiation			
	N	r	r_c	95% CI	N	r	r_c	95% CI	N	r	r_c	95% CI
Initiation												
Self-initiation	—	—	—	—	949	-.50	—	-.55, -.45	839	-.06	—	-.13, .01
Employer-initiation	949	-.50	—	-.55, -.45	—	—	—	—	833	-.21	—	-.28, -.15
Spouse-initiation	839	-.06	—	-.13, .01	833	-.21	—	-.28, -.15	—	—	—	—
Adjustment												
Overall adjustment	972	.05	**.06**	-.01, .13	951	.05	**.06**	-.01, .13	838	.00	**.00**	-.08, .07
Locational adjustment	973	.02	**.03**	-.05, .11	952	.08	**.10**	.03, .18	838	.03	**.04**	-.04, .12
Interaction adjustment	972	.10	**.11**	.04, .18	951	-.06	**-.07**	-.14, .00	838	-.04	**-.04**	-.12, .03
Work adjustment	971	-.04	**-.05**	-.12, .03	950	.12	**.14**	.06, .21	836	.00	**.00**	-.08, .08
Satisfaction												
Job satisfaction	948	-.06	**-.07**	-.14, .00	929	.12	**.13**	.06, .20	818	-.05	**-.06**	-.13, .02
Life satisfaction	948	-.02	**-.02**	-.09, .05	929	.07	**.08**	.01, .15	818	.02	**.02**	-.06, .10
Job performance												
Overall job performance	422	.09	**.13**	.00, .26	412	.02	**.02**	-.11, .16	385	.08	**.11**	-.03, .25
Technical performance	422	.08	**.11**	-.02, .24	412	.02	**.03**	-.11, .16	385	.03	**.04**	-.10, .18
Interpersonal relations	422	.10	**.13**	.00, .26	412	-.04	**-.05**	-.18, .08	385	.09	**.12**	-.02, .26
Management/supervision	419	.02	**.03**	-.10, .16	409	.17	**.24**	.11, .37	382	.05	**.07**	-.07, .21
Effort/initiative	414	.09	**.12**	-.01, .26	404	.00	**.00**	-.13, .14	377	.05	**.07**	-.07, .21
Personal discipline	420	.09	**.12**	-.01, .25	410	.00	**.00**	-.14, .13	383	.09	**.12**	-.02, .26

Note: N = sample size, r = observed correlation, r_c = observed correlation corrected for attenuation due to unreliability in the criterion variables, 95% CI = 95% confidence interval around r_c; adjustment and satisfaction were corrected using alpha estimates from the current sample; job performance variables was corrected using meta-analytic estimates of the supervisor interrater reliability for each performance dimension from Viswesvaran et al. (1996).

4   Discussion

In this chapter, we examined the differences between self-initiated and assigned expatriates on adjustment, job satisfaction, and job performance. Our results suggest that outcomes for these two groups are similar. While self-initiated expatriates tend to have stronger interaction adjustment than assigned expatriates, the size of this difference (as well as differences on other criteria) is relatively small. Based on other findings from the expatriate literature (e.g., Bhaskar-Shrinivas et al. 2005; Mol et al. 2005), other personal, environmental, and procedural factors appear to be more important for driving expatriate success than merely whether the decision to go abroad originated from the expatriate or their employer. Future research attempting to differentiate self-initiated from assigned expatriates would benefit from more nuanced investigations of specific decision-making processes and their impact on expatriate contexts and outcomes (e.g., how do potential expatriates evaluate the relative advantages and tradeoffs of alternative international and domestic options for advancing their careers?).

4.1   Initiative in Expatriate Research

Based on the similarities of these groups observed in this study, it is likely that findings from studies of self-initiated expatriates may apply to assigned expatriates (and vice versa). Considering these findings, we wish to highlight the limitations of self-initiation of expatriation as an operationalization of the broader construct of initiative/proactivity in expatriate research. Because differences between self-initiated and assigned expatriates appear to be weak to negligible, we believe that focusing on this distinction has little potential to enhance our understanding of expatriate success. Proactive personality, attitudes, and behaviors have been established as important drivers of success in studies of domestic employees (cf. Fuller/Marler 2009; Thomas et al. 2010). We suspect that proactivity/initiative are likely to be similarly important for expatriate success. However, it is the broader class of behaviors and variables associated with initiative, not merely whether employees initiated the sojourn itself, that makes initiative important in expatriate settings. Individuals who are more achievement-oriented, assertive, and open to change (characteristics associated with proactive personality; Fuller/Marler 2009), are likely more prone to initiate encounters with host country nationals and build a larger social network, ultimately leading to higher interaction adjustment. Self-initiation of expatriation is a poor indicator of proactivity and is likely unrelated to these more specific tendencies. Besides its poor construct validity as a measure of proactivity, self-initiation also treats this continuous quantitative trait (cf. Thomas et al. 2010) as a dichotomous variable. The profound consequences of dichotomization for measurement and statistical analyses have been aptly summarized elsewhere (e.g., MacCallum et al. 2002). The current study echoes much previous research finding that self-initiated expatriates do not differ strongly from assigned expatriates (Andresen et al. 2014; Tharenou 2015). Moving forward, studies of expatriate initiative and proactivity would benefit from measuring, rather than assuming, these employee characteristics.

References

Albrecht, Anne-Grit (2005): Untangling the Laundry List: General Mental Ability, the Big Five, and Context Related Variables as Predictors for Expatriate Success. Master's Thesis. Lüneburg, Germany: Leuphana Universität. [http://opus.uni-lueneburg.de/opus/volltexte/2006/344/].

Albrecht, Anne-Grit; Ones, Deniz S.; Sinangil, Handan Kepir (2018a): Expatriate Management. In: Ones, Deniz S. et al. (Eds.): The SAGE Handbook of Industrial, Work and Organizational Psychology. Volume 3: Managerial Psychology and Organizational Approaches. 2nd ed. London, United Kingdom: Sage: 429–468.

Albrecht, Anne-Grit et al. (2018b): Design, Implementation, and Analysis of the iGOES Project. In: Wiernik, Brenton M.; Rüger, Heiko; Ones, Deniz S. (Eds.): Managing Expatriates: Success Factors in Private and Public Domains, Series on Population Studies 50. Opladen, Germany: Barbara Budrich Publishers.

Al Ariss, Akram (2010): Modes of Engagement: Migration, Self-Initiated Expatriation, and Career Development. In: *Career Development International* 15,4: 338–358. [https://doi.org/10.1108/13620431011066231].

Andresen, Maike et al. (2014): Addressing International Mobility Confusion: Developing Definitions and Differentiations for Self-Initiated and Assigned Expatriates as Well as Migrants. In: *International Journal of Human Resource Management* 25,16: 2295–2318. [https://doi.org/10.1080/09585192.2013.877058].

Andresen, Maike; Al Ariss, Akram; Walther, Matthias (Eds.) (2012): Self-Initiated Expatriation: Individual, Organizational, and National Perspectives. New York: Routledge.

Andresen, Maike; Biemann, Torsten; Pattie, Marshall Wilson (2015): What Makes Them Move Abroad? Reviewing and Exploring Differences between Self-Initiated and Assigned Expatriation. In: *International Journal of Human Resource Management* 26,7: 932–947. [https://doi.org/10.1080/09585192.2012.669780].

Bhaskar-Shrinivas, Purnima et al. (2005): Input-Based and Time-Based Models of International Adjustment: Meta-Analytic Evidence and Theoretical Extensions. In: *Academy of Management Journal* 48,2: 257–281. [https://doi.org/10.5465/AMJ.2005.16928400].

Biemann, Torsten; Andresen, Maike (2010): Self-Initiated Foreign Expatriates versus Assigned Expatriates: Two Distinct Types of International Careers? In: *Journal of Managerial Psychology* 25: 430–448. [https://doi.org/10.1108/02683941011035313].

Black, J. Stewart; Stephens, Gregory K. (1989): The Influence of the Spouse on American Expatriate Adjustment and Intent to Stay in Pacific Rim Overseas Assignments. In: *Journal of Management* 15,4: 529–544. [https://doi.org/10.1177/014920638901500403].

Diener, Ed et al. (1985): The Satisfaction with Life Scale. In: *Journal of Personality Assessment* 49,1: 71–75. [https://doi.org/10.1207/s15327752jpa4901_13].

Doherty, Noeleen; Dickmann, Michael; Mills, Timothy (2011): Exploring the Motives of Company-Backed and Self-Initiated Expatriates. In: *International Journal of Human Resource Management* 22,3: 595–611. [https://doi.org/10.1080/09585192.2011.543637].

Fuller, Jerry Bryan, Jr.; Marler, Laura E. (2009): Change Driven by Nature: A Meta-Analytic Review of the Proactive Personality Literature. In: *Journal of Vocational Behavior* 75,3: 329–345. [https://doi.org/10.1016/j.jvb.2009.05.008].

Inkson, K. et al. (1997): Expatriate Assignment versus Overseas Experience: Contrasting Models of International Human Resource Development. In: *Journal of World Business* 32,4: 351–368. [https://doi.org/10.1016/S1090-9516(97)90017-1].

Jokinen, T.; Brewster, C.; Suutari, V. (2008): Career Capital during International Work Experiences: Contrasting Self-Initiated Expatriate Experiences and Assigned Expatriation. In: *International Journal of Human Resource Management* 19,6: 979–998. [https://doi.org/10.1080/09585190802051279].

Judge, Timothy A. et al. (1998): Dispositional Effects on Job and Life Satisfaction: The Role of Core Evaluations. In: *Journal of Applied Psychology* 83,1: 17–34. [https://doi.org/10.1037/0021-9010.83.1.17].

MacCallum, Robert C. et al. (2002): On the Practice of Dichotomization of Quantitative Variables. In: *Psychological Methods* 7,1: 19–40. [https://doi.org/10.1037/1082-989X.7.1.19].

Mol, Stefan T. et al. (2005): Predicting Expatriate Job Performance for Selection Purposes: A Quantitative Review. In: *Journal of Cross-Cultural Psychology* 36,5: 590–620. [https://doi.org/10.1177/0022022105278544].

Paterson, Ted A. et al. (2016): An Assessment of the Magnitude of Effect Sizes: Evidence from 30 Years of Meta-Analysis in Management. In: *Journal of Leadership & Organizational Studies* 23,1: 66–81. [https://doi.org/10/bjz9].

Peltokorpi, Vesa; Froese, Fabian Jintae (2009): Organizational Expatriates and Self-Initiated Expatriates: Who Adjusts Better to Work and Life in Japan? In: *International Journal of Human Resource Management* 20,5: 1096–1112. [https://doi.org/10.1080/09585190902850299].

Salgado, Jesús F. et al. (2003): A Meta-Analytic Study of General Mental Ability Validity for Different Occupations in the European Community. In: *Journal of Applied Psychology* 88,6: 1068–1081. [https://doi.org/10.1037/0021-9010.88.6.1068].

Selmer, Jan et al. (2015): Context Matters: Acculturation and Work-Related Outcomes of Self-Initiated Expatriates Employed by Foreign vs. Local Organizations. In: *International Journal of Intercultural Relations* 49: 251–264. [https://doi.org/10.1016/j.ijintrel.2015.05.004].

Stahl, Günter K.; Miller, Edwin L.; Tung, Rosalie L. (2002): Toward the Boundaryless Career: A Closer Look at the Expatriate Career Concept and the Perceived Implications of an International Assignment. In: *Journal of World Business* 37,3: 216–227. [https://doi.org/10/ddttgr].

Suutari, Vesa; Brewster, Chris (2000): Making Their Own Way: International Experience through Self-Initiated Foreign Assignments. In: *Journal of World Business* 35,4: 417–436. [https://doi.org/10.1016/S1090-9516(00)00046-8].

Tharenou, Phyllis (2015): Researching Expatriate Types: The Quest for Rigorous Methodological Approaches. In: *Human Resource Management Journal* 25,2: 149–165. [https://doi.org/10.1111/1748-8583.12070].

Thomas, Jeffrey P.; Whitman, Daniel S.; Viswesvaran, Chockalingam (2010): Employee Proactivity in Organizations: A Comparative Meta-Analysis of Emergent Proactive Constructs. In: *Journal of Occupational and Organizational Psychology* 83,2: 275–300. [https://doi.org/10.1348/096317910x502359].

Vance, Charles M. (2005): The Personal Quest for Building Global Competence: A Taxonomy of Self-Initiating Career Path Strategies for Gaining Business Experience Abroad. In: *Journal of World Business, Global Careers* 40,4: 374–385. [https://doi.org/10.1016/j.jwb.2005.08.005].

Viswesvaran, Chockalingam; Ones, Deniz S.; Schmidt, Frank L. (1996): Comparative Analysis of the Reliability of Job Performance Ratings. In: *Journal of Applied Psychology* 81,5: 557–574. [https://doi.org/10/c8f68f].

Wiernik, Brenton M.; Rüger, Heiko; Ones, Deniz S. (2018): Advancing Expatriate Research in Public and Private Sectors. In: Wiernik, Brenton M.; Rüger, Heiko; Ones, Deniz S. (Eds.): Managing Expatriates: Success Factors in Private and Public Domains, Series on Population Studies 50. Opladen, Germany: Barbara Budrich Publishers.

Lingua Necessaria? Language Proficiency and Expatriate Success

Brenton M. Wiernik, Anne-Grit Albrecht, Stephan Dilchert, Jürgen Deller, Deniz S. Ones, and Frieder M. Paulus

Abstract

Local language proficiency is often regarded as a key enabling factor for expatriate success. In this study, we use data from the iGOES project to examine how language proficiency contributes to expatriate outcomes. Language proficiency is negligibly to weakly related to most outcomes, but does show positive relations with interaction adjustment. Moderator analyses support the interpretation of this relation as reflecting increased comfort from being able to communicate effectively, rather than reflecting cultural engagement or social inclusion effects. Overall, results indicate that local language proficiency can contribute to expatriate comfort, but is not absolutely necessary for expatriate success.

1   Introduction

One of the most fundamental preparations expatriates can make in advance of an international assignment is to develop familiarity with or proficiency in their host country's language. Language proficiency[1] is frequently regarded as a necessary prerequisite for success on expatriate assignments (Jordan/Cartwright 1998) and has been associated with many positive expatriate outcomes, including locational and interaction adjustment (Bhaskar-Shrinivas et al. 2005) and performance (Mol et al. 2005). Language training forms a central part of many cross-cultural training programs and is often the only formal training expatriates receive before embarking on their assignments or after arrival (Morris/Robie 2001). Understanding the impact of language ability on expatriate outcomes is crucial for effectively managing expatriate employees, both because language proficiency can have strong main effects on expatriate outcomes and because language proficiency is a key moderator of the effectiveness of other management techniques (cf. the role of language in driving receipt and effectiveness of pre-departure training, Kostal et al. 2018, Chapter 13, this volume).

Proficiency in the languages spoken in a new location can facilitate adjustment and other positive outcomes for a variety of reasons. Speaking the local language facilitates effective communication between expatriates and host country nationals (Du-Babcock/Babcock 1996). Expatriates who cannot speak in host country nationals' local language may be perceived as outsiders and have difficulties managing local subordinates (Mol et al. 2005; though this perception could also encourage helping behavior in some contexts, see e.g., Leonardelli/Toh 2011). Inability to communicate with coworkers naturally can lead to unpleasant workplace climates (Takeuchi et al. 2005) and dissatisfaction (Li/Tse 1998).

---

[1]   Language proficiency can range in degree from complete absence of the ability to understand or communicate in a language to complete fluency, including various levels of rudimentary or intermediate ability.

Language fluency can also increase expatriates' confidence to handle cross-cultural adjustment challenges outside of work (Robinson 2003). Managing everyday tasks, navigating the local environment, and handling emergencies are all made easier when one can read and speak the local language (Bhaskar-Shrinivas et al. 2005).

Generally, the various ways that language proficiency can contribute to positive outcomes can be grouped into two broad mechanisms. First, the *comfort hypothesis* argues that language fluency contributes to positive outcomes by reducing the stress and negative experiences associated with not speaking the local language (e.g., inability to communicate effectively with coworkers). This hypothesis has two components — core workplace language proficiency (i.e., being able to communicate effectively with one's coworkers on work tasks) and incidental language proficiency (i.e., being able to understand less important communications, such as casual office conversations or printed signs and notices). Second, the *cultural engagement hypothesis* argues that facilitating communication is only one part of the benefit of language fluency for expatriates. Learning a language requires a substantial investment of time and effort and typically demands that learners engage deeply with the culture of the language in order to learn usage rules, customs, and idioms. Few other cross-cultural training methods provide as rich an introduction to another culture as language training (Puck et al. 2008). The cultural investment gained when learning the local language facilitates effective communication between expatriates and host country nationals by helping expatriates to adapt to local values, standards, and rules of conduct (Du-Babcock/ Babcock 1996; Gudykunst et al. 1988), but also facilitates other forms of adjustment due to expatriates' increased familiarity with their new culture. Thus, the cultural engagement hypothesis contends that it is not merely the effective communication, but the broader cultural competence that comes with language fluency, that contributes to expatriate success.

Previous meta-analyses have shown that local language ability (measured in various ways) is consistently positively related to self-rated locational[2] adjustment (ρ = .22, 95% credibility interval [CV] = .11, .34) and interaction adjustment (ρ = .43, 95% CV = .16, .70; Bhaskar-Shrinivas et al. 2005). Language proficiency appears to be positively, but inconsistently related to work adjustment (ρ = .18, 95% CV = -.25, .61; Bhaskar-Shrinivas et al. 2005) and self-rated job performance (ρ = .19, 95% CV = -.05, .43; Mol et al. 2005). The lack of consistent positive relations between local language ability and work-related outcomes is likely due to the focus of most previous expatriate research on expatriates from English-speaking countries moving to non-English-speaking locales. Given the status of English as the *de facto* language of world business, it is possible that knowing a local language is less critical for English speakers than non-English speakers (English is widely spoken internationally, whereas most English-speaking countries are limited in their capacity to accommodate non-speakers; Bhaskar-Shrinivas et al. 2005). Most of the samples included in the above-cited meta-analyses comprised natively English-speaking expatriates. In general, the scope of the impact of local language ability for expatriates who are not English-language natives is unknown.

---

[2]   Previous expatriate research has used to the terms "general" (Black/Stephens 1989) or "cultural" (Bhaskar-Shrinivas et al. 2005) adjustment to refer to expatriates' comfort handling everyday non-work demands, such as obtaining food, healthcare, safety, and transportation. We prefer the term "locational adjustment", as it captures that this construct refers to the management of the everyday challenges of living in one's current location (cf. Schlunze 2002). "General adjustment" is overly vague and may be confused with total or overall adjustment. "Cultural adjustment" is too narrow as a label, as the locational adjustment construct encompasses a broader set of challenges than merely adapting to a new culture.

This chapter explores the contribution of language proficiency to expatriate success using the iGOES samples. Across the 28 host countries included in the iGOES project, we asked participants to indicate the languages that are spoken most frequently in their workplaces and to indicate their levels of proficiency with those languages. A key benefit of the iGOES samples for these questions is that the participants share German as their native language, allowing us to examine the impact of local language ability on work-related outcomes for expatriates whose native language is not English. In addition, the design of the iGOES project allows us to compare the validity of the comfort and cultural engagement hypotheses by examining the moderating impact of speaking German (versus the culturally-dominant local language) at work on language proficiency–criterion relationships. Finally, in addition to adjustment and performance, the two criteria most frequently studied in the expatriate literature (Albrecht et al. 2018a), we also examine the impact of language fluency on expatriate job satisfaction and perceived social and organizational support.

2   Methods

2.1   Samples

Data for this chapter came from the iGOES project (see Wiernik et al., Chapter 1, this volume). This project simultaneously gathered data from German-speaking expatriates employed in a variety of jobs, organizations, and countries. Participants across countries were administered the same assessments to allow for examination of the international generalizability of expatriate success factors. Both Wave 1 and Wave 2 of the iGOES data contributed to these analyses. Additional details about the iGOES project are available in Albrecht et al. (2018b, Appendix A, this volume).

2.2   Measures

Language proficiency. Language proficiency was measured in two ways across the countries sampled. In 22 countries (Argentina, China, Costa Rica, Czech Republic, Egypt, Finland, France, Ghana, India, Ireland, Italy, Mexico, the Netherlands, Poland, Russia, South Korea, Spain, Sweden, Switzerland, Thailand, Turkey, the United States), language proficiency was measured with the question, "To what degree do you speak the local language?" This question was answered on a 5-point scale (1 = not at all, 2 = basic knowledge, 3 = can make myself understood, 4 = almost fluent, 5 = fluent).

In 17 countries (Austria, Denmark, Finland, France, Ireland, Italy, Malaysia, Mexico, Morocco, the Netherlands, Poland, Singapore, Spain, Switzerland, Thailand, Turkey, the United Kingdom), language proficiency was either instead or additionally assessed by asking participants to indicate all the languages that were commonly spoken in their workplace and to rate their proficiency with each language. We used these responses to compute two overall language proficiency scores for each participant.[3] First, we computed overall proficiency as the mean proficiency level across all languages spoken in the workplace.

---

[3] We also computed overall proficiency scores based on the maximum proficiency level across all languages spoken in the workplace. However, there was very little variance on this score (653 out of 657 respondents indicated proficiencies of 4 or 5 out of 5 for at least one language). This is understandable, as few companies would send an expatriate on an assignment where they are unable to communicate at work. Because of this lack of variance, we do not report results of maximum proficiency (all correlations are essentially zero).

This score represents expatriates' overall ability to communicate in the workplace. Second, we computed overall proficiency as the *minimum* proficiency level reported across all languages spoken in the workplace. This score captures the impact of there being *any* language spoken in the workplace that an individual doesn't understand. The presence of an incomprehensible language might be alienating for expatriates if they cannot participate in casual conversations (e.g., office gossip), even if they can make themselves understood in another language.

In a substantial portion of the sample, German (participants' native language) was commonly spoken in the workplace. This factor allowed us to test the cultural engagement versus comfort hypotheses of language proficiency. If expatriates primarily benefit from language proficiency by being able to communicate effectively with coworkers, we would expect relationships between language proficiency to be equally strong for analyses including and excluding expatriates who speak their native language in the workplace. In contrast, if language proficiency contributes to positive expatriate outcomes because it serves as a proxy for increased levels of expatriate engagement with the local culture (either in preparation before their trip or while on-location), then we would expect relationships between language proficiency (especially mean language proficiency) to be stronger when workplaces where German was spoken were excluded. Proficiency in non-German speaking contexts would then reflect a greater degree of engagement with the local culture to learn the locally-spoken languages.

Job performance. Supervisors, coworkers, or subordinates rated expatriates' job performance using a short job performance survey completed by one rater for each expatriate covering the following dimensions of job performance: technical performance (average Cronbach's α = .66 across countries for Wave 1, .90 for Wave 2), contextual performance (α = .45, wave 1 only), management and supervision (α = .58 for Wave 1, .86 for Wave 2), effort and initiative (α = .59 for Wave 1, .84 for Wave 2), interpersonal relations (α = .88, wave 2 only), and personal discipline (α = .85, wave 2 only). An overall performance score was computed combining all dimension measures (average α = .86 for wave 1, .96 for wave 2).

Adjustment. Self-rated adjustment was assessed using Black and Stephens' (1989) 14-item scale in Costa Rica, Czech Republic, Ghana, India, Ireland, the Netherlands, Sweden, and Turkey. This scale produces separate scores for locational, interaction, and work adjustment. Locational adjustment refers to an expatriate's perceived ability to manage everyday life demands (e.g., running errands, moving around, accessing food and healthcare) in their current location. Interaction adjustment refers to expatriates' comfort with communicating with host country nationals in both work and nonwork settings. Work adjustment refers to expatriates' perceived ability to carry out their work assignments in their current location. Total or overall adjustment was computed as the sum of all 14 items on the scale. In these countries, the average internal consistency estimates were α = .81 for total overall adjustment, α = .72 for locational adjustment, α = .83 for interaction adjustment, α = .71 for work adjustment.

In China, Egypt, Russia, South Korea, and the United States, adjustment was assessed using Albrecht's (2005) 3-item measure (the item measuring perceived overall adjustment was excluded). Consequently, only one value for total overall adjustment could be estimated for these countries (average α = .63).

Job satisfaction. Job satisfaction was assessed using the five-item scale provided by Judge et al. (1998). This scale assesses overall job satisfaction through a series of general judgments about the overall quality of the work experience (example item: "I feel fairly well satisfied with my present job"). Average internal consistency was α = .80 across country samples.

Life satisfaction. Life satisfaction was assessed using the short version of the Satisfaction with Life Scale developed by Diener et al. (1985), consisting of four items such as "In most ways my life is close to ideal" and "The conditions of my life are excellent". Expatriates were asked to rate their agreement with high scores indicating life satisfaction and low scores indicating dissatisfaction. The average internal consistency of this scale in this study was $\alpha = .74$; values ranged from .70 (Finland and Turkey) to .88 (Mexico) in individual country samples.

Social support. Social support was assessed using a multidimensional measure (Zimet et al. 1988). The overall scale contained 12 items assessing three factors with four items each, relating to support from family, friends, and one's significant other. Sample items include "My family really tries to help me" and "I can count on my friends when things go wrong". Internal consistency reliabilities for the total score combining the three dimensions ranged between .66 and .84 across countries, with an average of .78.

Organizational support. Organizational support was assessed using the measure developed by Kraimer et al. (2001). It contained 12 items with three organizational support dimensions (financial, career, adjustment). Sample items include "My company has taken care of me financially" (financial), "My company takes an interest in my career" (career), "My company has taken care of my family's well-being" (adjustment). Average internal consistency reliabilities for these subscales ranged between .73 and .84. Total scores for the measure had an average internal consistency of .84 across samples.

2.3 Analyses

Individual country samples from the iGOES data were combined using psychometric meta-analysis (Schmidt/Hunter 2015), weighting each country by sample size. Only countries with sample sizes of at least $N = 10$ were included. Correlations were corrected for unreliability in the criterion only; no reliability information was available for the language proficiency measures. Job performance correlations were corrected using meta-analytic supervisor inter-rater reliability distributions for each performance dimension from Viswesvaran et al. (1996). Correlations other criteria were corrected using alpha values from the current samples.

3   Results

3.1 Single-item Language Proficiency

Results for the single-item language proficiency surveys ("To what degree do you speak the local language?") are presented in Table 1. Across the countries included in this analysis, language proficiency showed negligible relations with most dimensions of job performance (overall performance $\rho = .09$, 80% credibility interval [CV] = -.02, .20). Only contextual performance showed a generalizable moderate positive relation with language proficiency ($\rho = .20$, CV = .20, .20). Some dimensions (e.g., technical performance, management and supervision) showed negligible mean correlations, but with large residual variance, suggesting the possibility of moderating factors. Two potential moderators are explored below.

Language proficiency showed more consistent moderate to large positive relationships with expatriate adjustment, particularly with interaction adjustment ($\rho = .38$, CV = .21, .56). This is expected, as ability to communicate with host country nationals (the essence of interaction adjustment) is heavily constrained without a shared language. Relations of language proficiency with locational and work adjustment were more modest ($\rho = .16$ for both dimensions).

Table 1: Meta-analytic results: Single-item language proficiency and expatriate success

Measure	k	N	r_{obs}	SD_{obs}	ρ	SD_ρ	90% CI		80% CV	
Overall job performance	21	739	.07	.18	**.09**	.06	.00	.17	-.02	.20
Technical performance	21	743	.06	.24	**.08**	.18	-.04	.19	-.22	.37
Interpersonal relations	8	226	-.03	.17	**-.03**	.00	-.12	.07	-.03	-.03
Management/supervision	21	733	.05	.20	**.07**	.10	-.03	.18	-.10	.24
Effort/initiative	21	734	.03	.17	**.05**	.02	-.05	.17	.01	.08
Personal discipline	8	225	-.07	.21	**-.10**	.08	-.27	.07	-.23	.03
Contextual performance	13	515	.15	.15	**.20**	.00.	.11	.29	.20	.20
Overall adjustment	24	1,681	.32	.17	**.42**	.12	.34	.49	.22	.62
Locational adjustment	16	996	.13	.17	**.16**	.11	.07	.25	-.01	.33
Interaction adjustment	16	996	.35	.17	**.38**	.12	.30	.46	.21	.56
Work adjustment	16	988	.13	.11	**.16**	.00	.10	.21	.16	.16
Job satisfaction	12	717	.03	.13	**.03**	.00	-.03	.09	.03	.03
Life satisfaction	9	480	-.01	.14	**-.01**	.04	-.09	.07	-.06	.05
Organizational support	9	467	-.12	.13	**-.13**	.00	-.21	-.05	-.13	-.13
Social support	9	479	-.02	.19	**-.02**	.13	-.12	.09	-.21	.18

Note: r_{obs} = Sample size weighted mean observed correlation, SD_{obs} = observed standard deviation, ρ = mean correlation corrected for criterion unreliability, 90% CI = 90% confidence interval around ρ, 80% CV = 80% credibility interval around ρ, SD_ρ = residual true standard deviation.

Beyond the oft-studied criteria of performance and adjustment, we also examined relations with satisfaction and perceived support. Language proficiency was consistently unrelated to job satisfaction (ρ = .03, CV = .03, .03) and life satisfaction (ρ = -.01, CV = -.06, .05). Relationships between language proficiency and social support were also small, but less consistent across countries (ρ = -.02, CV = -.21, .18). Organizational support showed a small *negative* relationship with language proficiency (ρ = -.13, CV = -.13, -.13). However, this result was not replicated in our analyses using either mean proficiency or minimum proficiency across multiple languages spoken in the workplace (see below), suggesting that they resulted from second-order sampling error or measurement artefacts. In short, language proficiency showed negligible relationships with satisfaction and support outcomes.

3.2 Mean Proficiency across Workplace Languages

Results of analyses examining relations of expatriate success with expatriates' mean level of proficiency across all languages commonly spoken in their workplaces are shown in Table 2. Results generally agreed with those for the single-item language proficiency analyses. Mean language proficiency was negligibly related to each performance dimension examined (contextual performance was not assessed in these samples) and was unrelated to all satisfaction and support outcomes.

Expatriate adjustment was moderately positively related to mean language proficiency (overall adjustment ρ = .19, CV = .19, .19). However, relations between adjustment (especially interaction adjustment) and mean language proficiency were much more muted than they were for the single-item language proficiency analyses presented above. This discrepancy may reflect differences in the diversity of individuals with whom expatriates can communicate implied by high scores on each of these measures. In the single-item samples, expatriates indicated their proficiency with "the local language" (i.e., the native language of most or all host country nationals). In contrast, in the multiple language proficiency samples, expatriates indicated their proficiency with all languages spoken in their workplaces, which may have included German, English, or other languages that are not widely spoken among host country nationals generally. High scores on the single-item measure imply a capacity to communicate with individuals generally, while high scores on the multiple language proficiency measure may imply ability to communicate with some coworkers, but not with all host country nationals within and outside the workplace. Additionally, the two language proficiency measures may also imply differences in the degree of expatriates' engagement with the local culture, as discussed in the German moderation analyses below.

3.3 Moderating Factor: Analyses Excluding German

In the introduction, we presented two competing hypotheses explaining the relation between language proficiency and expatriate outcomes. The comfort hypothesis argued that language proficiency leads to positive outcomes by reducing the stress and anxiety associated with being unable to communicate, while the cultural engagement hypothesis argued that language proficiency contributes to positive outcomes because learning the local language reflects a substantial investment in understanding the host country culture. We tested these competing hypotheses by examining whether excluding expatriates who reported that German (their native language) was spoken in the workplace would change relations between language proficiency and expatriate outcomes. If language proficiency primarily influenced outcomes via comfort, we would expect little change in relations.

Table 2: Meta-analytic results: Mean language proficiency and expatriate success

Measure	k	N	r_{obs}	SD_{obs}	ρ	SD_{ρ}	90% CI		80% CV	
Overall job performance	15	408	-.05	.14	**-.06**	.00	-.13	.01	-.06	-.06
Technical performance	15	408	-.04	.13	**-.05**	.00	-.13	.03	-.05	-.05
Interpersonal relations	15	408	-.04	.18	**-.05**	.00	-.15	.05	-.05	-.05
Management/supervision	15	405	.01	.15	**.01**	.00	-.06	.07	.01	.01
Effort/initiative	15	400	-.04	.17	**-.05**	.00	-.14	.04	-.05	-.05
Personal discipline	15	406	-.08	.18	**-.11**	.00	-.21	.00	-.11	-.11
Overall adjustment	17	979	.14	.13	**.19**	.00	.12	.26	.19	.19
Locational adjustment	17	979	.13	.15	**.16**	.06	.09	.23	.07	.26
Interaction adjustment	17	978	.12	.17	**.13**	.11	.05	.20	-.02	.28
Work adjustment	17	976	.06	.11	**.07**	.00	.02	.12	.07	.07
Job satisfaction	17	953	-.03	.11	**-.03**	.00	-.07	.02	-.03	-.03
Life satisfaction	17	954	-.02	.10	**-.03**	.00	-.09	.03	-.03	-.03
Organizational support	17	932	-.02	.10	**-.02**	.00	-.06	.02	-.02	-.02
Social support	17	951	.03	.14	**.03**	.04	-.03	.08	-.03	.09

Note: r_{obs} = Sample size weighted mean observed correlation, SD_{obs} = observed standard deviation, ρ = mean correlation corrected for criterion unreliability, 90% CI = 90% confidence interval around ρ, 80% CV = 80% credibility interval around ρ, SD_{ρ} = residual true standard deviation.

Table 3: Meta-analytic results: Mean language proficiency and expatriate success (excluding German-speaking workplaces)

Measure	k	N	r_{obs}	SD_{obs}	ρ	SD_{ρ}	90% CI		80% CV	
Overall job performance	9	184	-.12	.12	**-.16**	.00	-.24	-.08	-.16	-.16
Technical performance	9	184	-.15	.14	**-.21**	.00	-.32	-.10	-.21	-.21
Interpersonal relations	9	184	-.05	.16	**-.07**	.00	-.20	.06	-.07	-.07
Management/supervision	9	183	-.03	.14	**-.04**	.00	-.15	.07	-.04	-.04
Effort/initiative	9	183	-.12	.15	**-.15**	.00	-.25	-.04	-.15	-.15
Personal discipline	9	183	-.17	.14	**-.23**	.00	-.34	-.12	-.23	-.23
Overall adjustment	14	491	.17	.13	**.22**	.00	.14	.28	.22	.22
Locational adjustment	14	491	.17	.15	**.21**	.00	.12	.28	.21	.21
Interaction adjustment	14	491	.12	.12	**.13**	.00	.07	.18	.13	.13
Work adjustment	14	490	.10	.15	**.12**	.00	.04	.19	.12	.12
Job satisfaction	14	482	-.01	.17	**-.01**	.00	-.09	.06	-.01	-.01
Life satisfaction	14	482	-.06	.20	**-.07**	.09	-.18	.02	-.20	.06
Organizational support	14	470	-.05	.18	**-.06**	.06	-.16	.04	-.14	.03
Social support	14	481	-.03	.19	**-.04**	.08	-.16	.07	-.16	.09

Note: r_{obs} = Sample size weighted mean observed correlation, SD_{obs} = observed standard deviation, ρ = mean correlation corrected for criterion unreliability, 90% CI = 90% confidence interval around ρ, 80% CV = 80% credibility interval around ρ, SD_{ρ} = residual true standard deviation.

However, if language proficiency primarily benefits expatriates through cultural engagement, we would expect relations to become stronger when German-speaking workplaces were excluded, as high language proficiency scores would thus reflect greater investment in learning the local culture. Results are reported in Table 3.

Results show that relationships between mean language proficiency and satisfaction and support outcomes were not substantially different when German-speaking workplaces were excluded (mean $\Delta\rho$ = -.03, mean absolute $\Delta\rho$ = .04, range $\Delta\rho$ = -.07, .02). Language proficiency–adjustment relations were also largely unchanged (mean $\Delta\rho$ = .03, range .00, .05). Confidence intervals for each of these analyses overlapped substantially. These results support the comfort hypothesis – language proficiency leads to better expatriate adjustment because it relieves a key source of stress in the expatriate experience – difficulty communicating.

When German-speaking workplaces were excluded, language proficiency showed small to moderate *negative* relationships with overall performance (ρ = -.16) and several performance dimensions (technical performance, effort and initiative, personal discipline). However, the total sample size for these analyses was small (N = 183–184). Moreover, confidence intervals for the mean correlations were wide (e.g., overall performance 90% confidence interval [CI] = -.24, -.08) and overlapped substantially with the full-sample confidence interval; caution is warranted in interpreting this result.

3.4 Moderating Factor: Mean vs. Minimum Proficiency

Results of the German moderation analyses suggest that the influence of language proficiency on expatriate adjustment is primarily due to increased comfort, rather than because language proficiency indicates greater cultural engagement. With that being the case, the question remains what the nature of this increased comfort is. A key potential source of stress for expatriates is inability to communicate effectively on core work tasks. High levels of proficiency on only one or two of the languages spoken in the workplace (as indexed by expatriates' mean language proficiency score) would reduce this source of stress. However, another potential source of language-related stress for expatriates is the social exclusion that can result from not speaking the language commonly used in casual office conversations. For example, even if an expatriate can communicate about work tasks with coworkers in German or English, thex may still feel excluded from the office culture if most off-task conversations, posted messages, and other communications are conducted in Korean. This effect is indexed by expatriates' minimum language proficiency scores, as these scores can indicate the presence of such a socially-excluding language in the workplace. Results for relations between minimum language proficiency and expatriate outcomes are shown in Table 4.

Results for minimum language proficiency were generally the same as for mean language proficiency. Performance, satisfaction, and perceived support were all negligibly related to minimum language proficiency. Overall and interactional adjustment showed small positive relationships with minimum language proficiency. These results suggest that the detrimental effects of there being *any* incomprehensible language spoken in the workplace are not strong. The key factor influencing expatriate adjustment regarding language is whether they are generally able to understand others and make themselves understood, not whether they can understand *all* communications at work.

Table 4: Meta-analytic results: Minimum language proficiency and expatriate success

Measure	k	N	r_{obs}	SD_{obs}	ρ	SD_ρ	90% CI		80% CV	
Overall job performance	14	394	.01	.21	**.01**	.09	-.09	.10	-.15	.16
Technical performance	14	394	-.05	.17	**-.06**	.00	-.14	.04	-.06	-.06
Interpersonal relations	14	394	.06	.20	**.07**	.07	-.04	.18	-.04	.19
Management/supervision	14	391	.05	.19	**.07**	.00	-.04	.18	.07	.07
Effort/initiative	14	386	.01	.20	**.01**	.03	-.08	.10	-.04	.06
Personal discipline	14	392	-.02	.26	**-.03**	.18	-.21	.14	-.33	.27
Overall adjustment	17	975	.08	.15	**.11**	.06	.03	.19	.01	.21
Locational adjustment	17	975	.05	.19	**.06**	.13	-.04	.14	-.14	.27
Interaction adjustment	17	974	.10	.14	**.11**	.04	.06	.17	.06	.16
Work adjustment	17	972	.02	.14	**.02**	.05	-.04	.08	-.06	.10
Job satisfaction	17	949	-.01	.11	**-.01**	.00	-.05	.04	-.01	-.01
Life satisfaction	17	950	-.02	.11	**-.02**	.00	-.07	.03	-.02	-.02
Organizational support	17	928	.03	.18	**.04**	.12	-.05	.15	-.12	.20
Social support	17	947	.01	.13	**.01**	.00	-.05	.06	.01	.01

Note: r_{obs} = Sample size weighted mean observed correlation, SD_{obs} = observed standard deviation, ρ = mean correlation corrected for criterion unreliability, 90% CI = 90% confidence interval around ρ, 80% CV = 80% credibility interval around ρ, SD_ρ = residual true standard deviation.

4   Discussion

The present analyses examined the relations between language proficiency and expatriate outcomes, including the most popular expatriate criteria of adjustment and job performance, as well as the less-studied criteria of job satisfaction, life satisfaction, and perceived organizational and social support. Across the 28 countries in the iGOES samples, language proficiency was consistently positively related to interaction adjustment and contextual performance (magnitudes ranged from weak to strong), but showed negligible or inconsistent relationships with locational and work adjustment, other performance dimensions, satisfaction, and perceived support. These results are in line with previous meta-analyses of language proficiency in expatriates.

Several factors were investigated as moderators of the magnitude of the relations between language ability and interaction adjustment. Neither excluding German-speaking workplaces nor using minimum (versus mean) language proficiency substantially altered the relation between language proficiency and interactional adjustment. We interpreted these results as indicating that language proficiency benefits expatriates by facilitating effective communication on work tasks with coworkers, rather than by reducing social marginalization associated with not speaking all workplace languages or because language fluency served as a proxy for cultural engagement.

The one factor that did moderate the relation between language proficiency and interaction adjustment was whether proficiency was measured for all languages spoken in the workplace or only for a single dominant local language. When proficiency was assessed for a single dominant language, the relation with interaction adjustment was much stronger ($\rho = .38$ versus $\rho = .13$ for mean proficiency across all workplace languages) and closer to meta-analytic estimates of the language proficiency–interaction adjustment relation ($\rho = .43$; Bhaskar-Shrinivas et al. 2005). The measures of interaction adjustment used in this study and in most of the studies included in Bhaskar-Shrinivas et al.'s meta-analysis assess expatriates' comfort communicating in both work and non-work settings, so this pattern of results highlights the important role of communication competence outside the workplace in contributing to expatriate adjustment. While expatriates may be able to work with their coworkers using German, English, or another non-local language, if they cannot also ask for directions, read street signs, and otherwise communicate in the local language in their everyday lives, their ability to adjust will be inhibited. Local language proficiency is a key factor providing for comfort in carrying out everyday tasks.

That language contributes to success because of increased comfort and ease of interaction, rather than because learning a language reflects expatriates' efforts to grapple with another culture is also indirectly supported by results from the German Foreign Service sample (see Wiernik et al. 2018, Chapter 1, this volume; Rüger et al. 2018, Appendix B, this volume). In this sample, all respondents were conversant in the language of their host country. However, respondents differed widely in the number of different languages they spoke proficiently (mean = 3.16 languages, $SD = 1.02$; sample sizes for correlations below range from 1,351 to 1,462, mean = 1,418). Proficiency in many languages can be regarded as a form of broad cultural competence. Number of fluent languages was associated with increased mobility-specific self-efficacy ($r = .19$). However, number of languages spoken was unrelated to expatriate outcomes, including locational adjustment ($r = .02$), health ($r = -.01$), stress ($r = .05$), and general job satisfaction ($r = .07$). While proficiency with many languages and proficiency with the specific language spoken in one's current location do not necessarily reflect similar levels of engagement with other cultures, these results are nevertheless supportive of the interpretation that language benefits expatriates through comfort, rather than effort spent developing cultural understanding.

5   Conclusion

Language proficiency is frequently cited as one of the most important competencies for expatriates. The results presented in this chapter demonstrate that language is a key factor contributing to expatriates' ability to interact comfortably with host country nationals. However, language fluency has little impact on other expatriate outcomes, including job satisfaction and performance. Accordingly, while language can certainly help expatriates feel comfortable in their new surroundings, lack of fluency in the local language should not be regarded as an insurmountable barrier to expatriate success.

References

Albrecht, Anne-Grit (2005): Untangling the Laundry List: General Mental Ability, the Big Five, and Context Related Variables as Predictors for Expatriate Success. Master's Thesis. Lüneburg, Germany: Leuphana Universität. [http://opus.uni-lueneburg.de/opus/volltexte/2006/344/].

Albrecht, Anne-Grit; Ones, Deniz S.; Sinangil, Handan Kepir (2018a): Expatriate Management. In: Ones, Deniz S. et al. (Eds.): The SAGE Handbook of Industrial, Work and Organizational Psychology. Volume 3: Managerial Psychology and Organizational Approaches. 2nd ed. London, United Kingdom: Sage: 429–468.

Albrecht, Anne-Grit et al. (2018b): Design, Implementation, and Analysis of the iGOES Project. In: Wiernik, Brenton M.; Rüger, Heiko; Ones, Deniz S. (Eds.): Managing Expatriates: Success Factors in Private and Public Domains, Series on Population Studies 50. Opladen, Germany: Barbara Budrich Publishers.

Bhaskar-Shrinivas, Purnima et al. (2005): Input-Based and Time-Based Models of International Adjustment: Meta-Analytic Evidence and Theoretical Extensions. In: *Academy of Management Journal* 48,2: 257–281. [https://doi.org/10.5465/AMJ.2005.16928400].

Black, J. Stewart; Stephens, Gregory K. (1989): The Influence of the Spouse on American Expatriate Adjustment and Intent to Stay in Pacific Rim Overseas Assignments. In: *Journal of Management* 15,4: 529–544. [https://doi.org/10.1177/014920638901500403].

Diener, Ed et al. (1985): The Satisfaction with Life Scale. In: *Journal of Personality Assessment* 49,1: 71–75. [https://doi.org/10.1207/s15327752jpa4901_13].

Du-Babcock, Bertha; Babcock, Richard D. (1996): Patterns of Expatriate-Local Personnel Communication in Multinational Corporations. In: *Journal of Business Communication* 33,2: 141–164. [https://doi.org/10.1177/002194369603300204].

Gudykunst, William B.; Ting-Toomey, Stella; Chua, Elizabeth (1988): Culture and Interpersonal Communication. Sage Series in Interpersonal Communication 8. Thousand Oaks, CA: Sage.

Jordan, Joe; Cartwright, Sue (1998): Selecting Expatriate Managers: Key Traits and Competencies. In: *Leadership & Organization Development Journal* 19,2: 89–96. [https://doi.org/10.1108/01437739810208665].

Judge, Timothy A. et al. (1998): Dispositional Effects on Job and Life Satisfaction: The Role of Core Evaluations. In: *Journal of Applied Psychology* 83,1: 17–34. [https://doi.org/10.1037/0021-9010.83.1.17].

Kostal, Jack W. et al. (2018): Expatriate Training: Intercontextual Analyses from the iGOES Project. In: Wiernik, Brenton M.; Rüger, Heiko; Ones, Deniz S. (Eds.): Managing Expatriates: Success Factors in Private and Public Domains, Series on Population Studies 50. Opladen, Germany: Barbara Budrich Publishers.

Kraimer, Maria L.; Wayne, Sandy J.; Jaworski, Ren Ata A. (2001): Sources of Support and Expatriate Performance: The Mediating Role of Expatriate Adjustment. In: *Personnel Psychology* 54,1: 71–99. [https://doi.org/10.1111/j.1744-6570.2001.tb00086.x].

Leonardelli, Geoffrey J.; Toh, Soo Min (2011): Perceiving Expatriate Coworkers as Foreigners Encourages Aid. In: *Psychological Science* 22,1: 110–117. [https://doi.org/10/ftwk2t].

Li, Lan; Tse, Eliza (1998): Antecedents and Consequences of Expatriate Satisfaction in the Asian Pacific. In: *Tourism Management* 19,2: 135–143. [https://doi.org/10/dzsqsg].

Mol, Stefan T. et al. (2005): Predicting Expatriate Job Performance for Selection Purposes: A Quantitative Review. In: *Journal of Cross-Cultural Psychology* 36,5: 590–620. [https://doi.org/10.1177/0022022105278544].

Morris, Mark A.; Robie, C. (2001): A Meta-Analysis of the Effects of Cross-Cultural Training on Expatriate Performance and Adjustment. In: *International Journal of Training and Development* 5,2: 112–125. [https://doi.org/10.1111/1468-2419.00126].

Puck, Jonas F.; Kittler, Markus G.; Wright, Christopher (2008): Does It Really Work? Re-Assessing the Impact of Pre-Departure Cross-Cultural Training on Expatriate Adjustment. In: *International Journal of Human Resource Management* 19,12: 2182–2197. [https://doi.org/10.1080/09585190802479413].

Robinson, Gregory (2003): The Application of Social Cognitive Theory to the Prediction of Expatriate Success. Doctoral Dissertation. Albany, NY: University at Albany, SUNY. [http://search.proquest.com/dissertations/docview/305270127/]

Rüger, Heiko et al. (2018): Sampling and Procedures for the Mobility Skills in the German Foreign Service Study. In: Wiernik, Brenton M.; Rüger, Heiko; Ones, Deniz S. (Eds.): Managing Expatriates: Success Factors in Private and Public Domains, Series on Population Studies 50. Opladen, Germany: Barbara Budrich Publishers.

Schlunze, Rolf D. (2002): Locational Adjustment of Japanese Management in Europe. In: *Asian Business & Management* 1,2: 267–283. [https://doi.org/10.1057/palgrave.abm.9200014].

Schmidt, Frank L.; Hunter, John E. (2015): Methods of Meta-Analysis: Correcting Error and Bias in Research Findings. 3rd ed. Thousand Oaks, CA: Sage. [https://doi.org/10/b6mg].

Takeuchi, Riki; Wang, Mo; Marinova, Sophia V. (2005): Antecedents and Consequences of Psychological Workplace Strain during Expatriation: A Cross-Sectional and Longitudinal Investigation. In: *Personnel Psychology* 58,4: 925–948. [https://doi.org/10/bk93cd].

Visweswaran, Chockalingam; Ones, Deniz S.; Schmidt, Frank L. (1996): Comparative Analysis of the Reliability of Job Performance Ratings. In: *Journal of Applied Psychology* 81,5: 557–574. [https://doi.org/10/c8f68f].

Wiernik, Brenton M.; Rüger, Heiko; Ones, Deniz S. (2018): Advancing Expatriate Research in Public and Private Sectors. In: Wiernik, Brenton M.; Rüger, Heiko; Ones, Deniz S. (Eds.): Managing Expatriates: Success Factors in Private and Public Domains, Series on Population Studies 50. Opladen, Germany: Barbara Budrich Publishers.

Zimet, Gregory D. et al. (1988): The Multidimensional Scale of Perceived Social Support. In: *Journal of Personality Assessment* 52,1: 30–41. [https://doi.org/10.1207/s15327752jpa5201_2].

Expatriate Training: Intercontextual Analyses from the iGOES Project

Jack W. Kostal, Anne-Grit Albrecht, Stephan Dilchert, Jürgen Deller, Deniz S. Ones, and Frieder M. Paulus

Abstract

Cross-cultural training (CCT) is used to provide expatriates with the knowledge, skills, and abilities necessary to function effectively in the cultural contexts of their host countries. Previous meta-analyses of the effectiveness of CCT have found that, while CCT is on average beneficial for expatriates, there is large variability in effectiveness across studies. We use data from the iGOES project to examine potential moderators of CCT's effectiveness, including type of training, specificity of training to the host culture context, presence of a mentor in the host country, and length of training. In contrast to previous findings in this literature, we found that associations between participation in CCT and expatriate job performance, job satisfaction, and international adjustment were small, and sometimes negative.

1   Introduction

Expatriation presents many challenges to the international assignee. In addition to the need to adapt to a new work environment, managerial expatriates must also deal with pressures created by increased professional responsibility, unfamiliarity with the host country's language, norms, and customs, and isolation from family and friends at home. Success in meeting these challenges depends upon the severity of stressors encountered, as well as the resources expatriates can bring to bear in response (cf. Bhaskar-Shrinivas et al. 2005). Of the latter, the importance of the knowledge, skills, and abilities (KSAs) that expatriates possess cannot be understated. For example, if expatriates lack the knowledge and skill required to behave in accordance with the host country's social norms, poor relationships with host country nationals may result and hamper expatriate adjustment (Johnson et al. 2003). Training interventions may serve as one means to provide employees with these critical KSAs.

Following Campbell et al. (2018), we define training as a planned intervention designed to enhance knowledge, skills, and abilities that determine individual performance. Previous research in single-culture contexts indicates that the provision of training to employees can substantially improve their job-relevant KSAs as measured at the end of training and as indicated by subsequent job performance (meta-analytic standardized mean differences, corrected for criterion unreliability [Cohen's δs], of .62 and .63, respectively; Arthur et al. 2003). At a more fine-grained level, the best results for long-term retention and transfer of training tend to be associated with interventions that encourage trainees to actively process to-be-learned materials (vs. just passively absorb information, e.g., via error learning; Frese/ Keith 2015) or else provide opportunities for trainees to reproduce learned knowledge and skills following initial acquisition (cf. Roediger/Butler 2011). Although extended discussion of the general literature on training interventions exceeds the scope of this chapter, such results strongly suggest the potential of training interventions for improving expatriate success outcomes, including international adjustment, satisfaction, and job performance.

Before discussing the state of the literature on cross-cultural training (CCT), it is important to briefly describe some of the unique challenges that accompany expatriate training and what these challenges do, and do not, mean for the relevance of the general training literature to CCT. The goal of expatriate training is to facilitate *both* performance in the workplace *and* adjustment to the host culture, albeit with the latter serving the ends of the former (in line with our definition of training above; cf. discussions treating international adjustment as a mediator or facilitator of expatriate job performance and satisfaction, rather than a success outcome unto itself; Albrecht et al. 2018a; Mol et al. 2005). Accordingly, the scope of expatriate training is somewhat broader than that of other training interventions due to the need to prepare trainees for numerous aspects of life in an entirely new social environment. Nevertheless, CCT – which aims to provide trainees with KSAs needed for successful interactions abroad (Littrell et al. 2006) – is properly viewed as different from other training interventions *only* in its goal (cross-cultural adjustment) and the KSAs targeted to facilitate success in meeting this goal. The universals of training design (cf. Campbell et al. 2018) and the voluminous literature on learning (e.g., Dunlosky et al. 2013; Schmidt/Bjork 1992) still apply, even in the cross-cultural context. Accordingly, the most important questions for those implementing CCT to ask are *what* KSAs are most relevant for the international assignee, whether an employee *lacks* these KSAs, and if so, whether the KSAs are *amenable* to training. Once these questions have been answered, research from the larger literature on training, learning, and education has much to say about optimal instructional methods.

Turning to the cross-cultural training literature itself, the most recent meta-analysis on CCT's effectiveness (Morris/Robie 2001) produced estimated population correlations corrected for criterion unreliability of $\rho = .26$ between CCT and expatriate performance and $\rho = .13$ between CCT and adjustment (corresponding to δ values of .53 and .26, respectively); these values represent small to moderate effects (Paterson et al. 2016) but are substantially smaller than effects typically observed in general training research (Arthur et al. 2003). Despite these potentially promising mean values, however, Morris and Robie observed substantial true variance in observed training effects across studies that was not attributable to sampling error or measurement artefacts. This variance indicates that general effectiveness of a particular CCT intervention, regardless of design, targeted KSAs, and context, cannot be assumed. Cross-cultural training effectiveness likely differs across targeted KSAs, instructional methods, and other aspects of training design. Identifying factors that influence CCT effectiveness is essential to provide cross-cultural training practitioners with necessary tools to develop quality expatriate training programs. More research in this domain is sorely needed, including critical evaluations of whether current CCT practices are sufficient to meet expatriate training needs. To this end, Littrell et al. (2006), Mendenhall et al. (2004), and Kealey and Protheroe (1996) provide excellent reviews of the CCT literature that may be used as springboards for future research. Each review also calls for more attention to moderators of CCT effectiveness. To facilitate cross-pollination between research streams, the reader is also directed to Salas et al. (2012) and Campbell et al. (2018) for reviews of the current state of the broader training literature.

In this chapter, our goal is to contribute to the development of cumulative knowledge on cross-cultural training by presenting results from a large multinational sample of German-speaking expatriates. The expatriates in our sample came from a common cultural background (Germanic Europe) and were deployed in a diverse range of cultures and countries.

This intercontextual design (Ones et al. 2012) allows us to examine the cross-cultural generalizability of training effects without the confounding effects of varying home cultures. We focus especially on moderators of training effects, and report results of training interventions separately by training type, specificity of training content to the host culture context (vs. culture-general training), length of training, and availability of a mentor in the host country. Because the goals of expatriate training are often multiple, and may include improving performance, reducing early termination of assignments, or enhancing employees' affective well-being in their host country, we report results across three separate classes of criteria – job performance, job satisfaction, and adjustment. Our hope is that this study will serve as a guide for similar studies in the future.

2 Methods

2.1 Participants

The current sample consists of 1,155 German-speaking expatriates from Wave 1 of the iGOES project (see Wiernik et al. 2018b, Chapter 1, and Albrecht et al. 2018b, Appendix A, this volume, for more details).[1] As part of this project, expatriates located in any of 14 countries (Argentina, China, Costa Rica, Czech Republic, Egypt, Ghana, India, Italy, the Netherlands, Russia, South Korea, Sweden, Turkey, and the United States) reported on their participation in cross-cultural training interventions. Sample characteristics separated by training participation and all hypothesized moderators are shown in Table 1. Across training conditions, trainees were generally similar in age, educational level, gender, and presence of a romantic partner. More pronounced differences arose, however, for employees' organizational tenure and length of time in their current international location. The implications of these differences are considered in the discussion.

2.2 Measures

Job performance. In contrast to previous expatriate research, which has often relied on single-item or self-reported performance, we measured expatriate job performance using ratings by a supervisor or knowledgeable coworker for each expatriate on a 17-item scale adapted from Foldes et al. (2006; see also Ones et al. 2018, Chapter 15, this volume). Scores were reported for the following dimensions of job performance: technical performance (average Cronbach's $\alpha = .66$), contextual performance (support for organizational goals, extra-role engagement, local cultural knowledge; $\alpha = .45$), management and supervision ($\alpha = .58$), and effort and initiative ($\alpha = .59$). An overall job performance score was computed combining all 17 items of the measure ($\alpha = .86$).

    Adjustment. In China, Egypt, Russia, South Korea, and the United States, adjustment was assessed using the 3-item self-report measure from Albrecht (2005). For these countries, only total overall expatriate adjustment could be computed (average $\alpha = .63$). For the remaining countries, we measured adjustment using self-reports on the 14-item scale developed by Black and Stephens (1989). This scale contains subscales for locational (comfort managing everyday life demands), interaction (comfort communicating with host country nationals), and work (comfort with one's job role) adjustment. Overall adjustment

---

[1]   Several participants with more than 144 months of experience abroad were removed as outliers.

was computed as the sum of all 14 items on the scale. Across countries, the average internal consistency estimates were $\alpha = .81$ for total overall adjustment, $\alpha = .72$ for locational adjustment, $\alpha = .83$ for interaction adjustment, $\alpha = .71$ for work adjustment.

Job satisfaction. Job satisfaction was measured using the five-item scale by Judge et al. (1998). This scale assesses overall job satisfaction with global judgments about the quality of employees' work experiences (average $\alpha = .80$).

Training type. Participants were asked whether they had participated in any of nine different training interventions – short briefing, long (intensive) briefing, reading materials, movies, role plays, case studies, simulations, group language training, and individual language training. These interventions were further grouped into three classes – those which require minimal active cognitive processing by trainees (*passive training*; short briefing, long briefing, reading, movies), those which require a great deal of active processing or production of to-be-learned behaviors (*active training*; role plays, case studies, simulations), and *language training*. The distinction between passive and active interventions in this framework corresponds closely to that between didactic and experiential interventions in the cross-cultural training literature (cf. Kealey/Protheroe 1996), with the sole difference being that case studies have been grouped with skill-based interventions of the type traditionally deemed experiential. Nearly all (96%) of participants who received active training also received some form of passive training, so these variables were collapsed into two groups – those who received passive training without active training ("passive") and those who received both passive and active training ("active").

Table 1: Sample characteristics by training category

Training category	N	Gender (% male)	Partner (% yes)	Age	Years of education	Months of org. tenure	Months abroad
Complete sample	1,143	71	70	37.7	17.4	85.7	34.6
No training	401	68	66	38.2	17.2	72.9	43.7
Any Training	742	73	72	37.4	17.6	92.2	29.7
Training type							
Passive	497	73	72	37.5	17.6	93.3	29.4
Active	214	79	75	39.0	17.9	108.3	25.7
Language	148	69	70	35.2	17.2	78.0	35.3
Training duration							
Less than 3	159	81	79	37.4	17.8	103.2	19.5
3 or more days	159	75	71	40.7	17.9	115.4	32.0
Training specificity							
Culture-general	95	79	68	40.0	17.8	113.5	34.5
Culture-specific	320	77	76	38.5	17.5	103.3	23.6
Presence of mentor							
No	184	74	74	38.0	17.6	98.4	31.1
Yes	551	69	66	35.8	17.5	74.8	25.9

Note: Values computed across countries in Wave 1 of the iGOES data collection.

Other moderators. In addition to training type, we also assessed moderating effects of self-reported training duration, training specificity (culture-general vs. culture-specific), and availability of a mentor in the host country. For meta-analytic subgroup moderator analyses, self-reported training duration was dichotomized at the median value (3 days) in this sample.

2.3 Analyses

There were substantial mean-level differences across countries in training rates and outcome levels. These country-level differences can confound within-country training effects (cf. Ostroff/Harrison 1999). To remove these country-level effects and test the cross-cultural generalizability of findings, we applied transcultural meta-analysis (Ones et al. 2012). We computed associations between training and expatriate criteria individually within each host country, then aggregated across countries using psychometric meta-analysis (Schmidt/Hunter 2015). Only countries with sample sizes of at least $N = 10$ were included in analyses. All effect sizes were corrected for unreliability in the criterion. We corrected for criterion unreliability in international adjustment and job satisfaction using internal consistency estimates from the current samples. We corrected for job performance unreliability using the meta-analytic supervisor interrater reliability distribution for each performance dimension reported by Viswesvaran et al. (1996).

3   Results

3.1   Job Performance

Meta-analytic results for the association between training and job performance are reported in Table 2. There was little difference, on average, in performance between expatriates who received any form of training and those who did not ($\delta = .04$ for overall job performance; δs ranged from -.04 to .11 across performance facets). Confidence intervals included zero in all cases. However, credibility intervals around these meta-analytic means were quite wide (e.g., for overall performance the 80% credibility interval [CV] ranged from -.35 to .43), suggesting the potential for moderators for these relations.

We found a broadly similar pattern of results when examining relations between training and job performance across moderator levels. We found the largest moderating effects for training type. In line with findings from the broader training literature, active training showed larger relations with performance than passive training ($\delta = .26$ vs. .03 for overall job performance), particularly for the effort and initiative performance dimension ($\delta = .31$ vs. .08). Due to small k and total N for many of these analyses, confidence intervals were wide and overlapped across moderator levels. We caution against over-interpretation of differences in mean δ values across moderator levels, but do note that the current results are consistent with broader research on the superiority of active training methods (Arthur et al. 2003).

Table 2: Associations between training and expatriate job performance

Training	Criterion	k	N	$\bar{d}$	SD_d	SD_{res}	$SE_{\bar{d}}$	δ	SD_δ	90% CI	80% CV
Any training	Overall performance	13	512	.03	.40	.22	.11	**.04**	.31	-.21, .29	-.35, .43
	Technical performance	13	516	.00	.38	.00	.11	**.00**	.00	-.25, .25	.00, .00
	Contextual performance	13	514	.02	.43	.26	.12	**.03**	.36	-.25, .30	-.43, .49
	Management/supervision	13	507	-.03	.52	.39	.14	**-.04**	.53	-.36, .27	-.72, .64
	Effort and initiative	13	513	.08	.43	.27	.12	**.11**	.36	-.16, .37	-.36, .57
Training type: Passive	Overall performance	13	383	.02	.35	.00	.10	**.03**	.00	-.20, .26	.03, .03
	Technical performance	13	388	.02	.38	.00	.11	**.03**	.00	-.22, .28	.03, .03
	Contextual performance	13	386	.04	.38	.00	.11	**.06**	.00	-.20, .31	.06, .06
	Management/supervision	13	380	.01	.50	.31	.14	**.01**	.42	-.30, .33	-.53, .56
	Effort and initiative	13	384	.06	.43	.17	.12	**.08**	.23	-.18, .35	-.21, .37
Training type: Active	Overall performance	10	219	.19	.47	.06	.15	**.26**	.08	-.08, .61	.16, .37
	Technical performance	10	221	.15	.39	.00	.12	**.21**	.00	-.07, .48	.21, .21
	Contextual performance	10	219	.09	.51	.20	.16	**.13**	.28	-.24, .49	-.23, .48
	Management/supervision	10	217	-.02	.54	.27	.17	**-.03**	.37	-.41, .35	-.50, .45
	Effort and initiative	10	220	.23	.43	.00	.14	**.31**	.00	.00, .62	.31, .31
Training type: Language	Overall performance	9	204	-.09	.42	.00	.14	**-.13**	.00	-.44, .19	-.13, -.13
	Technical performance	9	205	.00	.29	.00	.10	**.00**	.00	-.23, .23	.00, .00
	Contextual performance	9	205	-.04	.68	.50	.23	**-.06**	.69	-.58, .47	-.94, .83
	Management/supervision	9	199	-.20	.95	.81	.32	**-.27**	1.11	-.99, .44	-1.69, 1.15
	Effort and initiative	9	204	.00	.40	.00	.13	**.00**	.00	-.29, .29	.00, .00

$\downarrow$

Table 2: Associations between training and expatriate job performance – continued

Training	Criterion	k	N	$\bar{d}$	SD_d	SD_{res}	$SE_{\bar{d}}$	δ	SD_δ	90% CI	80% CV
Length: Less than 3 days	Overall performance	8	171	.04	.20	.00	.07	**.06**	.00	-.10, .22	.06, .06
	Technical performance	8	173	.16	.24	.00	.09	**.22**	.00	.02, .43	.22, .22
	Contextual performance	8	174	.00	.42	.00	.15	**.00**	.00	-.34, .34	.00, .00
	Management/supervision	8	173	-.06	.45	.00	.16	**-.08**	.00	-.44, .28	-.08, -.08
	Effort and initiative	8	171	.02	.30	.00	.11	**.03**	.00	-.22, .27	.03, .03
Length: 3 or more days	Overall performance	10	180	.00	.67	.42	.21	**.00**	.58	-.48, .48	-.75, .75
	Technical performance	10	183	.01	.47	.00	.15	**.01**	.00	-.33, .36	.01, .01
	Contextual performance	10	180	-.03	.80	.59	.25	**-.04**	.82	-.61, .53	-1.09, 1.01
	Management/supervision	10	178	-.20	.95	.78	.30	**-.27**	1.07	-.95, .40	-1.64, 1.09
	Effort and initiative	10	181	.08	.61	.31	.19	**.11**	.42	-.31, .53	-.43, .64
Training specificity: Culture-general	Overall performance	8	127	.08	.90	.69	.32	**.11**	.96	-.62, .84	-1.12, 1.34
	Technical performance	8	129	.00	.79	.55	.28	**.00**	.76	-.64, .64	-.98, .98
	Contextual performance	8	127	.11	.57	.11	.20	**.15**	.15	-.30, .61	-.04, .35
	Management/supervision	8	126	-.10	.80	.57	.28	**-.14**	.78	-.77, .49	-1.14, .86
	Effort and initiative	8	127	.08	.90	.69	.32	**.11**	.93	-.60, .82	-1.09, 1.30
Training specificity: Culture-specific	Overall performance	10	259	.05	.41	.00	.13	**.07**	.00	-.23, .37	.07, .07
	Technical performance	10	263	.10	.39	.00	.12	**.14**	.00	-.13, .41	.14, .14
	Contextual performance	10	262	-.05	.34	.00	.11	**-.07**	.00	-.32, .18	-.07, -.07
	Management/supervision	10	260	-.08	.64	.48	.20	**-.11**	.66	-.56, .34	-.95, .73
	Effort and initiative	10	260	.13	.38	.00	.12	**.18**	.00	-.09, .44	.18, .18

$\rightarrow$

Table 2: Associations between training and expatriate job performance – continued

Training	Criterion	k	N	$\bar{d}$	SD_d	SD_{res}	$SE_{\bar{d}}$	δ	SD_δ	90% CI	80% CV
Mentor available: No	Overall performance	13	420	.04	.43	.21	.12	**.06**	.29	-.22, .33	-.32, .43
	Technical performance	13	423	.03	.34	.00	.09	**.04**	.00	-.16, .25	.04, .04
	Contextual performance	13	421	.01	.43	.22	.12	**.01**	.31	-.26, .29	-.38, .40
	Management/supervision	13	414	.01	.61	.48	.17	**.01**	.66	-.37, .40	-.83, .86
	Effort and initiative	13	421	.08	.42	.19	.12	**.11**	.26	-.16, .37	-.22, .44
Mentor available: Yes	Overall performance	12	243	.00	.55	.25	.16	**.00**	.35	-.36, .36	-.44, .44
	Technical performance	12	246	-.04	.47	.00	.14	**-.06**	.00	-.37, .26	-.06, -.06
	Contextual performance	12	245	.09	.52	.17	.15	**.13**	.24	-.22, .47	-.18, .43
	Management/supervision	12	241	-.09	.49	.05	.14	**-.12**	.07	-.44, .19	-.21, -.04
	Effort and initiative	12	243	.06	.76	.58	.22	**.08**	.78	-.41, .57	-.92, 1.08

Note: k = number of samples included in meta-analysis, N = total sample size, d = mean observed standardized mean difference (Cohen's d), SD_d = observed standard deviation of d, SD_{res} = residual standard deviation of d after accounting for sampling error and unreliability, $SE_{\bar{d}}$ = standard error of mean d; δ = mean d corrected for criterion unreliability, SD_δ = true distribution standard deviation; 90% CI = 90% confidence interval for δ; 80% CV = 80% credibility interval for δ.

Language training showed a somewhat perplexing result. Expatriates who received language training showed somewhat *worse* job performance ($\delta = -.13$, particularly for management and supervision, $\delta = -.27$). However, it may be that receipt of language training is negatively associated with language *proficiency*. Only employees with poor language skills may be likely to receive language training, so negative relations between language training and performance may reflect poor language proficiency as a third variable. We examined this possibility by estimating the relation between language training and performance in the pooled sample while controlling for self-reported language proficiency. Results were virtually unchanged ($d_c = -.01$ for overall performance, -.08 for technical performance, -.04 for contextual performance, -.08 for management and supervision, .10 for effort and initiative, Ns range 264–270). These results suggest that while language training is not harmful, it is unlikely to be especially beneficial, particularly compared to other KSAs that might be trained instead (cf. the modest relations observed for the iGOES samples between language proficiency and expatriate success, Wiernik et al. 2018a, Chapter 12, this volume).

Other moderators (training duration, cultural specificity, mentor availability) had generally negligible or inconsistent effects on training effectiveness for job performance.

3.2 Job Satisfaction

Meta-analytic results for the association between training and job satisfaction are shown in Table 3. Expatriates who had received any training reported slightly higher satisfaction than those who did not ($\delta = .14$). However, the overall sample size for this analysis was small, and the confidence interval around this mean value was wide (-.38, .65). For every moderator examined, confidence intervals included zero. As with job performance, confidence intervals overlapped for all comparisons between moderators.

3.3 International Adjustment

Meta-analytic results for the association between training and adjustment are also shown in Table 3. Expatriates who had received any form of training reported *lower* levels of overall adjustment ($\delta = -.45$; 90% confidence interval [CI] = -.65, -.26), work adjustment ($\delta = -.50$; CI = -.62, .37), and interaction adjustment ($\delta = -.28$; CI = -.42, .14). Credibility intervals excluded zero in all cases, suggesting that negative associations were generalizable across countries in our sample. Overall training was unrelated to locational adjustment.

When examining relations between training and adjustment separately by moderating variables, similar patterns of findings again emerged. Mean δ values were similar across all moderator variables, with small deviations likely attributable to second-order sampling error. Confidence intervals overlapped in every case. Although it is possible that impacts on international adjustment may vary across training moderator levels, the current analyses provide no evidence for such effects.

Table 3: Associations between training and expatriate adjustment and job satisfaction

Training	Criterion	k	N	$\bar{d}$	SD_d	SD_{res}	$SE_{\bar{d}}$	δ	SD_δ	90% CI	80% CV
Any training	Overall adjustment	13	959	-.34	.33	.23	.09	**-.45**	.30	-.65, -.26	-.84, -.07
	Locational adjustment	7	446	-.05	.27	.10	.10	**-.06**	.12	-.27, .14	-.22, .10
	Work adjustment	7	441	-.45	.17	.00	.07	**-.50**	.00	-.62, -.37	-.50, -.50
	Interaction adjustment	7	446	-.23	.23	.00	.07	**-.28**	.00	-.42, -.14	-.28, -.28
	Job satisfaction	3	237	.12	.48	.43	.28	**.14**	.49	-.38, .65	-.49, .76
Training type: Passive	Overall adjustment	13	745	-.35	.34	.20	.09	**-.47**	.26	-.66, -.27	-.80, -.14
	Locational adjustment	7	345	-.06	.30	.04	.11	**-.07**	.05	-.30, .15	-.14, -.01
	Work adjustment	7	342	-.44	.18	.00	.07	**-.48**	.00	-.61, -.36	-.48, -.48
	Interaction adjustment	7	345	-.17	.18	.00	.07	**-.21**	.00	-.35, -.07	-.21, -.21
	Job satisfaction	3	172	.12	.35	.22	.20	**.14**	.25	-.23, .51	-.18, .45
Training type: Active	Overall adjustment	11	478	-.33	.39	.23	.12	**-.44**	.30	-.70, -.18	-.82, -.06
	Locational adjustment	5	206	.03	.35	.13	.16	**.04**	.16	-.29, .36	-.17, .24
	Work adjustment	5	204	-.57	.33	.00	.15	**-.63**	.00	-.90, -.36	-.63, -.63
	Interaction adjustment	5	206	-.37	.44	.29	.20	**-.45**	.35	-.85, -.05	-.90, .00
	Job satisfaction	3	119	.14	.66	.57	.38	**.16**	.64	-.55, .86	-.67, .98
Training type: Language	Overall adjustment	13	446	-.22	.41	.20	.12	**-.29**	.26	-.56, -.03	-.63, .04
	Locational adjustment	7	211	.07	.28	.00	.10	**.09**	.00	-.12, .29	.09, .09
	Work adjustment	7	210	-.66	.41	.13	.16	**-.73**	.14	-1.02, -.44	-.91, -.55
	Interaction adjustment	7	211	.00	.68	.56	.26	**.00**	.68	-.52, .52	-.88, .88
	Job satisfaction	3	93	-.31	.30	.00	.17	**-.35**	.00	-.67, -.04	-.35, -.35

Table 3: Associations between training and expatriate adjustment and job satisfaction – continued

Training	Criterion	k	N	$\bar{d}$	SD_d	SD_{res}	$SE_{\bar{d}}$	δ	SD_δ	90% CI	80% CV
Length: Less than 3 days	Overall adjustment	10	411	-.37	.50	.38	.16	**-.49**	.50	-.84, -.14	-1.14, .15
	Locational adjustment	5	189	-.11	.55	.44	.25	**-.14**	.55	-.65, .37	-.84, .56
	Work adjustment	5	188	-.59	.41	.22	.19	**-.65**	.24	-.99, -.31	-.96, -.34
	Interaction adjustment	5	189	-.20	.34	.01	.15	**-.24**	.00	-.55, .06	-.24, -.24
	Job satisfaction	3	116	.40	.38	.18	.24	**.45**	.20	.01, .90	.19, .71
Length: 3 or more days	Overall adjustment	12	432	-.27	.31	.00	.09	**-.36**	.00	-.56, -.16	-.36, -.36
	Locational adjustment	6	200	.03	.32	.00	.13	**.04**	.00	-.23, .30	.04, .04
	Work adjustment	6	198	-.60	.64	.51	.26	**-.66**	.56	-1.13, -.19	-1.38, .06
	Interaction adjustment	6	200	-.18	.50	.34	.20	**-.22**	.41	-.62, .18	-.75, .31
	Job satisfaction	3	95	-.08	.42	.18	.24	**-.09**	.20	-.53, .35	-.35, .17
Training specificity: Culture-general	Overall adjustment	10	334	-.19	.63	.51	.20	**-.25**	.68	-.69, .18	-1.12, .62
	Locational adjustment	6	172	-.01	.68	.55	.28	**-.01**	.68	-.58, .56	-.89, .86
	Work adjustment	6	171	-.80	.78	.66	.32	**-.88**	.73	-1.46, -.30	-1.81, .05
	Interaction adjustment	6	172	.03	.72	.60	.29	**.04**	.73	-.54, .62	-.90, .98
	Job satisfaction	3	81	-.06	.61	.45	.35	**-.07**	.51	-.72, .58	-.72, .58
Training specificity: Culture-specific	Overall adjustment	12	573	-.30	.33	.14	.10	**-.40**	.18	-.62, -.18	-.63, -.17
	Locational adjustment	6	284	.00	.29	.00	.12	**.00**	.00	-.24, .24	.00, .00
	Work adjustment	6	282	-.43	.30	.00	.12	**-.47**	.00	-.69, -.26	-.47, -.47
	Interaction adjustment	6	284	-.24	.19	.00	.08	**-.29**	.00	-.45, -.13	-.29, -.29
	Job satisfaction	3	166	.19	.52	.43	.30	**.21**	.49	-.34, .77	-.41, .84

$\downarrow$

Table 3: Associations between training and expatriate job performance – continued

Training	Criterion	k	N	$\bar{d}$	SD_d	SD_{res}	$SE_{\bar{d}}$	δ	SD_δ	90% CI	80% CV
Mentor available: No	Overall adjustment	13	795	-.29	.40	.30	.11	**-.39**	.40	-.63, -.15	-.89, .12
	Locational adjustment	7	371	-.01	.24	.00	.09	**-.01**	.00	-.20, .17	-.01, -.01
	Work adjustment	7	367	-.45	.23	.00	.09	**-.50**	.00	-.66, -.33	-.50, -.50
	Interaction adjustment	7	371	-.20	.30	.08	.11	**-.24**	.09	-.46, -.02	-.36, -.12
	Job satisfaction	3	166	.19	.52	.43	.30	**.21**	.49	-.34, .77	-.41, .84
Mentor available: Yes	Overall adjustment	13	470	-.40	.33	.00	.09	**-.53**	.00	-.73, -.34	-.53, -.53
	Locational adjustment	7	219	-.10	.43	.20	.16	**-.12**	.25	-.45, .20	-.44, .19
	Work adjustment	7	217	-.58	.37	.00	.14	**-.64**	.00	-.89, -.39	-.64, -.64
	Interaction adjustment	7	219	-.34	.22	.00	.08	**-.42**	.00	-.58, -.26	-.42, -.42
	Job satisfaction	3	91	-.15	.60	.46	.35	**-.17**	.52	-.82, .48	-.83, .50

Note: k = number of samples included in meta-analysis, N = total sample size, d = mean observed standardized mean difference (Cohen's d), SD_d = observed standard deviation of d, SD_{res} = residual standard deviation of d after accounting for sampling error and unreliability, $SE_{\bar{d}}$ = standard error of mean d; δ = mean d corrected for criterion unreliability, SD_δ = true distribution standard deviation; 90% CI = 90% confidence interval for δ; 80% CV = 80% credibility interval for δ.

4   Discussion

The most pronounced findings from this study is the weak, and sometimes negative, association between cross-cultural training and various expatriate outcomes. This finding is in stark contrast to the positive benefits to training observed in the broader training literature (Arthur et al. 2003) and in meta-analyses of the cross-cultural training literature (Morris/ Robie 2001). There are several possible explanations for these divergent findings. First, participants were not randomly assigned to training groups in this study (see Table 1 for some examples of differences between groups). That is, our study design is correlational in nature. It is possible that training interventions were offered only to employees sent on higher risk (i.e., more challenging) assignments or to employees with weaker existing KSAs (who are most in need of training, particularly for language skills). Likewise, in some cases employees may not have been provided with training due to pre-existing familiarity with a country. The implication of these concerns can be illustrated by using our finding of higher adjustment for expatriates who did not receive training. If untrained individuals report better adjustment because they were sent on less strenuous assignments for which training was deemed unnecessary, then it is possible that these individuals' adjustment would be *even better* had they been provided with pre-departure training. Future studies using experimental designs are necessary to answer this type of question.

A second possible explanation for the present findings is that the KSAs targeted by the training interventions in our study may not have been relevant to expatriate job performance or adjustment. Previous reviews of the cross-cultural training literature have lamented that expatriate pre-departure training is often poorly-conceived and not designed to address the specific needs of expatriates for their assigned countries (Albrecht et al. 2018a; Deshpande/ Viswesvaran 1992). Limitations in survey space meant that we were unable to ask participants about the *exact list* of KSAs targeted in intercultural training and their relevance for their current assignments and contexts. Because expatriates in this sample are often more than a year removed from training, it is also possible that training effects were attenuated due to accumulated in-country experience across participants and that expatriate response reliability was decreased due to poor recall of the specifics of the interventions they received. Ideally, training information would be gathered from organizational managers who had administered or coordinated the training interventions, but these persons were not available for this study.

Third because the expatriates in the current sample worked in a variety of organizations and received a wide range of training interventions, it is possible that the nature and quality of training interventions may have varied widely across participants (even for inventions of the same type, such as readings or case studies). These variations in training quality would function in the same way as measurement error, systematically attenuating training effects across samples (Schmidt/Hunter 2015). Thus, it is likely that the current analyses underestimated CCT effectiveness to some extent, compared to experimental evaluations of the effectiveness of a single training intervention.

Finally, previous CCT meta-analyses did not specify whether performance was assessed using self-ratings, other-ratings, or objective criteria. In line with much of the expatriate research, it is likely that these analyses included many studies relying on self-reported performance. These designs may have inflated training effectiveness estimates in previous CCT meta-analyses due to common method bias.

4.1   The Future of Expatriate Training Research

Given the current findings and previous meta-analyses, where does the cross-cultural training literature go from here? First and foremost, more attention needs to be given to careful specification of the purpose of cross-cultural training and to expatriates' actual training needs. International assignments vary widely in their cultural contexts, adaptation challenges, and work expectations and responsibilities. It is unlikely that any one-size-fits-all cross-cultural training will be universally effective. For training to be beneficial, researchers and human resource managers must carefully design trainings that target necessary KSAs and gather rigorous data to evaluate the effectiveness of specific training programs for specific developmental goals. When evaluating whether a CCT program is effective, researchers must pay much more attention than has typically been the case to *which specific* KSAs were targeted, *how* the training was designed and implemented to improve these KSAs, and whether any improvements in expatriate outcomes (e.g., improved performance or adjustment) can be *causally attributed to increments in those KSAs* (as opposed to, for example, increased feelings of organizational support). Highly general descriptions of training programs or evaluations, such as a rating of overall "training rigor," fail to provide training practitioners with sufficient information or guidance needed to develop sound interventions. Rather than amorphous "rigor" or "hours taught," more precise information, such as time spent on each type of intervention, specific scenarios or concepts addressed, specific instructional strategies employed, and methods used to check learning progress, will shed light on optimal training practices. In addition, increased integration between the general training literature and research on CCT specifically is sorely needed. Recent developments in general training research (e.g., recognition of the importance of providing learners with opportunities to make errors and learn from their mistakes [error learning]; Frese/Keith 2015) suggest fruitful avenues through which current expatriate training practices may be improved. In addition to the above-cited studies, we also direct interested readers to Dunlosky et al. (2013) for a listing of easy-to-implement strategies that may be used to enhance learning during training. While the challenges of expatriation may be unique, learning processes and methods for effective instruction are more universal. Future research and practice of cross-cultural training should seek to generalize findings from the broader training, learning, and education fields to better promote expatriate learning and success.

References

Albrecht, Anne-Grit (2005): Untangling the Laundry List: General Mental Ability, the Big Five, and Context Related Variables as Predictors for Expatriate Success. Master's Thesis. Lüneburg, Germany: Leuphana Universität. [http://opus.uni-lueneburg.de/opus/volltexte/2006/344/].

Albrecht, Anne-Grit; Ones, Deniz S.; Sinangil, Handan Kepir (2018a): Expatriate Management. In: Ones, Deniz S. et al. (Eds.): The SAGE Handbook of Industrial, Work and Organizational Psychology. Volume 3: Managerial Psychology and Organizational Approaches. 2nd ed. London, United Kingdom: Sage: 429–468.

Albrecht, Anne-Grit et al. (2018b): Design, Implementation, and Analysis of the iGOES Project. In: Wiernik, Brenton M.; Rüger, Heiko; Ones, Deniz S. (Eds.): Managing Expatriates: Success Factors in Private and Public Domains, Series on Population Studies 50. Opladen, Germany: Barbara Budrich Publishers.

Arthur, Winfred, Jr. et al. (2003): Effectiveness of Training in Organizations: A Meta-Analysis of Design and Evaluation Features. In: *Journal of Applied Psychology* 88,2: 234–245. [https://doi.org/10.1037/0021-9010.88.2.234].

Bhaskar-Shrinivas, Purnima et al. (2005): Input-Based and Time-Based Models of International Adjustment: Meta-Analytic Evidence and Theoretical Extensions. In: *Academy of Management Journal* 48,2: 257–281. [https://doi.org/10.5465/AMJ.2005.16928400].

Black, J. Stewart; Stephens, Gregory K. (1989): The Influence of the Spouse on American Expatriate Adjustment and Intent to Stay in Pacific Rim Overseas Assignments. In: *Journal of Management* 15,4: 529–544. [https://doi.org/10.1177/014920638901500403].

Campbell, John P.; Kuncel, Nathan R.; Kostal, Jack W. (2018): Training and Learning in Work Roles. In: Ones, Deniz S. et al. (Eds.): The SAGE Handbook of Industrial, Work and Organizational Psychology. Volume 1: Personnel Psychology and Employee Performance. 2nd ed. London, United Kingdom: Sage: 533–610.

Deshpande, Satish P.; Viswesvaran, Chockalingam (1992): Is Cross-Cultural Training of Expatriate Managers Effective: A Meta Analysis. In: *International Journal of Intercultural Relations* 16,3: 295–310. [https://doi.org/10.1016/0147-1767(92)90054-X].

Dunlosky, John et al. (2013): Improving Students' Learning with Effective Learning Techniques: Promising Directions from Cognitive and Educational Psychology. In: *Psychological Science in the Public Interest* 14,1: 4–58. [https://doi.org/10.1177/1529100612453266].

Foldes, Hannah Jackson; Ones, Deniz S.; Sinangil, Handan Kepir (2006): Neither Here nor There: Impression Management Does Not Predict Expatriate Adjustment and Job Performance. In: *Psychology Science* 48,3: 357–368. [http://www.pabst-publishers.de/psychology-science/3-2006/ps_3_2006_357-368.pdf].

Frese, Michael; Keith, Nina (2015): Action Errors, Error Management, and Learning in Organizations. In: *Annual Review of Psychology* 66,1: 661–687. [https://doi.org/10/b6pz].

Johnson, Erin C. et al. (2003): Expatriate Social Ties: Personality Antecedents and Consequences for Adjustment. In: *International Journal of Selection and Assessment* 11,4: 277–288. [https://doi.org/10.1111/j.0965-075X.2003.00251.x].

Judge, Timothy A. et al. (1998): Dispositional Effects on Job and Life Satisfaction: The Role of Core Evaluations. In: *Journal of Applied Psychology* 83,1: 17–34. [https://doi.org/10/gdv].

Kealey, Daniel J.; Protheroe, David R. (1996): The Effectiveness of Cross-Cultural Training for Expatriates: An Assessment of the Literature on the Issues. In: *International Journal of Intercultural Relations* 20,2: 141–165. [https://doi.org/10.1016/0147-1767(96)00001-6].

Littrell, Lisa N. et al. (2006): Expatriate Preparation: A Critical Analysis of 25 Years of Cross-Cultural Training Research. In: *Human Resource Development Review* 5,3: 355–388. [https://doi.org/10.1177/1534484306290106].

Mendenhall, Mark E. et al. (2004): Evaluation Studies of Cross-Cultural Training Programs: A Review of the Literature from 1988 to 2000. In: Landis, Dan; Bennett, Janet M.; Bennett, Milton J. (Eds.): Handbook of Intercultural Training. Thousand Oaks, CA: Sage: 129–143. [https://doi.org/10/b6mb].

Mol, Stefan T.; Born, Marise Ph.; van der Molen, Henk T. (2005): Developing Criteria for Expatriate Effectiveness: Time to Jump off the Adjustment Bandwagon. In: *International Journal of Intercultural Relations* 29,3: 339–353. [https://doi.org/10/dk2vzk].

Morris, Mark A.; Robie, Chet (2001): A Meta-Analysis of the Effects of Cross-Cultural Training on Expatriate Performance and Adjustment. In: *International Journal of Training and Development* 5,2: 112–125. [https://doi.org/10.1111/1468-2419.00126].

Ones, Deniz S. et al. (2012): Cross-Cultural Generalization: Using Meta-Analysis to Test Hypotheses about Cultural Variability. In: Ryan, Ann Marie; Leong, Frederick T.L.; Oswald, Frederick L. (Eds.): Conducting Multinational Research Projects in Organizational Psychology: Challenges and Opportunities, APA/MSU Series on Multicultural Psychology 1. Washington, DC: American Psychological Association: 91–122. [https://doi.org/10/5kz].

Ones, Deniz S.; Foldes, Hannah Jackson; Sinangil, Handan Kepir (2018): A Family Affair: Spouse and Children's Role in Expatriate Adjustment and Job Performance. In: Wiernik, Brenton M.; Rüger, Heiko; Ones, Deniz S. (Eds.): Managing Expatriates: Success Factors in Private and Public Domains, Series on Population Studies 50. Opladen, Germany: Barbara Budrich Publishers.

Ostroff, Cheri; Harrison, David A. (1999): Meta-Analysis, Level of Analysis, and Best Estimates of Population Correlations: Cautions for Interpreting Meta-Analytical Results in Organizational Behavior. In: *Journal of Applied Psychology* 84,2: 260–270. [https://doi.org/10/cz7bx8].

Paterson, Ted A. et al. (2016): An Assessment of the Magnitude of Effect Sizes: Evidence from 30 Years of Meta-Analysis in Management. In: *Journal of Leadership & Organizational Studies* 23,1: 66–81. [https://doi.org/10/bjz9].

Roediger, Henry L.; Butler, Andrew C. (2011): The Critical Role of Retrieval Practice in Long-Term Retention. In: *Trends in Cognitive Sciences* 15,1: 20–27. [https://doi.org/10/fh5t8r].

Salas, Eduardo; Weaver, Sallie J.; Shuffler, Marissa L. (2012): Learning, Training, and Development in Organizations. In: Kozlowski, Steve W.J. (Ed.): The Oxford Handbook of Organizational Psychology. Volume 1. Oxford, United Kingdom: Oxford University Press: 330–372. [https://doi.org/10.1093/oxfordhb/9780199928309.013.0011].

Schmidt, Frank L.; Hunter, John E. (2015): Methods of Meta-Analysis: Correcting Error and Bias in Research Findings. 3rd ed. Thousand Oaks, CA: Sage. [https://doi.org/10/b6mg].

Schmidt, Richard A.; Bjork, Robert A. (1992): New Conceptualizations of Practice: Common Principles in Three Paradigms Suggest New Concepts for Training. In: *Psychological Science* 3,4: 207–217. [https://doi.org/10.1111/j.1467-9280.1992.tb00029.x].

Viswesvaran, Chockalingam; Ones, Deniz S.; Schmidt, Frank L. (1996): Comparative Analysis of the Reliability of Job Performance Ratings. In: *Journal of Applied Psychology* 81,5: 557–574. [https://doi.org/10/c8f68f].

Wiernik, Brenton M. et al. (2018a): Lingua Necessaria? Language Proficiency and Expatriate Success. In: Wiernik, Brenton M.; Rüger, Heiko; Ones, Deniz S. (Eds.): Managing Expatriates: Success Factors in Private and Public Domains, Series on Population Studies 50. Opladen, Germany: Barbara Budrich Publishers.

Wiernik, Brenton M.; Rüger, Heiko; Ones, Deniz S. (2018b): Advancing Expatriate Research in Public and Private Sectors. In: Wiernik, Brenton M.; Rüger, Heiko; Ones, Deniz S. (Eds.): Managing Expatriates: Success Factors in Private and Public Domains, Series on Population Studies 50. Opladen, Germany: Barbara Budrich Publishers.

Organizational and Social Support Among Foreign Service Diplomats

Maria M. Bellinger, Brenton M. Wiernik, and Herbert Fliege

Abstract

International relocation is increasingly common in a globalized world. In our sample of Federal Foreign Office staff, it is part of the lifelong job routine. This process is extremely demanding on employees and is associated with a variety of negative outcomes. External support systems are an important factor that can facilitate adjustment during international location and contribute to expatriate success. We describe support interventions implemented by the Federal Foreign Office to facilitate preparation for international rotation and adjustment of employees at their new postings. We distinguish between perceived organizational support and non-work social support. We find that employees' perceptions of these two forms of support differ by gender and family status. We find that organizational and social support show small to moderate relations with a variety of outcomes, including work attitudes, family and life attitudes, and mental health outcomes. The contributions of support systems to many of these outcomes appear to differ by gender and family status.

1   Introduction

International relocation is a source of stress for employees and their family members because it often causes feelings of uncertainty or ambiguity and reduces individual control over situations (Wilkinson/Singh 2010). As the number of international assignments increases, many organizations are challenged with how to support their expatriate employees as they face these stressors. These challenges are especially acute for organizations, like the Federal Foreign Office, whose employees relocate frequently. While most organizations send their staff abroad once or twice during a lifetime career, organizations like the Federal Foreign Office are based on the principle of continued job-rotation "until retirement and worldwide." This principle is one of the main organizational characteristics in diplomacy. Foreign Office employees commit themselves to frequent international moves, requiring them to move with their entire families every three to four years. Compared to other forms of job-related mobility, such as commuting or relocation within the same country, these repeated international transfers are exceptionally intense and challenging (Brandt/Buck 2005). In our study, we evaluated employees' subjective perceptions of the opportunities and risks associated with this lifetime rotation abroad in the Foreign Service with regard to employees' partnerships, family, and health. Additionally, we examined whether men and women and individuals with differing family structures differ in the degree to which they benefit from organizational and social support systems in dealing with relocation-associated stress.

1.1   Review of Empirical and Theoretical Literature

1.1.1   Perceived Organizational Support (POS)

There is some empirical evidence showing that the negative effects of relocation-associated stress can be mitigated, amongst other factors, by organizational and social support (Eisenberger et al. 1986; Mazerolle/Singh 2002). In this context, *perceived organizational support* refers to the degree to which employees believe that their organization values their contributions and cares about their and their family's well-being. Employees who feel valued and rewarded by their organizations tend to perform better than those who are disappointed with their perceived treatment (Rhoades/Eisenberger 2002). Organizations may offer important socio-emotional resources, such as respect and care, as well as material benefits and instrumental support, such as financial benefits, child care, and medical support. Being regarded highly by the organization helps to meet employees' needs for appreciation, esteem, and affiliation (Byrne/Hochwarter 2008). Being noticed and rewarded for increased effort within the organization is also perceived as very supportive. Because of these psychological and material benefits, employees usually take an active interest in the way they are regarded by their employer.

Organizational support theory (Eisenberger et al. 1986) posits that employees evaluate the degree to which their socio-emotional needs are met by forming a general perception of the extent to which the organization values their contributions and cares about their well-being. When employees perceive strong organizational support, they feel obligated to help the organization reach its objectives and accordingly increase the effort they exert for the organization (contributing to better performance; Rhoades/Eisenberger 2002). Perceived organizational support is strongly associated feelings of identification with the organization and an expectation that better performance will be rewarded (Rhoades/Eisenberger 2002). POS is also related to other positive work attitudes, such as job satisfaction and organizational commitment, as well as with reduced withdrawal behaviors, such as absenteeism and turnover (Rhoades/Eisenberger 2002).

In their meta-analysis of more than 70 studies, Rhoades and Eisenberger (2002) identified three primary antecedents of POS – supervisor support, fairness, and organizational rewards and favorable job conditions. An individual's supervisor often is the most proximal representative of the larger organization, so employees often regard treatment by their supervisors as direct indicators of the degree to which they are valued by the organization. Fairness refers to the degree to which employees feel that the processes through which decisions are made and rewards are allocated are just (i.e., procedural justice). A process can be perceived as fair even if employees' rewards differ in size, so long as the decision criteria (e.g., distribution according to hierarchical level) are understood and accepted by the employees affected. Finally, organizational rewards and favorable job conditions also play an important role in perceived organizational support. Employees feel more valued by their organizations when they are rewarded for their efforts and new ideas and when the organization provides them with job security, safe and comfortable workspaces, and promotion prospects.

As discussed above, Rhoades and Eisenberger's (2002) meta-analysis also showed that perceived organization support is, in turn, related to favorable outcomes on the part of employees (e.g., job satisfaction, positive mood) and on the part of the organization (e.g., affective organizational commitment, performance, reduced withdrawal). POS also impacts stress and strain outcomes (Viswesvaran et al. 1999). When employees feel supported by their organizations, they are more likely to perceive potential work stressors as manageable. As a result, when POS is high, strain is generally perceived as lower. The buffering effect of POS for strain and attitudinal outcomes depends on certain processes predicted by organizational support theory – employees must believe that the organization's actions are discretionary, feel obligated to help the organization in return, and perceive that their socio-emotional needs and performance-reward expectancies are fulfilled.

Organizational support is also a major contributor to outcomes that cross the boundaries between work and non-work domains. Kossek et al. (2011) conducted a meta-analysis examining the effects of general and work–family-specific supervisor and organizational support on employee perceptions of work–family conflict. Drawing on 115 samples from 85 studies comprising 72,507 employees, they compared the relative influence of four types of work-place social support on work–family conflict perceptions – perceived organizational support (POS), supervisor support, perceived organizational work–family support (also referred to as family-supportive organizational perceptions; FSOP), and supervisor work–family support. As would be expected, work–family-specific aspects of supervisor and organizational support were more strongly related to (low) work–family conflict than were general forms of support. These results demonstrate that, while different forms and sources of workplace support are highly related, it is important for organizations and managers to provide support structures that specifically address the particular employee outcomes of interest.

To sum up, POS is beneficial to employees' stress perceptions, work satisfaction, and job performance. Thus, POS can be instrumental with respect to the organization's goals. Importantly, the benefits of organization support are stronger when the forms of support provided are conceptually aligned with the particular outcome (e.g., work–family-specific support reduces perceptions of work–family conflict better than more general forms of support).

1.1.2   Perceived Social Support (PSS)

In contrast to POS, *perceived social support* is a more general construct that refers to the degree to which employees believe that assistance is available to them to manage problems in their lives. It includes perceptions that psychosocial resources are available, assistance actually received, and the degree to which the person feels integrated into a social network. PSS can come from many sources, including family, friends, neighbors, and even pets or coworkers (Hobfoll 2002, 1989) and it can be categorized in many different ways (e.g., emotional versus informational social support; structural versus functional social support). Moreover, organizations can provide resources that contribute to perceived social support, especially when, as in the case of expatriates, the organization forms a prominent part of an individual's social network. However, social support more often comes from sources outside the organization. Researchers in the late-1970s found that the absence of adequate social support could explain an increase in the likelihood of psychiatric disorders in the face of critical life events, such as change in marital status or geographic mobility (Cassel 1974; Cobb 1976). Subsequently, many studies confirmed the important buffering role of social support for mental health. Several studies also demonstrated that social support contributes to physical health outcomes, House (1981) found that social support is associated with increased psychological well-being in the workplace. Social support can also help to reduce psychological distress (e.g., anxiety or depression; Moyle/Parkes 1999) and to promote psychological adjustment to conditions with chronically-raised stress, such as severe health problems and work stress (Cobb 1976; Halbesleben 2006; Taylor 2011). Regarding the challenges faced by expatriates, in a four-year qualitative study of 264 expatriate trailing spouses in 54 host-locations, McNulty (2012) observed that professional support (factors helping them to maintain their own careers while abroad) and social support (factors alleviating marital stress) were perceived by trailing spouses as having the greatest impact on identity reconstruction and, in turn, their international adjustment. Similarly, in a survey of 166 expatriates in China from North America, Europe, and other Asian countries, Wang and Kanungo (2004) found that expatriate social network characteristics have direct and meaningful benefits for expatriate psychological well-being. Unfortunately, Engler et al. (2015) found that 43.5% of German expatriates reported that their expatriation had a negative impact on their social contacts (and only 15.6% reported a positive impact), suggesting that many expatriates are deprived of this important source of resiliency while abroad.

There are several hypotheses addressing the link between social support and health. The major difference between alternative hypotheses is whether they predict that social support is beneficial all the time or whether social support is theorized to be specifically beneficial during stressful periods. Evidence suggests that both hypotheses are correct to a degree (Taylor 2011). For example, individuals with strong social support networks tend to experience (or perceive) fewer negative life events, contributing to an overall positive effect of social support across time. However, when stressful events do occur, social support also appears to protect from negative health effects by influencing the way people think about and cope with the events. Individuals with strong social support have fewer negative thoughts about events, helping them to more effectively cope (Edwards 1992). In expatriate contexts, interventions that help employees to build their social networks and accumulate social support, such as intercultural/diversity training, strategic planning, and familiarization with the new environment, as well as individual differences with similar effects (e.g., managerial resourcefulness, acculturation attitudes, coping strategies, stability-related personality traits), contribute to successful international adjustment (Aycan 1997).

Gender differences have been repeatedly examined in social support research (Caligiuri/ Lazarova 2002; Tamres et al. 2002). Women are more likely to provide social support to others and to engage with their social networks. They are also more likely to seek out social support to deal with stress, especially from their spouses. Concerning the type of social support, women tend to specifically seek out more emotional support than men, and there is some evidence that this type of support is also more beneficial for women (Schwarzer/ Leppin 1989; Tamres et al. 2002). Taylor (2011) suggests that these gender differences in social support may stem from biological difference between men and women in the stress-response system (e.g., "flight or fight" versus "tend and befriend"). In contrast, men's behaviors tend be less prosocial and show less regard for the impact their coping strategies may have upon others. This difference in the degree to which men and women are concerned with the impacts of their coping behaviors on others may explain why women tend to find stressful situations more emotionally straining than men (Purvanova/Muros 2010).

Caligiuri and Lazarova (2002) propose a model that describes the manner in which female expatriates develop social relationships and utilize those relationships to become cross-culturally adjusted. It encompasses three predictive components affecting international adjustment. The first includes factors affecting whether a woman is able to form relationships on the expatriate assignment (e.g., the female expatriate's interpersonal personality traits, her language skills, availability of social interaction opportunities, and the environment's cultural norms towards women). The second component includes various sources of social interaction and social support, including family members, work colleagues, and host country nationals. The third component describes the nature of a female expatriate's social interactions and social support resources (i.e., emotional, informational, and instrumental). The general premise of this model is that when female expatriates are prevented from procuring the necessary social resources to address their particular expatriate challenges, their international adjustment suffers.

1.2   Organizational and Social Support Provided by the Federal Foreign Office

Frequent international mobility has important effects on family life and health (Lück/ Schneider 2010). With increasing mobility, expatriates face increasing difficulty forming a family and organizing family life. These challenges are especially present when mobility is unforeseeable or irregular. Fortunately, in the case of the Federal Foreign Office, staff rotations are mostly foreseeable and regular, and the organization implements a variety of procedures to ensure that employees perceive the rotation process to be as fair and transparent as possible. Employees are sent to new postings every three to four years. Usually, two postings abroad are followed by one stage in Germany. The diplomats are generally accompanied by their family members – only to crisis-postings like Kabul or Baghdad are they sent alone. Diplomats are required to apply for their next posting one year in advance by specifying 15 possible postings. Postings are organized into three difficulty levels: (A) proper infrastructure, few security- and health-risks; (B) moderate infrastructure, moderate security- and health-risks; and (C) poor infrastructure, high security- and health-risks. When diplomats are assigned to higher-risk postings, they receive higher compensation. Approximately six months before relocation, employees are informed about the location of their next posting (Brandt/Buck 2005). This allows for adequate time for preparatory activities, such as language training and house-hunting.

Despite the transparency of the rotation process, there remains several potential sources of stress for diplomats and their families. To give three examples, first, employees are often sent to countries other than the ones they had applied for. Second, due to delays in the complex rotation planning procedure, employees are sometimes only informed about their next posting one or two months in advance. Third, there are sometimes cases where, due to the demands from their current post, no advanced training or briefing is feasible. As a result, employees and their families arrive at their new posting without any specific preparations. These stressors, combined with challenges already inherent with international mobility, can make moving to a new posting extremely difficult for employees and their families.

The Federal Foreign Office has implemented several programs to help employees and families prepare for and adjust to their new locations and to mitigate the negative impacts of mobility on family life and health (Rüger et al. 2013). These include:

- Language training (both in advance and while abroad);
- Medical evaluations before and at the end of each posting;
- Stress-counseling and psychosocial support before and during the posting;
- Embassies' reports on current living-conditions;
- Predecessors' field-reports;
- Training for cultural diversity and applied geography;
- Specific briefings on the new posting;
- Peer support systems at the new posting, which facilitate family-adjustment during the first weeks of the posting through concrete actions by the incumbent employees, such as showing individuals around the local area, shopping guidance, and connecting individuals with craftsmen, car-garages, local administration, medical facilities, childcare facilities, and other helpful contacts; and
- Relocation facilitation kits, which provide employees and families with necessary housing and kitchen supplies while their personal belongings are still being moved.

In addition, recently several other support interventions were introduced in response to findings from this study or other organizational development processes:

- Leadership training before employees' first assignment as a manager/supervisor;
- Professional networking training to help spouses to find employment abroad;
- Dedicated staff to assist trailing spouses in finding paid employment;
- Financial support for spouses' job-education and licensure for employment abroad (e.g., for positions such as language teacher, physician, physiotherapist, or IT consultant);
- Special training programs aimed at employing spouses as embassy staff in several visa-sections worldwide;
- Specific preparatory courses for children and couples addressing their age- and relationship-specific requirements during expatriation; and
- Pilot projects in telecommuting and part-time-work on post abroad for employees with children.

Each of these support measures should help to reduce relocation-associated stress and should provide employees and their families with all necessary information and capabilities to cope with and adjust to the demands of their new posting. Many of these support measures also address the work–family conflict issues that are prevalent during expatriation.

1.3   Study Aims

The overall aim of this study was to identify risk factors and protective factors for German diplomatic staff working in Foreign Service, their partners, and their children, as well as factors that moderate these effects. In this chapter, based on findings from previous analyses (Rüger et al. 2013), we addressed the following questions:

5. How strongly are organizational and social support related to work and life attitudinal and health outcomes? What are their individual and joint contributions? While studies of organizational and social support are common in the expatriate literature, few studies have assessed both in one sample.
6. Previous studies have found that women benefit more from social support than men when dealing with relocation-associated stress (Caligiuri/Lazarova 2002). Does this gender difference also apply to organizational support?
7. Married individuals often have larger social networks than unmarried individuals, both because family can provide a ready source of social support and because one's spouse can facilitate the development of new social contacts. Do unmarried individuals, therefore, benefit more from organizational and social support than married persons?

2   Methods

At the end of 2011, a standardized online questionnaire was used for a cross-sectional survey of employees of the Federal Foreign Office ($N = 2,598$), as well as their partners ($N = 417$) and children ($N = 298$). The sample discussed in this chapter included 1,665 expatriates who provided information on their experiences of organizational or social support (see Wiernik et al. 2018, Chapter 1, and Rüger et al. 2018, Appendix B, this volume, for more details).

2.1 Measures

Organizational support. Perceived organizational support was measured with nine items assessing how helpful expatriates found the various services the Federal Foreign Office provided to facilitate adjustment in new locations (e.g., language training, psychosocial counseling, medical evaluations), as well as one item measuring overall feelings of support from the organization ("How satisfied are you with the support of the Federal Foreign Office?"; rated on scale from 1 [very satisfied] to 4 [very dissatisfied]). This combined measure had $\alpha = .77$. Higher scores indicate more support.

Social support. Perceived social support was measured with 4 items from the Berlin Social-Support Scales (Schulz/Schwarzer 2003) assessing the degree to which expatriates felt that people were available to offer support when needed, as well as expatriates' feelings of loneliness and connection with others. The items selected were the four showing the highest factor loadings on the Available Support scale ($\alpha = .85$).

We examine relations between these two forms of support and several other variables.

Gender and marital status. First, we examined whether perceptions of organizational and social support differed across gender (coded as $0 =$ male, $1 =$ female; $N = 803$ males, 716 females) and marital status (coded as $0 =$ unmarried, $1 =$ married; $N = 329$ unmarried, 1,243 married). Correlations between support and these variables are adjusted to reflect equal group sizes (Schmidt/Hunter 2015).

Work- and adjustment-related variables. Second, we examined the relations between these different forms of support and the following work- and adjustment-related variables:

1. *Extrinsic career success.* This includes self-reported organizational tenure, hierarchical level, and pay grade.
2. *Locational adjustment.* Individuals' comfort with completing everyday tasks and errands was measured with eight items developed for this study, assessing climate, local safety and amenities, social contacts, and recreational options ($\alpha = .84$).
3. *General job satisfaction.* This scale assessed employees' satisfaction with coworkers, pay, recognition, autonomy, task variety, job security, and the organization and work in general (measured with 13 items developed for this study; $\alpha = .77$).
4. *Satisfaction with the rotation process.* This scale assessed employees' satisfaction with the process leading to their current assignment locations (four items developed for this study, one global and three about specific aspects; $\alpha = .63$).

Family- and health-related variables. Third, we examined relations between these forms of support and the following family- and health-related variables:

1. *Hours worked per week.* Measured continuously in hours.
2. *Work–family conflict.* Perceptions of conflict between working for the Foreign Office and other life responsibilities were measured with 12 items developed for this study, including perceptions of interference of work demands with family life and perceptions family problems attributable to the frequent international moves (e.g., "My work is a burden to family life"; $\alpha = .81$).
3. *Satisfaction with romantic relationship.* Employees' satisfaction with their romantic relationships was assessed with three items developed for this study, including a global rating of satisfaction and questions addressing relationship conflict due to relocation ($\alpha = .61$).

4. *Satisfaction with friendships.* Employees' satisfaction with their friendships was assessed with three items developed for this study, including a global rating of satisfaction and questions addressing proximity to one's friends and interconnectedness of one's friendship network ($\alpha = .40$).
5. *Perceived stress.* Stress was measured with four items selected from the German version of the Perceived Stress Questionnaire (Fliege et al. 2005). The selected items were the ones showing the highest factor loadings on each of the four subscales ($\alpha = .72$).
6. *Subjective health.* Subjective health perceptions were measured using subscales from the Quality of Life Questionnaire (Aaronson et al. 1993). These scales included eight items assessing physical health symptoms, three items assessing mental health, and two items assessing overall evaluations of health. Cronbach's α for these scales were .88 (Physical), .83 (Mental), and .92 (Overall).

2.2   Analyses

We computed correlations between both organizational and social support and each of the variables described above. For variables measured with multi-item scales, we corrected correlations for attenuation due to measurement error using Cronbach's α. We also estimated the joint influence of organizational and social support on each outcome by computing multiple correlations. Based on the empirical benchmarks established by Hemphill (2003) for the magnitude of correlation coefficients, we interpreted values less than .10 as negligible, .10–.19 as small, .20–.29 as moderate, .30–.44 as large, and larger than .45 as very large.

Comparison of correlations. To address our second and third research questions, we computed correlations between organizational and social support and each outcome separately for men and women and for married and unmarried individuals. We computed the difference between these correlations and placed a confidence interval around these differences. Positive differences between the correlations indicate that the correlation is higher in the reference group (females; married), while negative differences indicate that the correlation is higher in the contrast group (males; unmarried).

3   Results

Organizational support and social support were weakly correlated ($r = .13$, corrected $r_c = .16$ [95% CI around $r_c = .10, .22$], $N = 1,440$). This shows that there is only a small relationship between these two forms of support, which is in line with the theoretical conceptualization of organizational and social support as distinct and complementary sources of employees' needs fulfilment. Gender showed negligible relations with organizational support ($r = -.04$, $r_c = -.05$ [95% CI -.11, .01], $N = 1,412$), but women perceived somewhat stronger social support than men ($r = .16$, $r_c = .18$ [95% CI .12, .23], $N = 1,386$). Similarly, marital status was negligibly related to organizational support ($r = .03$, $r_c = .03$ [95% CI -.03, .09], $N = 1,412$), but married individuals experienced moderately stronger social support than unmarried individuals ($r = .18$, $r_c = .20$ [95% CI .14, .26], $N = 1,386$). These patterns of gender and marital-status differences in support are also reflected in differences in correlations between support and outcomes (see below).

Correlations between organizational and social support and the outcome variables for the complete sample are shown in Table 1. Support showed small to moderate relations with a variety of outcomes. Organizational support was moderately related to hierarchical level and pay grade (r_c = .20, .24, respectively), but social support was negligibly related to these variables (but weakly negatively related to organizational tenure, r_c = -.18). Organizational support showed small relations to family and health outcomes (absolute r_c ranged .10 to .19); relations of these outcomes with social support were stronger, especially for relationship and friendship satisfaction (r_c = .34, .49, respectively). Work-related variables showed generally moderate relations with both organizational and social support (r_c ranged .13 to .36, mean = .22). The largest correlations for organizational support we found were with job satisfaction (r_c = .36) and with pay level (r_c = .24); for social support, the largest correlations were with romantic relationship satisfaction (r_c = .34) and with friendship satisfaction (r_c = .49). Joint contributions of organizational and social support with outcomes ranged from small (weekly work hours, R = .14) to large (friendship satisfaction, R = .50), with most multiple correlations in the range of R = .20 to .30.

When we examine relations separately by gender (Table 2), we see that perceived organizational support is more strongly related with hierarchical level, pay grade, and weekly work hours among men than among women, but more strongly related with friendship satisfaction among women (r_c = .34) than among men (r_c = .08). Social support was more strongly linked with romantic relationship satisfaction among women (r_c = .43) than among men (r_c = .33). Social support was also more strongly related to locational adjustment for women than men (r_c = .23 vs. .14). Other relations showed negligible to small gender differences.

Concerning family status, we also found several noteworthy differences between married and unmarried individuals (see Table 3). As expected, organizational and social support were more strongly related to satisfaction with the rotation process among unmarried (r_c = .36, .27, respectively) versus married (r_c = .21, .17) individuals. Social support was also much more strongly linked to friendship satisfaction for unmarried (r_c = .60) rather than married (r_c = .45) individuals. The most distinct difference we observed was for health outcomes. Organizational and social support were much more strongly connected with health for unmarried individuals (r_c = .22, .29 for overall subjective health, respectively) than for married individuals (r_c = .11, .17).

Table 1: Correlations between Support and Work, Life, and Health-related Outcomes

Outcome	Organizational support			Social support			Multiple R
	r	r_c	95% CI	r	r_c	95% CI	
Tenure	.04	.05	-.01, .10	-.17	-.18	-.24, -.13	.20
Occupational level	.18	.20	.15, .26	.06	.06	.01, .12	.20
Pay level	.21	.24	.18, .30	.03	.04	-.02, .09	.24
Locational adjustment	.10	.13	.06, .19	.16	.19	.13, .25	.21
Job satisfaction	.28	.36	.27, .40	.18	.22	.15, .27	.40
Satisfaction with rotation process	.17	.24	.17, .32	.14	.19	.12, .26	.28
Weekly work hours	.12	.14	.08, .19	.03	.03	-.02, .09	.14
Work–life conflict	-.15	-.19	-.25, -.13	-.16	-.19	-.25, -.13	.25
Relationship satisfaction	.07	.10	.01, .19	.24	.34	.25, .42	.34
Friendship satisfaction	.10	.18	.09, .27	.29	.49	.41, .59	.50
Stress	-.11	-.14	-.21, -.08	-.16	-.21	.14, .27	.24
Subjective health (overall)	.13	.15	.08, .20	.17	.19	.14, .25	.23
Subjective health (physical)	.10	.13	.06, .19	.12	.14	.08, .20	.18
Subjective health (mental)	.10	.12	.06, .18	.18	.21	.15, .27	.23

Note: Mean $N = 1,412$ for organizational support, 1,386 for social support; r = observed correlation; r_c = correlation corrected for unreliability; 95% CI = 95% confidence interval around r_c; Multiple R = multiple correlation of organizational and social support with outcomes, corrected for unreliability.

Table 2: Correlations between Support and Work, Life, and Health-related Outcomes by Gender

Outcome	Organizational support						Social support					
	Men		Women				Men		Women			
	r	r_c	r	r_c	Diff.	95% CI	r	r_c	r	r_c	Diff.	95% CI
Tenure	.06	.07	.01	.01	-.06	-.16, .05	-.14	-.15	-.16	-.18	-.03	-.14, .08
Occupational level	.25	.28	.14	.16	-.12	-.23, -.02	.13	.14	.11	.11	-.03	-.13, .07
Pay level	.25	.29	.14	.16	-.13	-.24, -.03	.09	.09	.02	.02	-.07	-.17, .04
Locational adjustment	.09	.11	.13	.16	.05	-.05, .15	.12	.14	.19	.23	.09	-.01, .19
Job satisfaction	.29	.38	.32	.41	.03	-.07, .14	.24	.29	.28	.35	.06	-.04, .17
Satisfaction with rotation process	.13	.19	.19	.27	.08	-.02, .19	.16	.22	.14	.19	-.03	-.14, .08
Weekly work hours	.16	.18	.06	.07	-.11	-.22, .00	.09	.10	.03	.03	-.07	-.18, .04
Work–life conflict	-.13	-.16	-.17	-.22	-.06	-.16, .04	-.17	-.21	-.20	-.24	-.03	-.13, .07
Relationship satisfaction	.07	.11	.07	.10	-.01	-.14, .12	.23	.33	.31	.43	.10	-.01, .24
Friendship satisfaction	.04	.08	.18	.33	.25	.15, .35	.29	.49	.32	.54	.05	-.04, .17
Stress	-.09	-.12	-.12	-.16	-.04	-.14, .06	-.16	-.21	-.20	-.25	-.04	-.14, .06
Subjective health (overall)	.10	.11	.14	.16	.05	-.06, .16	.20	.23	.20	.23	.00	-.11, .11
Subjective health (physical)	.07	.09	.13	.17	.08	-.03, .19	.14	.16	.16	.19	.03	-.08, .14
Subjective health (mental)	.09	.11	.11	.13	.02	-.09, .13	.21	.24	.19	.22	-.02	-.13, .09

Note: Mean $N = 712$ for men, 639 for women; $r =$ observed correlation; $r_c =$ correlation corrected for unreliability; Diff. = difference between r_c for men and women; 95% CI = 95% confidence interval around Diff.

Table 3: Correlations between Support and Work, Life, and Health-related Outcomes by Marital Status

	Organizational support						Social support					
	Unmarried		Married				Unmarried		Married			
Outcome	r	r_c	r	r_c	Diff.	95% CI	r	r_c	r	r_c	Diff.	95% CI
Tenure	-.01	-.01	.05	.05	.06	-.07, .19	-.16	-.17	-.19	-.21	-.04	-.17, .09
Occupational level	.19	.21	.17	.20	-.01	-.14, .11	.09	.10	.03	.03	-.07	-.19, .06
Pay level	.17	.20	.21	.24	.04	-.09, .17	.05	.06	.01	.01	-.05	-.18, .08
Locational adjustment	.09	.11	.11	.14	.03	-.09, .15	.20	.23	.14	.17	-.06	-.19, .06
Job satisfaction	.35	.45	.30	.39	-.06	-.20, .05	.28	.34	.21	.26	-.08	-.21, .04
Satisfaction with rotation process	.25	.36	.15	.21	-.15	-.29, -.03	.20	.27	.12	.17	-.10	-.23, .03
Weekly work hours	.15	.17	.12	.13	-.04	-.18, .10	.03	.03	.02	.02	-.01	-.14, .12
Work–life conflict	-.14	-.18	-.15	-.19	-.01	-.13, .11	-.17	-.20	-.14	-.17	.03	-.09, .15
Relationship satisfaction	—	—	.07	.10	—	—	—	—	.24	.34	—	—
Friendship satisfaction	.09	.16	.10	.19	.03	-.10, .16	.35	.60	.26	.45	-.15	-.32, -.08
Stress	-.13	-.18	-.10	-.13	.05	-.08, .18	-.23	-.29	-.15	-.19	.10	-.02, .23
Subjective health (overall)	.19	.22	.09	.11	-.11	-.24, .02	.25	.29	.15	.17	-.12	-.26, .01
Subjective health (physical)	.18	.23	.08	.10	-.13	-.26, .00	.19	.23	.11	.13	-.10	-.23, .03
Subjective health (mental)	.14	.16	.09	.11	-.05	-.18, .09	.28	.32	.15	.18	-.14	-.28, -.02

Note: Mean $N = 291$ for unmarried individuals, 1,096 for married individuals; r = observed correlation; r_c = correlation corrected for unreliability; Diff. = difference between r_c for unmarried and married individuals; 95% CI = 95% confidence interval around Diff.

4   Discussion

As introduced above, the Federal Foreign Office provides a wide variety of organizational support interventions for employees. In addition to the more general support measures, a number of initiatives specifically aim at alleviating the strains involved in the worldwide rotational scheme wherein diplomatic staff and their families frequently move across the world. The positive perception and impact of these organizational support measures were evaluated and compared to the impact of general social support perceptions.

Analyzing data from an online survey of German diplomats, we tested if the availability of and satisfaction with different types of organizational and social support show correlations with employees' locational adjustment, job satisfaction, life satisfaction, work–life conflict, stress, and health. Results demonstrated that POS had several significant correlations with the outcome measures. In line with Rhoades and Eisenberger's (2002) meta-analyses of studies in the general work context, our study demonstrated that expatriate diplomats' general job satisfaction and, more importantly, satisfaction with the rotation process were higher the more organizational support employees perceived. Also consistent with Rhoades and Eisenberger's meta-analysis, POS was associated with lower stress levels and with better feelings of health. Finally, consistent with Kossek et al.'s (2011) meta-analysis, POS correlated with lower work-life conflict. This finding is especially important because reconciliation between work and family life is a crucial issue for expatriates (Engler et al. 2015).

Most corrected correlations were small to moderate, indicating that, while POS and PSS are important contributors to expatriate outcomes, other factors, not captured in this study, are also relevant for these multi-faceted outcomes. Nonetheless, we conclude from the data that organizational support measures offered by the Foreign Office do fulfill their aim and have the potential to substantially alleviate the strains involved in working in the Foreign Service.

The data also show that social support is correlated with the outcome measures, yet the correlational pattern differs between social and organizational support. Social support seems to be specifically relevant for outcomes outside the workplace, including locational adjustment, partnership satisfaction, and friendship satisfaction. Social support, as it was conceptualized and assessed here, refers to general perceptions of the availability of psychosocial resources, not resources limited to work-related social support (e.g., support from colleagues or supervisor support). It is likely that sources of support outside the work context, such as partners, family members, and friends, were more salient for respondents when answering the questionnaire. Thus, it seems that this form of support is uniquely important for relationship and friendship satisfaction and locational adjustment. For organizations sending employees abroad, it is important to consider the specific relevance of social support for expatriate success. The present findings show that there are life domains where the influence of employers' organizational support is limited and demonstrate the importance of social support networks outside the workplace. In light of the well-documented negative impact of expatriation on social life (Engler et al., 2015), it is vital for personnel departments' agendas to create work conditions that enable employees to reconcile their private lives – here seen as enabling support systems – with their work lives. Additionally, and perhaps a bit unexpectedly, social support was even more strongly connected than organizational support with stress and health outcomes. This highlights the broad relevance of social support in the high-stress context of expatriation.

Also in line with the literature, we found that women in our sample showed higher levels of perceived social support and stronger associations between social support and locational adjustment than men. Women also tend to show a higher association than men between perceived organizational support and friendship satisfaction. While gender differences in relations between POS and work satisfaction outcomes are smaller, they also trend in the direction of being stronger among women. We interpret these findings as indicating that women benefit more strongly from social and/or organizational support than men, at least in some areas. The smaller gender differences in relations between POS and work attitudes are somewhat at odds with previous studies. One reason for this difference may be that women prefer other forms of organizational support than assessed in this study. McNulty (2012) reported that organizational support continues to disappoint expatriate trailing spouses (who were mostly women), many of whom believed that organizations were not genuinely interested in their personal welfare because the resources they offered did not address their particular needs (e.g., the dual-career dilemma, socialization difficulties within the expatriate community) sufficiently. Some of the support measures offered by the Foreign Office do address these issues, such as financial support for spouses' job-education, training programs aimed at employing spouses as local staff, and preparatory courses for couples. However, we did not evaluate specific effects of individual interventions, so we cannot conclude whether the resources assessed in this study address these specific needs better than those assessed by other researchers.

We predicted that unmarried persons would benefit more from social support than married persons because the latter group might have more support available from their partners and a usually larger social network. Our data supported this prediction and showed stronger relations in unmarried individuals between social support and many outcomes. With regard to POS, unmarried individuals also received an incremental benefit over married persons, but this effect was limited to only satisfaction with the rotation process and health outcomes. Our interpretation is that while both groups, married and unmarried individuals, profit from both forms of support, unmarried expatriates benefit more because they lack the reliable social support that can be provided by one's romantic partner.

Of course, our interpretations concerning the moderating effects of gender and marital status are limited by the cross-sectional study design, so firm causal inferences cannot be made.

4.1 *Recommendations for Organizations and Implications for Expatriate Success*

What practical recommendations for personnel managers in Foreign Offices and other organizations sending employees abroad can be derived from this study? Our finding that organizational support was positively associated with job satisfaction and satisfaction with the rotation system underscores that sending organizations should ensure that resources are provided to employees to facilitate their relocation and that employees perceive their availability. Interventions such as language training (preparatory and while abroad), regular medical evaluations before and at the end of postings, stress-counseling and psychosocial support before and during the posting, were perceived as supportive in our sample. Some of these interventions, such as language training, can also be supportive when offered to partners or children and may facilitate adjustment and reduce work–life–conflicts.

We found that relationship and friendship satisfaction were the outcomes that were most responsive to organizational and social support. Both of these attitudes are more or less direct indicators of balance between work and non-work demands, so sending organizations should make all efforts to improve the reconcilability of family and work for their expatriate employees. Such work–life balance could be achieved through interventions such as employment assistance for trailing spouses (e.g., obtaining work permits, offering career coaching) or by helping spouses to remain connected to their career during the international assignment (e.g., through advanced trainings). In future, expanding the possibilities for telework on international postings may also help to increase work–life reconciliation for expatriate employees.

References

Aaronson, Neil K. et al. (1993): The European Organization for Research and Treatment of Cancer QLQ-C30: A Quality-of-Life Instrument for Use in International Clinical Trials in Oncology. In: *Journal of the National Cancer Institute* 85,5: 365–376. [https://doi.org/10/d9d26h].

Aycan, Zeynep (1997): Expatriate Adjustment as a Multifaceted Phenomenon: Individual and Organizational Level Predictors. In: *International Journal of Human Resource Management* 8,4: 434–456. [https://doi.org/10.1080/095851997341540].

Brandt, Enrico; Buck, Christian (2005): Auswärtiges Amt: Diplomatie als Beruf. 4th ed. Wiesbaden, Germany: VS Verlag für Sozialwissenschaften. [https://doi.org/10/b6k9].

Byrne, Zinta S.; Hochwarter, Wayne A. (2008): Perceived Organizational Support and Performance: Relationships across Levels of Organizational Cynicism. In: *Journal of Managerial Psychology* 23,1: 54–72. [https://doi.org/10.1108/02683940810849666].

Caligiuri, Paula M.; Lazarova, M. (2002): A Model for the Influence of Social Interaction and Social Support on Female Expatriates' Cross-Cultural Adjustment. In: *International Journal of Human Resource Management* 13,5: 761–772. [https://doi.org/10/drscsj].

Cassel, John (1974): Psychosocial Processes and "Stress": Theoretical Formulation. In: *International Journal of Health Services* 4,3: 471–482. [https://doi.org/10.2190/WF7X-Y1L0-BFKH-9QU2].

Cobb, Sidney (1976): Social Support as a Moderator of Life Stress. In: *Psychosomatic Medicine* 38,5: 300–314. [https://doi.org/10.1097/00006842-197609000-00003].

Edwards, Jeffrey R. (1992): A Cybernetic Theory of Stress, Coping, and Well-Being in Organizations. In: *Academy of Management Review* 17,2: 238–274. [https://doi.org/10.5465/AMR.1992.4279536].

Eisenberger, Robert et al. (1986): Perceived Organizational Support. In: *Journal of Applied Psychology* 71,3: 500–507. [https://doi.org/10.1037/0021-9010.71.3.500].

Engler, Marcus et al. (2015): International Mobil: Motive, Rahmenbedingungen und Folgen der Aus- und Rückwanderung deutscher Staatsbürger. Studie des SVR-Forschungsbereichs 2015-1. Berlin, Germany: Sachverständigenrat deutscher Stiftungen für Integration und Migration. [https://www.svr-migration.de/wp-content/uploads/2015/03/Studie_International-Mobil_Web.pdf].

Fliege, Herbert et al. (2005): The Perceived Stress Questionnaire (PSQ) Reconsidered: Validation and Reference Values from Different Clinical and Healthy Adult Samples. In: *Psychosomatic Medicine* 67,1: 78–88. [https://doi.org/10.1097/01.psy.0000151491.80178.78].

Halbesleben, Jonathon R.B. (2006): Sources of Social Support and Burnout: A Meta-Analytic Test of the Conservation of Resources Model. In: *Journal of Applied Psychology* 91,5: 1134–1145. [https://doi.org/10.1037/0021-9010.91.5.1134].

Hemphill, James F. (2003): Interpreting the Magnitudes of Correlation Coefficients. In: *American Psychologist* 58,1: 78–79. [https://doi.org/10.1037/0003-066X.58.1.78].

Hobfoll, Stevan E. (2002): Social and Psychological Resources and Adaptation. In: *Review of General Psychology* 6,4: 307–324. [https://doi.org/10.1037//1089-2680.6.4.307].

Hobfoll, Stevan E. (1989): Conservation of Resources: A New Attempt at Conceptualizing Stress. In: *American Psychologist* 44,3: 513–524. [https://doi.org/10.1037/0003-066X.44.3.513].

House, James S. (1981): Work Stress and Social Support. Addison-Wesley Series on Occupational Stress 4. Reading, MA: Addison-Wesley.

Kossek, Ellen Ernst et al. (2011): Workplace Social Support and Work–family Conflict: A Meta-Analysis Clarifying the Influence of General and Work–family-Specific Supervisor and Organizational Support. In: *Personnel Psychology* 64,2: 289–313. [https://doi.org/10.1111/j.1744-6570.2011.01211.x].

Lück, Detlev; Schneider, Norbert F. (2010): Introduction to the Special Issue on Mobility and Family: Increasing Job Mobility – Changing Family Lives. In: *Zeitschrift für Familienforschung* 22,2. [http://nbn-resolving.de/urn:nbn:de:0168-ssoar-355447].

Mazerolle, Maurice J.; Singh, Gangaram (2002): Social Support and the Reduction of Discouragement after Job Displacement. In: *Journal of Socio-Economics* 31,4: 409–422. [https://doi.org/10.1016/S1053-5357(02)00132-4].

McNulty, Yvonne (2012): 'Being Dumped in to Sink or Swim': An Empirical Study of Organizational Support for the Trailing Spouse. In: *Human Resource Development International* 15,4: 417–434. [https://doi.org/10.1080/13678868.2012.721985].

Moyle, Penny; Parkes, Katharine (1999): The Effects of Transition Stress: A Relocation Study. In: *Journal of Organizational Behavior* 20,5: 625–646. [https://doi.org/10/fbrpw2].

Purvanova, Radostina K.; Muros, John P. (2010): Gender Differences in Burnout: A Meta-Analysis. In: *Journal of Vocational Behavior* 77,2: 168–185. [https://doi.org/10.1016/j.jvb.2010.04.006].

Rhoades, Linda; Eisenberger, Robert (2002): Perceived Organizational Support: A Review of the Literature. In: *Journal of Applied Psychology* 87,4: 698–714. [https://doi.org/10.1037/0021-9010.87.4.698].

Rüger, Heiko et al. (2018): Sampling and Procedures in the Mobility Skills in the German Foreign Service Study. In: Wiernik, Brenton M.; Rüger, Heiko; Ones, Deniz S. (Eds.): Managing Expatriates: Success Factors in Private and Public Domains, Series on Population Studies 50. Opladen, Germany: Barbara Budrich Publishers.

Rüger, Heiko et al. (2013): Mobilitätskompetenzen im Auswärtigen Dienst: Risiken und protektive Faktoren bei der Bewältigung der Auslandsrotation. Beiträge zur Bevölkerungswissenschaft. 44. Würzburg, Germany: Ergon.

Schmidt, Frank L.; Hunter, John E. (2015): Methods of Meta-Analysis: Correcting Error and Bias in Research Findings. 3rd ed. Thousand Oaks, CA: Sage. [https://doi.org/10/b6mg].

Schulz, Ute; Schwarzer, Ralf (2003): Soziale Unterstützung bei der Krankheitsbewältigung: Die Berliner Social Support Skalen (BSSS). In: *Diagnostica* 49,2: 73–82. [https://doi.org/10.1026//0012-1924.49.2.73].

Schwarzer, Ralf; Leppin, Anja (1989): Social Support and Health: A Meta-Analysis. In: *Psychology & Health* 3,1: 1–15. [https://doi.org/10.1080/08870448908400361].

Tamres, Lisa K.; Janicki, Denise; Helgeson, Vicki S. (2002): Sex Differences in Coping Behavior: A Meta-Analytic Review and an Examination of Relative Coping. In: *Personality and Social Psychology Review* 6,1: 2–30. [https://doi.org/10.1207/S15327957PSPR0601_1].

Taylor, Shelley E. (2011): Social Support: A Review. In: Friedman, Howard S. (Ed.): Oxford Handbook of Health Psychology. Oxford, United Kingdom: Oxford University Press: 192–217. [https://doi.org/10.1093/oxfordhb/9780195342819.013.0009].

Viswesvaran, Chockalingam; Sanchez, Juan I.; Fisher, Jeffrey (1999): The Role of Social Support in the Process of Work Stress: A Meta-Analysis. In: *Journal of Vocational Behavior* 54,2: 314–334. [https://doi.org/10.1006/jvbe.1998.1661].

Wang, Xiaoyun; Kanungo, Rabindra N. (2004): Nationality, Social Network and Psychological Well-Being: Expatriates in China. In: *International Journal of Human Resource Management* 15,4: 775–793. [https://doi.org/10.1080/0958519042000192942].

Wiernik, Brenton M.; Rüger, Heiko; Ones, Deniz S. (2018): Advancing Expatriate Research in Public and Private Sectors. In: Wiernik, Brenton M.; Rüger, Heiko; Ones, Deniz S. (Eds.): Managing Expatriates: Success Factors in Private and Public Domains, Series on Population Studies 50. Opladen, Germany: Barbara Budrich Publishers.

Wilkinson, Amanda; Singh, Gangaram (2010): Managing Stress in the Expatriate Family: A Case Study of the State Department of the United States of America. In: *Public Personnel Management* 39,2: 169–181. [https://doi.org/10.1177/009102601003900206].

A Family Affair: Spouse and Children's Role in Expatriate Adjustment and Job Performance

Deniz S. Ones, Hannah J. Foldes, and Handan Kepir Sinangil

Abstract

Previous research has consistently identified a relation between family and expatriate outcomes (e.g., adjustment, stay intentions, job performance), but little research has sought to isolate the various roles of the spouse and other family members (e.g., children) in relation to these outcomes. This study examined the influence that the spouse and family have on expatriate adjustment, stay intentions, and job performance in Turkey. Data were obtained for 311 expatriates and 308 Turkish host country national coworkers. Results indicated that marital status, presence and adjustment of family, and family support have a differential impact on various outcomes. The influence of children appeared to be more pronounced than that of spouses in terms of their presence in the assigned country and their adjustment. Also, family support influenced job performance strongly, but had no effect on adjustment or stay intentions. Organizations could benefit from attending more to family and spouse issues to increase the chances of successful expatriate assignments.

1 Introduction

In recent decades, expanding global competition has compelled organizations to face the assortment of challenges associated with international human resource management (Albrecht et al. 2018). Effective management of expatriates on international assignments is now a key requirement for any organization to be globally competitive (BGRS 2016; Guthridge/Komm 2008). Not only are these assignments important for an organization's success overseas, but they are also increasingly essential for employees' career development and advancement into high-level leadership roles (Stahl et al. 2002; Vance 2005). The success or failure of an international assignment can have significant consequences for both the organization (in terms of competitive position in local markets) and the expatriate (in terms of career advancement).

A frequently cited factor in the success or failure of international assignments is expatriates' families. Failed expatriate assignments are often attributed to the inability of expatriate family members to adjust to their new environments (BGRS 2012; Black/Gregersen 1991; Haslberger/Brewster 2008; Shaffer/Harrison 2001).

International assignments present a myriad of adaptation challenges – expatriates must learn how to navigate their everyday lives and needs in a foreign context (locational adjustment), as well as learn how to interact with host country nationals (interaction adjustment) and learn how to perform in new, often expanded, work roles (work adjustment; Black et al. 1991). Expatriate spouses and children face the same challenges; like expatriate employees, they also must learn to carry out their daily responsibilities and interact with others in new environments (Black/Gregersen 1991). Expatriate children also must adjust to new school environments, often with increased language difficulties. These adjustment challenges are often even more salient for expatriate families than for employees, as family members may more often encounter language and cultural difficulties in non-work settings than employees do while at work (Shaffer/Harrison 2001). Expatriate families must also adjust to changing family roles that often accompany international moves (e.g., expatriate spouses often are unable to find employment abroad and so transition to a family role as caretaker; Cole 2011; Lazarova et al. 2010; Mohr/Klein 2008). Adjustment can be more difficult for expatriate families than employees because spouses and children often receive less pre-departure preparation and training and less organizational and social support after arrival (Andreason 2008; Brown 2008; Caligiuri/Lazarova 2005; Pellico/Stroh 1997). Substantial empirical evidence demonstrates the detrimental impact poor family adjustment and other adverse family experiences have on expatriate outcomes (Bhaskar-Shrinivas et al. 2005; Black/Stephens 1989; Hechanova et al. 2003; Shaffer/Harrison 2001; Takeuchi et al. 2002). Despite these findings, this literature has focused almost exclusively on the role of family in driving expatriate employee adjustment and stay intentions. Contributions of family variables to other critical outcomes, such as job performance, job satisfaction, and well-being, have received comparatively little attention (Albrecht et al. 2018; Lazarova et al. 2010). The present study, therefore, sought to examine expand this literature by examining how expatriate families impact the critical criterion of expatriate job performance, in addition to adjustment and stay intentions (cf. Caligiuri 1997; Mol et al. 2005).

1.1   The Importance of Spouse and Family Experiences on Expatriate Outcomes

Research on expatriate families has drawn on models of work-family interface from domestic settings to examine how expatriate family life may interfere with, or facilitate, workplace outcomes (and vice versa; see, e.g., Lazarova et al. 2010; Takeuchi et al. 2002). These studies have noted that, in the context of international assignments, the stressors of international mobility may blur the line between work and non-work contexts, particularly if expatriates are uncommon in the host country region such that the expatriate family is constantly regarded as a representative of the sending organization and their origin country (Albrecht et al. 2018). Expatriate work–family interface is expected to demonstrate both spillover effects between work and non-work contexts (e.g., stress at home interferes with expatriate employees' ability to focus at work, support resources provided by the organization enhance both work and home adjustment) and crossover effects between expatriate family members (e.g., poor spouse adjustment creates a burden on expatriate employees, positive adjustment by expatriate parents reassures children; Shaffer et al. 2001; Takeuchi et al. 2002).

Broadly, the family is argued to influence expatriate employee outcomes through two primary mechanisms. First, expatriate families are most often conceptualized as a negative influence on expatriate employees. Researchers have examined the negative impact of poor spouse and family adjustment on expatriates and various factors that contribute to work-family conflict during international assignments (Andreason 2008; Caligiuri/Lazarova 2005). Expatriate families, particularly children, are also argued to create additional non-work responsibilities for expatriates that may further burden their adjustment, satisfaction, and performance (Caligiuri/Lazarova 2005; Haslberger/Brewster 2008). Second, more recently, researchers have begun to consider how families may facilitate expatriate success by providing social and emotional support during international transitions (Schütter/Boerner 2013). During difficult work transitions, the familiarity of coming home to one's family each night can be extremely fulfilling for expatriate employees. In fact, the alternatives to expatriate family presence – expatriates leaving their families in their home country or organizations only selecting unattached employees for international assignments – may be more socially isolating and stressful than any negative impact family's presence may have (Cui/Awa 1992; Schütter/Boerner 2013). Further, *effective* family adjustment can be a reassuring and stabilizing force for expatriate employees in the same manner as poor adjustment can be a burden.

This study examines both mechanisms by not only examining the impact of the presence of family members (which may have a positive, negative, or ambivalent effect on various outcomes), but also two specific factors – family adjustment (absence of which is likely to be a substantial burden on expatriate employees and a hindrance to their success) and family social/emotional support (which is likely to be an important success factor for expatriate employees). Moreover, in contrast to most research on expatriate families (Caligiuri et al. 1998; Caligiuri/Lazarova 2005; Haslberger/Brewster 2008; Takeuchi et al. 2002), this study examines the impacts of both expatriate *spouses* and *children* on employee success, seeking to identify potential differential impacts.

2   Methods

2.1   Sample and Procedure

This chapter analyzes Sample 2 of the studies of expatriate success in Turkey (see Wiernik et al. 2018, Chapter 1 of this volume). Data were collected from 311 expatriates currently working on an international assignment in Turkey and 308 host country national (HCN) coworkers (1 for each expatriate; we were unable to gather performance ratings for 3 expatriates). Participants were recruited by the third author and undergraduate research assistants who approached companies identified through the Istanbul Chamber of Commerce Guide and lists of the 500 largest companies in Istanbul. The sampled companies represented finance/banking, tourism, education, marketing, engineering, and other industries.

Expatriate sample. Expatriates completed a survey assessing demographics, details on their expatriate assignment, and a personality questionnaire (not used for the current study). Most expatriates were male ($N = 201$; female $N = 105$; 5 did not report their gender). Most expatriates were also married ($N = 162$, single $N = 95$; 54 did not report marital status). Among married expatriates, 133 reported having their spouse present in Turkey ($N = 29$ spouses were not present). Among expatriates with children, 88 had their children with them in Turkey ($N = 50$ expatriates' children were not present). Expatriates had a mean age of 38.2 years ($SD = 10.25$). Expatriates had an average of 13 years of full-time work experience and 6 years of tenure with their current organization. Expatriates had spent an average of 7.18 years ($SD = 7.52$) abroad on previous international assignments. Time spent on the current assignment in Turkey varied widely (mean 3.32 months, $SD = 48.14$). Expatriates included executive, mid- and lower-level managers, as well as non-managerial (primarily service and educational) employees. For more information on this sample, see Jackson et al. (2003) and Jackson Foldes et al. (2006).

Expatriates were citizens of 35 countries. For those expatriates providing citizenship information, citizenship frequencies were: Australia (7), Austria (4), Azerbaijan (8), Balkan countries (6), Canada (10), Denmark (12), Egypt (2), France (17), Germany (35), Ghana/ other West African countries (3), Hungary (2), India (3), Indonesia/Philippines (3), Iran (4), Israel (4), Italy (7), Japan (15), Jordan (1), Kirghizstan/other Central Asian countries (5),

Latin America (4), Malaysia (1), Morocco (1), the Netherlands (2), New Zealand (2), Russia (5), Saudi Arabia/other Arabian countries (3), South Africa (3), South Korea (3), Spain (4), Sudan/other Central African countries (1), Switzerland (4), Thailand (2), Turkey (dual citizenship; 4), the United Kingdom/Ireland (70), and the United States (49).

Host country national coworker sample. Host country national (HCN) coworkers provided confidential job performance ratings for the expatriate with whom they were working. HCNs had a mean age of 33.12 years ($SD = 8.99$). HCNs were 116 males and 175 females (17 did not report their gender). HCNs had an average of 8.33 years ($SD = 8.24$) of experience in their current occupation. HCNs had worked with the expatriates they were rating for an average of 12.98 months ($SD = 24.13$). Raters were recruited based on their experience working closely with the expatriates. Most raters were expatriates' peers ($N = 120$), with smaller numbers being expatriates' subordinates ($N = 80$) or supervisors ($N = 29$); 79 raters did not report their position.

2.2 Measures

Adjustment to local conditions. Expatriate locational adjustment (comfort living abroad) was measured using 9 items adapted from Black and Stephens (1989). Expatriates rated the conditions and environment they faced in Turkey on a 10-point scale, with higher scores indicating greater adjustment. The 9 items included adjustment to health care facilities, shopping, entertainment, housing conditions, food, cost of living, living conditions in general, daily interactions with Turks, and socialization with Turks ($\alpha = .81$).

Stay intentions. Expatriates' rated their intentions to stay for the duration of their assignment using 2 items from Black and Stephens (1989) rated on a 10-point scale – "I would do anything to keep this assignment for the full duration" and "I rarely discuss the possibility of returning to my home country early" ($\alpha = .96$).

Family adjustment. Expatriates rated the adjustment of their spouses and children to living in Turkey on a 10-point scale. We estimated the reliability of these single-item ratings to be $r_{yy} = .58$ (cf. Wanous/Hudy 2001; we used Wanous/Hudy's estimate of internal consistency for single-item ratings of others' behavior, rather than estimates of interrater reliability, as we are examining the impact of expatriate *perceptions* of family adjustment).

Job performance. HCNs completed a 53-item job performance measure rating expatriates on 10 dimensions of job performance. The instrument was adapted from Sinangil and Ones (2003) and was constructed directly in Turkish (i.e., was not a translated measure). HCNs rated expatriates on 10 performance dimensions (Table 1) based on existing models of job performance. An overall performance index was created using a composite of the 53 items and an overall job performance item. HCNs rated each item on a 9-point scale for its accuracy describing the expatriate's on-the-job behavior (1 = extremely inaccurate, 9 = extremely accurate). HCNs are uniquely positioned to provide culturally-contextualized and relevant evaluations expatriate job performance behaviors (Sinangil/Ones 2003, 1997), and HCN reactions to expatriate behavior have an important impact on expatriates' adjustment and effectiveness (Templer 2010). We estimated interrater reliability for the overall job performance *composite* as $r_{yy} = .89$ using the composite reliability method described by Wilmot et al. (2014) and the interrater reliability and performance facet intercorrelations reported by Viswesvaran et al. (1996, 2005). See Ones et al. (2018, Chapter 15, this volume) for more details. For interested readers, as a comparison, we also report correlations corrected using Viswesvaran et al.'s (1996) meta-analytic mean interrater reliability value for overall job performance measures ($r_{yy} = .52$).

Table 1: Job performance dimensions assessed

Performance Dimension	Description *(Sample Item)*	Source for Description/Measure	Item	α	IRR
Adjustment to foreign business practices	Knowledge and application of appropriate foreign business practices *(Has knowledge about Turkish work life applications)*	Hough & Dunnette (1992)	3	.74	.58
Establishing and maintaining business contacts	Identifying, developing, using, and maintaining business contacts to achieve goals *(Can develop a communication net with people that he/she encounters at work)*	Hough & Dunnette (1992)	4	.85	.58
Technical competence	Measure of the knowledge required to carry out the tasks of the job *(Uses technical knowledge in solving difficult problems and in helping reach high quality decisions)*	Hough & Dunnette (1992); Viswesvaran (1993)	3	.91	.63
Working with others	Proficiency in working with others, assisting others in the organization *(Has planful and effective work relations with superiors and coworkers)*	Hough & Dunnette (1992)	4	.84	.47
Communicating and persuading	Oral and written proficiency in gathering and transmitting information; persuading others *(Is effective in oral and written communication)*	Hough & Dunnette (1992)	3	.85	.45
Initiative and effort	Dedication to one's job; amount of work expended in striving to do a good job *(Has initiative and takes on extra responsibility)*	Hough & Dunnette (1992)	11	.90	.55
Personal discipline	The extent to which counterproductive behaviors at work are avoided *(Follows rules and regulations and respects authority)*	Campbell et al. (1990); Viswesvaran (1993)	8	.88	.56
Interpersonal relations	The degree to which the expatriate facilitates team performance; supports and champions others in the organization and unit *(Cooperates with others at work)*	Campbell et al. (1990); Viswesvaran (1993)	8	.90	.47
Management and supervision	Proficiency in the coordination of different roles in the organization *(Provides supervision to subordinates)*	Campbell et al. (1990); Viswesvaran (1993)	5	.79	.53
Productivity	Volume of work produced by the expatriate *(Is productive)*	Viswesvaran (1993)	4	.92	.57
Overall expatriate job performance	A unit-weighted composite of the 10 scales; α reliability computed as a Mosier reliability (stratified alpha)	Campbell et al. (1990); Hough & Dunnette (1992); Viswesvaran (1993)	54	.98	.89 *.52*

Note: IRR = estimated interrater reliability using meta-analytic values reported by Viswesvaran et al. (1996). For overall job performance, the first value is the estimated criterion interrater reliability for the overall job performance *composite* using the method by Wilmot et al. (2014). The second value (in italics) is the meta-analytic estimate for overall job performance *measures* reported by Viswesvaran et al. (1996).

Table 2: Comparison of success outcomes for married and single expatriates

	Married			Single				
	N	Mean	SD	N	Mean	SD	d_c	90% CI
Adjustment	155	7.07	1.49	89	7.24	1.22	-.14	-.38, .11
Stay intentions	145	4.78	1.54	82	4.58	1.78	.13	-.11, .35
Job performance	158	7.78	1.08	94	7.77	0.81	.01	-.22, .24
							.01	*-.28, .31*

Note: *d* values corrected for unreliability in the criterion, 90% CI = 90% confidence interval. For job performance, value on first row corrected for performance composite interrater reliability (estimated r_{yy} = .89). Value in italics on second row corrected for meta-analytic mean performance measure interrater reliability (r_{yy} = .52; Viswesvaran et al. 1996)

Table 3: Comparison of success outcomes for married expatriates with present and absent spouses

	Spouse present			Spouse absent				
	N	Mean	SD	N	Mean	SD	d_c	90% CI
Adjustment	128	7.08	1.48	27	7.12	1.46	-.03	-.42, .35
Stay intentions	118	4.89	1.64	27	4.78	1.39	.07	-.29, .43
Job performance	119	7.77	1.10	29	7.75	0.74	.02	-.34, .38
							.03	*-.44, .50*

Note: *d* values corrected for unreliability in the criterion, 90% CI = 90% confidence interval. For job performance, value on first row corrected for performance composite interrater reliability (estimated r_{yy} = .89). Value in italics on second row corrected for meta-analytic mean performance measure interrater reliability (r_{yy} = .52; Viswesvaran et al. 1996)

Table 4: Comparison of success outcomes for expatriate parents with present and absent children

	Children present			Children absent				
	N	Mean	SD	N	Mean	SD	d_c	90% CI
Adjustment	51	7.22	1.54	44	6.73	1.55	.35	-.02, .73
Stay intentions	47	4.87	1.68	42	4.55	1.65	.20	-.16, .55
Job performance	50	7.78	0.92	50	7.57	1.39	.19	-.16, .54
							.25	*-.21, .71*

Note: d values corrected for unreliability in the criterion, 90% CI = 90% confidence interval. For job performance, value on first row corrected for performance composite interrater reliability (estimated r_{yy} = .89). Value in italics on second row corrected for meta-analytic mean performance measure interrater reliability (r_{yy} = .52; Viswesvaran et al. 1996)

Table 5: Impact of poor spouse adjustment on expatriate outcomes

	Poorly adjusted			Not poorly adjusted[a]				
	N	Mean	SD	N	Mean	SD	d_c	90% CI
Adjustment	58	6.74	1.44	97	7.26	1.51	-.48	-.86, -.18
Stay intentions	50	4.92	1.77	81	5.07	1.77	-.11	-.47, .27
Job performance	57	7.91	0.83	96	7.77	1.07	.18	-.18, .54
							.24	*-.23, .71*

Note: d values corrected for unreliability in both variables, 90% CI = 90% confidence interval. For job performance, value on first row corrected for performance composite interrater reliability (estimated r_{yy} = 89). Value in italics on second row corrected for meta-analytic mean performance measure interrater reliability (r_{yy} = .52; Viswesvaran et al. 1996), [a] includes both well-adjusted and absent spouses.

Table 6: Impact of poor children adjustment on expatriate outcomes

	Poorly adjusted			Not poorly adjusted[a]				
	N	Mean	SD	N	Mean	SD	d_c	90% CI
Adjustment	50	6.59	1.36	53	7.64	1.57	-.91	-1.33, -.48
Stay intentions	40	5.04	1.87	40	5.35	1.89	-.19	-.61, .24
Job performance	50	7.87	0.79	50	7.75	1.26	.14	-.26, .52
							.18	*-.34, .69*

Note: d values corrected for unreliability in the criterion, 90% CI = 90% confidence interval. For job performance, value on first row corrected for performance composite interrater reliability (estimated r_{yy} = .89). Value in italics on second row corrected for meta-analytic mean performance measure interrater reliability (r_{yy} = .52; Viswesvaran et al. 1996), [a] includes both well-adjusted and absent children.

Table 7: Impact of family social and emotional support expatriate outcomes

	High support			Low support				
	N	Mean	SD	N	Mean	SD	d_c	90% CI
Adjustment	183	7.06	1.47	85	7.20	1.31	-.15	-.49, .18
Stay intentions	162	4.85	1.63	78	4.51	1.88	.28	-.04, .60
Job performance	194	8.07	0.69	92	7.18	1.13	1.53	1.21, 1.85
							2.00	*1.58, 2.42*

Note: d values corrected for unreliability in the criterion, 90% CI = 90% confidence interval. For job performance, value on first row corrected for performance composite interrater reliability (estimated r_{yy} = .89). Value in italics on second row corrected for meta-analytic mean performance measure interrater reliability (r_{yy} = .52; Viswesvaran et al. 1996)

Family social/emotional support. The host country nationals also rated the degree of social and emotional support they perceived their expatriate colleague's family as providing to the expatriate on a 10-point scale. We estimated the interrater reliability for these ratings to be $r_{yy} = .52$ (cf. Viswesvaran et al. 1996, 2014).

2.3   Analyses

We first compared adjustment, stay intentions, and performance for married and single expatriates using standardized mean differences (Cohen's d). Adjustment and stay intentions were corrected for unreliability using coefficient alpha; performance was corrected using interrater reliability. We then compared outcomes for married expatriates whose spouses were present versus absent and similarly for expatriate parents whose children were present versus absent. Next, we examined the negative impact of poorly adjusted spouses on expatriate outcomes by comparing expatriates who rated their spouses' adjustment as poor with a combined group of expatriates rating their spouses as well-adjusted and expatriates whose spouses were absent. We estimated "high" and "low" adjustment groups using a median split of the single-item adjustment rating. Reliability for spouse adjustment for these analyses was computed as a weighted average of .58 for present spouses (see above) and 1.0 for absent spouses. We then made similar comparisons and corrections for expatriate children adjustment. Finally, we compared expatriates with high HCN-rated family support to those with low HCN-rated family support, correcting family support for interrater reliability (again, we identified high and low support groups using a median split). We interpreted magnitudes of group differences in relation to findings from the management literature, using the quartiles for corrected effect sizes reported by Paterson et al. (2016), converted to d values - $d_c < .30$ as negligible/slight, .30–.51 as small, .52–.86 as moderate, and $\geq .87$ as large.

3   Results

Married and single expatriates showed slight differences on all criteria, as did married expatriates whose spouses were present versus absent (all $|d_c| \leq .15$). Expatriates whose children were present showed somewhat better outcomes than expatriates whose children did not accompany them on the overseas assignment, with magnitudes ranging from slight (job performance, $d_c = .19$; stay intentions, $d_c = .20$) to small (adjustment, $d_c = .35$). These results suggest that marital status and family presence have generally modest impacts on expatriate outcomes. These findings are heartening considering the wide diversity of family structures exhibited by contemporary expatriates (BGRS 2012). It must be noted that sample sizes for expatriates whose families did not accompany them are relatively small, leading to wide confidence intervals, so these findings should be regarded as suggestive and tentative.

In contrast to the generally small effects for family presence, poor family adjustment had a more substantial impact on expatriate employee adjustment. Compared to expatriates with absent or well-adjusted families, expatriates with poorly adjusted families showed weakly ($d_c = -.48$ for spouses) to strongly ($d_c = -.91$ for children) lower adjustment. We note the somewhat stronger influence of children's adjustment on expatriate adjustment than spouses' adjustment. Differences between expatriates with poorly-adjusted families and other groups were smaller for stay intentions and performance (with wide confidence intervals). Finally, family support as rated by host country national raters was negligibly to slightly related to expatriate adjustment (d_c = -.15) and stay intentions (d_c = .28), but very strongly related to job performance (d_c = 1.53).

4   Discussion

This study examined the potential impact of expatriate spouses and children on three critical employee criteria: locational adjustment, stay intentions, and job performance. We found that family presence had a minor impact on success, with separation of expatriate parents from their children having a stronger (but still modest) impact. We observed larger relations when we considered not only whether expatriates' families were *present*, but also whether they exhibited behaviors likely to function as burdens or resources for expatriate employees. We found evidence showing that poor family adjustment was a substantial burden on expatriate employee adjustment. Conversely, we found that family emotional and social support functioned as a resource for expatriates, contributing to stronger intentions to stay and, especially, much stronger job performance.

This pattern of findings suggests that research on expatriate families should avoid overgeneralizing family presence as universally a positive or negative influence on expatriate employees, but instead must consider the unique situation of each expatriate family and whether specific family structures, characteristics, and experiences are likely to enhance or hinder expatriate success outcomes. Our findings are generally in line with meta-analytic estimates of family impacts on expatriate adjustment (Bhaskar-Shrinivas et al. 2005; Hechanova et al. 2003), and we echo calls for more nuanced consideration of how family dynamics function in the context of international assignments (Kraimer et al. 2001; Lazarova et al. 2010).

Our data have several limitations that should be considered when interpreting our findings. First, unfortunately, family adjustment and support could only be assessed by single dichotomized items. These measures are likely associated with loss of statistical information, low reliability, and incomplete construct coverage (Hunter/Schmidt 1990). These factors are likely to have attenuated observed relations, as well as increased the sampling error in our results. Second, design features may have contributed to overestimates of some relations. The largest relation we observed was between expatriate job performance and family support. Both variables were rated by the same host country national at the same time point, so it is likely that this relation was inflated somewhat due to common method variance (Conway/Lance 2010). For example, halo may have influenced both HCNs' job performance and support ratings. HCNs may also have inferred expatriates' degree of family support from their perceived performance levels, relying on implicit theories of the role of support in expatriate success to make ratings. Similarly, expatriate adjustment also showed substantial relations with expatriate-rated spouse and children adjustment. It is possible that expatriates considered the same events (e.g., a negative shopping experience with one's spouse) when rating both their own and their family's adjustment; this effect may also have inflated relations due to common method variance. These caveats in mind, we again note that our findings are in line with previous studies of family influences on expatriates (Bhaskar-Shrinivas et al. 2005), suggesting that these potential positive and negative biasing effects may have cancelled out to some degree.

Our research is also characterized by some important strengths relative to many other studies in expatriate research. First, the expatriates sampled were *not* predominantly from the United States, but reflected a diverse cross-section of employees coming from many different countries. Second, we used a multifaceted job performance measure completed by a rater other than the expatriates themselves – this is a substantial improvement over the self-rated, unidimensional measures typically used in expatriate research. Using host country national performance evaluations also reflects an important step toward more deeply incorporating host country perspectives in expatriate research. Overall, this study suggests that the expatriate family, particularly expatriate children, are an important locus of consideration for expatriate research and practice. We call on expatriate researchers to distinguish influence of expatriate children versus expatriate spousal variables in examining family-based variables.

References

Albrecht, Anne-Grit; Ones, Deniz S.; Sinangil, Handan Kepir (2018): Expatriate Management. In: Ones, Deniz S. et al. (Eds.): The SAGE Handbook of Industrial, Work and Organizational Psychology. Volume 3: Managerial Psychology and Organizational Approaches. 2nd ed. London, United Kingdom: Sage: 429–468.

Andreason, Aaron W. (2008): Expatriate Adjustment of Spouses and Expatriate Managers: An Integrative Research View. In: *International Journal of Management* 25,2: 382–395. [https://search.proquest.com/docview/233229112].

BGRS (2016): Breakthrough to the Future of Global Talent Mobility: 2016 Global Mobility Trends Survey Report. Woodridge, IL: Brookfield Global Relocation Services. [http://globalmobilitytrends.brookfieldgrs.com].

BGRS (2012): Global Relocation Trends: 2012 Survey Report. Woodridge, IL: Brookfield Global Relocation Services. [http://globalmobilitytrends.brookfieldgrs.com].

Bhaskar-Shrinivas, Purnima et al. (2005): Input-Based and Time-Based Models of International Adjustment: Meta-Analytic Evidence and Theoretical Extensions. In: *Academy of Management Journal* 48,2: 257–281. [https://doi.org/10.5465/AMJ.2005.16928400].

Black, J. Stewart; Gregersen, Hal B. (1991): The Other Half of the Picture: Antecedents of Spouse Cross-Cultural Adjustment. In: *Journal of International Business Studies* 22,3: 461–477. [https://doi.org/10.1057/palgrave.jibs.8490311].

Black, J. Stewart; Mendenhall, Mark E.; Oddou, Gary R. (1991): Toward a Comprehensive Model of International Adjustment: An Integration of Multiple Theoretical Perspectives. In: *Academy of Management Review* 16,2: 291–317. [https://doi.org/10/fn7m8b].

Black, J. Stewart; Stephens, Gregory K. (1989): The Influence of the Spouse on American Expatriate Adjustment and Intent to Stay in Pacific Rim Overseas Assignments. In: *Journal of Management* 15,4: 529–544. [https://doi.org/10.1177/014920638901500403].

Brown, Robert J. (2008): Dominant Stressors on Expatriate Couples during International Assignments. In: *International Journal of Human Resource Management* 19,6: 1018–1034. [https://doi.org/10.1080/09585190802051303].

Caligiuri, Paula M. et al. (1998): Testing a Theoretical Model for Examining the Relationship between Family Adjustment and Expatriates' Work Adjustment. In: *Journal of Applied Psychology* 83,4: 598–614. [https://doi.org/10.1037/0021-9010.83.4.598].

Caligiuri, Paula M. (1997): Assessing Expatriate Success: Beyond Just "Being There." In: Aycan, Zeynep (Ed.): Expatriate Management: Theory and Research, New Approaches to Employee Management 4. Greenwich, CT: JAI Press: 117–140.

Caligiuri, Paula M.; Lazarova, Mila B. (2005): Expatriate Assignments and Work-Family Conflict. In: Poelmans, Steven A.Y. (Ed.): International Research in Work and Family. Mahwah, NJ: Erlbaum: 121–146.

Campbell, Charlotte H. et al. (1990): Development of Multiple Job Performance Measures in a Representative Sample of Jobs. In: *Personnel Psychology* 43,2: 277–300. [https://doi.org/10.1111/j.1744-6570.1990.tb01559.x].

Cole, Nina D. (2011): Managing Global Talent: Solving the Spousal Adjustment Problem. In: *International Journal of Human Resource Management* 22,7: 1504–1530. [https://doi.org/10.1080/09585192.2011.561963].

Conway, James M.; Lance, Charles E. (2010): What Reviewers Should Expect from Authors Regarding Common Method Bias in Organizational Research. In: *Journal of Business and Psychology* 25,3: 325–334. [https://doi.org/10.1007/s10869-010-9181-6].

Cui, Geng; Awa, Njoku E. (1992): Measuring Intercultural Effectiveness: An Integrative Approach. In: *International Journal of Intercultural Relations* 16,3: 311–328. [https://doi.org/10.1016/0147-1767(92)90055-Y].

Foldes, Hannah Jackson; Ones, Deniz S.; Sinangil, Handan Kepir (2006): Neither Here nor There: Impression Management Does Not Predict Expatriate Adjustment and Job Performance. In: *Psychology Science* 48,3: 357–368. [http://www.pabst-publishers.de/psychology-science/3-2006/ps_3_2006_357-368.pdf].

Guthridge, Matthew; Komm, Asmus B. (2008): Why Multinationals Struggle to Manage Talent. In: *The McKinsey Quarterly* 4: 1–5.

Haslberger, Arno; Brewster, Chris (2008): The Expatriate Family: An International Perspective. In: *Journal of Managerial Psychology* 23,3: 324–346. [https://doi.org/10/dwb3vt].

Hechanova, Regina; Beehr, Terry A.; Christiansen, Neil D. (2003): Antecedents and Consequences of Employees' Adjustment to Overseas Assignment: A Meta-Analytic Review. In: *Applied Psychology* 52,2: 213–236. [https://doi.org/10/d4f4xv].

Hough, Leaetta M.; Dunnette, Marvin D. (1992): US Managers Abroad: What It Takes to Succeed. Presented at the Academy of Management Conference. Las Vegas, NV.

Hunter, John E.; Schmidt, Frank L. (1990): Dichotomization of Continuous Variables: The Implications for Meta-Analysis. In: *Journal of Applied Psychology* 75,3: 334–349. [https://doi.org/10.1037/0021-9010.75.3.334].

Jackson, Hannah L.; Ones, Deniz S.; Sinangil, Handan Kepir (2003): Gender Differences in Overseas Adjustment: Do Women Exptriates Measure Up? In: Avallone, Francesco; Sinangil, Handan Kepir; Caetano, Antoni (Eds.): Identity and Diversity in Organizations. Milan, Spain: Guerini Studio: 185–191.

Kraimer, Maria L.; Wayne, Sandy J.; Jaworski, Ren Ata A. (2001): Sources of Support and Expatriate Performance: The Mediating Role of Expatriate Adjustment. In: *Personnel Psychology* 54,1: 71–99. [https://doi.org/10.1111/j.1744-6570.2001.tb00086.x].

Lazarova, Mila B.; Westman, Mina; Shaffer, Margaret A. (2010): Elucidating the Positive Side of the Work-Family Interface on International Assigments: A Model of Expatriate Work and Family Performance. In: *Academy of Management Review* 35,1: 93–117. [https://doi.org/10.1057/9781137006004_14].

Mohr, Alex T.; Klein, Simone (2008): Adjustment vs. Satisfaction: An Analysis of American Expatriate Spouses in Germany. In: Holtbrügge, Dirk (Ed.): Cultural Adjustment of Expatriates: Theoretical Concepts and Empirical Studies. München, Germany: Rainer Hampp: 49–59.

Mol, Stefan T.; Born, Marise Ph.; van der Molen, Henk T. (2005): Developing Criteria for Expatriate Effectiveness: Time to Jump off the Adjustment Bandwagon. In: *International Journal of Intercultural Relations* 29,3: 339–353. [https://doi.org/10/dk2vzk].

Ones, Deniz S.; Sinangil, Handan Kepir; Wiernik, Brenton M. (2018): Validity of Big Five Personality Traits for Expatriate Success: Results from Turkey. In: Wiernik, Brenton M.; Rüger, Heiko; Ones, Deniz S. (Eds.): Managing Expatriates: Success Factors in Private and Public Domains, Series on Population Studies 50. Opladen, Germany: Barbara Budrich Publishers.

Paterson, Ted A. et al. (2016): An Assessment of the Magnitude of Effect Sizes: Evidence from 30 Years of Meta-Analysis in Management. In: *Journal of Leadership & Organizational Studies* 23,1: 66–81. [https://doi.org/10/bjz9].

Pellico, Mary T.; Stroh, Linda K. (1997): Spousal Assistance Programs: An Integral Component of the International Assignment. In: Aycan, Zeynep (Ed.): Expatriate Management: Theory and Research, New Approaches to Employee Management 4. Greenwich, CT: JAI Press: 227–244.

Schütter, Heike; Boerner, Sabine (2013): Illuminating the Work-family Interface on International Assignments: An Exploratory Approach. In: *Journal of Global Mobility* 1,1: 46–71. [https://doi.org/10.1108/JGM-09-2012-0012].

Shaffer, Margaret A. et al. (2001): Struggling for Balance Ammid Turbulence on International Assignments: Work-Family Conflict, Support and Commitment. In: *Journal of Management* 27,1: 99–121. [https://doi.org/10.1177/014920630102700106].

Shaffer, Margaret A.; Harrison, David A. (2001): Forgotten Partners of International Assignments: Development and Test of a Model of Spouse Adjustment. In: *Journal of Applied Psychology* 86,2: 238–254. [https://doi.org/10.1037/0021-9010.86.2.238].

Sinangil, Handan Kepir; Ones, Deniz S. (2003): Gender Differences in Expatriate Job Performance. In: *Applied Psychology* 52,3: 461–475. [https://doi.org/10/c36tw5].

Sinangil, Handan Kepir; Ones, Deniz S. (1997): Empirical Investigations of the Host Country Perspective in Expatriate Management. In: Aycan, Zeynep (Ed.): Expatriate Management: Theory and Research, New Approaches to Employee Management 4. Greenwich, CT: JAI Press: 173–205.

Stahl, Günter K.; Miller, Edwin L.; Tung, Rosalie L. (2002): Toward the Boundaryless Career: A Closer Look at the Expatriate Career Concept and the Perceived Implications of an International Assignment. In: *Journal of World Business* 37,3: 216–227. [https://doi.org/10/ddttgr].

Takeuchi, Riki; Yun, Seokhwa; Tesluk, Paul E. (2002): An Examination of Crossover and Spillover Effects of Spousal and Expatriate Cross-Cultural Adjustment on Expatriate Outcomes. In: *Journal of Applied Psychology* 87,4: 655–666. [https://doi.org/10/d2ddkj].

Templer, Klaus J. (2010): Personal Attributes of Expatriate Managers, Subordinate Ethnocentrism, and Expatriate Success: A Host-Country Perspective. In: *International Journal of Human Resource Management* 21,10: 1754–1768. [https://doi.org/10.1080/09585192.2010.500493].

Vance, Charles M. (2005): The Personal Quest for Building Global Competence: A Taxonomy of Self-Initiating Career Path Strategies for Gaining Business Experience Abroad. In: *Journal of World Business, Global Careers* 40,4: 374–385. [https://doi.org/10.1016/j.jwb.2005.08.005].

Viswesvaran, Chockalingam et al. (2014): Measurement Error Obfuscates Scientific Knowledge: Path to Cumulative Knowledge Requires Corrections for Unreliability and Psychometric Meta-Analyses. In: *Industrial and Organizational Psychology* 7,4: 507–518. [https://doi.org/10/5k5].

Viswesvaran, Chockalingam (1993): Modeling Job Performance: Is There a General Factor? Doctoral Dissertation. Iowa City, IA: The University of Iowa. [http://www.dtic.mil/dtic/tr/fulltext/u2/a294282.pdf].

Viswesvaran, Chockalingam; Ones, Deniz S.; Schmidt, Frank L. (1996): Comparative Analysis of the Reliability of Job Performance Ratings. In: *Journal of Applied Psychology* 81,5: 557–574. [https://doi.org/10/c8f68f].

Viswesvaran, Chockalingam; Schmidt, Frank L.; Ones, Deniz S. (2005): Is There a General Factor in Job Performance Ratings? A Meta-Analytic Framework for Disentangling Substantive and Error Influences. In: *Journal of Applied Psychology* 90,1: 108–131. [https://doi.org/10.1037/0021-9010.90.1.108].

Wanous, John P.; Hudy, Michael J. (2001): Single-Item Reliability: A Replication and Extension. In: *Organizational Research Methods* 4,4: 361–375. [https://doi.org/10.1177/109442810144003].

Wiernik, Brenton M.; Rüger, Heiko; Ones, Deniz S. (2018): Advancing Expatriate Research in Public and Private Sectors. In: Wiernik, Brenton M.; Rüger, Heiko; Ones, Deniz S. (Eds.): Managing Expatriates: Success Factors in Private and Public Domains, Series on Population Studies 50. Opladen, Germany: Barbara Budrich Publishers.

Wilmot, Michael P.; Wiernik, Brenton M.; Kostal, Jack W. (2014): Increasing Interrater Reliability Using Composite Performance Measures. In: *Industrial and Organizational Psychology* 7,4: 539–542. [https://doi.org/10/38v].

Influence of Family Presence on Expatriate Outcomes

Brittany K. Mercado, Anne-Grit Albrecht, Frieder M. Paulus, Stephan Dilchert, Deniz S. Ones, and Jürgen Deller

Abstract

The role of expatriate families in the success or failure of international assignments is often overlooked. Organizations often consider employees' family status when making expatriate selection decisions, and as expatriates prepare for their travels, they must make important decisions about whether their partners and children will accompany them. In this chapter, we examine the impact of partner and children presence on expatriate outcomes. We find that family presence is generally beneficial, but note some important contexts where family may interfere with expatriate acculturation. We highlight implications for practice and areas for future study.

1 Introduction

Globalization has forced organizations to become internationally competitive by deploying prosperous strategies cross-culturally and harvesting innovation from many different sources. This heavy reliance on a multinational perspective has led many organizations to integrate international assignments into their development plans for employees with promising careers. If these employees are to be prepared for executive positions requiring immense international expertise, multinational organizations must provide opportunities for such knowledge acquisition. This continued focus on international assignments has created a mass of expatriate employees, raising the importance of managing employee expatriation and adjustment. Many critical predictors of expatriate success have received extensive scholarly attention, but the influence of family presence on the expatriate's experience is often overlooked. Expatriates often must make hard choices about moving their families with them on international assignments; with the rising rates of expatriation in contemporary organizations, understanding the consequences of family-related expatriate decisions is paramount. In the present study, we examine the influence of partner and children's presence on expatriate outcomes, including job and life satisfaction, as well as cross-cultural adjustment. Our findings, which rely on a large-scale sample of expatriates in 29 countries, provide important insights into the role that family accompaniment plays in expatriate success.

1.1 Expatriate Adjustment

Black et al. (1991) introduced a multifaceted conceptualization of expatriate adjustment that reflected three ways in which expatriates adapt to their environments. The first component is locational adjustment (called general/cultural adjustment by Black et al.), which consists of growing comfortable with nonwork general living conditions, such as local food, transportation, and healthcare, among other daily needs. Second, expatriates experience interaction adjustment, which consists of developing communication and socialization patterns that facilitate interactions with host country nationals. Finally, work adjustment consists of adjusting to the new work environment within the host country and the new job responsibilities that are often part of international assignments. Through each of these adaptation experiences, expatriates learn how to reduce their uncertainty in their new environments. Adjustment is an iterative process during which the expatriate's behavioral patterns become increasingly compatible with the norms of the host country (Mohr/Klein 2008). As expatriates adjust, they become more integrated into the daily life in their host location, and the difficulty associated with everyday tasks diminishes (Lauring/Selmer 2015).

Beyond enhancing expatriates' feelings of comfort and normalcy in their new environments, adjustment also relates to critically important outcomes of interest to expatriates' employers. Extensive evidence indicates that work adjustment and interaction adjustment are moderately to strongly positively related to job satisfaction (Bhaskar-Shrinivas et al. 2005; Shaffer/Harrison 1998), and cultural adjustment predicts nonwork satisfaction (Shaffer/ Harrison 1998). Perhaps of most interest to employing organizations, all forms of adjustment have demonstrated notable relationships with withdrawal cognitions (i.e., expatriates' intentions to return early from assignment) and technical, interpersonal, and overall job performance (Bhaskar-Shrinivas et al. 2005). Because expatriate adjustment is critical to a positive experience for both expatriates and their employers, a deeper understanding of the influence of family presence on adjustment, as well as other expatriate outcomes, motivated the present study.

1.2   Role of Family in Expatriation

Takeuchi (2010) argued that expatriates have three primary groups of stakeholders who greatly influence and are influenced by the expatriation experience: family members, parent company members, and host country nationals. According to a large-scale survey of top employers of international assignees, 60% of international assignees are married, 81% were accompanied by a spouse or partner, and 43% are accompanied by children (Brookfield GRS 2012). The report also found that expatriates reported that their greatest challenges are due to spouse/partner resistance, family adjustment, and children's educational needs, but that only 29% of companies assessed family suitability pre-assignment. Spouses and family members are a critical component of the expatriation process, and their roles in and influence on expatriate employees' experiences must be considered at each stage of the process.

The family plays a major role in every stage of the expatriation process, beginning with the decisions whether, when, and how to expatriate. Richardson (2006) found that some employees expect that children would be a burden during an international assignment and so consider expatriation without children to be optimal. However, Richardson found that other employees perceive that the expatriation process would provide a meaningful, developmental experience for the entire family. Employees must balance each family member's needs (e.g., the spouse's career progress, children's education, social contacts) when making their decision to move abroad. Even family members outside the immediate household often counsel and influence expatriates during their decision-making phase. Beyond the initial decisions whether and when to accept international assignments, family variables can also influence how expatriates go abroad. Expatriates might choose to be unaccompanied by some or all of their family members for a variety of reasons. For example, during periods of economic instability, some spouses may choose not to accompany expatriates abroad out of concern about the loss of the second income in their households (Brookfield GRS 2012). This concern is not unfounded, as although half of expatriates' spouses report being employed before assignment, only 12% are also employed during their tenure abroad.

When spouses and partners do move abroad with the expatriate employee, they also experience cross-cultural adjustment. Researchers have argued that this adjustment process differs from expatriate employees' adjustment in both nature and degree. In addition to the general and interaction components of adjustment that are part of expatriate employees' adjustment process, another spouse-specific role adjustment dimension has been proposed (Mohr/Klein 2008). Role adjustment refers to adaptation to a change in family and life roles that many spouses experience when they accompany expatriate employees on international assignments. Many spouses leave jobs and careers in their home countries to become stay-at-home parents or partners in a host country, particularly if they lack language skills or have insufficient social and organizational support to pursue local employment. This shift from active to more passive life roles profoundly affects their cross-cultural adjustment (Cole 2011). This shift also disturbs the household balance with the expatriate becoming a sole earner and the partner a caretaker (Lazarova et al. 2010). Mohr and Klein (2008) argue that even those who do not change their family role (i.e., those who are stay-at-home parents in both home and host country) still experience substantial role shifts, since their roles and their partners' participation in home life are likely to change. In some cases, the tasks within their roles change (e.g., when certain tasks are gendered in the host country), and in most cases, the tasks they carry out (e.g., childcare, shopping) require cross-cultural adjustment. Because expatriate spouses experience so many changes in their life roles and because they do not typically have the infrastructure of support employees do, spouse adjustment can be more difficult than expatriate adjustment (Andreason 2008). In fact, spouses experience many stressors more intensely than employees, including both local pressures and isolation (Brown 2008). Poor spousal adjustment can be a substantial burden on expatriate employees' own adjustment, as well as satisfaction, performance, intentions to remain on the international assignment, and other outcomes (Bhaskar-Shrinivas et al. 2005; Black/Stephens 1989; Shaffer/Harrison 2001; Takeuchi et al. 2002). Beyond spousal adjustment, expatriate children's adjustment also often poses a significant challenge for international employees, and the demands children place on parents can be particularly stressful during international transitions (Caligiuri/Lazarova 2005; Haslberger/Brewster 2008).

Whereas partners and children may potentially be a burden on expatriate employees, the presence of family can positively influence expatriates as well. For example, family can help expatriates by providing emotion-based coping and support in times of stress (Schütter/ Boerner 2013). Family members can also help instrumentally when they are more knowledgeable in the local language or culture. Pleasant family adjustment experiences can be beneficial and encouraging to the expatriate, just as much as poor adjustment can be a burden. In addition, while children can create stressful demands for expatriates (e.g., needs to accompany them to recreation, enroll them in schools, support extracurricular programs), these demands can also be sources of adjustment opportunity. Caring for children can have a developmental effect for parents by forcing them to engage with their new environment through interacting with children's teachers, taking children on errands, and helping them to build friend networks (Brown 2008; Mohr/Klein 2008). These demands increase the interactions parents have with the local culture, host country nationals, and, often, a wider established expatriate community. Interactions with host country nationals and the development of a local social support system are crucial predictors of spouse adjustment and expatriate employee outcomes (Black/Gregersen 1991; Copeland/Norell 2002).

Several studies have investigated the positive and negative effects of family responsibilities on expatriates. Shaffer and Harrison (1998) empirically examined the effects of family responsibilities on expatriate job satisfaction. They posited that expatriates with greater family responsibilities, including having a spouse and more children, may be more stressed due to the well-established relationship between work–family conflict and family responsibilities. They found a negative relation between family responsibility and expatriate job satisfaction; however, expatriates benefited both in terms of job satisfaction and adjustment if their spouse had a positive adjustment experience. Later, other scholars examined the presence of spouse and children in terms of psychological strain on expatriates (Takeuchi et al. 2005). They found that spouse *absence* and child *presence* both led to psychological strain, with the greatest strain experienced when both occurred (i.e., unaccompanied parenting). However, they also observed a nonlinear relationship between strain and performance, such that medium strain was optimal for expatriate employees' performance. As exemplified by these studies, scholars have only begun to examine the influence of family presence on expatriation. These studies suggest that family presence strongly influences important expatriate outcomes and therefore merits further study.

1.3   The Present Study

Just as family members create demands on employees, they also provide resources to buffer the inherently stressful process of expatriation. They reduce isolation and provide emotional and instrumental support. Expatriates report feeling relief and rejuvenation as their children embrace a new culture; experiencing gratitude as their spouses help with a difficult language; and generally appreciating the opportunity to focus on work tasks as their family members are nearby attending to nonwork demands (Schütter/Boerner 2013). Expatriates, and to some extent their sponsoring organizations, often must decide if they would like to be accompanied by family members. This influences their decisions whether or when to accept the international assignment. It could also influence the career outcomes of their spouses in addition to myriad variables for the entire family. Because family has been viewed as a source of both demands and resources for expatriate employees, we examine the effect of spouse and children presence on expatriate outcomes, specifically job and life satisfaction as well as cross-cultural adjustment in a large-scale study examining international assignees working in many host countries. Our findings offer insights into the effects of family presence on expatriates in addition to demonstrating the variance of those effects across host contexts, holding expatriate home country culture constant.

2   Methods

Data were collected between 2005 and 2010 using a standardized interview procedure as part of a larger intercontextual research endeavor, the International Generalizability of Expatriate Success (iGOES) study (see Wiernik et al., 2018, Chapter 1 of this volume).

2.1   Sample and Procedure

Both waves of the iGOES data collection were used in the current analyses. Participants were 2,096 German, German-speaking Swiss, and Austrian expatriates working abroad in

28 different countries (Argentina, Austria, China, Costa Rica, Czech Republic, Denmark, Egypt, Finland, France, Ghana, India, Ireland, Italy, Malaysia, Mexico, Morocco, Poland, Russia, Singapore, South Korea, Spain, Sweden, Switzerland, Thailand, the Netherlands, Turkey, United Kingdom, and the United States) representing all cultural clusters as defined by Project GLOBE. Expatriates were identified through membership lists of the German Chambers of Commerce in each country. Additional participants were recruited via corporate headquarters referrals, an internet platform for professional contacts (XING; www.xing.com) which lists individuals by country of employment, and recommendations from expatriates who had already participated. On average, participants were 36.8 years of age ($SD = 8.9$). They were predominantly male (68%) and highly educated ($M = 17.4$ years of formal education, $SD = 2.5$). Most reported being married or partnered (67.9%). The expatriates had spent an average of 33.6 months in their host country ($SD = 32.3$) and had a mean organizational tenure of 6.5 years ($SD = 7.0$).

2.2 Measures

Family variables. During the standardized interviews, intensively trained research assistants collected self-reported demographic and biographical information. The interviewers recorded expatriates' self-reported relationship status (i.e., whether they were married/ partnered or single), family status (i.e., whether they had non-adult children), as well as if they were accompanied by a spouse/partner and/or children. Henceforth, we refer to partners as the more inclusive term, including spouses and partners.

Job satisfaction. Global job satisfaction was assessed using an abbreviated, five-item version of the Brayfield and Rothe (1951) scale contained in Judge et al. (1998). Sample items include, "I feel fairly satisfied with my present job" and "Each day at work seems like it will never end" (reverse scored). Participants were asked to rate their agreement on a 5-point scale. Average internal consistency reliability was .81.

Life satisfaction. Life satisfaction was assessed using the short version of the Satisfaction with Life Scale (Diener et al. 1985). This abbreviated measure consists of four items such as "In most ways my life is close to ideal" or "The conditions of my life are excellent". Expatriates were again asked to rate their agreement with the statements. Average internal consistency reliability was .77.

Adjustment. Adjustment was measured using two self-report scales. In Wave 1 (8 samples in the current analyses from Argentina, China, Egypt, Italy, the Netherlands, Russia, South Korea, and the United States), Albrecht's (2005) 3-item scale was used to assess overall adjustment. Average internal consistency was .63. In Wave 2 (22 samples in the current analyses from Austria, Costa Rica, Czech Republic, Denmark, Finland, France, Ghana, India, Ireland, Italy, Malaysia, Mexico, Morocco, the Netherlands, Poland, Singapore, Spain, Sweden, Switzerland, Thailand, Turkey, and the United Kingdom), we administered Black and Stephens' (1989) 14-item scale, which assesses locational adjustment[1], interaction adjustment, and work adjustment. Participants rated their adjustment to local living conditions (e.g., food, housing, safety, health care), socialization with host country nationals, and specific job responsibilities to assess each dimension, respectively. Average internal consistencies were .68, .82, and .71, respectively.

---

[1] We use the term "locational adjustment" to refer to expatriates' adaptation to completing everyday tasks in their new location, rather than the more widely-used term "general adjustment", as the former more clearly describes the meaning of the construct and avoids confusion of "general adjustment" with the statistical general factor or composite measures of "overall adjustment".

2.3   Analyses

To test the influence of partner presence on expatriate outcomes, we compared expatriates accompanied by partners to those who were unaccompanied. The unaccompanied group included both single expatriates as well as expatriates whose partner was living in a different location, in line with previous research on the presence of family (Takeuchi et al. 2005). We also wanted to isolate the effect of single status from the stress of having a partner in another country, so we also compared these subgroups of unaccompanied expatriates. To test the influence of children presence, we first compared expatriates accompanied by their children to non-parent expatriates. We additionally compared each of these groups to expatriate parents whose children were living in another country.

For comparisons of expatriates accompanied by a partner versus not (including both single expatriates and expatriates with absent partners) and for comparisons of expatriates accompanied by their children with non-parents, we computed effect sizes separately within each sample and then combined them using psychometric meta-analysis (Schmidt/Hunter 2015). This approach allows us to statistically test international generalizability of relations and to control for country mean differences on adjustment and satisfaction outcomes (Ones et al. 2012). Many within-country sample sizes for expatriates with absent partners or children were too small for cross-cultural meta-analyses, so comparisons with these groups were conducted using a pooled sample across countries.

We compared group means using standardized mean differences (Cohen's d). For meta-analyses, we weighted each d value by its inverse sampling error variance; we computed sampling error variance for each sample assuming a constant δ and accounting for unequal group sizes (Schmidt/Hunter 2015). We corrected d values for unreliability in each criterion using artifact distributions from the current sample. We compared group variabilities using standard deviation ratios (u values). We meta-analyzed u values using the method by Hedges and Friedman (1993). Meta-analyses were performed using the log-transformed variance ratios (i.e., ln $[u^2]$), weighted by their inverse variance. The mean and residual standard deviation of the meta-analytic distribution of u values were estimated using the method of numerical integration described by Steel (2013).

3   Results

3.1   Partner Presence

Comparisons of cross-cultural adjustment between accompanied and unaccompanied expatriates showed large variability across samples (see Table 1). However, much of this variability was accounted for by sampling error and unreliability. After removing these artifacts, across samples, expatriates accompanied by their partners showed somewhat better overall adjustment ($\delta = .28$), particularly adjustment to their new living conditions ($\delta = .29$) and new job duties ($\delta = .19$). Differences on interaction adjustment showed a negligible mean effect, but were highly variable ($\delta = .09$, $SD_\delta = .28$). Examining the pattern of differences across countries, we found that positive d values were typically observed in European countries (e.g., Sweden, $d = .88$; Spain, $d = .32$; Ireland, $d = .30$; France, $d = .30$), while negative d values were observed mostly in countries more geographically- and culturally-distant to the German-speaking expatriates in our sample (e.g., Mexico, $d = -.52$; Thailand, $d = -.39$; Turkey,

d = -.37). This may reflect that when an expatriate's spouse is available, they may tend to spend less effort reaching out to host country nationals and trying to expand their social circle. Job satisfaction showed a similarly weak difference between accompanied and unaccompanied expatriates on average, but with large variability (δ = .09, SD_δ = .28). Examining the individual country correlations, we could identify no clear pattern indicating a specific moderator of these differences. Life satisfaction showed a homogeneous moderate difference favoring accompanied expatriates (δ = .43). Accompanied expatriates were also less variable on life satisfaction than unaccompanied expatriates (u = .83). Overall, having an accompanying partner appears to be a net positive influence for expatriates. While a partner may interfere with cultural immersion and job satisfaction in some circumstances, in general, having their partner abroad with them will facilitate expatriates' adjustment and satisfaction.

Comparisons of accompanied expatriates to single expatriates and those with absent partners separately revealed similar patterns of difference for these two groups (see Table 2). Expatriates with absent partners generally showed poorer interaction adjustment than single expatriates, but showed stronger life satisfaction.

3.2 Children Presence

As was the case for partner presence, adjustment differences between expatriates accompanied by their children and non-parent expatriates also showed large variability across samples (see Table 3). However, unlike partner presence, for children presence, this variability remained substantial after removing statistical artefacts (e.g., for overall adjustment, δ = .30, SD_δ = .28). On average, expatriates accompanied by their children showed moderately better overall (δ = .30), locational (δ = .25), and work (δ = .27) adjustment than non-parent expatriates. Like with spouse presence, interaction adjustment showed a negligible average difference between accompanied parents and non-parent expatriates (δ = .05). Examining individual country differences, the large variability in adjustment appeared to stem from a small number of very large positive and negative d values compared to the other samples (e.g., overall adjustment d = 1.35 for Austria, 1.24 for France, -.51 for Ghana, and -.36 for Finland). Trimming the two largest and small values (8% trim) from the meta-analytic sample negligibly impacted the mean difference (δ_{trim} = .33), but reduced the residual variability to $SD_{\delta \cdot trim}$ = .00. Similar results were obtained by trimming the single largest and smallest d values (6% trim) for locational adjustment (δ_{trim} = .31, $SD_{\delta \cdot trim}$ = .00) and work adjustment (δ_{trim} = .27, $SD_{\delta \cdot trim}$ = .00). Thus, it appears that the large residual variability for adjustment likely stems from second-order sampling error.

We examined the pattern of differences for interaction adjustment across countries and found a similar pattern as for spouse presence.[2] Positive d values were typically observed in European countries (e.g., France, d = .93; Austria, d = .63; Ireland, d = .31; Spain, d = .20), while negative d values were observed mostly in countries more geographically- and culturally-distant to the German-speaking expatriates in our sample (e.g., Mexico, d = -.55; Thailand, d = -.39; Turkey, d = -.29). Thus, having one's children present may have a similar insulating effect as spouse presence that interferes with expatriates' tendencies to immerse themselves in the local culture and interact with host country nationals.

---

[2]   Trimmed interaction adjustment results still showed substantial variability (δ_{trim} = -.09, $SD_{\delta \, trim}$ = .18).

Table 1: Comparisons between expatriates accompanied by a partner versus unaccompanied (single and partner absent) expatriates

Measure	k	N_{Acc}	N_{Unacc}	d_{obs}	SD_{obs}	δ	SD_δ	90% CI_δ		80% CV_δ	
Overall adjustment	30	1,194	916	.21	.24	**.28**	.00	.19	.38	.28	.28
Locational adjustment	22	811	621	.23	.27	**.29**	.11	.17	.41	.15	.42
Interaction adjustment	22	811	635	.09	.36	**.09**	.28	-.05	.23	-.26	.45
Work adjustment	22	805	633	.15	.27	**.18**	.09	.07	.30	.07	.30
Job satisfaction	20	669	484	.07	.36	**.08**	.25	-.06	.23	-.24	.41
Life satisfaction	16	529	393	.39	.24	**.43**	.00	.32	.55	.43	.43
Measure	k	N_{Acc}	N_{NonP}	VR	u	$SD_{obs.u}$	$SD_{res.u}$	90% CI_u		80% CV_u	
Overall adjustment	30	1,194	916	.95	**.98**	.13	.00	.94	1.02	.98	.98
Locational adjustment	22	811	621	.98	**.98**	.23	.12	.90	1.05	.83	1.14
Interaction adjustment	22	811	635	1.01	**.99**	.26	.18	.89	1.07	.78	1.22
Work adjustment	22	805	633	.92	**.95**	.21	.10	.88	1.02	.83	1.08
Job satisfaction	20	669	484	.98	**.98**	.26	.15	.88	1.06	.79	1.18
Life satisfaction	16	529	393	.70	**.83**	.21	.12	.74	.91	.69	.99

Note: N_{Acc} = total N accompanied by children, N_{NonP} = total N non-parent, d_{obs} = inverse variance weighted mean observed Cohen's d, SD_{obs} = inverse variance weighted observed standard deviation of d, δ = inverse variance weighted mean d corrected for criterion unreliability, SD_δ = residual true standard deviation of δ, 90% CI = 90% confidence interval, 80% CV = 80% credibility interval, VR = inverse variance weighted mean variance ratio, u = inverse variance weighted observed standard deviation ratio, $SD_{obs.u}$ = inverse variance weighted observed standard deviation of u, $SD_{res.u}$ = residual standard deviation of u, positive d values indicate that accompanied expatriates score higher, $u > 1$ indicated that accompanied expatriates are more variable.

Table 2: Comparisons between expatriates accompanied by a partner versus expatriates with absent partners and single expatriates

Measure	N_{Acc}	N_{Abs}	N_{Sing}	Accompanied vs. Partner Absent				Accompanied vs. Single			
				d	δ	90% CI_δ		d	δ	90% CI_δ	
Overall adjustment	1,197	106	914	.10	**.14**	-.07	.31	.08	**.11**	.01	.18
Locational adjustment	811	172	453	.15	**.19**	.02	.32	.23	**.29**	.15	.37
Interaction adjustment	811	172	452	.28	**.30**	.14	.43	.02	**.03**	-.08	.13
Work adjustment	805	171	452	.24	**.29**	.11	.42	.16	**.20**	.07	.29
Job satisfaction	669	134	354	.04	**.05**	-.12	.21	.10	**.11**	-.01	.22
Life satisfaction	532	108	297	.17	**.19**	.00	.36	.40	**.44**	.29	.55
Measure	N_{Acc}	N_{Abs}	N_{Sing}	VR	u	90% CI_u		VR	u	90% CI_u	
Overall adjustment	1,197	106	914	1.70	**1.31**	1.16	1.47	.86	**.93**	.88	.97
Locational adjustment	811	172	453	1.03	**1.02**	.92	1.12	.94	**.97**	.90	1.04
Interaction adjustment	811	172	452	1.17	**1.08**	.98	1.19	.93	**.96**	.90	1.03
Work adjustment	805	171	452	.74	**.86**	.78	.95	.94	**.97**	.90	1.04
Job satisfaction	669	134	354	1.09	**1.05**	.94	1.17	.92	**.96**	.89	1.03
Life satisfaction	532	108	297	.62	**.79**	.70	.89	.72	**.85**	.78	.92

Note: N_{Acc} = total N accompanied by partner, N_{Abs} = total N partnered, but partner absent, N_{Sing} = total N single, d = Cohen's d, δ = d corrected for criterion unreliability, 90% CI = 90% confidence interval, VR = variance ratio, u = observed standard deviation ratio, positive d values indicate that accompanied expatriates score higher, $VR > 1$ indicated that accompanied expatriates are more variable.

Table 3: Comparisons between expatriates accompanied by their children versus expatriate non-parents

Measure	k	N_{Acc}	N_{NonP}	d_{obs}	SD_{obs}	δ	SD_δ	90% CI_δ		80% CV_δ	
Overall adjustment	25	484	1,196	.23	.35	**.30**	.28	.15	.46	-.06	.66
Locational adjustment	18	328	704	.20	.41	**.25**	.34	.05	.45	-.19	.69
Interaction adjustment	17	325	684	-.05	.38	**-.05**	.26	-.22	.11	-.39	.28
Work adjustment	17	322	681	.22	.34	**.27**	.20	.10	.44	.01	.53
Job satisfaction	14	244	484	.31	.32	**.35**	.10	.19	.51	.22	.48
Life satisfaction	11	173	332	.21	.33	**.23**	.00	.05	.42	.23	.23

Measure	k	N_{Acc}	N_{NonP}	VR	u	$SD_{obs.u}$	$SD_{res.u}$	90% CI_u		80% CV_u	
Overall adjustment	25	484	1,196	.91	**.94**	.18	.00	.89	1.00	.94	.94
Locational adjustment	18	328	704	.93	**.94**	.30	.20	.82	1.04	.71	1.20
Interaction adjustment	17	325	684	.94	**.95**	.29	.19	.83	1.05	.72	1.20
Work adjustment	17	322	681	.77	**.88**	.20	.05	.80	.96	.81	.94
Job satisfaction	14	244	484	.57	**.75**	.17	.00	.68	.83	.75	.75
Life satisfaction	11	173	332	.65	**.81**	.15	.00	.74	.88	.81	.81

Note: N_{Acc} = total N accompanied by children, N_{NonP} = total N non-parent, dobs= inverse variance weighted mean observed Cohen's d, SD_{obs} = inverse variance weighted observed standard deviation of δ, δ = inverse variance weighted mean d corrected for criterion unreliability, SD_δ = residual true standard deviation of δ, 90% CI = 90% confidence interval, 80% CV = 80% credibility interval, VR = inverse variance weighted mean observed variance ratio, u = inverse variance weighted mean observed standard deviation ratio, $SD_{obs.u}$ = inverse variance weighted observed standard deviation of u, $SD_{res.u}$ = residual standard deviation of u, positive d values indicate that accompanied expatriates score higher, $u > 1$ indicated that accompanied expatriates are more variable.

Table 4: Comparisons between expatriates with absent children versus expatriates accompanied by children and non-parent expatriates

Measure	N_{Acc}	N_{Abs}	N_{NonP}	Children Absent vs. Accompanied				Children Absent vs. Non-Parents			
				d	δ	90% CI_δ		d	δ	90% CI_δ	
Overall adjustment	489	52	1,202	-.16	**-.21**	-.46	.10	-.07	**-.09**	-.35	.19
Locational adjustment	328	33	704	-.45	**-.55**	-.83	-.16	-.18	**-.23**	-.53	.12
Interaction adjustment	328	33	684	-.17	**-.19**	-.50	.13	-.21	**-.23**	-.53	.09
Work adjustment	325	33	681	-.21	**-.25**	-.56	.10	.05	**.06**	-.27	.38
Job satisfaction	247	24	484	-.19	**-.21**	-.57	.17	.18	**.21**	-.17	.56
Life satisfaction	176	7	332	-.51	**-.58**	-1.22	.13	-.15	**-.17**	-.83	.51
Measure	N_{Acc}	N_{Abs}	N_{NonP}	VR	u	90% CI_u		VR	u	90% CI_u	
Overall adjustment	489	52	1,202	.99	**.99**	.84	1.18	.99	**1.00**	.94	1.06
Locational adjustment	328	33	704	1.07	**1.03**	.83	1.28	.95	**.97**	.90	1.05
Interaction adjustment	328	33	684	.86	**.93**	.75	1.15	.84	**.92**	.85	.99
Work adjustment	325	33	681	1.22	**1.11**	.89	1.37	.93	**.96**	.89	1.04
Job satisfaction	247	24	484	1.42	**1.19**	.93	1.54	.75	**.86**	.79	.95
Life satisfaction	176	7	332	.78	**.88**	.55	1.43	.48	**.69**	.62	.77

Note: N_{Acc} = total N accompanied by partner, N_{Abs} = total N partnered, but partner absent, N_{Sing} = total N single, d = Cohen's d, δ = d corrected for criterion unreliability, 90% CI = 90% confidence interval, VR = observed variance ratio, u = observed standard deviation ratio, positive d values indicate that expatriates with absent children score higher, $u > 1$ indicated that expatriates with absent children are more variable.

In general, while children presence may negatively impact cultural immersion in some contexts, being accompanied by children appears to be a net benefit for expatriates' adjustment. Expatriates accompanied by children also showed weakly to moderately higher job and life satisfaction than non-parents, and these differences were relatively consistent across countries. Expatriates with present children were also somewhat more homogeneous than non-parents on job satisfaction, life satisfaction, and work adjustment.

Finally, we compared both non-parent expatriates and expatriates accompanied by their children to expatriate parents whose children were in a different country (see Table 4). Expatriate parents with absent children showed uniformly worse outcomes than parents with present children (δ ranged -.19 to -.58). Due to the small sample size for parents with absent children, confidence intervals were wide. However, the consistent negative trend across outcomes suggests that the deleterious impact of separating from one's family while on international assignment is an important area of inquiry for future expatriate research and practice. Expatriates with absent children showed inconsistent differences from non-parents, also with wide confidence intervals.

4 Discussion

Our findings demonstrate interesting patterns in expatriate outcomes based on family presence. Generally, expatriates who were accompanied by their partners fared better than those who were unaccompanied by their partners or single. Partner presence was particularly beneficial for life satisfaction, locational adjustment, and work adjustment. Interaction adjustment was inconsistently related to partner presence. In European countries, being accompanied by their partners enhanced interaction adjustment, like work and locational adjustment. However, in more culturally- and geographically-distant countries, expatriate partners may provide sufficient social contact that expatriates feel less need to venture outside their comfort zones and engage with host country nationals. The facilitative or inhibitory processes of spouse presence on expatriate interaction and engagement with the host country culture is an important area for future research, and organizations should ensure that expatriates who travel to distant countries with their partners are given sufficient encouragement and support to promote effective interaction adjustment.

We found that the benefits of partner accompaniment were generally consistent whether they were compared to single expatriates or expatriates whose partners were absent. Absent-partner expatriates showed poorer interaction adjustment, but, given the international heterogeneity of the samples for this analysis and the moderating effect discussed above, this difference is difficult to interpret. Somewhat surprisingly, expatriates with absent partners showed stronger life satisfaction (and to a lesser extent, locational adjustment) than single expatriates. Being separated from one's partner is likely to be a major stressor for expatriates, and yet, these separated partners still fared better than single expatriates in some ways. Perhaps the partner remotely provides substantial personal and even instrumental support for the expatriate. This effect may also reflect that married individuals tend to report higher life satisfaction in general (Haring-Hidore et al. 1985; Lucas et al. 2003). As technology continues to improve, many stressors associated with long distance relationships are lessened. Simple, inexpensive video calls and other readily available, synchronous communication forms alleviate many of the concerns of leaving a partner at home while also providing opportunities for the partner to provide critical support during challenging adjustment periods. These results, while surprising, suggest many opportunities for future research to better understand the ways that partners might contribute to the expatriate experience from afar.

The effects of children's presence were similarly enlightening. Generally, the presence of children benefited expatriates in this sample. Parents accompanied by their children experienced greater job and life satisfaction and better work and locational adjustment than non-parent expatriates. Notably, like the results for partner presence, the impact of children's presence on interaction adjustment varied across countries, with children having a positive effect in European countries and a negative impact in culturally- and geographically-distant countries. This pattern suggests that children may have a similar effect as partners in insulating expatriates from engaging with host country nationals when these interactions are more challenging.

The benefits experienced by parents accompanied by their children are unsurprising. Although children are a source of many nonwork demands, they are also a source of resources. In addition to instrumentally facilitating adjustment by forcing their parents to learn the local language and culture, children also provide emotional support and joy to their parents. Beyond the direct benefits of children's presence on assignment is the benefit of not being concerned about their absence. Children left behind may create greater guilt and concern for parents than those brought to a suboptimal (e.g., unclean, highly polluted, unsafe) environment. Further research into the strain of expatriates who are away from their children is needed, especially considering the dearth of studies examining the impact of separation on all members of the family, as well as on expatriate work outcomes.

4.1 Areas for Future Research

Throughout this data collection, we learned of several common expatriate family situations that fell beyond the scope of this study but present interesting avenues for future research. First, the age of expatriates' children may be incredibly important. Although typically unmeasured in investigations of expatriate families, some expatriates leave "adult children" behind in their home countries. Expatriates sometimes wait to work internationally until their children have grown and moved out; however, those children may still present notable stressors for their parents. Children leaving home is often a source of mixed emotional reactions for parents. If parents become expatriates, they may have fewer opportunities to visit their young adult children, may be less able to support their children's adaptation to adult life, and in some cases, will postpone valuable life experiences, such as meeting their grandchildren. These expatriates experience two enormous stressors at the same time; they must adjust to a new culture as well as a new family dynamic. More research on the interactive effects of these stressors is needed.

Second, we observed that behavioral responses to separation from their partners varied based on expatriates' location. For example, for our sample of largely German expatriates, unaccompanied expatriation to neighboring countries (e.g., France and Denmark) may be more akin to a domestic long distance relationship than other longer-distance expatriate situations (e.g., those traveling to a different continent). Expatriates whose families live in neighboring countries can more easily visit each other, and the daily strain may also be partially alleviated due to similar time zones and other factors that facilitate easier communication.

Third, just as there are many forms of expatriation (e.g., self-initiated, short-term corporate troubleshooting, career developmental), there are also many reasons why partners and children may not accompany an expatriate. The reason for family's absence may influence expatriate outcomes. For example, if the family does not accompany the employee because the living conditions are undesirable, the employee may feel secure and pleased that their family is safe in their home country. Similarly, if the partner chooses to stay in the home country for career advancement, the costs associated with separation might be fewer than the financial and psychological impact of the partner sacrificing a career to accompany the expatriate. These nuances are critical to understanding not only the optimal configurations for expatriate families, but also how organizations and communities can best support these families during their challenging times apart.

Finally, as organizations incorporate more holistic assessments of expatriate families into their selection, preparation, and support processes, more information on the benefits of family members who are host-country nationals would be incredibly useful. There are many reasons why expatriates partnered with host-country nationals might fare better. These partners provide critical cultural knowledge. The expatriate employees might also have a history of exposure to the culture as well as a developed social network prior to arrival, both of which have substantial benefits for adjustment (Bhaskar-Shrinivas et al. 2005; Shaffer/Harrison 2001). In a similar vein, Herleman et al. (2008) highlighted the importance of Ibasho, a "sense of comfort and psychological security that a person feels in specific locations they regularly visit" (p. 282). Ibasho encompasses the feeling that one knows what to expect and has a developed routine in that setting. Herleman showed that Ibasho positively influenced expatriate spouses' adjustment. For expatriates whose partners are host-country nationals, it is possible that Ibasho occurs more readily and facilitates other critical spouse and expatriate outcomes.

5   Conclusion

The present study demonstrates the influence of partner and children's presence on a variety of important expatriate outcomes in a large sample of expatriates from homogeneous cultural backgrounds assigned to many different host country contexts. The findings demonstrate the benefits of family presence in many situations, as well as notable potential pitfalls. The specific processes that contribute to family's benefits or hindrances for expatriates, as well as interventions that can enhance expatriate outcomes in different family configurations, are important areas for further research. In addition to our current findings, our experiences with a large group of expatriates in various family situations and expatriation processes suggested many important directions for future research on expatriate family processes. From this study's findings and the many questions sparked, we can conclusively recognize the critical role of families in expatriation and argue that employers and employees carefully integrate consideration of family characteristics into each aspect of the expatriation process.

References

Albrecht, Anne-Grit (2005): Untangling the Laundry List: General Mental Ability, the Big Five, and Context Related Variables as Predictors for Expatriate Success. Master's Thesis. Lüneburg, Germany: Leuphana Universität. [http://opus.uni-lueneburg.de/opus/volltexte/2006/344/].
Andreason, Aaron W. (2008): Expatriate Adjustment of Spouses and Expatriate Managers: An Integrative Research View. In: *International Journal of Management* 25,2: 382–395. [https://search.proquest.com/docview/233229112].

BGRS (2012): Global Relocation Trends: 2012 *Survey Report*. Toronto, Canda: Brookfield Global Relocation Services. [http://globalmobilitytrends.brookfieldgrs.com].

Bhaskar-Shrinivas, Purnima et al. (2005): Input-Based and Time-Based Models of International Adjustment: Meta-Analytic Evidence and Theoretical Extensions. In: *Academy of Management Journal* 48,2: 257–281. [https://doi.org/10.5465/AMJ.2005.16928400].

Black, J. Stewart; Gregersen, Hal B. (1991): The Other Half of the Picture: Antecedents of Spouse Cross-Cultural Adjustment. In: *Journal of International Business Studies* 22,3: 461–477. [https://doi.org/10.1057/palgrave.jibs.8490311].

Black, J. Stewart; Mendenhall, Mark E.; Oddou, Gary R. (1991): Toward a Comprehensive Model of International Adjustment: An Integration of Multiple Theoretical Perspectives. In: *Academy of Management Review* 16,2: 291–317. [https://doi.org/10.5465/AMR.1991.4278938].

Black, J. Stewart; Stephens, Gregory K. (1989): The Influence of the Spouse on American Expatriate Adjustment and Intent to Stay in Pacific Rim Overseas Assignments. In: *Journal of Management* 15,4: 529–544. [https://doi.org/10.1177/014920638901500403].

Brayfield, Arthur H.; Rothe, Harold F. (1951): An Index of Job Satisfaction. In: *Journal of Applied Psychology* 35,5: 307–311. [https://doi.org/10.1037/h0055617].

Brown, Robert J. (2008): Dominant Stressors on Expatriate Couples during International Assignments. In: *International Journal of Human Resource Management* 19,6: 1018–1034. [https://doi.org/10.1080/09585190802051303].

Caligiuri, Paula M.; Lazarova, Mila B. (2005): Expatriate Assignments and Work-Family Conflict. In: Poelmans, Steven A.Y. (Ed.): International Research in Work and Family. Mahwah, NJ: Lawrence Erlbaum Associates: 121–146.

Cole, Nina D. (2011): Managing Global Talent: Solving the Spousal Adjustment Problem. In: *International Journal of Human Resource Management* 22,7: 1504–1530. [https://doi.org/10.1080/09585192.2011.561963].

Copeland, Anne P.; Norell, Sara K. (2002): Spousal Adjustment on International Assignments: The Role of Social Support. In: *International Journal of Intercultural Relations* 26,3: 255–272. [https://doi.org/10.1016/S0147-1767(02)00003-2].

Diener, Ed et al. (1985): The Satisfaction with Life Scale. In: *Journal of Personality Assessment* 49,1: 71–75. [https://doi.org/10.1207/s15327752jpa4901_13].

Haring-Hidore, Marilyn et al. (1985): Marital Status and Subjective Well-Being: A Research Synthesis. In: *Journal of Marriage and the Family* 47,4: 947. [https://doi.org/10.2307/352338].

Haslberger, Arno; Brewster, Chris (2008): The Expatriate Family: An International Perspective. In: *Journal of Managerial Psychology* 23,3: 324–346. [https://doi.org/10.1108/02683940810861400].

Hedges, Larry V.; Friedman, Lynn (1993): Gender Differences in Variability in Intellectual Abilities: A Reanalysis of Feingold's Results. In: *Review of Educational Research* 63,1: 94–105. [https://doi.org/10.3102/00346543063001094].

Herleman, Hailey A.; Britt, Thomas W.; Hashima, Patricia Y. (2008): Ibasho and the Adjustment, Satisfaction, and Well-Being of Expatriate Spouses. In: *International Journal of Intercultural Relations* 32,3: 282–299. [https://doi.org/10.1016/j.ijintrel.2008.01.004].

Judge, Timothy A. et al. (1998): Dispositional Effects on Job and Life Satisfaction: The Role of Core Evaluations. In: *Journal of Applied Psychology* 83,1: 17–34. [https://doi.org/10.1037/0021-9010.83.1.17].

Lauring, Jakob; Selmer, Jan (2015): Adjustment of Spouses of Self-Initiated Expatriates: Feeling Different vs. Feeling Welcome. In: Mäkelä, Liisa; Suutari, Vesa (Eds.): Work and Family Interface in the International Career Context. Cham, Switzerland: Springer International: 117–138. [https://doi.org/10.1007/978-3-319-17647-5_7].

Lazarova, Mila; Westman, Mina; Shaffer, Margaret A. (2010): Elucidating the Positive Side of the Work-Family Interface on International Assignments: A Model of Expatriate Work and Family Performance. In: *Academy of Management Review* 35,1: 93–117. [https://doi.org/10/cd4c].

Lucas, Richard E. et al. (2003): Reexamining Adaptation and the Set Point Model of Happiness: Reactions to Changes in Marital Status. In: *Journal of Personality and Social Psychology* 84,3: 527–539. [https://doi.org/10.1037/0022-3514.84.3.527].

Mohr, Alex T.; Klein, Simone (2008): Adjustment vs. Satisfaction: An Analsyis of American Expatriate Spouses in Germany. In: Holtbrügge, Dirk (Ed.): Cultural Adjustment of Expatriates: Theoretical Concepts and Empirical Studies. München, Germany: Rainer Hampp: 49–59.

Ones, Deniz S. et al. (2012): Cross-Cultural Generalization: Using Meta-Analysis to Test Hypotheses about Cultural Variability. In: Ryan, Ann Marie; Leong, Frederick T.L.; Oswald, Frederick L. (Eds.): Conducting Multinational Research Projects in Organizational Psychology: Challenges and Opportunities, APA/MSU Series on Multicultural Psychology. Washington, DC: American Psychological Association: 91–122. [https://doi.org/10/5kz].

Richardson, Julia (2006): Self-Directed Expatriation: Family Matters. In: *Personnel Review* 35,4: 469–486. [https://doi.org/10.1108/00483480610670616].

Schmidt, Frank L.; Hunter, John E. (2015): Methods of Meta-Analysis: Correcting Error and Bias in Research Findings. 3rd ed. Thousand Oaks, CA: Sage. [https://doi.org/10/b6mg].

Schütter, Heike; Boerner, Sabine (2013): Illuminating the Work-family Interface on International Assignments: An Exploratory Approach. In: *Journal of Global Mobility* 1,1: 46–71. [https://doi.org/10.1108/JGM-09-2012-0012].

Shaffer, Margaret A.; Harrison, David A. (2001): Forgotten Partners of International Assignments: Development and Test of a Model of Spouse Adjustment. In: *Journal of Applied Psychology* 86,2: 238–254. [https://doi.org/10.1037/0021-9010.86.2.238].

Shaffer, Margaret A.; Harrison, David A. (1998): Expatriates' Psychological Withdrawal from International Assignments: Work, Nonwork, and Family Influences. In: *Personnel Psychology* 51,1: 87–118. [https://doi.org/10.1111/j.1744-6570.1998.tb00717.x].

Steel, Piers D. (2013): Converting between Meta-Analytic Variance Estimates Based on Correlations and Fisher *z*. Presented at the 8th Annual Meeting of the Society for Research Synthesis Methodology. Providence, RI.

Takeuchi, Riki (2010): A Critical Review of Expatriate Adjustment Research through a Multiple Stakeholder View: Progress, Emerging Trends, and Prospects. In: *Journal of Management* 36,4: 1040–1064. [https://doi.org/10.1177/0149206309349308].

Takeuchi, Riki; Wang, Mo; Marinova, Sophia V. (2005): Antecedents and Consequences of Psychological Workplace Strain during Expatriation: A Cross-Sectional and Longitudinal Investigation. In: *Personnel Psychology* 58,4: 925–948. [https://doi.org/10/bk93cd].

Takeuchi, Riki; Yun, Seokhwa; Tesluk, Paul E. (2002): An Examination of Crossover and Spillover Effects of Spousal and Expatriate Cross-Cultural Adjustment on Expatriate Outcomes. In: *Journal of Applied Psychology* 87,4: 655–666. [https://doi.org/10.1037/0021-9010.87.4.655].

Wiernik, Brenton M.; Rüger, Heiko; Ones, Deniz S. (2018): Advancing Expatriate Research in Public and Private Sectors. In: Wiernik, Brenton M.; Rüger, Heiko; Ones, Deniz S. (Eds.): Managing Expatriates: Success Factors in Private and Public Domains, Series on Population Studies 50. Opladen, Germany: Barbara Budrich Publishers.

Gender Differences in Job Performance and Adjustment: Do Women Expatriates Measure Up?

Hannah J. Foldes, Deniz S. Ones, and Handan Kepir Sinangil

Abstract

This study examined gender differences in expatriate job performance and general adjustment to living abroad to determine whether women effectively perform job duties and adjust in Turkey, an environment potentially perceived to be unfriendly to women managers (N = 308 expatriates). Findings lend support to the employment of women expatriates. Men and women expatriates rated themselves similarly in terms of adjustment to local conditions. Host country national (HCN) ratings of job performance revealed that men and women expatriates were rated similarly in terms of job performance. However, moderator analyses revealed that HCN subordinates gave lower ratings to women than HCN co-workers and supervisors. Additional moderator analyses revealed rater-ratee gender effects in expatriate ratings: women HCNs gave women expatriates higher ratings than their male counterparts.

1 Introduction

In today's global economy, two of the greatest challenges faced by human resources practitioners include finding people willing to accept international assignments and managing them effectively (Albrecht et al. 2018). Identifying high-potential employees to fill international management positions can both contribute to organizational strategic goals (Guthridge/Komm 2008) and enhance employees' career success by providing opportunities for skill development and advancement (Stahl et al. 2002; Vance 2005). However, despite the importance of selecting high-quality candidates for expatriation, selection processes for international assignments are often haphazard and prone to unintended biases (BGRS 2016; Harris/Brewster 1999). For example, organizational decision-makers often overlook women for these vital positions (Andresen et al. 2015; Baruch/Reis 2015; BGRS 2011; Vance/McNulty 2014). Under-representation of women among organizationally-assigned expatriates may stem from implicit or explicit beliefs that women will be less able to adjust and perform effectively in a new international context, particularly in areas that are traditionally viewed as hostile to women, such as the Middle East (Caligiuri/Cascio 1998). If inaccurate, such beliefs may lead to women having fewer opportunities to serve in expatriate roles, depriving them of the career opportunities provided by international assignments and potentially harming organizational global interests.

In this study, we evaluate the veracity of beliefs about women's ability to succeed abroad using a sample of expatriates in a country traditionally perceived to have high levels of gender inequity, Turkey. By Western standards, many of the male-dominated, patriarchal, and Islamic institutions in Turkey may appear to create a hostile environment for women, particularly women in positions of power, such as expatriate managers (House et al. 2004;

Müftüler-Bac 1999). Such an environment may make it difficult for female expatriates to become comfortable working in the Turkish context and leading their subordinates. Indeed, local superiors and coworkers may evaluate their performance less favorably than their male counterparts. However, in a previous study of gender differences in expatriate job performance in Turkey, Sinangil and Ones (2003) found that men and women tended to be evaluated similarly across a range of job performance dimensions. Sinangil and Ones concluded that, even in the ostensibly unwelcoming environment of Turkey, increasing the gender diversity of expatriate workforces was unlikely to negatively impact job performance (and, indeed, increased diversity may have positive benefits for adjustment and social outcomes). In this study, we use a new sample of expatriates in Turkey to replicate and extend Sinangil and Ones (2003). We examine both expatriate job performance and another critical expatriate success criterion – international adjustment (Black et al. 1991). In addition, we examine the impact of gender biases and social power dynamics by examining host country national rater gender and relative hierarchical level (i.e., supervisor, peer, or subordinate to the expatriate being rated) as potential moderators of gender differences in expatriate job performance ratings (cf. Bowen et al. 2000; Cochran 1999; Eagly et al. 1992; Facteau/Craig 2001; Roth et al. 2012).

2   Methods

2.1   Sample and Procedure

This chapter analyzes Sample 2 of the studies of expatriate success in Turkey (see Wiernik et al. 2018, Chapter 1 of this volume). Data were collected from 311 expatriates currently working on an international assignment in Turkey and 308 host country national (HCN) coworkers (1 for each expatriate). Participants were volunteers recruited by the third author and a group of 50 senior level industrial-organizational psychology students as part of a course research project. Initially, several major multinational and national organizations were selected through the Istanbul Chamber of Commerce Guide, in conjunction with lists of the 500 largest companies in Istanbul. Each student was tasked with contacting at least 5 organizations where expatriates were known to be employed. A broad range of industries was represented among the organizations from which data were gathered. These included finance/banking, tourism, education, marketing, and engineering. In most organizations, data were collected with the cooperation of the Human Resources department. During the first stage of data collection, the in-country researcher conducted in-depth interviews with the expatriates, their coworkers, and the HR directors about selection, training, adjustment, and performance. During the second stage of data collection, the researcher returned to the organizations to collect data via questionnaires. The latter were used for the present study.

Expatriate sample. Expatriates completed a survey assessing demographics, details on their expatriate assignment, and a personality questionnaire (not used for the current study). Expatriates were more often male ($N = 201$) than female ($N = 105$; 5 did not report their gender). Expatriates had a mean age of 38.2 years ($SD = 10.25$). Expatriates had an average of 13 years of full-time work experience and 6 years of tenure with their current organization. Expatriates had spent an average of 7.18 years ($SD = 7.52$) abroad on previous international assignments. Time spent on the current assignment in Turkey varied widely (mean 3.32 months, $SD = 48.14$). Female expatriates tended to be somewhat older than males, to have somewhat more general work and international experience, and to have somewhat more organizational tenure (see Table 1). Males and females did not differ in time on current assignment. Expatriates included executive, mid- and lower-level managers, as well as non-managerial (primarily service and educational) employees.

Expatriates were citizens of 35 countries. For those expatriate providing citizenship information, citizenship frequencies were: Australia (7), Austria (4), Azerbaijan (8), Balkan countries (6), Canada (10), Denmark (12), Egypt (2), France (17), Germany (35), Ghana/other West African countries (3), Hungary (2), India (3), Indonesia/Philippines (3), Iran (4), Israel (4), Italy (7), Japan (15), Jordan (1), Kirghizstan/other Central Asian countries (5), Latin America (4), Malaysia (1), Morocco (1), the Netherlands (2), New Zealand (2), Russia (5), Saudi Arabia/other Arabian countries (3), South Africa (3), South Korea (3), Spain (4), Sudan/other Central African countries (1), Switzerland (4), Thailand (2), Turkey (dual citizenship; 4), the United Kingdom/Ireland (70), and the United States (49).

Host country national coworker sample. Host country national (HCN) coworkers provided confidential job performance ratings for the expatriate with whom they were working. HCNs had a mean age of 33.12 years ($SD = 8.99$). HCNs were 116 males and 175 females (17 did not report their gender). HCNs had an average of 8.33 years ($SD = 8.24$) of experience in their current occupation. HCNs had worked with the expatriates they were rating for an average of 12.98 months ($SD = 24.13$). Raters were recruited based on their experience working closely with the expatriates. Most raters were expatriates' peers ($N = 120$), with smaller numbers being expatriates' subordinates ($N = 80$) or supervisors ($N = 29$); 79 raters did not report their position.

2.2 Measures

Job performance. HCNs completed a 53-item job performance measure rating expatriates on 10 dimensions of job performance. The instrument was adapted from Sinangil and Ones (2003) and was constructed directly in Turkish (i.e., was not a translated measure). HCNs rated expatriates on 10 performance dimensions based on existing models of job performance (for details, see Ones et al. 2018, Chapter 15, this volume). An overall performance index was created using a composite of the 53 items and an overall job performance item ($\alpha = .98$). HCNs rated each item on a 9-point scale for its accuracy describing the expatriate's on-the-job behavior (1 = extremely inaccurate, 9 = extremely accurate).

HCNs are uniquely positioned to provide culturally-contextualized and relevant evaluations expatriate job performance behaviors (Sinangil/Ones 1997), and HCN reactions to expatriate behavior have an important impact on expatriates' adjustment and effectiveness (Templer 2010). HCNs are thus the ideal source for expatriate job performance information. Our use of data from the HCN perspective also supports recent calls for further consideration of multiple stakeholders in expatriate research (Takeuchi 2010).

Adjustment to local conditions. Expatriate locational adjustment (comfort living abroad) was measured using 9 items adapted from Black and Stephens (1989). Expatriates rated the conditions and environment they faced in Turkey on a 10-point scale, with higher scores indicating greater adjustment. The 9 items included adjustment to health care facilities, shopping, entertainment, housing conditions, food, cost of living, living conditions in general, daily interactions with Turks, and socialization with Turks ($\alpha = .81$).

3 Results

Descriptive statistics and correlations for all variables are shown in Table 1. Cohen's *d* values for overall comparisons of male and female expatriates on performance and adjustment are shown in Table 3. Effect sizes were computed such that positive values indicated male expatriates scored higher than female expatriates.

The results in Table 2 are striking. They show very small gender differences across all measured job performance dimensions and adjustment to local conditions. As such, overall, there appear to be no performance- or adjustment-related concerns for sending women to Turkey as expatriates; they adjust and perform as well as male expatriates in this culture. If anything, women were rated slightly *higher* on most performance dimensions. However, our moderator analyses revealed that these negligible differences for the full sample masked more complex relations for HCN rater subsamples.

Table 3 reports gender differences in expatriate performance across rater position (i.e., subordinate, peer, or supervisor) relative to the expatriate being rated. An apparent trend is present for HCN subordinates to rate male expatriates slightly more highly (note the generally positive *d* values for subordinates), but for HCN peers to rate female expatriates somewhat more highly (note the uniformly negative *d* values for peers). The largest divergences were for the performance dimensions of adjustment to foreign business practices ($d = .21$ for subordinates, -.55 for peers; $\Delta_d = .76$ [95% CI = .14, 1.38]), establishing and maintaining business contacts ($d = .13$ for subordinates, -.45 for peers; $\Delta_d = .58$ [95% CI = -.04, 1.20]), and personal discipline ($d = .19$ for subordinates, -.26 for peers; $\Delta_d = .45$ [95% CI = -.17, 1.07]).

Table 4 reports gender differences in expatriate performance across HCN gender. Results clearly show that male raters gave higher performance ratings to male expatriates (*d* values uniformly positive) but female raters gave higher ratings to female expatriates (*d* values uniformly negative); mean $\Delta_d = .59$, range .42 to .89, with most confidence intervals excluding zero.

4 Discussion

This study examined gender differences in expatriate job performance and adjustment to local conditions in Turkey, a context typically regarded as relatively hostile to women. It also examined the moderating effects of HCN rater hierarchical position and gender on expatriate gender differences in performance ratings. Consistent with previous findings from the expatriate literature (Hechanova et al. 2003), we found negligible gender differences for adjustment. Similarly, our full sample analyses for expatriate job performance were consistent with Sinangil and Ones (1997) in finding negligible gender differences. However, we found some evidence for moderator effects for rater position and gender.

For rater position, we found that subordinate HCNs tended to favor male expatriates in their ratings, while peer HCNs favored women, particularly for the dimensions of establishing business contacts, adjusting to foreign practices, and maintaining personal discipline. This effect may reflect that subordinate HCNs may be less educated and of lower socioeconomic status than peer HCNs; such individuals may be more invested in traditional patriarchal social structures and less open to women working in positions of authority.

Table 1: Descriptive statistics and correlations among study variables

	Variable	Mean	SD	N	1	2	3	4	5	6	7	8	9	10
1	HCN gender	1.60	.49	288	—									
2	HCN age	33.13	8.99	288	-.15	—								
3	HCN years in occupation	8.33	8.24	270	-.15	.79	—							
4	HCN working months with expatriate	12.98	24.13	224	.02	.16	.13	—						
5	Expatriate gender	1.34	.48	306	.19	-.03	-.03	.01	—					
6	Expatriate age	38.19	1.27	300	-.02	.16	.15	-.01	-.19	—				
7	Expatriate full-time work experience (years)	12.99	9.77	264	-.07	.20	.17	.04	-.17	.76	—			
8	Expatriate years working abroad	7.18	7.52	142	.06	.06	.06	-.03	-.13	.51	.55	—		
9	Expatriate organizational tenure (years)	6.04	6.59	268	-.12	.05	.02	.09	-.20	.48	.47	.43	—	
10	Expat months on current assignment	3.32	48.14	251	.03	.06	.03	.11	.03	.24	.30	.31	.09	—
11	Establishing and maintaining business contacts	7.51	1.28	294	.03	.05	.02	.10	.07	-.04	-.01	-.01	-.10	-.08
12	Technical competence	7.59	1.46	298	-.03	.09	.04	-.03	-.03	.02	-.02	-.05	.08	-.02
13	Working with others	7.77	1.24	288	.07	.07	.04	.01	.05	-.03	-.03	-.14	-.09	-.10
14	Communicating and persuading	7.73	1.21	297	.02	.12	.07	.14	.03	-.07	-.03	-.13	-.05	-.11
15	Initiative and effort	7.73	1.04	285	.02	.05	.03	.09	.06	-.06	-.02	-.01	-.07	-.09
16	Personal discipline	8.15	.81	292	.03	.08	.09	.14	.04	.02	.02	-.04	-.04	-.10
17	Interpersonal relations	7.74	1.13	283	-.01	.13	.07	.07	.06	-.07	-.05	-.17	-.06	-.14
18	Management and supervision	7.65	1.08	285	.07	.04	-.04	.16	-.01	.00	.03	-.02	.07	-.06
19	Productivity	8.08	1.14	293	.03	.06	.04	.10	.02	-.05	-.08	-.13	-.05	-.05
20	Adjustment to foreign business practices	7.68	1.20	297	.00	.11	.04	.10	.10	-.02	.05	-.03	-.05	-.03
21	Overall job performance composite	7.77	.99	231	.01	.09	.06	.11	.06	-.07	-.07	-.10	-.08	-.08
22	Adjustment to local conditions	6.24	1.23	263	.05	-.06	-.05	-.15	.03	-.09	.11	.03	-.03	.09

Note: HCN = host country national; bivariate N ranges 170-298.

Table 1: Descriptive statistics and correlations among study variables – continued

	Variable	11	12	13	14	15	16	17	18	19	20	21	22
11	Establishing and maintaining business contacts	—											
12	Technical competence	.48	—										
13	Working with others	.75	.56	—									
14	Communicating and persuading	.74	.62	.77	—								
15	Initiative and effort	.72	.61	.76	.80	—							
16	Personal discipline	.59	.54	.66	.65	.72	—						
17	Interpersonal relations	.82	.63	.86	.85	.81	.72	—					
18	Management and supervision	.61	.64	.67	.71	.77	.69	.72	—				
19	Productivity	.67	.70	.77	.78	.79	.70	.81	.74	—			
20	Adjustment to foreign business practices	.64	.49	.57	.63	.61	.62	.66	.62	.57	—		
21	Overall job performance composite	.84	.72	.88	.90	.92	.82	.94	.87	.90	.75	—	
22	Adjustment to local conditions	-.10	-.12	-.13	-.05	-.04	-.10	-.10	-.03	-.05	-.03	-.12	—

Table 2: Gender differences for expatriate job performance and adjustment - full sample

	Variable	d	95% CI
1	Establishing and maintaining business contacts	**-.15**	-.39 to .09
2	Technical competence	**.06**	-.18 to .30
3	Working with others	**-.10**	-.35 to .14
4	Communicating and persuading	**-.07**	-.31 to .18
5	Initiative and effort	**-.11**	-.36 to .13
6	Personal discipline	**-.07**	-.32 to .17
7	Interpersonal relations	**-.12**	-.37 to .12
8	Management and supervision	**.02**	-.23 to .26
9	Productivity	**-.03**	-.28 to .21
10	Adjustment to foreign business practices	**-.23**	-.47 to .02
11	Overall job performance composite	**-.13**	-.41 to .14
12	Adjustment to local conditions	**-.06**	-.31 to .20

Note: male N = 151-191; female N = 76-102; positive d values indicate that males score higher; 95% CI = 95% confidence interval.

Table 3: Gender differences for expatriate job performance by rater position

	Variable	Subordinate[a]		Peer[b]		Supervisor[c]	
		d	95% CI	d	95% CI	d	95% CI
1	Establishing and maintaining business contacts	**.13**	-.37 to .62	**-.45**	-.83 to -.07	**.30**	-.45 to 1.04
2	Technical competence	**.17**	-.32 to .67	**-.15**	-.52 to .23	**.03**	-.70 to .76
3	Working with others	**-.02**	-.51 to .47	**-.22**	-.61 to .16	**.03**	-.69 to .76
4	Communicating and persuading	**.03**	-.46 to .52	**-.23**	-.61 to .14	**.02**	-.71 to .75
5	Initiative and effort	**-.13**	-.62 to .37	**-.21**	-.60 to .17	**.06**	-.68 to .80
6	Personal discipline	**.19**	-.30 to .68	**-.26**	-.64 to .12	**-.13**	-.87 to .62
7	Interpersonal relations	**.03**	-.42 to .52	**-.33**	-.72 to .07	**.19**	-.56 to .93
8	Management and supervision	**.20**	-.31 to .71	**-.10**	-.48 to .29	**-.17**	-.90 to .56
9	Productivity	**.01**	-.48 to .51	**-.15**	-.53 to .23	**-.20**	-.96 to .56
10	Adjustment to foreign business practices	**.21**	-.28 to .70	**-.55**	-.93 to -.17	**-.67**	-1.42 to .08
11	Overall job performance composite	**.06**	-.49 to .62	**-.27**	-.70 to .17	**-.31**	-1.14 to .52

Note: [a] male $N = 50$-54; female $N = 21$-23; [b] male $N = 65$-68; female $N = 41$-46; [c] male $N = 14$-15; female $N = 12$-14; positive d values indicate that males score higher; 95% CI = 95% confidence interval.

Table 4: Gender differences for expatriate job performance by rater gender

	Variable	Male[a]		Female[b]	
		d	95% CI	d	95% CI
1	Establishing and maintaining business contacts	**.15**	-.28 to .58	**-.29**	-.61 to .02
2	Technical competence	**.28**	-.16 to .71	**-.14**	-.44 to .17
3	Working with others	**.28**	-.16 to .71	**-.30**	-.62 to .02
4	Communicating and persuading	**.25**	-.18 to .69	**-.21**	-.52 to .10
5	Initiative and effort	**.24**	-.20 to .69	**-.28**	-.60 to .03
6	Personal discipline	**.45**	.02 to .89	**-.33**	-.64 to -.01
7	Interpersonal relations	**.26**	-.18 to .70	**-.33**	-.65 to -.01
8	Management and supervision	**.40**	-.05 to .84	**-.11**	-.43 to .20
9	Productivity	**.55**	.10 to 1.01	**-.34**	-.65 to -.02
10	Adjustment to foreign business practices	**.24**	-.20 to .80	**-.42**	-.73 to -.11
11	Overall job performance composite	**.32**	-.16 to .80	**-.37**	-.73 to -.01

Note: [a] male $N = 71$-89; female $N = 22$-27; [b] male $N = 81$-101; female $N = 57$-71; positive d values indicate that males score higher; 95% CI = 95% confidence interval.

These results may also reflect differences across raters in each position in the performance behaviors observed and attended to, as well as the relative importance attached to different behaviors (Mount et al. 1998). Subordinate HCNs may attend more to traditionally-masculine leadership behaviors, whereas peer HCNs may favor more interpersonally-sensitive leadership (cf. Eagly et al. 1992). Notably, of the subordinate HCNs reporting their gender, more were female than male (47 versus 32), so the subordinate effect cannot be explained as merely covariation between moderators (see below).[1]

For gender, we found that same-gender ratings tended to be substantially higher than cross-gender HCN ratings of expatriate performance. This trend was consistent across all job performance dimensions. These differences may also reflect preferences and attention to divergent sets of expatriate performance behaviors for male and female HCNs; male HCNs may favor more masculine leadership styles, while female HCNs prefer more feminine approaches. The differences may also reflect cultural effects. HCNs may be more comfortable and accustomed to observing and interpreting the behavior of members of their own gender.

4.1   Limitations, Strengths, and Directions for Future Research

The findings from this study are limited by the nature of the sample. The expatriates sampled were working in Turkey, and the host country perspective examined in this study could carry with it the idiosyncrasies unique to that country. Therefore, it will be necessary to replicate the results of the present research with host country nationals from other countries that vary along the continua of gender equity and acceptance of women in positions of authority. We expect that the rater position and gender effects observed in this study may be even stronger in countries with great gender inequity, but attenuated in countries where parity in men's and women's societal roles is more common.

This study also has several unique strengths. First, we conducted a direction replication of previous research on expatriate gender differences in the same context (Sinangil/Ones 2003), while also extending the findings using additional criteria and a sample with representation from many nationalities and a diversity of additional expatriate experiences in countries other than Turkey. This study also considered the host country perspective on expatriate performance. Using HCN performance ratings ensured that our findings reflect the individuals whose perceptions of expatriate behaviors are most important and do not suffer from the common method bias that plagues much of expatriate research.

There is growing evidence that, contrary to the notion that women will be disadvantaged in male-dominant cultures, male and female expatriates tend to report similar levels of adjustment and to receive similar performance ratings. Hence, from a practical perspective, HR managers must ensure that they do not overlook female employees for international assignments based on such ill-founded assumptions. However, the moderating effects observed in the current study indicate that more research is needed to better understand the various social dynamics in specific host country contexts that may advantage or disadvantage women in their interactions with HCNs. Identifying the nature and source of frictions between expatriates and HCNs will better enable managers to reduce or accommodate them, as well as adapt specific practices (e.g., 360-degree feedback systems) to fit local cultures.

Overall, the present study supports the assertion that cross-cultural contexts can sustain meaningful participation of diverse groups, including women, in international assignments.

---

[1]   Of the peer HCNs reporting their gender, 69 were female, and 46 were male.

Even when differences were found, their magnitudes were moderate at most and often quite small. Deploying more women on overseas assignments will contribute to global gender equity and enhance workplace diversity for the future. Enhancing gender diversity need not lead to decrements in expatriate success.

References

Albrecht, Anne-Grit; Ones, Deniz S.; Sinangil, Handan Kepir (2018): Expatriate Management. In: Ones, Deniz S. et al. (Eds.): The SAGE Handbook of Industrial, Work and Organizational Psychology. Volume 3: Managerial Psychology and Organizational Approaches. 2nd ed. London, United Kingdom: Sage: 429–468.

Andresen, Maike; Biemann, Torsten; Pattie, Marshall Wilson (2015): What Makes Them Move Abroad? Reviewing and Exploring Differences between Self-Initiated and Assigned Expatriation. In: *International Journal of Human Resource Management* 26,7: 932–947. [https://doi.org/10.1080/09585192.2012.669780].

Baruch, Yehuda; Reis, Cristina (2015): Global Career Challenges for Women Crossing International Borders. In: Broadbridge, Adelina M.; Fielden, Sandra L. (Eds.): Handbook of Gendered Careers in Management: Getting in, Getting on, Getting Out. Cheltenham, United Kingdom: Elgar: 341–356. [https://doi.org/10.4337/9781782547709].

BGRS (2016): Breakthrough to the Future of Global Talent Mobility: 2016 Global Mobility Trends Survey Report. Woodridge, IL: Brookfield Global Relocation Services. [http://globalmobilitytrends.brookfieldgrs.com].

BGRS (2011): Global Relocation Trends: 2011 Survey Report. Woodridge, IL: Brookfield Global Relocation Services. [http://globalmobilitytrends.brookfieldgrs.com].

Black, J. Stewart; Mendenhall, Mark E.; Oddou, Gary R. (1991): Toward a Comprehensive Model of International Adjustment: An Integration of Multiple Theoretical Perspectives. In: *Academy of Management Review* 16,2: 291–317. [https://doi.org/10/fn7m8b].

Black, J. Stewart; Stephens, Gregory K. (1989): The Influence of the Spouse on American Expatriate Adjustment and Intent to Stay in Pacific Rim Overseas Assignments. In: *Journal of Management* 15,4: 529–544. [https://doi.org/10.1177/014920638901500403].

Bowen, Chieh-Chen; Swim, Janet K.; Jacobs, Rick R. (2000): Evaluating Gender Biases on Actual Job Performance of Real People: A Meta-Analysis. In: *Journal of Applied Social Psychology* 30,10: 2194–2215. [https://doi.org/10.1111/j.1559-1816.2000.tb02432.x].

Caligiuri, Paula M.; Cascio, Wayne F. (1998): Can We Send Her There? Maximizing the Success of Western Women on Global Assignments. In: *Journal of World Business* 33,4: 394–416. [https://doi.org/10.1016/S1090-9516(98)90024-4].

Cochran, Caroline Carter (1999): Gender Influences on the Process and Outcomes of Rating Performance. Doctoral Dissertation. Minneapolis, MN: University of Minnesota. [http://search.proquest.com/dissertations/docview/304509257/].

Eagly, Alice H.; Makhijani, Mona G.; Klonsky, Bruce G. (1992): Gender and the Evaluation of Leaders: A Meta-Analysis. In: *Psychological Bulletin* 111,1: 3–22. [https://doi.org/10.1037/0033-2909.111.1.3].

Facteau, Jeffrey D.; Craig, S. Bartholomew (2001): Are Performance Ratings from Different Rater Sources Comparable? In: *Journal of Applied Psychology* 86,2: 215–227. [https://doi.org/10.1037/0021-9010.86.2.215].

Guthridge, Matthew; Komm, Asmus B. (2008): Why Multinationals Struggle to Manage Talent. In: *The McKinsey Quarterly* 4: 1–5.

Harris, Hilary; Brewster, Chris (1999): The Coffee-Machine System: How International Selection Really Works. In: *International Journal of Human Resource Management* 10,3: 488–500. [https://doi.org/10.1080/095851999340440].

Hechanova, Regina; Beehr, Terry A.; Christiansen, Neil D. (2003): Antecedents and Consequences of Employees' Adjustment to Overseas Assignment: A Meta-Analytic Review. In: *Applied Psychology* 52,2: 213–236. [https://doi.org/10/d4f4xv].

House, Robert J. et al. (Eds.) (2004): Culture, Leadership, and Organizations: The GLOBE Study of 62 Societies. Thousand Oaks, CA: Sage.

Mount, Michael K. et al. (1998): Trait, Rater and Level Effects in 360-Degree Performance Ratings. In: *Personnel Psychology* 51,3: 557–576. [https://doi.org/10.1111/j.1744-6570.1998.tb00251.x].

Müftüler-Bac, Meltem (1999): Turkish Women's Predicament. In: *Women's Studies International Forum* 22,3: 303–315. [https://doi.org/10.1016/S0277-5395(99)00029-1].

Ones, Deniz S.; Foldes, Hannah Jackson; Sinangil, Handan Kepir (2018): A Family Affair: Spouse and Children's Role in Expatriate Adjustment and Job Performance. In: Wiernik, Brenton M.; Rüger, Heiko; Ones, Deniz S. (Eds.): Managing Expatriates: Success Factors in Private and Public Domains, Series on Population Studies 50. Opladen, Germany: Barbara Budrich Publishers.

Roth, Philip L.; Purvis, Kristen L.; Bobko, Philip (2012): A Meta-Analysis of Gender Group Differences for Measures of Job Performance in Field Studies. In: *Journal of Management* 38,2: 719–739. [https://doi.org/10.1177/0149206310374774].

Sinangil, Handan Kepir; Ones, Deniz S. (2003): Gender Differences in Expatriate Job Performance. In: *Applied Psychology* 52,3: 461–475. [https://doi.org/10/c36tw5].

Sinangil, Handan Kepir; Ones, Deniz S. (1997): Empirical Investigations of the Host Country Perspective in Expatriate Management. In: Aycan, Zeynep (Ed.): Expatriate Management: Theory and Research, New Approaches to Employee Management 4. Greenwich, CT: JAI Press: 173–205.

Stahl, Günter K.; Miller, Edwin L.; Tung, Rosalie L. (2002): Toward the Boundaryless Career: A Closer Look at the Expatriate Career Concept and the Perceived Implications of an International Assignment. In: *Journal of World Business* 37,3: 216–227. [https://doi.org/10/ddttgr].

Takeuchi, Riki (2010): A Critical Review of Expatriate Adjustment Research through a Multiple Stakeholder View: Progress, Emerging Trends, and Prospects. In: *Journal of Management* 36,4: 1040–1064. [https://doi.org/10.1177/0149206309349308].

Templer, Klaus J. (2010): Personal Attributes of Expatriate Managers, Subordinate Ethnocentrism, and Expatriate Success: A Host-Country Perspective. In: *International Journal of Human Resource Management* 21,10: 1754–1768. [https://doi.org/10.1080/09585192.2010.500493].

Vance, Charles M. (2005): The Personal Quest for Building Global Competence: A Taxonomy of Self-Initiating Career Path Strategies for Gaining Business Experience Abroad. In: *Journal of World Business* 40,4: 374–385. [https://doi.org/10.1016/j.jwb.2005.08.005].

Vance, Charles M.; McNulty, Yvonne (2014): Why and How Women and Men Acquire Global Career Experience: A Study of American Expatriates in Europe. In: *International Studies of Management & Organization* 44,2: 34–54. [https://doi.org/10.2753/IMO0020-8825440202].

Wiernik, Brenton M.; Rüger, Heiko; Ones, Deniz S. (2018): Advancing Expatriate Research in Public and Private Sectors. In: Wiernik, Brenton M.; Rüger, Heiko; Ones, Deniz S. (Eds.): Managing Expatriates: Success Factors in Private and Public Domains, Series on Population Studies 50. Opladen, Germany: Barbara Budrich Publishers.

Influence of Gender and Family Status on Expatriate Well-Being

Stine Waibel and Heiko Rüger

Abstract

This chapter examines how gender and family status interact to impact expatriate outcomes (locational adjustment, job satisfaction, satisfaction with relocation, health-related quality of life, work-life balance, and perceived stress) in a sample of 1,771 German Foreign Service diplomats on post abroad. Results reveal that both female and male diplomats who are single parents report a significantly lower health-related quality of life than diplomats in other family arrangements. Moreover, single male diplomats with children report significantly lower adjustment levels. Irrespective of the presence of children, single women are particularly uncomfortable with how their profession and frequent moves affect their personal life. We discuss the need for further studies of the challenges of family formation during expatriation, especially for women, as well as issues connected to geographically-separated families.

1   Introduction

Over the past decades, organizational expatriate management policies and practices have become increasingly supportive of expatriates' families and the pivotal role they play in employees' adjustment and success (BGRS 2012; Takeuchi 2010). International human resource practitioners widely believe that families are an important source of emotional, social and practical support for expatriates, an assumption that has received substantial support in expatriate research (e.g., Adelman 1988; Caligiuri/Cascio 1998; Copeland/Norell 2002; Lazarova et al. 2010; Shaffer/Harrison 1998). Therefore, the adjustment and well-being of expatriates' accompanying partners and other family members continue to be investigated as crucial "non-work factors" contributing to expatriate employees' own adjustment and ultimately work performance (cf. Bhaskar-Shrinivas et al. 2005; Black/Stephens 1989; Caligiuri/Cascio 1998; Haslberger/ Brewster 2008; Lazarova et al. 2010; Richardson 2006; Shaffer/Harrison 2001; Takeuchi 2010).

Associated with general societal demographic and cultural shifts, the mechanisms through which family is posited to impact expatriate outcomes has changed over time. In the early 1980s, expatriate family research focused on the "inability of expatriates' spouses to adjust to a different physical or cultural environment" as a critical risk factor for international assignment failure (Tung 1982: 67). Tung (1982: 70) recommended that sending organizations "prepare them [the spouses] for living in a different cultural environment" as well as assess and develop expatriates' "relational abilities". As married couples began to develop more co-equal roles for each partner (and as more female employees became expatriates), expatriate researchers sought to understand the implications of these more diverse family models for expatriate success. Emphasis shifted toward studying organizational support measures that can reduce expatriate families' work–family conflicts (Fischlmayr/Kollinger

2010; Shaffer/Harrison 1998; Takeuchi 2010) and that provide tailored assistance for expatriate spouses, particularly regarding maintaining their own career goals while they accompany their partners abroad (Eby et al. 2002; Harvey 1997; Mäkelä et al. 2011a; McNulty 2012; Shaffer/Harrison 2001). Most recently, researchers have begun to consider the facilitative and supportive role that expatriate families may play during international adjustment (Insch/ Daniels 2002; Lazarova et al. 2010).

From the very beginning, gender issues have been deeply intertwined with research on work–family interface (cf. Lyness/Judiesch 2008). This is because, despite the decreasing prominence of traditional gender roles over time, women still often bear the brunt of family responsibilities, face unique obstacles balancing work and personal life, and take more ownership of work–life challenges then men (Duxbury/Higgins 1991; Eccles 1987; Gutek et al. 1991; Martinengo et al. 2010; Thompson/Walker 1989). Extensive travel or the profound challenges of international relocation are likely to exacerbate these gender differences in coping with competing work and family demands (Fischlmayr/Kollinger 2010; Harris 2004; Shoemaker/ Park 2009). Family barriers and considerations reduce women's willingness to accept international assignments more than men's (Hofbauer/Fischlmayr 2004; Linehan/Walsh 2000; Tharenou 2008). Expatriate assignments are also often associated with gendered stereotypes that lead women to be overlooked, even if they are qualified and willing (Hearn et al. 2008; Kofman 2012; Meil 2010; Sinangil/Ones 2003; see also Foldes et al. 2018, Chapter 17, this volume).

Despite these challenges, the proportion of female international assignees in the private sector has increased steadily from 3% in the early 1980s (Adler 1984) to around 25% today (BGRS 2016; Cartus 2016). This increase raises the question of whether women experience similar outcomes as men, particularly for the personal satisfaction and well-being outcomes that have rarely been investigated in expatriate research (Albrecht et al. 2018). Previous research has suggested that women adjust and perform equally well as men during expatriate assignments (Albrecht et al. 2018; Sinangil/Ones 2003), but do these nil differences extend to well-being? Moreover, how do gender differences intersect with family challenges during expatriation? Previous studies have suggested that female expatriates are more often single, divorced, or childless compared to their male counterparts (Hearn et al. 2008; Shoemaker/ Park 2009; Tzeng 2006; Wiese 2004). Do these family structure lead to differences in well-being? We explore these questions in this chapter.

1.1   The Current Study

Given the changing nature of family forms and gender roles, this chapter examines how gender and family status (having a partner and/or children) interact to impact expatriate well-being outcomes. Few studies have explicitly addressed and empirically examined how family or relationship status itself impacts expatriate experiences and if there are gender differences (Kollinger-Santer/Fischlmayr 2013; but cf. Mayerhofer et al. 2004; Selmer/ Lauring 2011).

Interactions between gender and family status have primarily been addressed from the perspective of willingness to expatriate (e.g., Dupuis et al. 2008; Kim/Froese 2012), and research on family issues and work-life balance has mainly focused on dual career couples or married (female) expatriates with family obligations, thus, neglecting non-traditional family structures, such as expatriates without children, single parents, or geographically separated families (Hamilton et al. 2006; McNulty 2014; see also Mercado et al. 2018, Chapter 16, this volume).

Previous research has characterized family as both a support system (Insch/Daniels 2002) and source of personal responsibility and organizational commitment (Shaffer/Harrison 1998), as well as a potentially destabilizing force (see above). Family adjustment challenges may be even more challenging for female expatriates due to the discomfort felt by both partners in practicing non-traditional family models with men as stay-at-home parent or secondary breadwinner (Harris 2004; Hofbauer/Fischlmayr 2004; Mäkelä et al. 2011b; Mohr/Klein 2008), though the intense challenges of international assignments may also lead men and women to evaluate work–family reconciliation challenges more similarly than in domestic settings (Mayerhofer et al. 2004).

We investigate the interaction between gender and family status on expatriate well-being using a sample of employees in the German Foreign Service (GFS) on international assignments (in short, diplomats). Although frequent international mobility is a fundamental part of diplomats' profession, they have rarely been the subject of expatriate research (Davoine et al. 2013; Groeneveld 2008). In contrast to business expatriates, GFS employees are part of a rotation system wherein they are assigned to a new host country every three to five years (see Brandt/Buck 2005). After approximately two assignments abroad, diplomats return home to Germany to work at the ministry for 3–5 years before starting the next overseas assignment. Consequently, diplomats have (perhaps more than one-time or short-term business expatriates) traditionally relied on spouses who follow them to each new post, focus on managing the household and family, and suspend their own career opportunities (though diplomat spouses may have significant "vicarious achievements" through being involved in the diplomats' careers; Whip 1982; Wood 2005).

As is the case for private-sector expatriates, employee demographics have also changed over the past decades within foreign services (Brandt/Buck 2005). As the number of female employees, dual career couples, and geographically-separated families is increasing, it will be insightful to see how men and women and diplomats with diverse family structures differ in their experience of moving internationally. These questions are particularly relevant given that foreign services are often highly conservative and traditionally-oriented professional environments. For example, even in the United States, a liberal country with a strong commitment to equity, women's opportunities for advancement in the State Department were limited well into the 1970s (Grunig 1995). Until 1972, women were required to quit the Foreign Service as soon as they married, and it was common for women to be questioned about their marriage plans when applying for Foreign Service positions (Shoemaker/Park 2009).

2   Methods

2.1   Participants

We examined 1,771 diplomats on post abroad from the German Foreign Service (GFS) sample (see Wiernik et al. 2018, Chapter 1, and Rüger et al. 2018, Appendix B, this volume, for more details). As shown in Table 1, 47% of the sample was female. On average, diplomats were 45 years old (men were 48 and women 42 years old, respectively) and had been part of the GFS organizational rotation process for 18 years (male = 20, female = 16.5 years). The mean number of posts (including the current one) diplomats had been assigned to was 5.9 (male = 6.5, female = 5.2). Ninety percent of male diplomats had partners, while only 66% of female diplomats did. Similarly, 69% of male diplomats had children, while only 53% of female diplomats did.

Stine Waibel and Heiko Rüger

Table 1: Sample Characteristics

Variable	Total				Male		Female	
	Mean	SD	Min	Max	Mean	SD	Mean	SD
Gender (female = 0, male = 1)	.53	.50	0	1				
Age	45.15	9.86	21	67	47.70	9.65	42.31	9.33
Organizational tenure	18.13	9.73	1	44	19.87	9.82	16.52	9.35
No. of previous assignments	5.85	3.00	1	19	6.48	3.09	5.22	2.80
Higher CS[a]	.20	.40	0	1	.27	.44	.10	.30
Higher intermediate CS[a]	.37	.48	0	1	.32	.47	.44	.50
Intermediate CS[a]	.25	.43	0	1	.34	.47	.14	.35
Ordinary CS[a]	.04	.19	0	1	.06	.24	.01	.08
Secretarial pool[a]	.15	.36	0	1	.01	.11	.31	.46
Partnered, no children[b]	.23	.42	0	1	.23	.42	.23	.42
Partnered, children[b]	.56	.50	0	1	.67	.47	.43	.50
Single, children[b]	.06	.24	0	1	.02	.15	.11	.31
Single, no children[b]	.15	.36	0	1	.08	.27	.24	.42

Note: CS = civil service; [a] dummy coded versus other civil service grades; [b] dummy coded versus other family structures.

In Germany, there are four professional tracks for civil servants, depending on their education level – ordinary service, intermediate service, higher intermediate service, and higher service. The German Foreign Service also employs a secretarial pool. In this sample, 20% of diplomats held the highest rank (higher civil service), but this level was more common among men (27%) than women (10%). In contrast to the male-dominated higher civil service positions, the secretarial pool is almost exclusively female (1% of men, 31% of women).

2.2 Measures

Family status. We compared expatriate outcomes for four family structures – diplomats who were partnered with children, partnered without children, single with children (i.e., single parents), and single without children. Note that having a partner and/or children does not imply that employees are necessarily *accompanied* by these family members (though separated families are rare in our sample, see below). Family members could reside in a different location or country; we consider such situations when interpreting our results.

Locational adjustment. Locational adjustment was measured using eight statements assessing diplomats' feelings of comfort in their new location with regards to everyday needs and activities (e.g., "I can easily look after every day errands."; $\alpha = .81$).

Job satisfaction. Job satisfaction was measured using seven items assessing individuals' evaluations of their working conditions, compensation, career progress, and jobs overall. An example item was "How satisfied are you with the working atmosphere at your current post?" Items were standardized before summing to bring variables with different response scales to a comparable metric ($\alpha = .67$).

Satisfaction with rotation process. We measured diplomats' satisfaction with the rotation process using 9 items, including evaluations of life in rotation in general and the way the rotation system works in specific (e.g., "How satisfied are you with the rotation process?"). Items were standardized before summing ($\alpha = .73$).

Health-related quality of life. Health-related quality of life (i.e., subjective health) was measured using 13 items from the German language version of the Quality of Life Questionnaire (Aaronson et al. 1993). Respondents self-rated their physical and mental health; high scores indicate better subjective health. Items were standardized before summing ($\alpha = .92$).

Work–life conflict. Perceived conflict between work and non-work responsibilities was measured using eleven items assessing the degree to which diplomats felt conflict between their work in the GFS and their personal and family life ($\alpha = .82$; e.g. "The frequent moves are a burden to family life"). Assessed demands of diplomats' work in the GFS capture both general work characteristics as well as the demands of frequent rotation to new countries.

Stress. Perceived stress was measured using three items from the German version of the Perceived Stress Questionnaire (Fliege et al. 2005). Items assessed general feelings of being overwhelmed and unable to manage demands across life domains ($\alpha = .77$; e.g. "Your problems seem to be piling up").

2.3 Analyses

For each outcome variable, we compared gender and family status group differences by computing means and standard deviations for each subgroup and computing standardized mean differences (Cohen's *d*) for each subgroup, referenced to the largest subgroup for comparison.

Table 2: Correlations of Expatriate Outcomes with Age and Civil Service Grade

	Variable	1	2	3	4	5	6	7	8
1	Age	1.00							
2	Civil service grade[a]	-.04	1.00						
		(-.08, .01)							
3	Locational adjustment	.01	.15	1.00					
		(-.04, .06)	(.10, .20)						
4	Job satisfaction	.00	.33	.35	1.00				
		(-.06, .06)	(.28, .39)	(.29, .41)					
5	Satisfaction with rotation	-.01	.17	.25	.66	1.00			
		(-.07, .06)	(.12, .23)	(.19, .31)	(.60, .72)				
6	Health-related quality of life	.03	.01	.28	.39	.36	1.00		
		(-.02, .08)	(-.03, .06)	(.23, .33)	(.33, .45)	(.30, .46)			
7	Work–life conflict	-.13	.04	-.26	-.42	-.54	-.51	1.00	
		(-.20, -.06)	(-.03, .10)	(-.33, -.19)	(-.50, -.35)	(-.61, -.47)	(-.56, -.45)		
8	Stress	-.05	.09	-.23	-.35	-.27	-.58	.51	1.00
		(-.10, .00)	(.04, .14)	(-.28, -.17)	(-.41, -.28)	(-.34, -.21)	(-.62, -.54)	(.44, .57)	

Note: Correlations corrected for unreliability in measured variables with 90% confidence intervals; [a] higher/higher intermediate civil service versus lower-level groups (including secretarial pool).

We observed substantial relations of age and civil service grade with both gender and many outcome variables (see Tables 1 and 2, as well as Waibel et al. 2018, Chapter 9, this volume), so we additionally computed Cohen's *d* values while controlling for these two potential confounds using factorial ANCOVA[1]. We corrected all *d* values for criterion unreliability. Measurement error in criterion variables systematically downwardly biases group differences and other variable relations (Schmidt/Hunter 2015); failure to correct for measurement error thus leads underestimates of the effects of gender and family status on diplomat well-being outcomes.

3 Results

3.1 Gender Differences in Family Structure

The data revealed substantial family status differences between male and female German diplomats. As shown in Table 1, most male diplomats had a partner and at least one child (67%), but only 43% of female diplomats reported this classic family structure. Men and women were in relationships without children at equal rates (23%), but women were more often single parents (11% versus 2% for men) and single without children (24% versus 8% for men). Some diplomats reported that they were in long-distance relationships. In couples without children, 22% of partners (27% of women, 18% of men) did not accompany the diplomat to their current location. Among couples with children, 7.5% of partners did not live in the same country as the diplomat; rates of long-distance relationships did not differ substantially by gender among couples without children (7.7% for male diplomats, 7.4% for female diplomats). Many diplomats also reported that maintaining relationships was an issue. Thirty-five percent of diplomats (39% of females and 31% of males) reported that they at least once experienced a relationship breakup due to an international move associated with their job. Moreover, 60% of diplomats reported experiencing problems forming and establishing intimate relationships (particularly women – 73% of females versus 47% of males). Given substantial gender differences in family structure, we explored whether these translate to corresponding differences in family-related outcomes.

3.2 Gender Differences in Expatriate Outcomes

Table 3 shows gender differences for the six expatriate well-being outcomes investigated in this study. We report both zero-order Cohen's *d* values, as well as *d* values controlling for civil service (CS) grade and age. All *d* values were corrected for criterion unreliability.

Women report somewhat poorer subjective health than men (*d* = -.23, 90% confidence interval [CI] -.32, -.13), somewhat more work-life conflict (*d* = .24, CI .13, .36), and slightly more stress (*d* = .11, CI .01, .20). These differences decreased somewhat when controlling for age and CS grade. Gender differences for locational adjustment, job satisfaction, and satisfaction with rotation were negligible.

---

[1] We additionally checked whether these covariates interacted with gender or family status to predict any outcomes. We found no substantial interactions and so omitted these higher-order terms from the ANCOVA models.

Table 3: Gender and expatriate outcomes

	Locational adjustment				Job satisfaction				Satisfaction with rotation			
	N	M	SD	d	N	M	SD	d	N	M	SD	d
Male	734	2.73	.61		657	.02	.58		608	.02	.54	
Female	654	2.77	.57	**.08** (-.02, .18) *.08 (-.02, .19)*	544	.00	.57	**-.05** (-.16, .07) *.00 (-.12, .12)*	479	-.01	.59	**-.05** (-.17, .07) *.00 (-.12, .12)*

	Health-related quality of life				Work-life conflict				Stress			
	N	M	SD	d	N	M	SD	d	N	M	SD	d
Male	751	.07	.67		571	2.56	.52		794	2.31	.71	
Female	651	-.08	.74	**-.23** (-.32, -.13) *-.17 (-.26, .07)*	455	2.67	.50	**.24** (.13, .36) *.12 (.00, .24)*	706	2.38	.73	**.11** (.01, .20) *.08 (-.02, .18)*

Note: d = standardized mean difference (Cohen's d), corrected for criterion unreliability, with 90% confidence intervals; d values in bold are zero-order differences; d values in italics are controlled for civil service grade and age (Ns, means, and SDs unadjusted); positive d values indicate that females score higher than males.

3.3   Family Status Differences in Expatriate Outcomes

Expatriate outcome differences across family status groups are shown in Table 4. Diplomats who were single parents showed the worst outcomes, with somewhat lower health-related quality of life (d = -.28, CI -.41, -.09) and job satisfaction (d = -.22, CI -.46, .02) and much worse rotation satisfaction (d = -.38, CI -.62, -.15) and work–life conflict (d = .60, CI .37, .82), compared to partnered diplomats with children. Job satisfaction differences became negligible when controlling for age and CS grade (d_{adj} = -.06), but other differences remained substantial. Somewhat surprisingly, we also observed that single diplomats without children perceived more work-life conflict than partnered diplomat parents (d = .39, CI .20, .58; d_{adj} = .22 controlling for age and CS grade). However, examinations of the interactions between gender and family status (see below), revealed that these differences are specific to women. Locational adjustment and stress consistently showed negligible differences across family status groups.

3.4   Influence of Gender and Family Status on Expatriate Outcomes

Table 5 shows expatriate outcome differences across family status groups separately by gender. Results revealed several intriguing interactions between gender and family status. The negative effects of single parenthood on rotation satisfaction were consistent across gender (d = .55 for men, -.38 for women), but for women, these differences were largely attributable to CS grade (d_{adj} = -.09). Compared to male partnered diplomats with children, all other groups reported more work–life conflict, with effect sizes ranging from negligible (d = .09 for partnered men without children) to very large (d = 1.06 for male single parents). Excluding male single parents (see below), the largest work–life conflict effects were observed for single women, who reported much greater reconcilability challenges regardless of parenthood (d = .54 for both single female parents and non-parents). This difference may reflect that many single diplomat women perceive that working in the GFS interferes with their ability to establish and maintain personal relationships (see the discussion above). Female parents (regardless of partner status) also reported substantially lower health-related quality of life (d = -.43 single, -.29 partnered) and higher stress (d = .22 single, .23 partnered) than other groups. Most other group differences were negligible to slight ($|d| < .20$).

Male single parents showed especially poor outcomes across criteria (e.g., d = 1.06 for work-life conflict, -.66 for locational adjustment, compared to male partnered diplomats with children), but the sample size for this group was very small (N = 17), so these exceptionally large effects may be attributable to sampling error.

Table 4: Family status and expatriate outcomes

		Locational adjustment				Job satisfaction				Satisfaction with rotation			
		N	M	SD	d	N	M	SD	d	N	M	SD	d
Partnered	Children	803	2.74	.61		320	.02	.58		543	.01	.57	
	No children	314	2.75	.59	**.02** (-.10, .15) *.00 (-.13, .13)*	236	.00	.58	**-.06** (-.20, .09) *-.07 (-.23, .08)*	229	.02	.54	**-.05** (-.17, .07) *.00 (-.12, .12)*
Single	Children	89	2.72	.62	**-.03** (-.23, .18) *.00 (-.22, .22)*	66	-.08	.57	**-.22** (-.46, .02) *-.06 (-.32, .20)*	73	-.18	.65	**-.38** (-.62, -.15) *-.19 (-.44, .06)*
	No children	211	2.77	.54	**.06** (-.08, .20) *.00 (-.15, .15)*	173	.00	.52	**-.05** (-.22, .12) *-.06 (-.24, .11)*	150	.02	.51	**.03** (-.15, .20) *-.01 (-.19, .16)*

		Health-related quality of life				Work-life conflict				Stress			
		N	M	SD	d	N	M	SD	d	N	M	SD	d
Partnered	Children	803	-.01	.72		642	2.56	.52		834	2.36	.73	
	No children	329	.05	.67	**.09** (-.02, .20) *.12 (.00, .24)*	228	2.62	.50	**.13** (-.01, .27) *.04 (-.11, .19)*	345	2.32	.72	**-.06** (-.18, .07) *-.05 (-.18, .08)*
Single	Children	85	-.20	.78	**-.28** (-.48, -.09) *-.24 (-.44, -.03)*	73	2.84	.50	**.60** (.37, .82) *.44 (.20, .68)*	92	2.41	.63	**.09** (-.12, .29) *.10 (-.12, .32)*
	No children	186	.06	.64	**.09** (-.05, .23) *.16 (.01, .30)*	109	2.74	.49	**.39** (.20, .58) *.22 (.02, .42)*	228	2.31	.72	**-.07** (-.21, .07) *-.12 (-.27, .03)*

Note: *d* = standardized mean difference (Cohen's *d*), corrected for criterion unreliability, with 90% confidence intervals; *d* values in bold are zero-order differences; *d* values in italics are controlled for civil service grade and age (*N*s, means, and *SD*s unadjusted); positive *d* values indicate that specified group scores higher than partnered expatriates with children.

Table 5: Interaction of gender and family status on expatriate outcomes

		Locational adjustment				Job satisfaction				Satisfaction with rotation			
		N	*M*	*SD*	*d*	*N*	*M*	*SD*	*d*	*N*	*M*	*SD*	*d*
Male													
Partnered	Children	492	2.72	.62		444	.03	.58		418	.01	.55	
	No children	159	2.74	.61	**-.03** (-.20, .13) *-.06 (-.23, .11)*	141	.05	.59	**.04** (-.16, .23) *.02 (-.17, .22)*	124	.06	.52	**.10** (-.09, .30) *.10 (-.10, .31)*
Single	Children	16	2.37	.75	**-.66** (-1.13, -.20) *-.60 (-1.08, -.13)*	15	-.21	.48	**-.50** (-1.03, .03) *-.51 (-1.04, .01)*	16	-.24	.56	**-.55** (-1.04, -.06) *-.40 (-.90, .09)*
	No children	54	2.74	.53	**.00** (-.26, .26) *.06 (-.35, .24)*	46	-.03	.53	**-.13** (-.44, .18) *-.15 (-.48, .18)*	43	.01	.54	**-.02** (-.32, .29) *.03 (-.30, .36)*
Female													
Partnered	Children	253	2.75	.59	**.03** (-.11, .16) *.02 (-.12, .17)*	236	.03	.58	**-.01** (-.17, .15) *.03 (-.13, .19)*	210	.03	.61	**.04** (-.12, .21) *.08 (-.09, .25)*
	No children	125	2.80	.57	**.15** (-.04, .33) *.09 (-.06, .29)*	119	-.03	.57	**-.12** (-.33, .09) *-.17 (-.38, .04)*	98	.00	.56	**-.04** (-.25, .18) *-.02 (-.24, .20)*
Single	Children	61	2.79	.57	**.10** (-.13, .33) *.17 (-.08, .41)*	59	-.05	.60	**-.17** (-.45, .11) *.07 (-.21, .35)*	56	-.17	.67	**-.38** (-.66, -.11) *-.09 (-.38, .20)*
	No children	137	2.77	.54	**.06** (-.11, .23) *.03 (-.15, .21)*	120	.03	.52	**.00** (-.21, .20) *-.03 (-.24, .17)*	103	.03	.50	**.03** (-.19, .24) *.01 (-.20, .22)*

Table 5: Interaction of gender and family status on expatriate outcomes – continued

		Health-related quality of life				Work–life conflict				Stress			
		N	M	SD	d	N	M	SD	d	N	M	SD	d
Male													
Partnered	Children	512	.07	.67		402	2.53	.51		525	2.30	.70	
	No children	169	.12	.64	**.08** (-.07, .23) *.08 (-.08, .24)*	122	2.57	.51	**.09** (-.10, .28) *.02 (-.17, .22)*	180	2.34	.71	**.06** (-.10, .22) *.05 (-.12, .22)*
Single	Children	16	-.13	.78	**-.31** (-.74, .13) *-.24 (-.69, .21)*	17	3.02	.41	**1.06** (.61, 1.52) *.79 (.32, 1.25)*	17	2.31	.55	**.03** (-.44, .49) *.03 (-.44, .51)*
	No children	45	.05	.68	**-.02** (-.29, .25) *.09 (-.20, .38)*	24	2.59	.57	**.14** (-.24, .52) *-.02 (-.42, .37)*	60	2.28	.83	**-.03** (-.29, .22) *-.12 (-.41, .16)*
Female													
Partnered	Children	278	-.13	.78	**-.29** (-.42, -.16) *-.21 (-.34, -.08)*	218	2.60	.50	**.16** (.01, .32) *.06 (-.10, .22)*	294	2.44	.76	**.22** (.08, .35) *.15 (.14, .16)*
	No children	151	-.01	.68	**-.12** (-.27, .04) *-.04 (-.20, .13)*	96	2.67	.49	**.30** (.09, .51) *.13 (-.09, .34)*	156	2.32	.75	**.03** (-.14, .20) *-.02 (-.20, .16)*
Single	Children	68	-.22	.80	**-.43** (-.65, -.21) *-.33 (-.56, -.09)*	54	2.78	.53	**.54** (.28, .81) *.35 (.07, .63)*	73	2.44	.65	**.23** (.00, .47) *.19 (-.06, .44)*
	No children	137	.06	.63	**-.01** (-.18, .15) *.04 (-.13, .21)*	77	2.77	.46	**.54** (.31, .77) *.33 (.10, .56)*	162	2.31	.67	**.02** (-.15, .19) *-.03 (-.20, .15)*

Note: d = standardized mean difference (Cohen's d), corrected for criterion unreliability, with 90% confidence intervals; d values in bold are zero-order differences; d values in italics are controlled for civil service grade and age (Ns, means, and SDs unadjusted); positive d values indicate that specified group scores higher than partnered expatriates with children.

4   Discussion

We found that female GFS employees were more likely to be single and childless than male employees and to report that life in rotation interfered with their ability to establish relationships, supporting the thesis that women face greater trade-offs than men and may find it more difficult to have both a family and an expatriate career. Given this stratification of family status along gender lines, we explored the impacts of gender and family on diplomats' outcomes.

4.1   Gender and Diplomat Well-Being

We found that male and female diplomats did not differ in their locational adjustment, job satisfaction, or satisfaction with rotation. These findings are consistent with existing research documenting that women are equally suited to adapting to and working in foreign countries as men (Froese/Peltokorpi 2011; Hechanova et al. 2003; Selmer/Leung 2003; Sinangil/Ones 2003), despite characterizations that foreign societies with masculine values might create more challenges for female expatriates (Caligiuri/Tung 1999). Indeed, female expatriates are often seen more as "foreigners" than as "women" by host country nationals and may be better able to perform effectively than men in terms of building and maintaining work relationships, negotiation, and interacting (Adler 1987).

However, compared to male diplomats, female diplomats reported lower subjective health, more stress, and more work-life conflict. These findings are consistent with research across life domains finding higher levels of depression, distress, chronic illnesses, and anxiety about social roles among women than men (Verbrugge 1985), but contrasts domestic employee research finding similar levels of work–family conflict for men and women (Byron 2005). This suggests that the additional challenges of frequent mobility may exacerbate the obstacles women may face meeting both their personal and professional goals, particularly for women in challenging family structures (see below).

4.2   Family Status and Diplomat Well-Being

Concerning diplomats with different family structures, we identified single parents as the most vulnerable group. Having children but no partner was associated with job and rotation dissatisfaction, poor subjective health, and high work–life conflict. Consistent with applications of the job demands-resources model to expatriate contexts (Lazarova et al. 2010; Qin et al. 2014; Shaffer et al. 2012), our findings suggest that, for single parent diplomats, their family and mobility demands are not offset by social support resources from their partners, leading to lower well-being. Moreover, negative affective experiences related to their family situation, such as experiences of divorce or separation, feelings of time deficits with their children, or experiences of isolation without a partner, may also create additional psychological demands on single parents. However, it is difficult to confirm the causal direction in these relations, as it may be that individuals more prone to health problems, dissatisfaction, and work–life conflict are also more likely to experience separation or divorce (cf. Carr/Springer 2010).

4.3   Interaction between Family Status and Gender

We also found several substantial interactions between gender and family status on diplomat well-being outcomes. First, the negative impact of single parenthood was especially pronounced for men in our sample. For men, separation from a partner in most cases implies separation from the couple's children. Having geographically distant children likely creates additional psychological and social costs (e.g., feelings of guilt and deprivation) that hinder adjustment and coping (cf. Mayerhofer et al. 2004). Male single diplomats who are the active parents for their children may also face additional societal pressures and stigma compared to female single parents (cf. Waters 2010) and may be less able than women to compensate for the demands of single parenthood through expanding external support (Caligiuri/Lazarova 2002). These findings may also qualify simplistic generalizations, such as the "[o]bvious fact that single or divorced women with children have one of the highest work/life balance tensions" (Fischlmayr/Kollinger-Santer 2014: 62). However, as noted above, our sample of male single parents was extremely small, so these large negative effects should not be overinterpreted.

We also found that female (but not male) parents, regardless of partnership status, reported higher stress and poorer health than either men or female non-parents. These differences support voluminous findings of gender imbalances in parenting responsibility (e.g., Katz-Wise et al. 2010) and suggest that female expatriate parents may face unique obstacles, even in the presence of a supportive (and even non-employed) partner.

Finally, we found that female single diplomats, regardless of parenthood, reported much higher levels of work–life conflict than most male subgroups. This finding (combined with similar levels of work–life conflict between male and female single parents) suggests that aggregate gender differences in work–life conflict (i.e., women reporting more conflicts) reflect less parenting issues than they do partnering issues. Female expatriates are more likely to experience problems finding (new) partners who are willing to sacrifice their own career to accompany their spouse abroad (Cole 2011; Selmer/Leung 2003) and more often feel that they must choose between having a career and having a family (Linehan/ Walsh 2000; Shoemaker/Park 2009; Tzeng 2006). Not having children may similarly reflect a "creeping non-choice" among professional women who put off family formation from year to year for the sake of work (Hewlett 2002). Female diplomats in this sample are also more likely to experience a relationship ending because of an international move. Together, these findings also point toward complications in the family formation process being more common among female diplomats. For women, life in the Foreign Service, where international moves are typically non-negotiable, may seem fundamentally irreconcilable with family life (cf. Mincer 1978).

5   Conclusion

Integration of women and new family models into the German Foreign Service has not come about without frictions. Our current findings underscore the need for continued investigation into how personal and family goals can be supported as employees pursue their careers in the diplomatic service. We continue to observe the influence of traditional cultural practices on not only women's but (perhaps increasingly so) also men's well-being, depending on their family context. Future expatriate research should delve more deeply into the complexities of the intersection between family structure, gender, work, and the organizational environment in expatriation contexts. In particular, the challenges of family formation and stabilization, especially for women, deserve attention (cf. Ackers 2004). Moreover, the challenges associated with geographic separation between family members and other emerging non-traditional expatriate family structures should also receive greater attention (for example, see Mercado et al. 2018, Chapter 16, this volume; cf. Waters 2010).

References

Aaronson, Neil K. et al. (1993): The European Organization for Research and Treatment of Cancer QLQ-C30: A Quality-of-Life Instrument for Use in International Clinical Trials in Oncology. In: *Journal of the National Cancer Institute* 85,5: 365–376. [https://doi.org/10/d9d26h].

Ackers, Louise (2004): Managing Relationships in Peripatetic Careers: Scientific Mobility in the European Union. In: *Women's Studies International Forum* 27,3: 189–201. [https://doi.org/10.1016/j.wsif.2004.03.001].

Adelman, Mara B. (1988): Cross-Cultural Adjustment: A Theoretical Perspective on Social Support. In: *International Journal of Intercultural Relations* 12,3: 183–204. [https://doi.org/10.1016/0147-1767(88)90015-6].

Adler, Nancy J. (1987): Pacific Basin Managers: A Gaijin, Not a Woman. In: *Human Resource Management* 26,2: 169–191. [https://doi.org/10.1002/hrm.3930260205].

Adler, Nancy J. (1984): Women Do Not Want International Careers: And Other Myths about International Management. In: *Organizational Dynamics* 13,2: 66–79. [https://doi.org/10.1016/0090-2616(84)90019-6].

Albrecht, Anne-Grit; Ones, Deniz S.; Sinangil, Handan Kepir (2018): Expatriate Management. In: Ones, Deniz S. et al. (Eds.): The SAGE Handbook of Industrial, Work and Organizational Psychology. Volume 3: Managerial Psychology and Organizational Approaches. 2nd ed. London, United Kingdom: Sage: 429–468.

BGRS (2016): Breakthrough to the Future of Global Talent Mobility: 2016 Global Mobility Trends Survey Report. Woodridge, IL: Brookfield Global Relocation Services. [http://globalmobilitytrends.brookfieldgrs.com].

BGRS (2012): Global Relocation Trends: 2012 Survey Report. Woodridge, IL: Brookfield Global Relocation Services. [http://globalmobilitytrends.brookfieldgrs.com].

Bhaskar-Shrinivas, Purnima et al. (2005): Input-Based and Time-Based Models of International Adjustment: Meta-Analytic Evidence and Theoretical Extensions. In: *Academy of Management Journal* 48,2: 257–281. [https://doi.org/10.5465/AMJ.2005.16928400].

Black, J. Stewart; Stephens, Gregory K. (1989): The Influence of the Spouse on American Expatriate Adjustment and Intent to Stay in Pacific Rim Overseas Assignments. In: *Journal of Management* 15,4: 529–544. [https://doi.org/10.1177/014920638901500403].

Brandt, Enrico; Buck, Christian (2005): Auswärtiges Amt: Diplomatie als Beruf. 4th ed. Wiesbaden, Germany: VS Verlag für Sozialwissenschaften. [https://doi.org/10/b6k9].

Byron, Kristin (2005): A Meta-Analytic Review of Work-Family Conflict and Its Antecedents. In: *Journal of Vocational Behavior* 67,2: 169–198. [https://doi.org/10/b4kdmm].

Caligiuri, Paula M.; Cascio, Wayne F. (1998): Can We Send Her There? Maximizing the Success of Western Women on Global Assignments. In: *Journal of World Business* 33,4: 394–416. [https://doi.org/10.1016/S1090-9516(98)90024-4].

Caligiuri, Paula M.; Lazarova, Mila (2002): A Model for the Influence of Social Interaction and Social Support on Female Expatriates' Cross-Cultural Adjustment. In: *International Journal of Human Resource Management* 13,5: 761–772. [https://doi.org/10/drscsj].

Caligiuri, Paula M.; Tung, Rosalie L. (1999): Comparing the Success of Male and Female Expatriates from a US-Based Multinational Company. In: *International Journal of Human Resource Management* 10,5: 763–782. [https://doi.org/10/d3nkdr].

Carr, Deborah; Springer, Kristen W. (2010): Advances in Families and Health Research in the 21st Century. In: *Journal of Marriage and Family* 72,3: 743–761. [https://doi.org/10.1111/j.1741-3737.2010.00728.x].

Cartus (2016): Trends in Global Relocation: 2016 Global Mobility Policy & Practices Survey. Danburry, CT: Cartus Corporation. [http://guidance.cartusrelocation.com/global-mobility-policy-and-practices-survey-2016.html].

Cole, Nina D. (2011): Managing Global Talent: Solving the Spousal Adjustment Problem. In: *International Journal of Human Resource Management* 22,7: 1504–1530. [https://doi.org/10.1080/09585192.2011.561963].

Copeland, Anne P.; Norell, Sara K. (2002): Spousal Adjustment on International Assignments: The Role of Social Support. In: *International Journal of Intercultural Relations* 26,3: 255–272. [https://doi.org/10.1016/S0147-1767(02)00003-2].

Davoine, Eric et al. (2013): A "Dramaturgical" Analysis of Spouse Role Enactment in Expatriation: An Exploratory Gender Comparative Study in the Diplomatic and Consular Field. In: *Journal of Global Mobility* 1,1: 92–112. [https://doi.org/10.1108/JGM-09-2012-0005].

Dupuis, Marie-Josée; Haines, Victor Y., III; Saba, Tania (2008): Gender, Family Ties, and International Mobility: Cultural Distance Matters. In: *International Journal of Human Resource Management* 19,2: 274–295. [https://doi.org/10.1080/09585190701799846].

Duxbury, Linda E.; Higgins, Christopher A. (1991): Gender Differences in Work-Family Conflict. In: *Journal of Applied Psychology* 76,1: 60–74. [https://doi.org/10.1037/0021-9010.76.1.60].

Eby, Lillian T. et al. (2002): Managerial Support for Dual-Career Relocation Dilemmas. In: *Journal of Vocational Behavior* 60,3: 354–373. [https://doi.org/10.1006/jvbe.2001.1818].

Eccles, Jacquelynne S. (1987): Gender Roles and Women's Achievement-Related Decisions. In: *Psychology of Women Quarterly* 11,2: 135–172. [https://doi.org/10.1111/j.1471-6402.1987.tb00781.x].

Fischlmayr, Iris C.; Kollinger, Iris (2010): Work-Life Balance: A Neglected Issue among Austrian Female Expatriates. In: *International Journal of Human Resource Management* 21,4: 455–487. [https://doi.org/10.1080/09585191003611978].

Fischlmayr, Iris C.; Kollinger-Santer, Iris (2014): Female Frequent Flyers: How Women Travelling Internationally Handle Their Work/Life Balance. In: Hutchings, Kate; Michailova, Snejina (Eds.): Research Handbook on Women in International Management. Cheltenham, United Kingdom: Elgar: 47–70. [https://doi.org/10.4337/9781781955031.00013].

Fliege, Herbert et al. (2005): The Perceived Stress Questionnaire (PSQ) Reconsidered: Validation and Reference Values from Different Clinical and Healthy Adult Samples. In: *Psychosomatic Medicine* 67,1: 78–88. [https://doi.org/10.1097/01.psy.0000151491.80178.78].

Foldes, Hannah Jackson; Ones, Deniz S.; Sinangil, Handan Kepir (2018): Gender Differences in Job Performance and Adjustment: Do Women Expatriates Measure Up? In: Wiernik, Brenton M.; Rüger, Heiko; Ones, Deniz S. (Eds.): Managing Expatriates: Success Factors in Private and Public Domains, Series on Population Studies 50. Opladen, Germany: Barbara Budrich Publishers.

Froese, Fabian Jintae; Peltokorpi, Vesa (2011): Cultural Distance and Expatriate Job Satisfaction. In: *International Journal of Intercultural Relations* 35,1: 49–60. [https://doi.org/10.1016/j.ijintrel.2010.10.002].

Groeneveld, Sandra (2008): Dual Careers and Diplomacy: The Willingness of Dual-Career Couples to Accept an International Assignment within the Dutch Foreign Services. In: *Review of Public Personnel Administration* 28,1: 20–43. [https://doi.org/10.1177/0734371X07309540].

Grunig, Larissa A. (1995): The Consequences of Culture for Public Relations: The Case of Women in the Foreign Service. In: *Journal of Public Relations Research* 7,2: 139–161. [https://doi.org/10.1207/s1532754xjprr0702_03].

Gutek, Barbara A.; Searle, Sabrina; Klepa, Lilian (1991): Rational versus Gender Role Explanations for Work-Family Conflict. In: *Journal of Applied Psychology* 76,4: 560-568. [https://doi.org/10.1037/0021-9010.76.4.560].

Hamilton, Elizabeth A.; Gordon, Judith R.; Whelan-Berry, Karen S. (2006): Understanding the Work-Life Conflict of Never-Married Women without Children. In: *Women in Management Review* 21,5: 393–415. [https://doi.org/10.1108/09649420610676208].

Harris, Hilary (2004): Global Careers: Work-Life Issues and the Adjustment of Women International Managers. In: *Journal of Management Development* 23,9: 818–832. [https://doi.org/10.1108/02621710410558431].

Harvey, Michael G. (1997): Dual-Career Expatriates: Expectations, Adjustment and Satisfaction with International Relocation. In: *Journal of International Business Studies* 28,3: 627–658. [https://doi.org/10.1016/1053-4822(95)90003-9].

Haslberger, Arno; Brewster, Chris (2008): The Expatriate Family: An International Perspective. In: *Journal of Managerial Psychology* 23,3: 324–346. [https://doi.org/10/dwb3vt].

Hearn, Jeff et al. (2008): "Women Home and Away": Transnational Managerial Work and Gender Relations. In: *Journal of Business Ethics* 83,1: 41-54. [https://doi.org/10.1007/s10551-007-9655-2].

Hechanova, Regina; Beehr, Terry A.; Christiansen, Neil D. (2003): Antecedents and Consequences of Employees' Adjustment to Overseas Assignment: A Meta-Analytic Review. In: *Applied Psychology* 52,2: 213–236. [https://doi.org/10/d4f4xv].

Hewlett, Sylvia Ann (2002): Executive Women and the Myth of Having It All. In: *Harvard Business Review* 80,4: 66–73. [https://doi.org/10.1225/R0204E].

Hofbauer, Johanna; Fischlmayr, Iris C. (2004): Feminization of International Assignments: Conquering Empty Castles? In: *International Studies of Management & Organization* 34,3: 46–67. [https://doi.org/10.1080/00208825.2004.11043706].

Insch, Gary S.; Daniels, John D. (2002): Causes and Consequences of Declining Early Departures from Foreign Assignments. In: *Business Horizons* 45,6: 39–48. [https://doi.org/10.1016/S0007-6813(02)00259-8].

Katz-Wise, Sabra L.; Priess, Heather A.; Hyde, Janet S. (2010): Gender-Role Attitudes and Behavior across the Transition to Parenthood. In: *Developmental Psychology* 46,1: 18–28. [https://doi.org/10.1037/a0017820].

Kim, Jisun; Froese, Fabian Jintae (2012): Expatriation Willingness in Asia: The Importance of Host-Country Characteristics and Employees' Role Commitments. In: *The International Journal of Human Resource Management* 23,16: 3414–3433. [https://doi.org/10.1080/09585192.2011.637068].

Kofman, Eleonore (2012): Gender and skilled migration in Europe. In: *Cuadernos de Relaciones Laborales* 30,1. [https://doi.org/10.5209/rev_CRLA.2012.v30.n1.39115].

Kollinger-Santer, Iris; Fischlmayr, Iris C. (2013): Work Life Balance up in the Air: Does Gender Make a Difference between Female and Male International Business Travelers? In: *German Journal of Human Resource Management* 27,3: 195–223. [https://doi.org/10.1177/239700221302700303].

Lazarova, Mila B.; Westman, Mina; Shaffer, Margaret A. (2010): Elucidating the Positive Side of the Work-Family Interface on International Assigments: A Model of Expatriate Work and Family Performance. In: *Academy of Management Review* 35,1: 93–117. [https://doi.org/10.1057/9781137006004_14].

Linehan, Margaret; Walsh, James S. (2000): Work-Family Conflict and the Senior Female International Manager. In: *British Journal of Management* 11,1: 49–58. [https://doi.org/10.1111/1467-8551.11.s1.5].

Lyness, Karen S.; Judiesch, Michael K. (2008): Can a Manager Have a Life and a Career? International and Multisource Perspectives on Work-Life Balance and Career Advancement Potential. In: *Journal of Applied Psychology* 93,4: 789–805. [https://doi.org/10.1037/0021-9010.93.4.789].

Mäkelä, Liisa; Känsälä, Marja; Suutari, Vesa (2011a): The Roles of Expatriates' Spouses among Dual Career Couples. In: *Cross Cultural Management* 18,2: 185–197. [https://doi.org/10.1108/13527601111126012].

Mäkelä, Liisa; Suutari, Vesa; Mayerhofer, Helene (2011b): Lives of Female Expatriates: Work-Life Balance Concerns. In: *Gender in Management* 26,4: 256–274. [https://doi.org/10.1108/17542411111144283].

Martinengo, Giuseppe; Jacob, Jenet I.; Hill, E. Jeffrey (2010): Gender and the Work-Family Interface: Exploring Differences across the Family Life Course. In: *Journal of Family Issues* 31,10: 1363–1390. [https://doi.org/10.1177/0192513X10361709].

Mayerhofer, Helene; Hartmann, Linley C.; Herbert, Anne (2004): Career Management Issues for Flexpatriate International Staff. In: *Thunderbird International Business Review* 46,6: 647–666. [https://doi.org/10.1002/tie.20029].

McNulty, Yvonne (2014): Women as Female Breadwinners in Non-Traditional Expatriate Families: Status-Reversal Marriages, Single Parents, Split Families, and Lesbian Partnerships. In: Hutchings, Kate; Michailova, Snejina (Eds.): Research Handbook on Women in International Management. Cheltenham, United Kingdom: Elgar: 332–366. [https://doi.org/10.4337/9781781955031.00025].

McNulty, Yvonne (2012): 'Being Dumped in to Sink or Swim': An Empirical Study of Organizational Support for the Trailing Spouse. In: *Human Resource Development International* 15,4: 417–434. [https://doi.org/10.1080/13678868.2012.721985].

Meil, Gerardo (2010): Geographic Job Mobility and Parenthood Decisions. In: *Journal of Family Research* 22,2: 171–195. [https://doi.org/10.3224/zff.v22i2.4025].

Mercado, Brittany K. et al. (2018): Influence of Family Presence on Expatriate Adjustment and Satisfaction. In: Wiernik, Brenton M.; Rüger, Heiko; Ones, Deniz S. (Eds.): Managing Expatriates: Success Factors in Private and Public Domains, Series on Population Studies 50. Opladen, Germany: Barbara Budrich Publishers.

Mincer, Jacob (1978): Family Migration Decisions. In: *Journal of Political Economy* 86,5: 749–773. [https://doi.org/10.1086/260710].

Mohr, Alex T.; Klein, Simone (2008): Adjustment vs. Satisfaction: An Analysis of American Expatriate Spouses in Germany. In: Holtbrügge, Dirk (Ed.): Cultural Adjustment of Expatriates: Theoretical Concepts and Empirical Studies. München, Germany: Rainer Hampp: 49–59.

Qin, Xin et al. (2014): Applying the Job Demands-Resources Model to Migrant Workers: Exploring How and When Geographical Distance Increases Quit Propensity. In: *Journal of Occupational and Organizational Psychology* 87,2: 303–328. [https://doi.org/10.1111/joop.12047].

Richardson, Julia (2006): Self-Directed Expatriation: Family Matters. In: *Personnel Review* 35,4: 469–486. [https://doi.org/10.1108/00483480610670616].

Rüger, Heiko et al. (2018): Sampling and Procedures for the Mobility Skills in the German Foreign Service Study. In: Wiernik, Brenton M.; Rüger, Heiko; Ones, Deniz S. (Eds.): Managing Expatriates: Success Factors in Private and Public Domains, Series on Population Studies 50. Opladen, Germany: Barbara Budrich Publishers.

Schmidt, Frank L.; Hunter, John E. (2015): Methods of Meta-Analysis: Correcting Error and Bias in Research Findings. 3rd ed. Thousand Oaks, CA: Sage. [https://doi.org/10/b6mg].

Selmer, Jan; Lauring, Jakob (2011): Marital Status and Work Outcomes of Self-initiated Expatriates: Is There a Moderating Effect of Gender? In: *Cross Cultural Management* 18,2: 198–213. [https://doi.org/10.1108/13527601111126021].

Selmer, Jan; Leung, Alicia S.M. (2003): International Adjustment of Female vs Male Business Expatriates. In: *International Journal of Human Resource Management* 14,7: 1117–1131. [https://doi.org/10.1080/0958519032000114237].

Shaffer, Margaret A. et al. (2012): Choices, Challenges, and Career Consequences of Global Work Experiences: A Review and Future Agenda. In: *Journal of Management* 38,4: 1282–1327. [https://doi.org/10.1177/0149206312441834].

Shaffer, Margaret A.; Harrison, David A. (2001): Forgotten Partners of International Assignments: Development and Test of a Model of Spouse Adjustment. In: *Journal of Applied Psychology* 86,2: 238–254. [https://doi.org/10.1037/0021-9010.86.2.238].

Shaffer, Margaret A.; Harrison, David A. (1998): Expatriates' Psychological Withdrawal from International Assignments: Work, Nonwork, and Family Influences. In: *Personnel Psychology* 51,1: 87–118. [https://doi.org/10.1111/j.1744-6570.1998.tb00717.x].

Shoemaker, Jolynn; Park, Jennifer (2009): Progress Report on Women in Peace and Security Careers: U.S. Executive Branch. WIIS Leadership Series. Washington, DC: Georgetown University, Center for Strategic and International Studies, Women in International Security. [https://www.csis.org/analysis/progress-report-women-peace-security-careers].

Sinangil, Handan Kepir; Ones, Deniz S. (2003): Gender Differences in Expatriate Job Performance. In: *Applied Psychology* 52,3: 461–475. [https://doi.org/10/c36tw5].

Takeuchi, Riki (2010): A Critical Review of Expatriate Adjustment Research through a Multiple Stakeholder View: Progress, Emerging Trends, and Prospects. In: *Journal of Management* 36,4: 1040–1064. [https://doi.org/10.1177/0149206309349308].

Tharenou, Phyllis (2008): Disruptive Decisions to Leave Home: Gender and Family Differences in Expatriation Choices. In: *Organizational Behavior and Human Decision Processes* 105,2: 183–200. [https://doi.org/10.1016/j.obhdp.2007.08.004].

Thompson, Linda; Walker, Alexis J. (1989): Gender in Families: Women and Men in Marriage, Work, and Parenthood. In: *Journal of Marriage and the Family* 51,4: 845. [https://doi.org/10.2307/353201].

Tung, Rosalie L. (1982): Selection and Training Procedures of U.S., European, and Japanese Multinationals. In: *California Management Review* 25,2: 57–71. [https://doi.org/10.1002/tie.5060250204].

Tzeng, Rueyling (2006): Gender Issues and Family Concerns for Women with International Careers: Female Expatriates in Western Multinational Corporations in Taiwan. In: *Women in Management Review* 21,5: 376–392. [https://doi.org/10.1108/09649420610676190].

Verbrugge, Lois M. (1985): Gender and Health: An Update on Hypotheses and Evidence. In: *Journal of Health and Social Behavior* 26,3: 156. [https://doi.org/10.2307/2136750].

Waibel, Stine et al. (2018): Impacts of Age, Tenure, and Experience on Expatriate Adjustment and Job Satisfaction. In: Wiernik, Brenton M.; Rüger, Heiko; Ones, Deniz S. (Eds.): Managing Expatriates: Success Factors in Private and Public Domains, Series on Population Studies 50. Opladen, Germany: Barbara Budrich Publishers.

Waters, Johanna L. (2010): Becoming a Father, Missing a Wife: Chinese Transnational Families and the Male Experience of Lone Parenting in Canada. In: *Population, Space and Place*, Special Issue: Embodied Transnationalism: Bodies in Transnational Spaces 16,1: 63–74. [https://doi.org/10.1002/psp.578].

Whip, Rosemary (1982): The Parliamentary Wife: Participant in the Two-Person Single Career. In: *Australian Journal of Political Science* 17,2: 38–44. [https://doi.org/10.1080/00323268208401852].

Wiernik, Brenton M.; Rüger, Heiko; Ones, Deniz S. (2018): Advancing Expatriate Research in Public and Private Sectors. In: Wiernik, Brenton M.; Rüger, Heiko; Ones, Deniz S. (Eds.): Managing Expatriates: Success Factors in Private and Public Domains, Series on Population Studies 50. Opladen, Germany: Barbara Budrich Publishers.

Wiese, Bettina S. (2004): Konflikte zwischen Beruf und Familie im Alltagserleben erwerbstätiger Paare. In: *Zeitschrift für Sozialpsychologie* 35,1: 45–58. [https://doi.org/10.1024/0044-3514.35.1.45].

Wood, Molly M. (2005): Diplomatic Wives: The Politics of Domesticity and the "Social Game" in the United States Foreign Service, 1905-1941. In: *Journal of Women's History* 17,2: 142–165. [https://doi.org/10.1353/jowh.2005.0025].

Appendix A: Design, Implementation, and Analysis of the iGOES Project

Anne-Grit Albrecht, Jürgen Deller, Deniz S. Ones, Stephan Dilchert, and Frieder M. Paulus

1 Introduction

The iGOES project was launched to provide a rigorous evaluation of the international generalizability of factors contributing to success and failure for expatriate employees. The project was a large-scale multinational collaboration designed with four guiding principles.

First, we sought to assess expatriates using the same instruments in countries spanning the full range of global cultural dimensions. Nearly all existing expatriate research examines variable relations within one, two, or, at most, three countries (Franke/Richey 2010). These designs sample a limited range of cultural characteristics and are thus severely constrained in the conclusions about cross-cultural generalizability or specificity that can be drawn. In contrast, iGOES sampled expatriates from 28 countries covering each of the major world cultural clusters.

Second, participants in the iGOES project were drawn from culturally-homogeneous backgrounds. Most expatriate studies include expatriates from a range of origin countries. This sampling heterogeneity confounds the effects of expatriates' host-country cultures with their home-country cultures (and the interactions between specific home- and host-country cultural characteristics; Ones et al. 2012; Spector et al. 2002). In contrast, iGOES sampled only German-speaking expatriates originating from Germanic European countries (i.e., Germany, Austria, and Switzerland). This "intercontextual" (versus merely "intercultural"; Ones et al. 2012: 111) research design allowed the iGOES project to examine the influence of foreign cultural contexts free from the confounding influence of expatriates' home cultures.

Third, iGOES sought to include a diverse range of predictor measures. Beyond predictor constructs commonly measured in expatriate research (e.g., self-efficacy, cross-cultural training, social support, language proficiency, tolerance of ambiguity), iGOES also sought to examine antecedent constructs that are widely-studied in domestic employee research, but which have been generally overlooked in expatriate studies. These include demographic characteristics, such as gender, age, and experience, as well as individual differences traits, such as cognitive ability and the Big Five personality traits (Campbell 2013). Widening the range of predictor constructs considered in expatriate research allows iGOES to better connect expatriate findings with broader theories of job performance, satisfaction, and persistence, and to more clearly specify which success factors are shared with domestic employees and which are unique to the international work context.

Fourth, iGOES sought to rigorously measure a range of critical expatriate criterion constructs. Most expatriate research has focused exclusively on international adjustment, the degree to which expatriates feel comfortable living, working, and interacting in their new locations (Black et al. 1991), assuming that adjustment is the most (and perhaps only) important antecedent for expatriate success (Albrecht et al. 2018; Mol et al. 2005; Sinangil/ Ones 2001). However, other criteria, such as job performance, withdrawal cognitions, and job satisfaction are likely to be more important for both sending organizations and expatriates themselves; adjustment should best be regarded as a mediator variable, rather than a success criterion in and of itself (Sinangil/Ones 2001). iGOES thus sought to examine a wide range of important expatriate outcomes and to do so using psychometrically-rigorous, construct valid, and contextually-appropriate measures.

Below, we provide an overview of the sampling methods, criterion measures, and statistical analyses used in the iGOES analyses reported in this volume. Predictor measures are described in their respective chapters.

2 Selection of Countries

Participants in the iGOES project were expatriates working in 28 countries across the world covering all of the GLOBE cultural clusters (House et al. 2004) – *Anglo* (Ireland, the United Kingdom, the United States), *Confucian Asia* (China, Singapore, South Korea), *Germanic Europe* (Austria, the Netherlands, Switzerland), *Eastern Europe* (Czech Republic, Poland, Russia), *Latin America* (Argentina, Costa Rica, Mexico), *Latin Europe* (France, Italy, Spain), *Nordic Europe* (Denmark, Finland, Sweden), *Middle East* (Egypt, Morocco, Turkey), *Southern Asia* (India, Malaysia, Thailand), and *Sub-Saharan Africa* (Ghana). The countries included were chosen to not only meet our goal of sampling from each of the 10 GLOBE cultural clusters, but also based on countries' ability to provide a sufficient sample of German-speaking expatriates.

3 Data Collection

The iGOES data collection took place in two large waves between 2005 and 2010. Forty-six research assistants conducted interviews with expatriates living in each of the 28 sampled countries. iGOES recruited participants in four ways: (1) from German chamber of commerce membership lists in each host country, (2) by contacting German multinational company headquarters and asking for contact with their expatriates in each country, (3) by contacting individuals working abroad through a social networking site (www.xing.com), and (4) by asking participating expatriates for further potential contacts. Research assistants interviewed expatriates in-person in their host countries. Research assistants were business psychology students, all of whom received intensive training prior to data collection. Each interview took about 1.5 hours during which expatriates were asked to provide demographic/biographic information, rate themselves on several personality scales, complete a cognitive ability test, and evaluate their adjustment and satisfaction. At the end of the interview, expatriates named a supervisor, peer, or subordinate who was sufficiently knowledgeable to rate their job performance. Performance rating forms were sent directly to these knowledgeable others, who returned them to the researchers.[1]

---

[1] Due to time and technical constraints, some expatriates in Wave 1 delivered the rating form to their knowledgeable other themselves.

4   Criterion Measures

Due to time and operational constraints, the number and framing of questions differed slightly across the two data collection waves. Analyses in each chapter are therefore based on somewhat varying samples of countries.

International adjustment. Adjustment was measured with two different scales. Wave 1 used a three-item scale (Albrecht 2005) including the statements "How confident are you in interacting with [country] individuals?", "How well have you adapted to work processes in [country]?" and "How well have you personally adjusted to life outside of work (food, transportation, health care, etc.) in [country]?". The item measuring perceived overall adjustment was excluded. Wave 2 used a German version of the 14-item scale developed by Black and Stephens (1989). Four I/O psychologists with expertise in the field of expatriate management independently translated the English version to German. Translation disagreements were resolved through discussion. The final German version was subsequently back-translated to English by a native speaker. Both the 3-item and 14-item scales were rated on a five-point scale.

Ratings on both adjustment scales were obtained for a subsample of $N = 469$ participants. Corrected for unreliability, the short and long adjustment scales correlated $r_c = .76$, indicating that the two measures tap equivalent constructs. When both scales were available, we used the 14-item scale for analyses, as this is the more comprehensive measure.

Job satisfaction. Job satisfaction is "a pleasurable emotional state resulting from the appraisal of one's job or experiences" (Locke 1976). Job satisfaction was measured with 5 items rated on a 5-point scale (Judge et al. 1998) with items assessing global evaluations of the job (e.g., "I feel fairly satisfied with my present job").

Life satisfaction. Life satisfaction is an evaluation "of one's life according to subjectively determined standards" (Schimmack et al. 2002: 582). Life satisfaction was measured using the 4-item short version of the Satisfaction with Life Scale developed by Diener et al. (1985). Items included "In most ways my life is close to ideal" and "The conditions of my life are excellent".

Job performance. We conceptualized job performance according to the models presented by Campbell and colleagues (Campbell et al. 1993; Campbell/Wiernik 2015) and Viswesvaran and Ones (2000), who define job performance as individual employee behaviors that contribute to or detract from an organization's legitimate goals and which are scalable in terms of their level of proficiency. The hierarchical models of performance presented by Campbell et al. and by Viswesvaran and Ones, with a general factor at the apex and increasingly specific lower-order dimensions, describe dimensions of job performance that generalize across jobs and settings, including expatriate contexts. Separate expatriate-specific performance dimensions are not needed to cover the construct space when each dimension is substantiated with behavioral descriptions relating to the job in question (though the relative importance of dimensions and the specific behaviors reflective of particular proficiency levels may vary across cultural contexts, see Campbell/Wiernik 2015). Moreover, multinational companies usually have company-wide performance criteria which neither differentiate between "regular" and expatriate employees nor between different cultures (Ployhart et al. 2003). Thus, using a generalizable model of job performance makes sense from a conceptual perspective, reflects how performance is measured in practice, and facilitates commensurate comparisons across countries.

In Wave 1, we assessed the performance dimensions of technical performance (core aspects of expatriates' job role; 3 items), contextual performance (behaviors aimed at supporting organizational values and initiatives, local cultural knowledge and skill; 3 items), effort and initiative (persistence in goal striving, exceptional effort, proactive work behaviors; 4 items), and management and supervision (behaviors aimed at enhancing subordinate and coworker performance by motivating, inspiring, and coordinating them; 3 items). Four items tapped global ratings of overall job performance (total number of items = 17).

Wave 2 job performance dimensions were slightly different. We slightly changed some of the items and assessed additional dimensions – technical performance (5 items), management and supervision (5 items), effort and initiative (3 items), interpersonal relations (behaviors that promote cooperation and increase acceptance by coworkers, including working well with others; 5 items), and personal discipline (avoiding counterproductive work behaviors [behaviors that detract from legitimate organizational goals]; 4 items).

Ratings from two different raters were available for a subset of 117 expatriates of the Wave 2 iGOES sample, allowing us to compute interrater reliabilities. The interrater reliability estimate for overall job performance was .35. Most interrater reliabilities for performance dimensions were in the .30s (min = .16, max = .55), thus falling near the lower tail of the distribution of interrater reliabilities observed in meta-analyses (Salgado et al. 2003; Viswesvaran et al. 1996).

5   Transcultural Meta-Analysis

Most of the analyses using the iGOES samples in this volume (as well as comparisons of expatriate and domestic managers reported by Kostal et al. 2018a, 2018b, Chapters 10 and 2) were conducted using transcultural meta-analysis (Ones et al. 2012), a novel powerful statistical technique which allows researchers to statistically evaluate the extent to which variable relations vary or generalize cross-culturally. When different relationships between the same two variables are observed across cultures, these can be due to chance (i.e., sampling error), statistical artefacts (e.g., measurement error or range restriction), or true cultural variation (or other substantive moderators; Ones et al. 2012). Transcultural meta-analysis is a methodologically innovative approach to testing these alternative artefactual and cultural explanations for cross-country differences using psychometric meta-analysis (Schmidt/Hunter 2015). In transcultural meta-analysis, for each predictor and criterion studied, the relationship is estimated separately in each country. The single-country correlations are then pooled using meta-analysis. This technique allowed us to decompose the observed variance in relations across countries into (1) artefactual variance due to sampling error and measurement error, and (2) true variation due to moderators (including cultural differences). If most or all the variability in relations across countries is accounted for by statistical artefacts (i.e., if SD_ρ is near zero), this indicates that culture has little moderating effect because the relation is largely consistent across contexts. Therefore, if SD_ρ is small, this offers strong evidence for the cross-cultural generalizability of results (Ones et al. 2012). The strength of this conclusion depends on both the total number of individuals assessed (total N) and the number and diversity of countries sampled (k).

References

Albrecht, Anne-Grit (2005): Untangling the Laundry List: General Mental Ability, the Big Five, and Context Related Variables as Predictors for Expatriate Success. Master's Thesis. Lüneburg, Germany: Leuphana Universität. [http://opus.uni-lueneburg.de/opus/volltexte/2006/344/].

Albrecht, Anne-Grit; Ones, Deniz S.; Sinangil, Handan Kepir (2018): Expatriate Management. In: Ones, Deniz S. et al. (Eds.): The SAGE Handbook of Industrial, Work and Organizational Psychology. Volume 3: Managerial Psychology and Organizational Approaches. 2nd ed. London, United Kingdom: Sage: 429–468.

Black, J. Stewart; Mendenhall, Mark E.; Oddou, Gary R. (1991): Toward a Comprehensive Model of International Adjustment: An Integration of Multiple Theoretical Perspectives. In: *Academy of Management Review* 16,2: 291–317. [https://doi.org/10/fn7m8b].

Black, J. Stewart; Stephens, Gregory K. (1989): The Influence of the Spouse on American Expatriate Adjustment and Intent to Stay in Pacific Rim Overseas Assignments. In: *Journal of Management* 15,4: 529–544. [https://doi.org/10.1177/014920638901500403].

Campbell, John P. (2013): Assessment in Industrial and Organizational Psychology: An Overview. In: Geisinger, Kurt F. et al. (Eds.): APA Handbook of Testing and Assessment in Psychology. Volume 1, APA Handbooks in Psychology. Washington, DC: American Psychological Association: 355–395. [https://doi.org/10.1037/14047-022].

Campbell, John P. et al. (1993): A Theory of Performance. In: Schmitt, Neal; Borman, Walter C. (Eds.): Personnel Selection in Organizations. San Francisco, CA: Jossey-Bass: 35–70.

Campbell, John P.; Wiernik, Brenton M. (2015): The Modeling and Assessment of Work Performance. In: *Annual Review of Organizational Psychology and Organizational Behavior* 2: 47–74. [https://doi.org/10/bc4k].

Diener, Ed et al. (1985): The Satisfaction with Life Scale. In: *Journal of Personality Assessment* 49,1: 71–75. [https://doi.org/10.1207/s15327752jpa4901_13].

Franke, George R.; Richey, R. Glenn (2010): Improving Generalizations from Multi-Country Comparisons in International Business Research. In: *Journal of International Business Studies* 41,8: 1275–1293. [https://doi.org/10.1057/jibs.2010.21].

House, Robert J. et al. (Eds.) (2004): Culture, Leadership, and Organizations: The GLOBE Study of 62 Societies. Thousand Oaks, CA: Sage.

Judge, Timothy A. et al. (1998): Dispositional Effects on Job and Life Satisfaction: The Role of Core Evaluations. In: *Journal of Applied Psychology* 83,1: 17–34. [https://doi.org/10/gdv].

Kostal, Jack W. et al. (2018a): Expatriate Leadership Experience: A Host Country Burden or Resource? In: Wiernik, Brenton M.; Rüger, Heiko; Ones, Deniz S. (Eds.): Managing Expatriates: Success Factors in Private and Public Domains, Series on Population Studies 50. Opladen, Germany: Barbara Budrich Publishers.

Kostal, Jack W. et al. (2018b): Expatriate Personality: Facet-Level Comparisons with Domestic Counterparts. In: Wiernik, Brenton M.; Rüger, Heiko; Ones, Deniz S. (Eds.): Managing Expatriates: Success Factors in Private and Public Domains, Series on Population Studies 50. Opladen, Germany: Barbara Budrich Publishers.

Locke, Edwin A. (1976): The Nature and Causes of Job Satisfaction. In: Dunnette, Marvin D. (Ed.): Handbook of Industrial and Organizational Psychology. 1st ed. Chicago: Rand-McNally: 1297–1343.

Mol, Stefan T.; Born, Marise Ph.; van der Molen, Henk T. (2005): Developing Criteria for Expatriate Effectiveness: Time to Jump off the Adjustment Bandwagon. In: *International Journal of Intercultural Relations* 29,3: 339–353. [https://doi.org/10/dk2vzk].

Ones, Deniz S. et al. (2012): Cross-Cultural Generalization: Using Meta-Analysis to Test Hypotheses about Cultural Variability. In: Ryan, Ann Marie; Leong, Frederick T.L.; Oswald, Frederick L. (Eds.): Conducting Multinational Research Projects in Organizational Psychology: Challenges and Opportunities, APA/MSU Series on Multicultural Psychology 1. Washington, DC: American Psychological Association: 91–122. [https://doi.org/10/5kz].

Ployhart, Robert E. et al. (2003): The Cross-Cultural Equivalene of Job Performance Ratings. In: *Human Performance* 16,1: 49–79. [https://doi.org/10.1207/S15327043HUP1601_3].

Salgado, Jesús F. et al. (2003): A Meta-Analytic Study of General Mental Ability Validity for Different Occupations in the European Community. In: *Journal of Applied Psychology* 88,6: 1068–1081. [https://doi.org/10.1037/0021-9010.88.6.1068].

Schimmack, Ulrich; Diener, Ed; Oishi, Shigehiro (2002): Life-Satisfaction Is a Momentary Judgment and a Stable Personality Characteristic: The Use of Chronically Accessible and Stable Sources. In: *Journal of Personality* 70,3: 345–384. [https://doi.org/10.1111/1467-6494.05008].

Schmidt, Frank L.; Hunter, John E. (2015): Methods of Meta-Analysis: Correcting Error and Bias in Research Findings. 3rd ed. Thousand Oaks, CA: Sage. [https://doi.org/10/b6mg].

Sinangil, Handan Kepir; Ones, Deniz S. (2001): Expatriate Management. In: Anderson, Neil et al. (Eds.): Handbook of Industrial, Work and Organizational Psychology. Volume 1: Personnel Psychology. Thousand Oaks, CA: Sage: 424–443. [https://doi.org/10/b6pn].

Spector, Paul E. et al. (2002): Locus of Control and Well-Being at Work: How Generalizable Are Western Findings? In: *Academy of Management Journal* 45,2: 453–466. [https://doi.org/10.2307/3069359].

Viswesvaran, Chockalingam; Ones, Deniz S. (2000): Perspectives on Models of Job Performance. In: *International Journal of Selection and Assessment* 8,4: 216–226. [https://doi.org/10/ctcc82].

Viswesvaran, Chockalingam; Ones, Deniz S.; Schmidt, Frank L. (1996): Comparative Analysis of the Reliability of Job Performance Ratings. In: *Journal of Applied Psychology* 81,5: 557–574. [https://doi.org/10/c8f68f].

Appendix B: Sampling and Procedures for the Mobility Skills in the German Foreign Service Study

Heiko Rüger, Herbert Fliege, Stine Waibel, and Maria M. Bellinger

1 Introduction

The Mobility Skills in the German Foreign Service study was initiated to identify risk and protective factors that support or hinder Foreign Service employees' and their families' ability to cope with frequent international mobility. The study sought to explore individual and family characteristics that foster effective adaptation, evaluate the effectiveness of various Foreign Office preparation, support, and developmental programs, and uncover areas in need of further attention for promoting diplomats' and other employees' well-being in rotation. The study was designed in collaboration between the Federal Foreign Office in Berlin, Germany (Auswärtiges Amt – GFS) and the German Federal Institute for Population Research (Bundesinstitut für Bevölkerungsforschung – BiB) in Wiesbaden, Germany.

2 Survey Design

The study was conducted using a set of online surveys. The online format ensured that all employees and their family members deployed worldwide could easily take part in the study by avoiding problems related to time differences (which would have interfered with telephone interviews) and high postage costs and delays (which would have limited written surveys). Three standardized questionnaires were constructed for the study – one each for GFS employees, their partners/spouses, and their children. In this volume, only the employee surveys were analyzed. Analyses of expatriate family members are part of the BiB's and the GFS's ongoing research and evaluation of diplomat management.

The employee questionnaire addressed a wide range of topics. These included a variety of potential risk and protective factors, including procedural and background information (e.g., whether employees were in rotation and abroad, previous international experiences in and before entering the Foreign Service), sociodemographic and family characteristics (e.g., gender, age, marital status, number and age of children, family living arrangements), physical mobility demands of their current jobs (e.g., commuting time, business trips), general personality traits (self-efficacy, optimism, pessimism, locus of control), international rotation-specific traits (e.g., mobility self-efficacy, mobility-specific coping strategies and control beliefs), features of work in the Foreign Office (e.g., evaluations of support measures offered by the Foreign Office and of positive characteristics of their current jobs), and features of employees' social network (e.g., size of network, feelings of social support). The questionnaire also assessed a variety of important outcomes for GFS employees. These include adjustment to their new location (i.e., comfort completing everyday tasks and meeting their needs for food, healthcare, social contacts, recreation, etc.), work-related outcomes (e.g., job satisfaction, satisfaction with the rotation process), social and family outcomes (e.g., perceived work-life conflict, relationship satisfaction, friendship satisfaction, beliefs about reconcilability of family life with work in the Foreign Service), and health-related outcomes (i.e., perceived stress, subjective heath/health-related quality of life).

The survey was extensively pre-tested to assess both usability of the online survey platform and comprehensibility of the questions. Thirty-eight former employees and employees on leave from the Foreign Office and their family members took part in the pre-test. Pre-test participants were given the opportunity to comment on the questionnaires and offer suggestions for improvement. In the full sample of GFS employees participating in the main survey phase (see below), the survey took an average of 40 minutes to complete.

3   Study Procedure

The survey phase commenced in mid-November 2011 and ended on 31 December 2011. During this period, GFS employees and their family members could access and complete the online questionnaire. All employees of the Foreign Office other than local employees at the diplomatic missions (who are not on rotation and who frequently are host-country nationals) were asked by the Foreign Office health service and the Federal Institute for Population Research via email to take part in the study. These invitations were forwarded to the employees via the Office's internal email distribution list, along with login data for the password-protected online questionnaires. Over the course of the survey phase, two reminders were sent out to request further participation. Of course, participation in the study was voluntary for all employees (and their family members and the pre-test participants). The study was anonymous; it was impossible to trace any information back to individuals. All data protection requirements were accounted for, and the Foreign Office legal counsel was involved in designing instructions and invitations for participation.

The employees themselves requested that their partners and children take part in the study. At the end of their questionnaire they were given the chance to invite their partners and their children (aged 8–21) to participate in the study if they lived in the same household. Employees could either send invitations to their family members directly from the online system with an email containing the login data and password for the corresponding online questionnaire or they could note down the data and pass it on personally to their family members. Partners' and children's questionnaire responses were connected to employees' data using family codes contained in the login data.

4   Study Participants

About one-third of all Foreign Office employees ($N = 2{,}598$ out of 7,321 total employees) took part in the study (responses, not used in the current analyses, were also obtained from $N = 417$ partners and $N = 265$ children). This 35.5% response rate corresponds closely to typical rates for web-based surveys (cf. Cook et al. 2000) and expatriate research (cf. Bhaskar-Shrinivas et al. 2005). Of the 2,598 participants, at the time of the survey 135 employees were *not* in rotation and were excluded from the current analyses. Another 30 respondents provided no information about their rotation status and were also excluded. Finally, about a third of the respondents ($N = 821$) were currently stationed in Germany (and thus were not on an international/expatriate assignment; cf. to 41% of all GFS employees stationed in Germany) and were also excluded from the current analyses.

Respondent employees were about equally female as male (48.8% women, 51.2% men). Women make up 40.9% of the employees in the Foreign Office, so our response rates indicate that women were somewhat more willing to participate in the survey than men. The average age of study participants was 44.8 years. This corresponds roughly to the average age of 45.6 years for all employees in the Foreign Service (not including local staff). The youngest participating employee was 20, and the oldest was 67 years old. Participation was greatest among the 40–49 year olds, who also represent the largest age group among all Foreign Office employees.

The German civil service has four hierarchical levels based on education level – ordinary, intermediate, higher intermediate, and higher. The Foreign Service additionally includes a secretarial pool. The largest group of respondents was in the higher intermediate civil service grade (37.8%, cf. 28.6% of all Foreign Office employees). The second-largest group of respondents was intermediate grade (23.4%, cf. 25.3% of all GFS employees). Only 21.8% of respondents were higher civil service grade (a rate substantially below the rate among all GFS employees, 28.9%). Employees in the ordinary civil service grade were also somewhat underrepresented among respondents (3.6% compared to 5.9% among all employees). Finally, 13.3% of respondents were in the secretarial pool in the sample, a slightly higher rate than among all employees (11.3%).

The large majority of employees who took part in the survey were married (66.1%, cf. 62.1% of all employees). The second-largest group among both the respondents and all employees were single individuals (21.5% or 27.4% respectively). Rates of widowed and divorced individuals were similar among respondents and all employees (6% divorced, 0.6% widowed). Separated employees and employees living in a registered civil union are slightly over-represented in the survey (2.4% of respondents were separated, cf. 1.7% of all employees; 2.4% of participants were in registered civil unions, cf. 0.9% of all employees).

Rates of employees with children were much higher among respondents (62.9%) than among all Foreign Office employees (51.1%). This overrepresentation suggests great interest in the topics of the study (e.g., adaptation, well-being, work-family balance) among parents.

All in all, there were relatively minor deviations of study participants from the general population of Foreign Office employees in terms of sociodemographic and family structure characteristics. The general representativeness of the sample suggests that findings from this study likely generalize well the total Foreign Service population.

References

Bhaskar-Shrinivas, Purnima et al. (2005): Input-Based and Time-Based Models of International Adjustment: Meta-Analytic Evidence and Theoretical Extensions. In: *Academy of Management Journal* 48,2: 257–281. [https://doi.org/10.5465/AMJ.2005.16928400].

Cook, Colleen; Heath, Fred; Thompson, Russel L. (2000): A Meta-Analysis of Response Rates in Web- or Internet-Based Surveys. In: *Educational and Psychological Measurement* 60,6: 821–836. [https://doi.org/10.1177/00131640021970934].

About the Editors

Dr. Brenton M. Wiernik is an assistant professor of industrial-organizational psychology at the University of South Florida. His research focuses on how individuals make career decisions and adapt and change throughout their careers, particularly with respect to the role of interests, personality, abilities, and other dispositional characteristics on these processes. He additionally studies how individuals and organizations adapt to promote environmental sustainability and develops techniques for meta-analysis and other quantitative research methods. Dr. Wiernik teaches courses in psychometrics and personnel psychology, and he serves on the editorial boards for the *Journal of Managerial Psychology*, the *Journal of Environmental Psychology*, and the *International Journal of Selection and Assessment*. As part of his academic and applied work, he has worked as an expatriate in Germany, France, Belgium, and South Africa. Dr. Wiernik received his B.S. and Ph.D. in industrial-organizational psychology from the University of Minnesota.

Dr. Heiko Rüger is a senior researcher at the Federal Institute for Population Research (BiB) in Wiesbaden, Germany, holding a Master's degree in sociology and a Ph.D. in physiological sciences from the University Medical Centre of the Johannes Gutenberg University Mainz. His research focuses on spatial mobility, family, health, and the interrelations between spatial mobility, family development, and personal/familial relationships from a life course perspective. He joined the Federal Institute for Population Research in 2009 and since 2011 has led its research group on spatial mobility. He is the coordinator of the cross-national longitudinal research project "Job Mobilities and Family Lives in Europe" (http://www.jobmob-and-famlives.eu), as well as the 2011 study "Mobility Skills in the Foreign Service", which surveyed employees of the German Foreign Service, as well as their life partners and children.

Dr. Deniz S. Ones is the Hellervik Professor of Industrial Psychology, a Distinguished McKnight Professor, and Distinguished University Teaching Professor at the University of Minnesota. Dr. Ones received her Ph.D. in business administration from the University of Iowa. She has received numerous prestigious awards for her research on individual differences, among them the Ernest J. McCormick Award and the S. Rains Wallace Award from the Society for Industrial and Organizational Psychology and the Cattell Award from the Society for Multivariate Experimental Psychology. She is a Fellow of the Association for Psychological Science and the American Psychological Association (Divisions 5, 8, and 14), for which she previously chaired the Committee on Psychological Testing and Assessment. Professor Ones is a co-editor of the bestselling *Handbook of Industrial, Work and Organizational Psychology* and has served as editor or on the editorial boards of a dozen scientific journals.

About the Authors

Dr. Anne-Grit Albrecht is a visiting scientist of business psychology at the Institute of Management & Organization (IMO) at Leuphana Universität Lüneburg, Germany. She also works as an independent HR consultant in Heidelberg, Germany. Her research and consulting interests are in the areas of expatriate management and positive supervisor–subordinate relationships. She received her doctorate (Dr. phil., Leuphana Universität Lüneburg, Germany) on the role of core self-evaluations in expatriate assignments. Prior to her current position, she worked at the global leadership development department of a financial services company and as postdoctoral researcher at the University of Mannheim.

Dr. Maria M. Bellinger is a medical doctor specialized in neurology, psychiatry, and psychotherapy, with more than 20 years of experience in the clinical field and a master's degree in health management. She has headed the Psychosocial Counseling Service of the Federal Foreign Office of Germany since 2008, and is engaged in research concerning work-related stress and resilience factors. She also addresses mental illness at the workplace and seeks to manage the impact of mobility and the demands of rotation on staff. The development and dissemination of preventive measures against work-related strains is one of her primary goals.

Dr. Jürgen Deller is a professor of business psychology and speaker at Institute of Management & Organization (IMO) at Leuphana University of Lüneburg, Germany. He is a founding member of Goinger Kreis e. V., a think tank of German HR Executives. Jürgen Deller worked with Commerzbank for three years and the Daimler group for more than eight years. As a senior manager, he was responsible for the office of the executive board member HR of DaimlerChrysler services (debis) AG, Berlin. Before he joined academia, he had senior responsibility in HR for Daimler's IT service company. His current research focuses on employee development and adaptation, particularly regarding older workers and transitions to retirement. He has conducted cross-cultural and expatriate research for more than 30 years.

Dr. Stephan Dilchert is an associate professor of management at the Zicklin School of Business at Baruch College, City University of New York. His research focuses on the role of personality, intelligence, and other individual differences variables in personnel decisions. He is particularly interested in how these characteristics relate to creativity, counterproductive behaviors, and pro-environmental behaviors among employees. His work on creativity was recognized with the Meredith P. Crawford Fellowship from the Human Resources Research Organization and the S. Rains Wallace Award from the Society for Industrial and Organizational Psychology. Dr. Dilchert teaches management and HR courses in the Zicklin School's MBA, doctoral, and executive programs, and regularly conducts executive and corporate education programs in the United States, Europe, and Asia. Dr. Dilchert currently serves as Editor-in-Chief of the *International Journal of Selection and Assessment*. Before becoming an academic, he has worked as a German expatriate in France, Singapore, and Malaysia. In addition to a Ph.D. in industrial and organizational psychology from the University of Minnesota, he holds SHRM-SCP certification from the Society for Human Resource Management as well as SPHR certification from the Human Resources Certification Institute.

Dr. Herbert Fliege is a clinical psychologist and psychotherapist (CBT) with long experience in the practice and research of stress and health-related quality of life. He has been with the Federal Foreign Office of Germany since 2010 as deputy head of the Psychosocial Counseling Service. His activities include preventive health measures for highly mobile employees and their accompanying families, providing in-house training on coping with stress in critical environments, as well as consultancy services to the management on questions regarding healthy leadership in a mobile context.

Dr. Hannah J. Foldes holds a Ph.D. in industrial and organizational psychology from the University of Minnesota and currently serves as the Practice Director for the Enterprise and Functional Excellence practice in CEB Talent Assessment. She has more than 13 years of experience applying psychology in work settings. In her role with CEB, Dr. Foldes leads projects with clients to help improve individual and organizational performance through better talent management. This includes studying job requirements and developing, implementing, and evaluating human capital systems in a variety of private and public sector organizations. With expertise in competency modelling, employee selection, and leadership development, Dr. Foldes has provided assessment and consulting services to numerous organizations across a variety of industries including Finance, Consumer Goods, Manufacturing, Retail, and Telecommunications. In addition to her consulting activities, Dr. Foldes is a past Board Member of Minnesota Professionals for Psychology Applied to Work (MPPAW) and has presented her research to practitioner and academic audiences at meetings of the Society for Industrial and Organizational Psychology (SIOP), American Psychological Association (APA), and European Association of Work and Organizational Psychology (EAWOP). Hannah has published her research in technical reports and peer-reviewed journals including the *Journal of Applied Psychology* and *Personnel Psychology*.

Jack W. Kostal is a doctoral candidate in industrial-organizational psychology at the University of Minnesota. His research focuses on training, employee development, and assessment of cognitive ability and learning, particularly with respect to how training and educational opportunities can be extended to disadvantaged and underrepresented groups. He is also interested in developing quantitative methods for modeling and analyzing psychological data. Kostal's research has been published in numerous journals, including *Assessment*, *Educational Measurement*, and *Industrial and Organizational Psychology*. In his applied work, Kostal uses quantitative analytic techniques to inform organizational human resource management decisions.

Dr. Brittany K. Mercado is an assistant professor of management at the Love School of Business at Elon University. Her scholarly and applied work consists of three primary streams: 1) predicting and conceptualizing employee performance with a focus on counterproductive work behaviors, 2) examining the validity of measures, and 3) identifying sources of bias in employment decisions. Across endeavors, she investigates fair, valid, and effective solutions for enhancing employee performance and well-being. She received her Ph.D. in management at the Zicklin School of Business, Baruch College, CUNY.

Dr. Frieder Paulus is assistant professor for social neuroscience methods at the Department of Psychiatry and Psychotherapy, University of Lübeck, Germany. His research focuses on the neural foundations of social behavior that shape human sociality. He studied psychology at Bielefeld University, Germany and started his graduate studies on expatriate management in the iGOES project (International Generalizability of Expatriate Success factors) at the Institute for Strategic Human Resource Management Research and Development at Leuphana University of Lüneburg, Germany. He later received his Ph.D. in neuroscience at the University of Marburg, Germany with his dissertation on social context and genetic risk dependent modulations of brain networks. Afterwards, he represented the vacant chair for Research Methods and Statistics at the Department of Psychology at the University of Lübeck.

Dr. Handan Kepir Sinangil is professor of work and organizational psychology at Marmara University, Organizational Behaviour Graduate Program, and adjunct professor at Bogazici University. She has served as the General Secretary of European Association of Work and Organizational Psychology (EAWOP). She is a member of the American Psychological Association (APA), the Society for Industrial and Organizational Psychology (SIOP, APA Division 14), the International Association of Applied Psychology (IAAP), and the International Association of Cross-Cultural Psychology (IACCP). Dr. Sinangil's international and national publications exceed 70 book chapters and conference papers. She is also an associate editor of the International Journal of Selection and Assessment (IJSA). Her ongoing research projects, either with international collaboration or alone, include expatriate management, organizational culture and change, performance appraisal, and selection. Additionally, her current teaching interests include assessment, training and development, and psychology of management.

Stine Waibel is a political scientist and has been a researcher at the German Federal Institute for Population Research since 2013. She is currently pursuing her doctoral degree at the Department of Social Science at Hamburg University. Her research interests include spatial and social mobility, educational inequality, transnational mobility, and expatriation, as well as related policy issues. Her research activities aim at identifying environments where the mobility demands of a globalized economy do not reinforce social inequality or negatively affect family life and individual well-being.

Name Index

Subject Index

work contexts, 225
   autonomy, 154, 159–60, 183
   complexity, 23, 71–72, 122, 166–67, 296
   job demands, 17–18, 23, 107, 120, 145,
       159, 174, 209, 256, 259–60, 271, 295
   living conditions, 107
   organizational climate, 107, 195, 204, 231
   recognition, 53, 57, 61, 107, 222, 231
   security, 107, 150, 160, 226, 229, 231, 256
   task meaningfulness, 107

CPSIA information can be obtained
at www.ICGtesting.com
Printed in the USA
LVOW04*0414210218
567304LV00001B/1/P